A Grammar of Present-Day English

von
Friedrich Ungerer
Gerhard E. H. Meier
Klaus Schäfer
Shirley B. Lechler

unter Mitwirkung und Leitung der Verlagsredaktion Neue Sprachen

Ernst Klett Verlag
Stuttgart Düsseldorf Leipzig

A Grammar of Present-Day English

von
Prof. Dr. Friedrich Ungerer, Rostock; Gerhard E. H. Meier, Saarbrücken;
Klaus Schäfer, Ludwigsburg; Shirley B. Lechler, Esslingen;

Bearbeitung dieser englischsprachigen Version von
Shirley B. Lechler, Esslingen und Jill Schrafnagl, London;

An den Arbeiten nahmen beratend teil:
Hans-Joachim Lechler, Esslingen; Dr. Peter Pasch, Tübingen.

Dieses Werk ist auch in deutschsprachiger Version erhältlich:

Grammatik des heutigen Englisch

Klettnummer 5057

1. Auflage   1 14 13 12 11 | 2005 2004 2003 2002

Alle Drucke dieser Auflage können im Unterricht nebeneinander benutzt werden, sie sind untereinander unverändert.
Die letzte Zahl bezeichnet das Jahr dieses Druckes.

Internetadresse: http://www.klett-verlag.de

Redaktion: Noreen O'Donovan und Inge Schäfer.
Umschlag: Hans Lämmle, Stuttgart.
Druck: SCHNITZER DRUCK GmbH, 71404 Korb
ISBN 3-12-505800-7

Preface

Aims of this Grammar

This Grammar has been designed mainly for students of the upper level of the Gymnasium. It should also be found useful by those going on to study English or aiming at a good command of the English language for professional or personal reasons.
A Grammar of Present-Day English has two main functions. One is to give a general outline of all the essential grammatical features of English and so refresh and expand the reader's existing knowledge and proficiency in the language; the other is to serve as a reference book for particular grammatical problems.

The presentation of the material

A grammar of this scope is bound to contain a great and varied amount of information. Therefore, care has been taken to present the material as clearly as possible and in graded steps.

- At the beginning of each chapter – or, in the case of longer chapters, at the beginning of each new section – comes a 'summary' which gives a general outline of the material to be dealt with.
- The most important points – especially of the summaries – are set in a frame of double lines.
- In the further detailed discussion of grammatical features, the examples are printed on a blue background usually on the left of the page, facing the appropriate explanations on the right.
- Less common features, exceptions, etc. are dealt with in the form of notes (in smaller print).
- An appendix deals with a number of additional features of the language (e.g. word formation, spelling rules) which do not, strictly speaking, belong to its grammar, but whose inclusion should make the book more valuable as a work of reference.
- Cross-references, a detailed index and a clear system of numbering all help to make it easy for readers to find their way about.

The importance of context

It is obvious that grammatical forms and structures always occur in spoken or written contexts. In fact, certain phenomena (e.g. the passive, use of tenses, indirect speech, emphatic word order) can only be properly explained in terms of the contexts in which they are used. In the relevant chapters these features are illustrated to a large extent in longer text passages, including some authentic published material.
Fortunately for the length of the book, however, most of the individual parts of speech (nouns, adjectives, etc.), could be adequately contextualized on the level of sentences – or even, in a few cases, in sentence fragments. But even these examples are not presented in total isolation: as a rule, they are arranged in groups treating of related subject matter.

Stylistic levels and varieties of English

With a view to general usefulness, stylistically neutral sentences predominate as examples, except where the structures themselves are typically colloquial or formal. Both examples and explanations concentrate on standard British English, but important variants, especially those occurring in American English, are also pointed out.

Linguistic background, terminology

This *Grammar of Present-Day English* sets out not merely to describe linguistic phenomena but also to explain the logic underlying their use, especially where the structure of the English language differs noticeably from that of German. On the whole, traditional grammatical terminology is employed, with the addition of only a very few new terms, which are in each case explained in full. In spite of this deliberate terminological restraint, the book incorporates many insights deriving from recent linguistic research. The aim of awakening some understanding of the workings of language is given special prominence in the introductory chapter. With the aid of simple examples it presents a number of different ways of looking at language, and shows what these have to do with grammar and the way it is presented in the chapters that follow.

Contents

Paragraph | Page

Introduction: Language, Communication and Grammar

Chapter 1: Types of Sentences

Chapter 2: The Patterns of the Simple Sentence

Chapter 3: Nouns and Noun Phrases

5

Chapter 4: Adjectives and Adjective Phrases

Chapter 5: Adverbs and Adverbial Phrases

Chapter 6: The Finite Verb Forms

Chapter 7: The Auxiliaries

Chapter 8: Non-Finite Constructions

Chapter 9: Subordinate Clauses

Chapter 10: Direct and Reported Speech

Chapter 11: Cohesion and Emphasis

Appendix

Introduction: Language, Communication and Grammar

When using one's native language, one will seldom need to consult aids such as grammars or dictionaries. Communication between speaker and listener or writer and reader normally functions quite well without them. This is not so in a foreign language. A speaker or writer may be uncertain how to formulate what he or she wants to say and the listener or reader may have difficulty in understanding. A systematic description of the grammar of a language can be of considerable help, by supplying answers to the following questions:

- How are words arranged into meaningful utterances?
- What linguistic means establish the connection between an utterance and reality? (For instance, how do a speaker and a listener know that they are thinking of the same thing or person?)
- How does one put information across in the most effective way possible?
- What intentions or perspective may underlie a certain utterance?
- Is the language used standard or non-standard? What is the level of style?
- To what extent do the linguistic means used to express an idea differ from those which would be used in one's native language?

In this introductory chapter we set out to show what part these considerations play in verbal communication and how they will be approached in the chapters that follow.

1–3 Communication and Word Order

Communication is only possible if words are arranged in a certain order. Compare the following two examples:

our indeed holiday enjoyable very was last
our last holiday was very enjoyable indeed

Only the second example has the right word order to produce a meaningful English utterance. The order of words depends on various factors, which will be discussed in sections **1–3** below.

1 Word Order and Structural Patterns (Phrases, Simple Sentences, Complex Sentences)

The smallest unit in which word order is important is the **phrase.** A phrase consists of items belonging to one or more **parts of speech.** The example given above, for instance, contains a noun phrase *(our last holiday)* with the following constituents:

our	last	holiday
possessive determiner	adjective	noun

The example also contains an adjective phrase *(very enjoyable).* Other possible phrases include adverb phrases (e.g. *very nicely*), prepositional phrases (e.g. *in Italy*) and verb phrases (e.g. *must visit*).

A larger unit in which word order is involved is the **simple sentence.** Here, phrases or single words function as **constituent parts of the sentence.** The way those words and phrases are combined into a sentence is described as a **sentence pattern.** One of the commonest sentence patterns consists of a subject, a predicate and its complementation; this pattern (here with the addition of an adverbial) is illustrated below:

Our last holiday	was	very enjoyable	indeed.
subject	predicate	complementation	adverbial

A simple sentence can be expanded into a **complex sentence.** Complex sentences include as their constituent parts not only words and phrases but also **subordinate clauses** or **non-finite constructions** (infinitive, gerund and participle constructions):

Sailing around the Greek islands	was very enjoyable	as you may imagine.
gerund construction as subject		subordinate clause as adverbial

This Grammar describes how words are combined into sentences according to certain structural patterns. Its aim is not only to help learners to speak and write correctly but also to help them to understand sentences like the following:

> To start with the development of tourism must be aimed at once the basic problems of food and housing have been solved.

You will probably not find this sentence easy to understand at first sight. It would be analysed as follows:

To start with	the development of tourism	must be aimed at	once the basic problems of food and housing have been solved.
infinitive construction as an adverbial	subject	predicate	subordinate clause introduced by *once* as an adverbial

The main chapters dealing with these patterns are Chapter 2 (sentence patterns), Chapters 3–5 (structure and function of the various kinds of phrases), and Chapters 8 and 9 (non-finite constructions and subordinate clauses).

2 Word Order and Types of Sentence

So far, we have only considered the patterns of statements, i.e. declarative sentences. In other types of sentence the word order may be different, as shown, for example, in the following comparison between a statement and a question, where the question is expressed through the inversion of the subject and the auxiliary verb (partial inversion):

Statement:		We subject	have brought back predicate	plenty of holiday snapshots. complementation (object)
Question:	Have part of predicate (auxiliary verb)	you subject	brought back part of predicate (main verb)	any holiday snapshots? complementation (object)

The structures of the different types of sentence are described in detail in Chapter 1.

3 Word Order, Cohesion and the Structuring of Information

Although word order is largely determined by the sentence patterns and types of sentence used, there are some cases where variations of the word order are possible. This, however, does not mean that the order in which the elements of the sentence are arranged is arbitrary; rather it is determined by the need to provide logical links between sentences (i.e. **cohesion**) and to **structure the information** so that it will be readily understood. (For the structuring of information see **6**.) The positioning of an adverbial of place, for instance, will depend on how the content of the sentence is related to the content of a preceding sentence or sentences:

Spanish food is quite different from English food.	**In Torremolinos,** however, some restaurants serve fish and chips. adverbial of place in front-position
You needn't do without your fish and chips completely.	You can get them **in Torremolinos.** adverbial of place in end-position

In the first of these two examples, the positioning of the adverbial of place at the beginning of the sentence has a 'scene-setting' effect: it indicates right away that what follows has to be seen as related particularly or exclusively to this place. At the same time, there is a definite contrast to the preceding sentence (a contrast between Spain as a whole and Torremolinos).

In the second example, the positioning of the adverbial at the end of the sentence puts the focus of the statement on the place adverbial itself. It is the place adverbial that conveys new information, whereas the other elements of the sentence merely take up what is already known from the preceding sentence.

In order to achieve special effects in text cohesion and information structuring, a speaker may even depart from the order subject – predicate – complementation which is normally used in statements:

Tourism has become essential to the country's economy.

A lot less beneficial	**have been**	**its effects on the natural beauty of the south coast.**
complementation	predicate	subject

The effects of cohesion and the structuring of information on word order are discussed in more detail in Chapter 11.

4–5 Language and Reality

4 In any meaningful verbal utterance, a speaker will refer to people, things, processes or states which form part of a reality beyond language (or to abstract ideas or an imaginary reality). But, as the following two representations of one and the same event show, utterances may differ in how explicitly they refer to reality.

HOSTAGES FREE
The hostages of the Taunton bank robbery were freed by a special police task force from a remote farmhouse last night.

In the first version the meanings of the two words used make it clear that the message has something to do with the freeing of hostages (the plural -s showing that there was more than one). But there is no indication as to what hostages are referred to or when, where and by whom they were freed. It only makes sense to express something in this way if, for example, it is a newspaper headline used at the beginning of an article which gives all the necessary details. The second version answers all of these questions. This is done not only by adding further words with particular meanings, but also by using certain **grammatical means:**

- The definite article ***the*** in *the hostages* shows that a particular, defined group of hostages are being referred to. (The exact definition is given by the following *of*-phrase: *of the Taunton bank robbery.*)
- The finite verb form ***were freed*** shows, amongst other things, that, in relation to the time of speaking, the action happened in past time. (The time adverbial *last night* tells us more exactly when it happened.)
- The preposition ***by*** introduces the person or persons who carried out the action (called the *by*-agent).
- The preposition ***from*** introduces the noun phrase *(a remote farmhouse)* which tells us where the hostages had been held captive.

5 In the above example the relation to reality is mainly indicated by the meanings of the nouns, adjectives and verbs; grammatical words and forms serve only to make the relation even clearer. But there are cases where grammatical means have a much more important function. For instance, two people who have been following the events on television or the radio can communicate with each other on the subject of the freeing of the hostages in a reduced form like the following:

A: They've freed them at last.
B: Thank God they have.
A: I never thought they would.
B: Nor did I.

In this example, the specific word meanings (e.g. *free*) play only a minor role in establishing the reference to reality. Otherwise we find pronouns *(they, them)* instead of the nouns/noun phrases *(police task force, hostages)*. In the second and third sentences, *free them* is represented only by the auxiliaries *have* and *would*. And in the last sentence the auxiliary *did* combined with *nor* replaces an even larger portion of the preceding sentences (namely: *think they would free them*).
This example is in fact quite typical of informal conversation with its many short sentences in which pronouns, auxiliaries and words like *so, nor* or *neither* occur as so-called pro-forms, replacing other words or phrases. The example illustrates how important these grammatical means are for making a reference to reality. It also shows that the choice of grammatical means depends to a large extent on the situation in which the speakers find themselves. This is why so much space in this book is given over to the description of these phenomena.
(For details on short sentences see Chapter 1; for pronouns, articles and other determiners and for singular and plural see Chapter 3; for prepositions in adverbials see Chapter 5; for finite verb forms see Chapter 6.)

6–7 Language and the Structuring of Information

6 If someone says the same thing several times without any particular reason the listener will soon lose interest. We normally expect utterances to present us with new information. On the other hand, the listener will find it hard to follow if the speaker keeps on adding new pieces of information, new points or ideas, stringing them together one after the other.

For effective communication it is better to steer a middle course. For example, one can take as a starting point something that is already known (e.g. from what has been said before) and then link it with a new item of information, or show it in a new light. This interchange between what is known (i.e. 'given') and what is new is illustrated in the following excerpt from a speech given at the opening of a new arts centre:

This beautifully converted building is the result of ***long and careful planning.***
known | new →

The first plans were in fact drawn up ten years ago ***by our Department of Works.***
known | new →

The Department originally suggested retaining ***only the façade of the old building.***
known | new →

This suggestion was rejected ***by the council.***
known | new →

As you read this text you see that the information it contains is conveyed step by step, in portions that are easy to assimilate. This is done by using sentences which are very similar in **the way the information is structured:**

- The **first element** of the sentence (in this text it is always the subject) relates to something that is **known** (usually something mentioned in the preceding sentence).
- The new information is contained in the remaining part of the sentence (the predicate and its complementation) whereby the **final element** (printed in bold italics) carries particular weight:
  - It is usually the longest element and therefore conveys the most information.
  - It contains the **most important information** and so also contains the syllable with the heaviest stress (underlined in each case).

This method of organizing a sentence according to known and new information with the greatest weight at the end of the sentence is the most straightforward way of communicating information. It fits in with the typical subject – predicate – complementation pattern of English sentences. The effect is often achieved – as in the above text – by **alternating between active and passive sentences.** (For passive sentences see **58–65.**)
The same principle of end weight also applies to phrases. For example, in the case of longer expressions, an *of*-phrase – which comes after the noun it refers to – would be preferred to an *s*-genitive (cf **92**); adjectives with complementation always follow the noun they modify (cf **130**).

the mayor's speech	but: the speech **of the newly-elected mayor of York**
pleasant colours	but: colours **pleasant to the eye**

7 Despite the obvious advantages of this method of structuring information, it does not necessarily produce ideal texts if it is carried too far. A text soon becomes monotonous if the same principle is applied over and over again. To keep a listener's or reader's interest it is best to deviate occasionally from the normal, straightforward way of organizing information. Most of these deviations are forms of **emphasis.** There are various ways of giving an utterance emphasis. In the spoken language this is often done through **stress.** The speaker shows which word has the highest information value by putting the greatest stress on this word (the stressed syllable is underlined). It is thus possible to bring the focus of information forward from the end of the sentence if this is justified by the context:

This suggestion was rejected ***by the council.***
This suggestion ***was rejected*** by the council. (It wasn't accepted as you seem to believe.)
This suggestion was rejected by the council. (The other suggestion was accepted.)

There are also **grammatical** ways of achieving emphasis, both in spoken and in written language. The following version of the above speech illustrates some of the possibilities:

May I remind my critics that *it was* ***our Department of Works*** *that* drew up the first plans for converting the old chocolate factory into an Arts Centre. *What* the Department originally suggested *was* ***that the interior of the building should be completely renewed.*** But, as you will remember, the estimated cost of such an extensive renovation caused the majority of the council to have some doubts about the project. So *back came* ***the old plans for demolishing and rebuilding.*** But *there was* considerable opposition to this among local residents. They were able to put forward numerous ideas on how the substance of this historic building could be retained and renovated at a relatively low cost. *I* ***do appreciate*** that *it was* mainly ***their initiative*** *that* convinced the council ...

This text contains several examples of emphasis. The construction *it was ... that ...* (a so-called *it* cleft sentence) serves to emphasize the subjects in the first and in the last sentence *(our Department of Works/their initiative).* In the second sentence, the construction *what ... was ...* (a so-called *what* cleft sentence) gives additional emphasis to the last element of the sentence (a *that*-clause as object), although it would carry weight in any case by being at the end of the sentence. An emphatic effect is also achieved by the unusual choice of word order in *So back came the old plans ...* and by the use of the form *do appreciate* (emphatic *do*).
The sentence *But there was ...* also deviates from the **'known – new'** order of information structuring by having a *there* -construction to introduce a new element (namely: *opposition among local residents*). These and other grammatical means which serve to make a text more structured and cohesive and to keep the interest of the listener or reader are discussed in Chapter 11.

8–9 Speech Intentions and Speaker Perspective

8 Verbal communication is a way of acting through the medium of words. Behind every utterance there lies some speech intention, i.e. the speaker or writer tries to achieve a certain effect on the listener or reader. Yet there is rarely a simple one-to-one equivalence between speech intentions and particular utterances; the relationship is almost always a complex one.

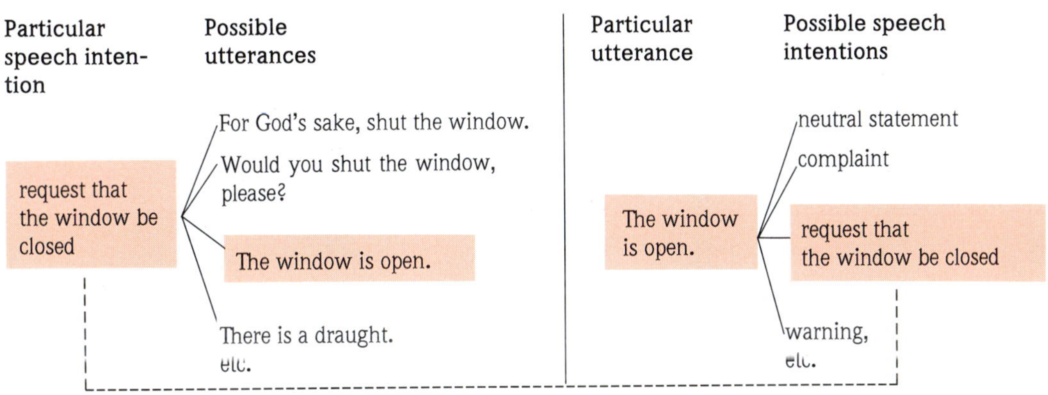

As this diagram shows, a speech intention can be expressed in various ways; similarly, behind any utterance there can lie several different speech intentions. So even in the simplest conversation, the participants are confronted with the following choices:

– The speaker has to choose from a range of words and grammatical possibilities an appropriate form of utterance to give expression to his or her intentions.
– The listener, hearing a certain utterance, has to decide what speech intention lies behind it.

In making these choices, both speaker and listener take account of the situation they are in. A grammar can only give systematic guidance in areas where a range of speech intentions can be expressed by similar grammatical means, e.g.:

- in the case of the modal auxiliaries, which can express speech intentions such as permission, wishes, reproaches, etc. (cf Ch. 7),
- in describing sentence types which, when given a certain intonation, can be used to express statements, questions, commands, etc. (cf Ch. 1).

9 Some grammatical phenomena cannot be directly related to particular speech intentions; they can, however, be expressions of the personal expectations and attitudes of the speaker. The following examples illustrate some such cases:

(a) The team **was** lined up for **its** group photo. The team **were** discussing tactics for **their** final match.	choice between singular and plural for the verb and possessive determiners
(b) Jane **is playing** in the school orchestra (this year). Jane **plays** the oboe in the school orchestra.	choice between the progressive form and the simple form
(c) What else are we running out of? Is there **any** orange juice in the fridge? I'm thirsty – is there **some** orange juice in the fridge?	choice between *some* and *any*

These pairs of sentences differ in the **perspective** from which the speaker views groups of people, actions, situations, etc.:

- In the first sentence of (a), the team is viewed as a whole; in the second, it is viewed as a number of individuals.
  The same choice exists with most other words denoting groups, e.g. *family, class, government,* etc. (cf **74**). (But there are some nouns also denoting groups of people which can only be used with the plural of verbs, determiners and pronouns, e.g. *police, people, clergy,* etc.: see **73**.4.)
- In the first sentence of (b), Jane's membership of the school orchestra is presented as existing at a particular time *(this year).* In the second sentence, her playing in the orchestra is presented as a fact which is not restricted to any particular period of time.
  There is the same choice between progressive form and simple form with other verbs which describe an action or a process. (There are, however, verbs which can only be used in the simple form, e.g. verbs which describe a state or a relationship, such as *seem, belong to, possess,* etc.: cf **181–185**.)
- In the first sentence of (c), the speaker is expressing uncertainty about whether there is any orange juice there at all. In the second sentence the speaker thinks there probably is, and expects an affirmative answer.
  Similar differences in speaker perspective can be expressed by the compounds with *some* and *any* (*someone, anything,* etc.) and by some pairs of adverbs (*already/yet, sometimes/ever,* etc.). (These choices only exist in questions. In other types of sentence the speaker perspective is fixed: cf **20, 22** and **113**.)

English has a wider choice of grammatical means to express such different speaker perspectives than German. In this Grammar care has been taken to describe the possible alternatives in some detail (and also to show where no choice is possible). The examples above can only give a limited impression of how important perspective is in English grammar. The main points affected are:

- the use of nouns, pronouns and determiners and the concord between noun and verb form (Chapter 3; see also examples (a) and (c))
- the use of certain tense forms, especially the simple and progressive forms (example (b)), past tense and present perfect and the various ways of expressing future time (Chapter 6)
- the choice between infinitive, gerund and participle as complementation (Chapter 8)
- the choice between active and passive sentences. This choice not only plays an important part in the structuring of information (cf **6**), but also depends on whether an action is seen from the point of view of the person (or thing) carrying out the action or the person (or thing) affected by the action (cf **58**).

Sometimes there is a close link between speaker perspective and speech intentions, e.g. in questions with *any* or *some* (cf example (c)). Since *any* expresses uncertainty what the answer to the question will be, the sentence with *any* can be seen as a genuine request for information. The sentence with *some* could, for example, be regarded as a request by the speaker to be given something to drink *(Can I have some orange juice?).* When one asks for something, one is assuming that it is available and one therefore uses *some.* We shall be looking at these aspects of the language more closely in the chapters dealing with the relevant grammatical phenomena.

10–12 Standard English and Levels of Style

10 What kind of English should a grammar like this describe? The following excerpt from a play illustrates one of the many varieties of English which differ quite considerably from the language variety used in our examples so far:

Mama: Who that round here slamming doors at this hour?
Ruth: That was Walter Lee. He and Bennie was at it again.
Mama: My children and they tempers. Lord, if this little old plant don't get more sun than it's been getting it ain't never going to see spring again. What's the matter with you this morning, Ruth? You looks right peaked. You aiming to iron all them things?

(Lorraine Hansberry, *A Raisin in the Sun*)

Here we have a form of English which is spoken by many blacks in the USA (Black English). It differs from the English described in most grammars (including this one) in a number of ways. Some of these deviations from the norm are also found in various British dialects (e.g. the forms *it don't, it ain't, them things* and the double negative in *it ain't never going . . .*).
These regional varieties of English are typically found in the usage of certain, usually lower, social classes. Although these varieties are in themselves just as effective for communication as the language used in our examples elsewhere in this book, they are often regarded as incorrect, unacceptable and uneducated, since they are not **Standard English.**
The generally recognized standard is based on the language of the middle and upper classes. But as language development has diverged somewhat in the different English-speaking countries, different **national standards** have evolved: Standard British English (with so-called Received Pronunciation, or RP, the pronunciation found in Southern England), Standard American English (General American), Standard Irish, South African, Australian English, and so on. Some standard forms of English are also emerging in countries where English is used as a lingua franca, e.g. in India and some African countries.
The differences between the various national standards are most obvious in pronunciation; there are also considerable differences in vocabulary, but in grammar the differences are relatively slight. We can therefore concentrate on just one of these standards, British English. Any important grammatical differences in American English are explained in the notes. (In addition, the main differences in pronunciation, spelling, etc. between British and American English are summarized in the Appendix, **362–365.**)

11 Limiting ourselves to Standard English does not, however, mean uniformity. A speaker or writer may keep within a particular standard variety and still have a wide choice of styles (registers). The style chosen will depend on the subject matter dealt with, the person addressed, the social situation, and the form of the communication (oral or written).
We will distinguish between three types of style: **colloquial English**, which is used typically in informal conversation and personal letters; **formal English**, which is found, for instance, in official speeches or documents and in business correspondence; and **neutral style.**
In the context of speech intentions and speaker perspective (cf **8–9**), one can also make a distinction between differing degrees of politeness and of personal, or emotional, involvement. This can influence the choice of grammatical means, e.g. modal auxiliaries (cf Ch. 7), the progressive form (cf **184.1** Note 1, **188, 206**), and types of sentence, intonation and stress (cf Ch. 1).
The stylistic effect of an utterance is determined by various factors, for instance, vocabulary. There are words and expressions which are considered to be outright colloquialisms. Some of them come from the **slang** of a particular group (e.g. Army slang, teenage slang, etc.). An example of this would be the use of *guy* or *bloke* for the stylistically neutral *man* or the more formal *gentleman.* In grammar, too, there are, in addition to the many stylistically neutral forms and structures, some phenomena which are typical of colloquial or formal style. Compare the following examples:

- How about doing our homework together this evening, Sue? You're so much better than me at maths.
- Sorry, Chris, but I can't help you today.
- Why not?
- Well, you see, those American friends I was telling you about have just arrived. I've got to show them around town.
- So you'll be gallivanting around town with the Yanks, while I struggle with the calculus all on my own.
- Too bad! Perhaps another time.

The director of our firm, to whom you had addressed your request, has instructed me to inform you that we shall unfortunately be unable to offer our assistance in making arrangements for the visit of the American Youth Orchestra to our town.
At the period in question, our facilities will be fully occupied by a business conference. However, international cultural exchange being of such vital importance, we wish to make a contribution to your expenses . . .

The dialogue on the left-hand side is typical of colloquial speech. It contains several of the grammatical features which characterize this style: short forms of auxiliary verbs (*you're, can't,* etc.), the object form of the personal pronoun instead of the subject form *(better than me),* omission of the relative pronoun in a relative clause and the final position of the preposition in the relative clause *(those American friends I was telling you about),* shortened sentences *(Why not? Too bad! Perhaps another time.)* including the question with *how about.* Some of the vocabulary is also typical of colloquial speech: *maths* (mathematics), *gallivanting* (wandering around enjoying oneself), *Yanks* (slang for: Americans).
In comparison with this, the excerpt from a letter on the right-hand side, with its long, complex first sentence, sounds very formal. There are also other grammatical features of formal style here: the full forms of auxiliaries (*we shall,* etc.), the non-defining relative clauses (and especially the positioning of the preposition *to* in front of the relative pronoun *whom* in the relative clause), and the absolute participle construction in the last sentence *(international cultural exchange being . . .).* Many of the words and phrases used here are formal, too: *addressed your request* (asked for help), *we shall be unable to offer our assistance* (we can't help you), *at the period in question* (at the time you mentioned), etc.

12 So-called **literary style** is a special case. It does not belong to any of the above categories. Depending on what type of literature it is and when it was written, a literary text may contain many features of either formal or colloquial style. In literary texts it is quite common to find that, although the writer essentially observes the grammatical rules of the language, certain things may be modified to achieve some special effect. Let us take as an example the following opening passage of a short story:

> It was raining **that** morning, and still very dark. When **the** boy reached **the** streetcar café he had almost finished his route . . . (Carson McCullers, *A Tree. A Rock. A Cloud*)

Normally, definite articles or demonstrative determiners are only used to refer to persons or things which have been mentioned before and are therefore already known (cf **4** and **100**). But in our example they are used in the very first sentence, which suggests that one ought to know what morning, what boy and what café are being referred to here. This device serves to arouse the reader's curiosity.
In order to be able to recognize when grammatical phenomena are being used in a special stylistic way, one first has to know how these phenomena are normally used. This is what our grammatical description of the English language aims to show.

13–15 English and German

13 Of all the modern languages widely taught in German-speaking countries, English is the one that appears most similar to German. This is because the two languages are closely related; they both developed from West Germanic dialects. (French, Spanish and Italian, on the other hand, are Romance languages and have a common origin in Latin.) English has evolved from the language spoken by the Angles, Saxons and Jutes, who had settled along the coast of the North Sea in what is now Holland, northwest Germany and Denmark. When these tribes invaded England in the 5th century A. D. and settled there, they took their language with them. This language is generally called Old English (or Anglo-Saxon). Its later development via Middle English to Modern English has always been strongly influenced by other languages. The Viking invasions between the 8th and the

11th centuries introduced North Germanic (Scandinavian) elements into English. The most lasting influence, however, followed on the conquest of England in 1066 by the French-speaking Normans. From the vocabulary point of view, English became a hybrid language, and Modern English has more words of Romance origin than of Germanic origin. (But the Germanic words are, on average, used much more frequently.) This chequered history explains why, over the centuries, English has always readily assimilated loan words from the classical languages Latin and Greek, from other modern European languages and from the languages of the former colonies (e.g. Indic languages):

From Scandinavian languages	From French	From Latin (some originally from Greek)	From other languages
egg, skirt, wrong, get, take, die, they, them, their, etc.	beauty, colour, country, peace, courage, justice, catch, pay, receive, etc.	stimulus, album, population, crisis, physics, paternal, attract, etc.	yacht [jɒt] (Dutch); canyon (Span.); bungalow (Ind.), etc.

14 In its grammatical structures, however, English has always remained in essence a Germanic language. Hardly any structures were adopted from other languages. The only signs of non-Germanic influence that can be identified with any certainty are from Latin: the absolute participle construction (*The people working hard, the damage was quickly repaired* – cf **294**) and the object + infinitive construction following verbs which express an opinion (*We thought him to be very cruel* – cf **266**). The development of other grammatical phenomena was furthered, but not, it is thought, actually brought about by the existence of French or Latin parallels. This applies, for example, to the comparison of adjectives and adverbs with *more/most* and the use as relative pronouns of the pronouns *who, whom, which,* etc., which were originally interrogatives only. Where the grammar of English diverges most from that of German, it is as a result of developments within the English language itself, many of which can be traced back to Old English. The major differences are:

- the disappearance of most inflections to nouns, verbs and adjectives, which means that the function of nouns in Modern English sentences (subject, object, etc.) is determined mainly by word order and prepositions. (This gives English its 'analytic' character.)
- the change from grammatical gender to biological gender in nouns (compare German *der Hut – er* and English *the hat – it*). As a result, the pronoun and determiner systems also had to change (e.g. with the relative pronoun: *who* for persons and *which* for things, etc.).
- the so-called *do*-paraphrase (*do* as an auxiliary in negative sentences and questions, etc.), and the development of systematic distinctions between past tense and present perfect, progressive form and simple form, gerund and infinitive constructions.

15 In a grammar of English for German speakers, it is obviously important to pay special attention to those areas of grammar where English differs from German. This does not mean, however, that the grammatically similar features can be ignored. It is particularly vital for advanced learners, for whom this Grammar is intended, to be provided with detailed guidance on such parallels: the more familiar they become with a language so closely related to their own, the more cautious they will be about using any grammatical structures or forms which resemble those of their native language. This is not only the case with individual problem areas (e.g. prepositions), often seen as 'idiomatic' difficulties. Advanced learners often experience difficulty with those aspects of grammar which concern the combining of sentences into a coherent written or spoken text. It is therefore essential to explain the basic principles of cohesion, emphasis and reporting, (for instance, the conversion of direct speech into reported speech), although the same or similar principles may apply in German and often differ in English only in the linguistic forms they take (cf Chs. 10 and 11). The resulting insight into the grammatical system of the English language should be of considerable help to learners who wish to become as confident in English, both as speakers and listeners, as they are in their native language.

Chapter 1: Types of Sentences

16–18 Types of Sentences and Speech Intentions; Complete and Shortened Sentences (Summary)

16 Types of Sentences

In English, as in German, there are four structurally different types of sentence. With the exception of exclamations, they can be either affirmative or negative.

Public transport is gaining ground in big cities. In the country, however, you can't do without a private car.	• Statements (cf **19**)
Do you enjoy driving on motorways? Didn't you read the latest statistics on accidents?	• Questions: – *yes/no* questions (cf **21**)
When did you pass your driving test? Why don't the police enforce speed limits more rigorously?	– questions with interrogatives ('*wh*-questions') (cf **24**)
Drive carefully on wet roads. Don't try to overtake on bends.	• Imperatives (commands) (cf **35**)
What a bottleneck this stretch of road is!	• Exclamations (cf **37**)

17 Types of Sentences, Intonation and Speech Intentions

Each type of sentence has a typical function in communication, which is indicated by the name given to it. For instance, one normally uses the statement form to make a statement about something. However, this effect is only achieved if the speaker uses a falling intonation pattern. If, instead, a particular kind of rising intonation is used, the effect is that of a question. As a general rule, a speaker will use

- falling intonation when something is regarded as complete or certain,
- rising intonation when something is regarded as uncertain, undecided or surprising.

The following examples show how widely differing speech intentions can be expressed through particular combinations of sentence type and intonation pattern:

	Sentence type	Intonation	Possible speech intention
Bread is a staple food in Europe.	statement	falling	assertion
You're throwing away that loaf? (– Yes, it's gone mouldy.)		rising	surprised question
Does this windmill still grind corn?	*yes/no* question	rising	neutral question
Doesn't that mill look picturesque?		falling	exclamation
How many pounds of flour do you need?	*wh*-question	falling	neutral question
(Ten pounds please.) – How many did you say?		rising	surprised question
Go to the baker's and don't take all day.	imperative	falling	command
Try some of my sponge cake. (It's really good.)		rising	neutral suggestion

18 Short Sentences, Set Phrases and Block Language

In addition to the types of sentence listed in **16**, a number of other categories can be distinguished, according to their form and their communicative function:

I forgot to wish you a happy birthday, **didn't I?**

Have you opened your presents yet? – **No, I haven't.**

Can you guess what's in this parcel?
– **I think *so.*/I'm afraid *not.*/I don't know.**

I enjoyed the party. – **So did I.**
We weren't home till late. – **Nor/neither was I.**

Short sentences

In short sentences, parts of the sentence are replaced by auxiliary verbs or other pro-forms, or are dropped altogether. They include

- question tags (cf **27–28**)
- short answers with *yes* and *no* (cf **29–30**)
- short sentences of comment or opinion with *so, not* or without pro-forms (cf **31–33**)
- short sentences of comparison with *so, nor, neither* (cf **34**).

Good morning. Hello. Welcome home.
Goodbye. See you (later/tomorrow).
Excuse me. Sorry.
Happy birthday (to you). Good luck.

Set phrases

These are short expressions of fixed form used in certain communicative situations, e.g. for greeting someone, taking one's leave, apologizing, etc. (cf **38–39**.)

A History of the English Language
Conservatives re-elected
Down with racism No entry

Block language

This refers to sentence fragments used, for instance, in titles, headlines, slogans, public notices, etc. (cf **40**).

Note:
The types of sentence listed in **16** can also be shortened by leaving out parts of the sentence which will be understood:

(I) Think he's at home now. – (I) Wish he were.	(statement)
(Do you) Want some more tea?	(*yes/no* question)
I'm going to Paris. – When (are you going)?	(question with interrogative)
(Get) Out!	(imperative)
What a wonderful idea (that is)!	(exclamation)

19–20 Affirmative and Negative Statements

19 Structures

	Subject	Predicate	Necessary complementation
	Bob	has passed	his exam.
Today	he	got	the results.
Of course	he	is	very pleased.

The normal word order of statements in English is: subject – predicate – necessary complementation (cf **41**).

Unlike in German, this word order is normally retained even when a sentence begins with an adverbial. (For exceptions see **337–338**.)

The word order subject – predicate – complementation also applies to negative statements. Two types of negation can be distinguished:

Negative element *not* added to the predicate

Subject	Predicate		Complementation		
(Compare: Ann	has	finished	her essay.)		Predicates consisting of auxiliary verb(s) + main verb either have *-n't* added to the first auxiliary, or the full form *not* following this auxiliary. (The latter is either formal or – with stressed *not* – emphatic.)
Tom	**hasn't**	finished	his essay	yet.	
I	**can't**	have lost	that page.		
Candidates	**may not**	leave	the room.		
(No,) I	**was not**	trying	to copy.		
(Compare: Joe		likes	poems.)		With the simple present and simple past active forms of the main verb a negated form of the auxiliary *do* is used (*do* paraphrase, cf **243**; for *be* see Note 1 below).
Jim	**doesn't**	like	poems.		
I	**didn't**	understand	that verse.		
Poetry	**does not**	appeal	to everyone.		

Negative element in a different part of the sentence

Nobody	could explain	that passage.	In sentences with *no, nobody, never,* etc. there is no paraphrase with *do* (but see **337**.3).
The notes	offered	**no** real help.	
He **never**	uses	a dictionary	

Notes:

1. As a main verb *be* never takes a *do* paraphrase (except in a negated imperative; cf **255**.2). But with the simple tenses of *have* as a main verb a paraphrase with *do* is always possible and, in fact, often necessary (cf **246–251**):
   The book shop **isn't** open now. They **don't have** any foreign language books anyway.

2. Instead of the negated shortened form with *-n't* one sometimes uses the shortened form of the auxiliary followed by *not* (cf **219, 246, 252**). This form is particularly common in the north of the British Isles. Other speakers use this form generally when they want to emphasize the negation:
   John's **not** done it. (Compare: John **hasn't** done it.) – He's **not** working at the moment.

3. Although the negative element *not* usually follows an auxiliary, it can also be combined with other words, e.g.
   - in shortened sentences without a predicate: Who wants to start? – **Not** me.
   - to express a contrast: I need a pencil, **not** a pen.
   - with non-finite constructions (cf **256** Note): She pretended **not** to hear me.
   - in coordinating constructions with *not only . . . but also:* She plays **not** only the piano, but also the flute.
   - for emphatic negation of the subject (only in combination with certain words: *not a, not even, not all,* and others): **Not** a sound could be heard.

20 The Choice of Negative, Non-Assertive and Assertive Words in Statements

In addition to **negative** words such as *not, no, nobody, nowhere, never,* etc., which have a negating effect, there are also **assertive** words with an affirmative effect (e.g. *some, somebody, somewhere, sometimes, some time, already, too, as well*). There is a third category, namely **non-assertive** words, which have neither an affirmative nor a negative effect (e.g. *any, anybody, anywhere, ever, yet, either*). Certain adverbs, pronouns and determiners can be assigned to one of these three categories. (For pronouns and determiners see **113** as well.)

Sorry, there are **no** eggs for breakfast this morning. Or: There **aren't any** eggs ...
Don't take my cup away. I **haven't** finished my breakfast **yet.** (Compare: You can take his cup first, he has **already** finished his breakfast.)
I'm not a coffee drinker. – I **don't** drink coffee in the morning, **either,** but I do in the afternoon. (Compare: Sue always has tea for breakfast. – My wife prefers tea, **too.**)

Just one negative word is sufficient to make a sentence negative. The rest of the sentence then contains non-assertive words (if required). The assertive equivalents cannot normally be combined with a negative element.
In negative sentences one can therefore only use the adverbs *yet* and *either* (Ger. *auch*), for example, but not *already, too/as well/also.*

I **don't** like **some** spices *(Gewürze)*. (= There are some spices which I don't like.)
I **don't** like **any** spices. (= I like no spices at all.)

They **didn't** offer us **any** alcoholic drinks.
I **haven't** tried **any** of your pastries yet.
No, thanks, I **don't** want **anything** to drink.
No drinks will be served during the performance.
As she is a vegetarian, she could eat **none** of the sandwiches.
There's **nothing** more refreshing than a cool beer.

The assertive word *some* and its compounds can sometimes occur in negative sentences, but the meaning is then quite different from that of *any* and its compounds (cf **115**).

Sentences with a negated auxiliary and non-assertive determiners or pronouns (*not ... any/anybody*, etc.)are much commoner than sentences where the negation is expressed with negative determiners or pronouns; the latter are used mainly in formal style or for giving special emphasis to the negation (cf **121**, **123**).

21–23 *Yes/No* Questions

21 Structures

Yes/no questions contain no interrogative word and are formed by reversing the position of the subject and the (first) auxiliary (partial inversion). In the simple tenses (which have no auxiliary) a paraphrase with *do* is used:

	(Statement: He	is working.)		**Affirmative *yes/no* questions:**
Is	he	working	on a new symphony?	With predicates consisting of auxiliary verb(s) + main verb, the (first) auxiliary is placed at the beginning of the sentence.
Would	you	have bought	the new album?	
	(Statement: Sue	likes	opera.)	
Does	she	like	ballet, too?	In the simple tenses a form of the auxiliary *do* is used at the beginning of the sentence (except with *be*, cf **19** Note 1). This is followed by the subject and the infinitive of the main verb.
Do	you	recognize	this music?	
Did	you	enjoy	the performance?	
				Negative *yes/no* questions:
Isn't	he	conducting	tonight?	Normally, *-n't* is added to the auxiliary in front-position.
Doesn't	Ann	like	going to concerts?	
Are	they	**not** playing	the Brahms after all?	In formal style or for special emphasis *not* is inserted after the subject.
Did	Tim	**not** want	to come?	

22 Speech Intentions and Assertive and Non-Assertive Words

Like their German equivalents, *yes/no* questions are usually given rising intonation. They can express a variety of intentions. The underlying intention will determine whether one uses assertive words such as *already*, *some*, etc. or non-assertive words such as *yet*, *any*, etc. (cf **20**).

Do you sell stamps?
Have the girls paid for their postcards?
Is there **anything** else you want?
Did you **ever** write to Fred?
Has the post gone **yet**? (I'm hoping this letter will catch it.)
Has **either** of you 5 p for a phone call?
(**But:** Was that telephone out of order, **too**?)

Affirmative *yes/no* questions are normally used when asking for information, i.e. when one does not know whether the answer will be *yes* or *no*. In such cases **non-assertive words** are used (if required), e.g. *any* and its compounds, *ever*, *yet* and *either* (= Ger. *einer von beiden*). (However, *either* is not used here in the sense of *auch; too, as well* or *also* are used instead.)

Examples	Explanation
Will you be writing to Fred **some time**? *(... irgendwann?)* Has the post gone **already**? (It looks as if it has.) Has **one** of you got 5 p for a phone call? Can I borrow **some** money from you? Is that enough or would you like **some** more?	If one wants an assumption to be confirmed, however, and therefore expects the affirmative answer *yes,* one will use **assertive words** such as *some, some time, sometimes, already, one (of the two).* Assertive words are also used when the intention behind the question is to make a request or an offer (cf **115**).
Didn't Jim write down the address of that American boy we met? *(Hat Jim denn nicht ... aufgeschrieben?)* Hasn't **anyone** written to the Youth Hostel **yet**? *(Hat denn noch niemand ... geschrieben?)* Haven't you got **any** more film left **either**? Weren't those pictures **ever** developed?	**Negative *yes/no* questions** can be used to express surprise (and often also disappointment or anger) that something is not as one expected it to be. Since one then assumes that the question will get a negative answer, one uses **non-assertive words** (if required).
Nobody seems to have thought of a thermos flask. – Hasn't Gwen brought one? We need some bread. – Hasn't Jane bought **some already**? *(Hat Jane nicht schon welches gekauft?)* Don't we need **some** tea, **too**? Isn't there a shop **somewhere** down the road?	Negative questions can also be used when one assumes that something is the case and is asking for confirmation of this assumption. In these questions **assertive words** will be used (if required).

Note:
Yes/no questions are given falling intonation if the question form is being used in the function of an exclamation, to express enthusiasm, astonishment, horror, etc. (in writing an exclamation mark is frequently used instead of a question mark here), and also if the speaker is impatiently repeating a question that has been asked before:

Wouldn't that be marvellous! Isn't that shocking!
... Yes, but what I still don't know is: Have you fixed the date?

23 Questions through Intonation

Sentences which have the same word order as statements are sometimes spoken with rising intonation, which gives them the character of questions. Such questions are a way of asking for confirmation of something which the speaker has concluded or realized – they often have an undertone of surprise. In some cases the speaker may not expect any answer at all. Questions through intonation occur mainly in colloquial speech. In written texts they would be written with a question mark.

Examples	Explanation
It took me over half an hour from the station. – You mean you walked all the way? (Taxi-driver to a customer with a load of parcels:) You've been doing **some** shopping? – Yes, I'm almost broke. Your taxi has arrived. – It's here **already?**	When they are in affirmative form, the answer is also expected to be in the affirmative and therefore **assertive words** are used (if required).
You have to change planes at Frankfurt. – There's no direct flight to Stuttgart in the evening? (At the airport check-in desk:) You haven't got **any** luggage? – No, just this small briefcase. I've got to get my ticket. – What, you haven't got it **yet?**	When they are in negative form, a negative answer is expected and so **non-assertive words** are used (if required).

Note:
As in German, statements containing verbs or adverbs which express a supposition or some degree of probability can be used in the function of *yes/no* questions:

You don't happen to know her telephone number, I **suppose?**
But **surely** she gave you a forwarding address?

24–26 Questions with Interrogatives

24 Structures

These questions are always introduced by an interrogative element. This may be a single interrogative (*who, why,* etc.) or an interrogative + noun or *of*-phrase (*what colour, which of you,* etc.).
Questions with interrogatives normally have falling intonation, just as they do in German.
The word order depends on whether the interrogative element is the subject of the sentence or not:

Interrogative element: subject

Who	wrote	'Treasure Island'?	These so-called subject questions always have the same word order as statements: subject – predicate – complementation.
What characters	appear	in the book?	
Which one	tells	the story?	
(Compare: Jim	tells	the story.)	Affirmative subject questions never have a paraphrase with *do.*
Which of you	**hasn't** read	to the end?	Negative subject questions are formed in the same way as negative statements (cf **19**).
Who	**did not** like	it?	

Interrogative element: some other part of the sentence

Where	**can**	we	go for the weekend?	In this case there is partial inversion (as in *yes/no* questions): inversion of the subject and the (first) auxiliary, *do*-paraphrase with simple tenses.
Who	**will**	we	be meeting there?	
What	**did**	you	do on Sunday?	
(Compare:	**Did**	you	go to the match?)	
Why	**won't**	Pat	join us?	Negation takes the same form as in negative *yes/no* questions (cf **21**).
Who	**did**	you	not invite?	
Who	**were**	you	talking **to?**	In questions with interrogatives, prepositions are usually in the same position as in the corresponding statements, i.e. after the predicate (+ direct object). In formal English, however, they are placed in front of the interrogative.
What remarks	**did**	he	get upset **about?**	
(Compare:		He	got upset about something.)	
To whom	**did**	you	turn for assistance?	
With whom	**did**	you	discuss the problem?	

Notes:

1. As in German, questions with interrogatives have rising intonation when a speaker has not understood what was said (and therefore wants it repeated) or finds it astonishing:
   She lives in Doddiscombeleigh. – (Sorry, I didn't get that.) Where does she live?
   I lent my pocket-knife to John. – Who did you lend it to? You will never get it back.

2. In informal conversation, questions with interrogatives are – as in German – frequently shortened, either to the interrogative word itself or to the interrogative plus preposition. The speaker uses
a) falling intonation to ask for additional information:
   Tom called. – When?/Where from?
b) rising intonation to express amazement or ask for something to be repeated. (Here, part or all of the original statement may be taken up and repeated with the same word order.)
   I opened the tin with a ballpoint pen. – With what?/You opened it with what?
   I was talking to Jimmy Peterson the other day. – Jimmy who?

3. When it is an adverbial that is being asked about, the preposition in some instances has to follow the predicate (and complementation) or is omitted altogether, and in other instances it must precede the interrogative:
   Where will he be going **(to)**? *(Wohin ...?)*
   Where have they come **from**? *(Woher ...?)*
   Since when have you known her? *(Seit wann ...?)*
   What do you need that **for**? *(Wozu ...?)*
   For what purpose do you need this certificate? (formal) *(Zu welchem Zweck ...?)*

25 The Choice between the Interrogatives *Who, Whom, Whose, What, Which*

The following points need to be considered when choosing between these interrogative:

a) Is one asking about persons or things? (Compare: *Who's this? – What's this?*),

b) Are the persons or things one is asking about part of an indefinite or a definite number? (Compare: *What* countries have you visited? – *Which* of them did you like best?),

c) Are the interrogatives pronouns or determiners used with a noun? (Compare: *Who* did this? – *What* fool did this?).

(However, as with the German *wer?* and *was?*, it makes no difference whether one is asking about just one person or thing or about more than one.)

Who phoned you just now? *(Wer . . .?)* **Who** did Susan phone this morning? *(Wen . . .?)* **Who** is this message intended for? *(Für wen . . .?)*	***Who*** is used to ask about persons; this may be anybody from an indefinite number of persons. It is used for subjects (Ger. *wer?*) and, in colloquial speech, also for objects (Ger. *wen? wem?*).
Whom shall I ring about the repair? *(Wen . . .?)* **To whom** did you want to speak? *(Mit wem . . .?)* **Who(m)** did she put you through **to**? *(Mit wem hat sie dich verbunden?)*	In formal style the object case form *whom* is used. When the interrogative is preceded by a preposition (formal) the form is always *whom*. (When there is a preposition in end-position *whom* can be used, but the colloquial *who* is more common.)
Whose telephone number is this? **Whose** call will you deal with first? What awful handwriting. **Whose** is it?	***Whose*** + noun (or sometimes *whose* on its own) is used for persons when asking about possession or origin, etc. (Ger. *wessen?*).
What's got teeth but can't bite? (A comb.) **What** does a winner lose in a race? (His breath.) **What** does the sea say to the sand? (Nothing, it just waves.)	***What*** can be a pronoun or a determiner. **As a pronoun** *what* is used to ask about things (or events, etc.) where there is a possible choice from an indefinite number (Ger. *was?*).
What drivers always go in circles? (Screw drivers.) **What ring** is a square? (A boxing ring.) **What (kind of) bed** can't you sleep in? (A river bed.)	**As a determiner** *what* can be used to ask about either persons or things in cases where there is a possible choice from an indefinite number (Ger. *was für?/welcher?*). *What kind(s) of/what sort(s) of* can often be used instead.
Which was discovered first, Australia or New Zealand? **Which navigator** was America named after? **Which country** is the larger, Canada or the USA? **Which of the Channel Islands** is nearest France? **Which of you** scored most points in the quiz?	***Which*** is used to ask about persons or things where there is a possible choice from a definite number (Ger. usually: *welcher?*). It is sometimes used on its own but more often precedes a noun or an *of*-phrase. Since the *of*-phrase always makes it clear that the choice is limited, it cannot be combined with *who* or *what*. (Compare: ***Wer*** *von uns/euch/ihnen* – ***Which*** *of us/you/them*.)

Notes:

1. As an interrogative pronoun *what* can also be used to refer to persons when one is asking about their job or profession, religion, nationality, etc:

   My elder sister is a librarian. – And **what**'s your younger sister?

2. In a number of cases the English *what* corresponds to the German *wie*, e.g. when asking about the time, someone's name or age. When asking about the characteristics of something one uses *What . . . like?* and a linking verb *(be, look, sound, taste, smell)*:

   What time is it? **What**'s the exact time? *(Wie spät/wieviel Uhr . . .?)*
   What is your name? **What** is *Verdacht* in English? **What** do you call this? *(Wie heißt/Wie nennt man . . .?)*
   What are the ages of your sisters?/**What** age are your sisters?/How old are your sisters?
   What is your new teacher like? *(Wie ist . . .?)* **What** does a mango look/taste **like?**
   (But: How is she? = *Wie geht es ihr?*)

26 Complex Questions: Questions within Questions

	Main clause	*That*-clause	
	They said	the boys had gone	to the zoo.
Who	did they say	had gone	to the zoo?
Where	did they say	the boys had gone?	

Where do you think the main entrance is?
When do you suppose they shut?
Why do you imagine they don't allow dogs?
What time did she suggest we should meet?
How much did you say they charge for admission?

Questions with interrogatives can also be used to ask about parts of a *that*-clause. The main clause is inserted (without a pause or a comma) between the interrogative element and the rest of the *that*-clause. In the main clause there is partial inversion (auxiliary – subject), whereas the rest of the *that*-clause keeps its normal word order.

This kind of question is formed with verbs of saying, thinking and supposing (in the main clause). By using them one can avoid being abrupt when asking for information; instead, one is casually asking somebody else's opinion, or taking up something that has already been mentioned.

	Greg was thinking of buying a cashmere scarf.
What	was Greg thinking of buying?

What shop did you see them going into?
How much are you prepared to pay?
What kind of gloves would you like me to show you?

Similarly, questions with interrogatives can be used to ask about parts of a non-finite construction (gerund, participle, infinitive).
This is possible with all verbs and verbal complexes which can take a non-finite construction as their complementation.

Notes:

1. Questions beginning with *why, when, where, how often* may have two possible meanings in cases where the interrogative can relate to either a main clause or a subordinate clause or non-finite construction:
   Why did they tell you John bought the car in Germany?
   a) Why did they tell you this? b) Why did John buy the car in Germany?
   When did you ask him to pay back the money?
   a) When did you ask him? b) When was he to pay back the money?

2. Instead of including a main clause with a verb of saying or supposing within the question, as described above, it is possible in colloquial speech to use a normal, straightforward question and add the 'main clause' at the end:
   Where have the boys gone, did they say?

27–28 Question Tags

27 Structures

Question tags are added on to the end of a statement and repeat its content in the shortened form of auxiliary + subject (in the form of a personal pronoun).

Joe Miller	**has**	changed,	**hasn't**	he?
You	**wouldn't**	have believed it,	**would**	you?
We	**don't**	envy him,	**do**	we?
That		helps a lot,	**doesn't**	it?
Even Mum		liked the idea,	**didn't**	she?

If the predicate of the statement has one or more auxiliaries, the first auxiliary is repeated. Otherwise a form of the auxiliary *do* is used (except with *be*, cf 19 Note 1).

The Lees	**are**	rather snobbish,	**aren't**	they?
They	**aren't**	very friendly either,	**are**	they?

Normally, a positive statement is followed by a negative question tag and a negative statement by a positive tag.

Grandpa	**has rarely**	let us down,	**has**	he?
(He has not often let us down.)				
Your cousin	**hardly**	opens her mouth,	**does**	she?

Restricting adverbs such as *hardly, scarcely, seldom, rarely* are more or less negative in meaning and are therefore followed by positive question tags.

Notes:

1. If there is a formal subject *there*, this is repeated in the question tag:
   There aren't many places to go in this town, are **there?**

2. Question tags can also be used after shortened sentences where the subject and the verb *be* have been omitted (these are supplied in the question tag):
   Terribly boring, isn't it, Fred?

28 Speech Intentions

Question tags belong essentially to the spoken language. In German one often finds *nicht (wahr)?/oder (nicht)?* used in a similar way.

1. Positive statement – negative question tag and vice versa (the general rule)

Mary Alice **can** come to the beach with us tomorrow, **can't** she? *(. . ., nicht?)*
You **didn't** bring an insect repellent *(Abwehrmittel)*, **did** you? *(. . ., oder?)*

Three miles. That's rather a long walk, **isn't** it? *(. . ., nicht wahr?)*
Well, we **have no** other choice, **have** we? *(. . ., nicht wahr?)*

We could take a taxi to the station. – Yes, we **could, couldn't** we? *(Ja, nicht wahr?)*
You **mustn't** miss the bus. – No, I **mustn't, must** I? *(Nein, da hast du recht.)*

Rising intonation is used for the question tag if one is asking for confirmation (or, alternatively, correction) of an assumption. This makes it a real question which one expects to be answered.

Falling intonation indicates that the speaker assumes that the person spoken to will agree. In this case, one does not necessarily expect any answer. The statement + question tag is then more like an assertion.

Question tags can also be added to short answers expressing agreement. Here, too, falling intonation is used and naturally no answer is expected.

Note:
Other sentence patterns can also be used when asking for something to be confirmed, e.g.:
   Rather strange, **don't you think?**
   That's his idea of a joke, **I suppose?**
   Don't you think that's going a bit too far?

2. Statement and question tag: both positive or both negative

I've got to pick up my little brother from the kindergarten. – Oh, you**'ve** got a little brother, **have** you? *(Ach, du hast einen kleinen Bruder?)*
So that**'s** what you call a tidy room, **is** it? *(Das nennst du also ein aufgeräumtes Zimmer?)*

There's a lion in the garden, Mummy. – Oh, there **is, is** there? *(Ach, was du nicht sagst.)*
I **won't** eat my porridge. – Oh you **won't, won't** you? *(So, du willst nicht? Das wollen wir doch mal sehen.)*

A positive statement with a positive question tag (rising intonation) is used to express a conclusion which a speaker has arrived at from the situation or from what has been said before. The tone is often ironic or sarcastic.

When a speaker responds to a remark with a short answer + question tag, both of which are either positive or negative, the tone is quite definitely ironic, and may even be threatening.

Note:
For question tags used after imperatives (*will you, shall we,* etc.) cf **36.2**.

Short Answers with *Yes* and *No*

29 Structures

These shortened sentences generally begin with a *yes* or *no* and are usually answers to questions. They consist of a personal pronoun and a (positive or negative) auxiliary:

Are you ready now?	– Yes,	**I am.**
Won't Ed be coming?	– No,	**he won't.**
Would you rather go home?	– Yes,	**we would.**
Did Jane want to stay?	– Yes,	**she did.**
You always **arrive** late.	– No,	**I don't.**

The pronoun takes up the subject of the preceding sentence and the auxiliary is a repetition of the preceding (first) auxiliary. For the simple tenses, a form of the auxiliary *do* is used (except with *be*, cf **19** Note 1).

Have you finished?	– Yes,	**I have.**
Are the Wells leaving now?	– Yes,	**they are.**
Didn't you want to come, too?	– No,	**I didn't.**
Has Dad actually said so?	– No,	**he hasn't.**
Isn't Shirley driving there?	– No,	**she's not.**
Did the others help you?	– No,	**they did not.**

In positive short answers one always uses the stressed full form of the auxiliary. In negative short answers one normally uses the stressed full form of the auxiliary with the shortened form *-n't* added on to it. To make the negation more emphatic the unstressed auxiliary + stressed *not* is used.

Notes:

1. A preceding formal subject *there* is repeated in short answers (cf **27** Note 1):
   Is **there** a bus stop near here? – Yes, **there** is./No, **there** isn't.

2. If the auxiliary is *must*, the same form *must* is used in positive short answers, whereas in negative short answers one uses *needn't:*
   Must we wait for the others? – Yes, we **must.**/No, we **needn't.**

30 Speech Intentions

Did you get what you wanted? – Yes, **I did.**/No, **I didn't,** but Pat did.
Size 12 is not in stock? – I'm afraid **it's not,** but it's on order./Yes, **it is.** You'll find it over there on the other rail.
We're being a bit extravagant, aren't we? – Yes, I think **we are.**/Oh, I don't think **we are.** We can afford it.

Short answers can be used in response to questions, e.g. *yes/no* questions, questions through intonation or question tags with rising intonation.
A short answer can be used to affirm or deny something, to confirm/correct an assumption or to express agreement/disagreement with an opinion.

The staff will never agree to working overtime. – No, **they** certainly **won't.**/Oh, I'm sure **they will,** if the pay is attractive.
There isn't much sense in arguing over details right now, is there? – Of course **there isn't.**
What a difficult decision! – Yes, **it was,** wasn't it?
Wasn't the old man hard to convince! – I should think **he was.**

Short answers can also be used to express a reaction to what has been said even though this does not call for any answer, e.g. statements and question tags spoken with falling intonation or exclamations and *yes/no* questions which function as exclamations. In such cases short answers generally express agreement or disagreement.

As the above examples show, short answers are frequently intensified or toned down by adverbs (*certainly, of course,* etc.), by verbs or verbal complexes (*I think, I'm afraid,* etc.), by the addition of question tags (cf **28.1**), etc. *Yes* or *no* are often omitted, particularly when the answers are expanded in this way or when a further sentence or clause is added.

Notes:

1. *Yes* and *no* are usually used without a following shortened sentence if the answer is expanded with a further sentence or clause:

   You'll have some more salad? – **Yes,** it's delicious. You don't like cucumber? – **No,** I hate it.

2. Shortened imperative sentences can be used to react to requests, offers or orders which are addressed to a third person:

   Can I open the window?/Shall I turn the heating up?/Shut the door, Angie. – **Yes, do./No, don't.**

31–33 Short Sentences of Comment or Opinion with *so/not* or without Pro-Forms

31 Structures

Short sentences of comment or opinion always refer back to a preceding sentence, the content of which is not repeated as a subordinate clause. They normally contain a pro-form.
So represents a positive and *not* a negative subordinate clause:

Is he badly hurt? – I wouldn't say **so.** (that he is badly hurt.) – I hope **not.** (that he is not badly hurt.)

There are three basic structures for this type of short sentence:

				1. Pro-form *so/not* in end-position
Will the champion keep the title?	–	It seems	**so.**	positive
Mike's sure to lose the match.	–	He **doesn't** think	**so.**	negative
Have our team a chance of winning?	–	I'm afraid	**not.**	negative
				2. No pro-form
Sheila's training hard at present.	–	I see.		positive
Has Philip got over his injury?	–	I **don't** know.		negative
				3. Proform *so* in front-position
Molly will be fit by then, won't she?	–	**So** she says.		positive

This type of short sentence is found mainly with verbs of reporting, opinion, supposition and appearance. With the equivalent verbs in German the preceding sentence is often replaced by *es, das, so: Ich weiß (es) nicht/Das glaube ich nicht/Es scheint so,* etc.

Note:
In short sentences containing this kind of verb the preceding sentence can be repeated in a shortened form, i.e. with a personal pronoun + auxiliary (cf **29**). In some cases the sentence can also be replaced by *that/this:*

Was Roger among the first ten? – I don't think **he was.**
Colin's sister won the competition. – I know **she did.**/I know **that.**

32 Use with Certain Verbs

At the races:

Are all the horses lined up?	– I *think* **so.**
	– I **don't** *think* **so.**
	– I *think* **not.**
Beach Boy's going to lose.	– I *hope* **so.**
	– I *hope* **not.**
Is Black Prince second?	– It *appears* **so.**
	– It **doesn't** *appear* **so.**
	– It *appears* **not.**

So and *not* can follow

- verbs of opinion, supposition, expectation, etc.: *think, believe, assume, suppose, imagine, expect; I should say* (= *I think*)

  (Negation only with the pro-form *not:*) *hope, guess, be afraid*
- verbs expressing appearance: *appear, seem*

The road is so icy I slipped and fell. – I *told* you **so.** *(Ich hab dich doch gewarnt.)* Will it snow? – The weather forecast didn't *say* **so,** but it certainly looks like it.	*So* (but not *not*) can be used after some verbs of reporting: *say, tell, s.o.;* it is possible, but rare, after: *claim, state, hint, indicate.*
Most economists believe that business will improve in the coming year. – **So** I *hope.* Watson & Day's is to close. – **So** I *have heard.* The firm's gone bankrupt, or **so** I *understand.* He owes at least £ 50,000. – **So** I *gather.* They got into debt, **so** John *was told.*	Short sentences with *so* in front-position can be formed with most of the verbs listed here so far and also with some of the verbs of perception and those expressing the idea of being informed (usually in the passive): *hear, notice, see; understand/ gather* (Ger. *erfahren haben*), *be told, be informed,* etc.
There's going to be a public inquiry into the Patterson tax scandal. – We *know.* When will the hearing be? – I *forget.* I shan't be here then. – I *see.*	There is no pro-form after the following verbs of knowledge, understanding, etc.: *know, remember, forget, understand, I see* (Ger. *ich verstehe*).

Note:
After some linking verbs such as *be, remain, seem,* etc. the pro-form *so* can also replace a subject complement:
I thought he was rather *arrogant,* but perhaps he really only seems so.

33 Speech Intentions

This kind of short sentence can be used to answer a question or to comment on a statement (one's own or someone else's) by giving one's opinion or citing another person's opinion on the matter.

The story about the Prime Minister's son must be true. 'The Times' and 'The Guardian' both *say* **so.** – Yes, I *know.*	Neutral confirmation is normally expressed by using a short sentence followed by *so* or (in the case of some verbs) without a pro-form.
Is there anything in these rumours? – I **wouldn't** *say* **so.**/Oh, I **don't** *think* **so.**/I **don't** *know.*	For negation one generally uses a negated verb (+ *so*).
Will the editor accept responsibility for the blunder? – I *should imagine* **not.** Are they going to apologize for the false accusation? – I'*m afraid* **not.**	Negation using the pro-form *not* is either formal or emphatic, except in the case of those verbs where *not* is the only possible form of negation *(hope, guess, be afraid).*
	Short sentences with *so* in front-position are mainly used when one is reacting to an assertion or a supposition. They can express a whole range of speech intentions:
The wrong figures are probably due to computer error. – **So** we *assume.* Everything points to it.	– cautious, guarded confirmation (often formal)
They are planning to reduce income tax, aren't they? – **So** I'*ve heard.* But I'll believe it when I see it.	– scepticism (one may, for example, wish to stress that one knows something only from hearsay)
Marion is seriously thinking of changing her job. Or **so** she *tells me.*	– toning down an assertion one has just made (here, the shortened sentence is introduced by *or*)
We've been having a little celebration here. – **So** I *see.* Now would you please get back to work.	– sarcastic comment

Note:
There are also short sentences with *so* in front position which take up the subject and auxiliary of a preceding statement (a *do*-auxiliary is used for the simple tense forms). These generally express surprised agreement:
Have you noticed? John always reads the newspaper backwards. – **So** he does! *(Ja, tatsächlich!)*

34 Short Sentences of Comparison with *So, Nor, Neither*

Short sentences consisting of *so/nor/neither* + auxiliary + subject (in German: subject + *auch/auch nicht*) are used to express a comparison with a preceding statement.
So, nor or *neither* together with the auxiliary represent the predicate and its complementation. The subject in end-position carries the main stress in the short sentence since it is given prominence by the comparison.

We	**'ve** often been to France.	–	So **have**	I.	(I've often been to France, too.)
I	**don't** speak French.	–	Nor **do**	we.	(We don't speak French, either.)
Ted	speaks it fluently.	–	So **does**	Sally.	(Sally speaks it fluently, too.)
He	learnt it in France.	–	So **did**	she.	(She learnt it there, too.)

If there is one, the (first) auxiliary of the preceding sentence is repeated in its unstressed full form. Otherwise a form of the auxiliary *do* is used (except with *be* as a main verb, cf **19** Note 1).

Positive sentence:	French fashions are most imaginative.	– **So** is French food.
	I usually bring back some wine.	– **So** do we.
Negative or restricted sentence:	My Paris hotel **wasn't** cheap at all.	– **Neither** was mine.
	I'll **never** go to Paris over Easter again.	– **Nor** will I.
	We **rarely** book in advance.	– **Neither** do we.
	I've **hardly** seen anything of the countryside.	– **Nor** have I.

A positive statement can be followed by a short sentence beginning with *so,* and a negated statement can be followed by a short sentence beginning with *nor* or *neither.* Because the meaning of sentences containing restricting adverbs such as *seldom, rarely, scarcely, hardly* is more or less negative (= *not often, not much*), they are followed by short sentences beginning with *nor* or *neither.*

I've never been to Nice, (and) **nor** has Mary.

Short sentences beginning with *so/nor/neither* are normally used in reaction to what somebody else has just said. However, they can basically be used in any sequence of two sentences.

Notes:

1. In colloquial speech, short sentences with subject + negated auxiliary + *either* (normal word order) are often used instead of ones beginning with *nor* or *neither,* and short sentences with *too* instead of beginning with *so.*

   I'm not hungry. – I'm not either.
   I'm thirsty. – I am, too.

2. If the preceding sentence and the short sentence do not refer to the same time, there will be a corresponding difference in tense:

   We enjoy travelling, and **so did** my parents till recently.

Imperative Sentences

35 Structures

Get up straight away. **Be** quick and **get** dressed.	**Positive** imperative sentences directed at one or more persons are constructed using the imperative form of the main verb. This has the same form as the infinitive.
Don't wake anybody. **Don't be** so noisy. **Do not neglect** dental hygiene. ['haɪdʒiːn]	**Negative** imperative sentences are constructed with the negative imperative form *don't* (colloquial) or *do not* (formal) + infinitive.
Let's go to the evening service. **Let us pray.**	Imperative sentences in which one includes oneself are constructed with *let's* or (very formal, ceremonious) *let us* + infinitive.
Let's not set off too late. **Let us not forget** the dear departed. **Don't let's lose** hope.	Negative imperative sentences of this type are constructed with *let's not, let us not* or – especially in British English – *don't let's.*

Notes:

1. Imperative sentences are sometimes constructed with an indefinite subject in the third person:
   Somebody help me carry these heavy books. *(Hilf mir mal einer, . . .)*
   Don't any of the boys touch these documents. *(Keiner der Jungen rühre mir . . . an.)*

2. Imperative sentences are normally followed by a full stop in English. Exclamation marks are only used when issuing strict orders or shouting in a state of anger or extreme agitation:
   Sit down, you fool! You stay out!
   Mind! Don't move. "Get out of my house!" she screamed.

36 Downtoning and Intensifying

1. Speech intentions and intonation

Get off that trolley! It's meant for carrying luggage, not for playing with.
Don't lean out of the window. It's dangerous.
Be careful! Don't drop this bag. It's got the thermos flask in it.

Imperative sentences spoken with falling intonation sound forceful, insistent and binding. Falling intonation is therefore used for orders, prohibitions, instructions, warnings, etc.

Just give me a ring, and I'll pick you up from the airport.
Don't be angry with me. It wasn't my fault that I'm late.
Try and be a bit more punctual in future. You could always take a taxi.

Imperative sentences spoken with rising intonation sound much less insistent or binding. They can sometimes have an undertone of entreaty or reproach.

2. Special ways of downtoning and intensifying

Fetch the sugar, **will you.** *(Hol doch bitte mal den Zucker.)*
Let's have some coffee, **shall we.**
Don't let the cat get on the table, **will you.**

By adding an unstressed *will you* (or with *let's: shall we*) – without pausing – to a positive or negative imperative sentence, one makes it less abrupt, and more like a request or suggestion.

Examples	Explanation
Try a bit of this cake, **won't you**. *(Versuchen Sie doch mal...)* Take a taxi, **won't you**. It's snowing. **Please** take your coat off and sit down. Don't go just yet, **please**.	When one is offering something to somebody or suggesting a course of action, one can add *won't you* to a positive imperative sentence. If one wants to be more polite, one can begin or end an imperative sentence with *please* (without a pause).
Do give me a ring next week. **Do** let's arrange another meeting. **Do** be ready on time. *(Sei bitte unbedingt...)* Oh, there you are Bridget. **Do** come in.	By using a stressed (emphatic) *do* in positive imperative sentences one can make requests, offers and suggestions more persuasive and invitations more polite. (For further details on the use of *do* for emphasis see **335–336**.)
You keep out of this. *(Du hältst dich gefälligst da raus.)* **You** be quiet. **Don't you** be so cheeky. *(Sei mir ja nicht so frech.)* **Don't you** shout at me like this.	A more abrupt and impolite type of order is constructed with *you* (stressed) + imperative. For the negative of this one uses *don't + you*. (*Don't* is stressed more heavily than *you* here.)

Notes:

1. Polite exhortations can take the form of a question and are then more like requests than commands. The question is constructed with *will/would* or *can/could*. *Would* and *could* sound especially polite:
   (Let's read the story first.) **Will** you start, Peter?/**Would** you (like to) start Peter?
   Can/Could you tell me where the headmaster's office is? *(Können/Könnten Sie...)*
2. Another form of command, expressing anger or impatience, is constructed with *will* and spoken with falling intonation:
   Will you be quiet. *(Wirst/Willst du wohl endlich ruhig sein!)*

37 Exclamations

Examples	Explanation
What lies he told! **What** a tedious speaker he is. **How** fast she talks! **How** I hate long speeches!	Exclamations (usually punctuated with an exclamation mark) express an emotional reaction such as enthusiasm, pity, malice, etc. They have falling intonation and are introduced by *what* or *how*.
What a terrible bore he is! **What a fool** I was to believe them. **How easy** she made it all sound! **How slowly** he grasped the situation. **How** he raged!	*What* is used before noun phrases (with or without an adjective). *How* is used with adjectives not followed by a noun or with adverbs, and sometimes on its own.
What a knowledgeable man **your father is.**	The rest of the exclamation has the normal subject – predicate word order.
What a silly argument (that is)! *(Was für ein dummes Argument!)*	As in German, exclamations are often shortened to the introductory part of the sentence.

Note:
For exclamations in the form of *yes/no* questions see **22** Note.

38–39 Set Phrases

Set phrases are fixed expressions used in certain situations.

38 Structures

Excuse me.	(I beg your) pardon.		Set phrases rarely consist of whole sentences. The sentence pattern is usually incomplete. In some cases they consist of just one single word.
Happy New Year.	Merry/Happy Christmas.		
Same to you.	Thank you.	Thanks.	
Hello.	Hi.	Bye.	
May I introduce you to Mr Williams? – How do you do? – How do you do?			Most of them cannot be changed grammatically, for example, the greeting *How do you do?*

39 Speech Intentions

Set phrases serve to establish or maintain contact in certain social situations. There are also set phrases which are used to express certain emotions. A selection of these phrases is given below. (They are stylistically neutral except where marked c – for colloquial or f – for formal usage.)

Phrases	Speech intention
Good morning/evening/... Hello. Hi. (c) How are you? (– Fine, thanks, and how are you?) *Only on meeting someone for the first time:* How do you do? (f) *(Response:* How do you do?) Pleased to meet you.	Greeting and establishing contact
Goodbye. Cheerio. (c) So long. (c) See you (later). (c)	Taking one's leave
Good luck. (– Same to you.) Merry/Happy Christmas. Happy New Year. Happy birthday (to you). Many happy returns. *Drinking (toasting):* Cheers! Your health. Here's to you/your health/...	Expressing good will or congratulations
Regards to Kate. Give my love to ... Please remember me to ... Please give my best wishes to ... (f)	Giving one's regards to a third person
Thank you. Many thanks. Thanks (very much). (c) *(It is not necessary to reply, but one can say:* Not at all./Don't mention it./ You're welcome.)	Expressing thanks
(I'm) sorry. Excuse me. (I beg your) pardon. (That's all right./ – Please don't worry. / – No harm done.)	Apologizing
Pardon? Sorry? What?	Asking for something to be repeated
Beginning: Dear Alan, Dear Mrs Brown, Dear Sir/Madam, (f) *Ending:* Love, (c) Yours, (c) Yours sincerely, Yours faithfully, (f)	Conventional forms of address and salutation in letters
(Good) Heavens! (Good) God! Gosh! Good gracious! Oh, my. Ouch! Damn! Blast (you/it)! Shame on ... Go to hell!	Expressing emotions (mainly colloquial)

40 Block Language

Block language consists of single words, phrases or 'sentences' in which all the elements not essential to the understanding of the message have been left out.
The function of block language is to convey information in the most concise way possible. It may also in some cases have the function of an order or prohibition. It occurs mainly in:

Entrance Push Way out Private Pull One Way Danger: Falling Rock No smoking Press	• notices and signs (directions, prohibitions, etc.)
SMITH'S INSTANT COFFEE PURE WOOL Ingredients: flour, sugar,... Produce of Spain *Stainless steel*	• labels on manufactured goods
UP THE REPUBLIC Down with war SMITH FOR PRESIDENT LUCINI - that certain style FOR REAL MEN: ARCTIC AFTER SHAVE	• slogans
The Old Man and the Sea A Grammar of Present-Day English Introduction Contents Chapter 3: Nouns and Noun Phrases	• titles, headings
Millionaire's Son Free 39 killed in plane crash Queen to meet Pope McNeill resigns	• headlines
ARRIVING HEATHROW TUESDAY 5 P.M. – BRENDA	• telegrams

Chapter 2: The Patterns of the Simple Sentence

41–43 The Verb and its Complementation: Summary

41 The Verb as the Basis of Different Sentence Patterns

Simple sentences can have a number of different patterns, which are all based on the predicate. The predicate is either a finite main verb (e.g. *listened*) or a verb phrase made up of one or more auxiliaries + main verb (e.g. *had listened, may be listening*). Depending on the type of verb used, the predicate may be (and often must be) accompanied by an object or some other form of complementation (apart from the subject). The complementation is sometimes linked to the predicate by means of a preposition. The patterns of the active sentence are shown in the following table.

Subject	Predicate		Necessary complementation		
The concert	has started.				
The orchestra	were playing		Beethoven's Fifth. direct object		
We	listened	to	the old songs. prepositional object		
He	has promised		his guitar direct object	to	his daughter. indirect prepositional object
My friend	can give		you indirect object		the new LP. direct object
The melody	reminded		the old man direct object	of	his youth prepositional object
Music	is		the language of feeling. subject complement		
Some critics	consider		Louis Armstrong direct object		the king of jazz. object complement
I	think	of	modern music prepositional object	as	very difficult. object complement
The origins of jazz	lie		in New Orleans. adverbial		
The player	put		his violin direct object		in the case. adverbial

They	awarded	the Dutch pianist indirect object		the first prize. direct object
The Dutch pianist subject	was awarded			the first prize. direct object
The first prize subject	was awarded		to	the Dutch pianist. indirect object

The objects of an active sentence can in many cases be made the subject of a passive sentence. The patterns of passive sentences are also dependent on the type of verb used. (Further details on passive sentences in **58–65**.)

Notes:

1. Some grammars use the term 'predicate' to mean the verb (or verb phrase) plus its necessary complementation, and call the verb (phrase) itself the 'predicator'.

2. All sentence patterns can be extended by the use of (additional, non-essential) adverbials:
   My friend gave me the Stones' new LP **last week.** He **slowly** put his violin in the case.

3. A predicate can be complemented not only by noun phrases and adjective phrases, but also by subordinate clauses and non-finite constructions (cf **302, 257**). Such sentences are called 'complex sentences':
   Everyone would agree **that the Beatles produced some wonderful songs.** (subordinate clause)
   The dream of many youngsters is **to become famous as a pop star.** (infinitive construction)
   Many singers dislike **performing live on TV.** (gerund construction)

42 Verbs with Several Sentence Patterns

Some very common verbs can be used – with different meanings – in a number of different sentence patterns. This is illustrated by the two examples given here (see also **45**). Details about other verbs can be found in dictionaries.

Look how the sunflowers **have grown!**
My friend Mike **is growing** ***a beard.***
My grandparents **have grown** ***old.***

Jane's **getting** ***a new carpet*** for her room.
Who **got** ***her that nice picture?***
The old chairs **had got** ***very shabby.***
We're **getting** ***the room ready*** for the painters.
How **did** the needles **get** ***into these cushions?***
However **will** you **get** ***that piano through the door?***

grow		
–		*wachsen*
+ direct object		*(sich) wachsen lassen*
+ subject complement		*werden*
get		
+ direct object		*bekommen, erhalten*
+ indir. obj. + dir. obj.		*besorgen, beschaffen*
+ subject complement		*werden*
+ dir. obj. + object compl.		*(fertig) machen*
+ adverbial		*gelangen*
+ dir. obj. + adverbial		*bringen, schaffen*

43 Verbs and Verbal Complexes

A verb is often so closely connected with an adjective or noun that together they form one unit of meaning, even though it can be analysed as consisting of predicate + subject complement or predicate + object. We call such units **verbal complexes**. They are formed mainly with the verbs *be, have, do, make, take* and *give.* They often correspond in meaning to single-word verbs.
Like the single-word verbs, many verbal complexes can be (or must be) complemented by the addition of a noun phrase, a non-finite construction, etc. These are often linked by a preposition to the verbal complex.

My father	**is fond**	**of**	painting.	verb + adjective (subject complement)
(My father	likes		painting.)	
It	**is a pity**		you missed the exhibition.	verb + noun (subject complement)
My sister	**had thoughts**	**of**	studying art once.	verb + noun (direct object)
(My sister	thought	of	studying art once.)	
No portrait	**does justice**	**to**	her beauty.	verb + noun (direct object)

44–46 Verbs without an Object and Verbs with a Direct Object

44 Sentence patterns

They were **dancing.** (intransitive: no object)
They were **dancing** ***a tango.*** (transitive: with a direct object)

Many English verbs can be used without an object (intransitively), or with a direct object (transitively), without any real difference in meaning.

The band turned up and the music **started.**
Tom and Mavis **arrived** ***at ten o'clock.***
Some of the guests **were dancing** ***in the hall.***
Excitement **mounted** ***rapidly.***

An intransitive verb, however, seldom appears as the last word in a sentence, where its effect tends to be rather dramatic (especially if it is in the simple form). Usually something needs to be said about the manner or the circumstances in which the action takes place, in which case adverbials (of time, manner, place, etc.) follow the intransitive verb.

After his long solo the clarinettist **had a drink.**
Shortly before midnight, the musicians **took a rest.**

Whereas intransitive verbs at the end of a sentence are rare, it is quite common to find verbal complexes consisting of verb + noun in this position (cf **46**). Such verbal complexes are less dramatic in their effect than single-word verbs.

Notes:

1. The direct object in English may correspond to an accusative or dative object in German (cf **59**):

I greeted	**her**	direct object	Ich begrüßte	**sie**	accusative object
and thanked	**her**		und dankte	**ihr**	dative object
for the invitation.			für die Einladung.		

2. Some verbs, when used intransitively, have passive meaning in spite of their active form (cf **65**):
   These dresses **wash** easily. His new story **reads** well.

45 Verbs which can be either Intransitive or Causative-Transitive

A number of English verbs can be used either intransitively or transitively. When transitive, they express the idea of causing something to happen (causative meaning). In this case we speak of causative-transitive use.

The plane **flew** and **landed** safely.	*fliegen, landen* (intransitive)	In German there are only a few verbs used like this.
The pilot **flew** and **landed** the plane safely.	*fliegen, landen* (causative-transitive)	
Some candidates **failed.**	*durchfallen*	Causative meaning is often expressed in German by adding *lassen*.
The examiners **failed** no candidate.	*durchfallen lassen*	
a horse races/to race a horse	*rennen/rennen lassen*	
s.o. starves/to starve s.o. to death	*verhungern/verh. lassen*	
a man works/to work a man hard	*arbeiten/arbeiten lassen*	
cabbages grow/to grow cabbages	*wachsen/anbauen*	Sometimes a different verb is used in German, which may be related to the intransitive verb (e.g. *sinken – versenken*).
the athlete runs/to run a firm	*laufen/leiten*	
the ship sinks/to sink a ship	*sinken/versenken*	
a chair stands s.wh./to stand a chair s.wh.	*stehen/stellen*	
s.o. walks/to walk one's dog	*spazierengehen/ausführen*	

The leaves **had fallen** from the trees.				*(waren gefallen)*	
The old oak tree **has been felled.**				*(ist gefällt worden)*	
Examples:	lie	lay	lain	*liegen*	(intransitive)
	lay	laid	laid s.th. s.wh.	*legen*	(transitive)
	fall	fell	fallen	*fallen*	(intransitive)
	fell	felled	felled s.th.	*fällen*	(transitive)
	rise	rose	risen	*aufstehen*	(intransitive)
	raise	raised	raised s.th.	*heben*	(transitive)

A few intransitive English verbs also form pairs with related causative-transitive verbs.
(The similarity of their forms can give rise to mistakes.)

Note:
Sit, sat, sat is usually intransitive, but can be causative-transitive, meaning 'to put s.o. in a sitting position':
The children **sat** on the sofa. *(... saßen ...)*
The mother **sat** her baby in an armchair. *(... setzte ...)*
Set, set, set on the other hand, is usually causative-transitive, but is intransitive when it is used for the going-down of the sun or moon, etc.:
The cook **set** the casserole on the table. *(... stellte ...)*
By the time they had finished supper, the sun **was setting.** *(... ging ... unter.)*

46 Verbal Complexes and Intransitive Verbs

When did you **have breakfast?**
My grandparents have **made arrangements** to have 'meals on wheels' in future.

Grandfather always **has a rest / rests** before tea, then he **takes a stroll / strolls** round the garden.
Grandfather always **has a long rest** before tea, then he **strolls slowly** round the garden.

Let's **take a walk** after lunch. (= walk for pleasure)
Shall we **walk** or take the bus? (= go on foot)

Verbs like *do, give, have, make, take* are often closely connected to a following noun and form a verbal complex with it. Formally, the noun is a direct object. (See also **43**.)
Sometimes either a verbal complex or a corresponding intransitive verb can be used for the same action. To describe the action more precisely, it is sometimes more convenient to use an adjective in a verbal complex, and sometimes easier to use an adverb with an intransitive verb.
There are often differences in meaning between verbal complexes and the corresponding single-word verbs.

Note:
Some verbs can be followed immediately by a direct object or by a preposition + object. The meaning remains the same. (This prepositional object can also be regarded as an adverbial.)
Every year there are several attempts to **swim** **the Channel.** (direct object)
Every year there are several attempts to **swim across the Channel.** (prepositional object or adverbial)
Similarly: fly (across) the ocean/...; jump (across) a ditch/...; fight (against) poverty/...; play (against) a team/... .

47–48 Prepositional Verbs and Phrasal Verbs

47 Comparison of the Sentence Patterns

Many English verbs can combine with prepositions (*for, at,* etc.) or adverbial particles (*out, up,* etc.) to form what are called prepositional verbs and phrasal verbs:

1. Prepositional Verbs

The passengers **were hoping for** *a good crossing.*
(**were hoping for** = prepositional verb; *a good crossing* = prepositional object)

Prepositional verbs in active sentences are always followed by an object, called the prepositional object.

A steward **looked after** *the old lady.*
A steward **looked after** *her.*
The captain **listened** attentively **to** *the weather forecast.*

The prepositional object cannot come between the verb and the preposition. Occasionally, however, adverbs come between the verb and preposition. (For the position of the preposition in passive sentences see **60**, in relative clauses **311**, in questions **24**.)

2. Phrasal Verbs

At last the ferry **moved off.**
(**moved off** = phrasal verb)

All the tourists **took out** *their cameras.*
(**took out** = phrasal verb; *their cameras* = direct object)

Some phrasal verbs occur without an object (intransitive use), others have a direct object (transitive use).

Someone **pointed out** *the Roman lighthouse.*
Someone **pointed** *the Roman lighthouse* **out.**
Someone **pointed out** *the ruins of the famous Roman lighthouse.*
Someone **pointed** *it* **out.**

If the direct object is a noun or short noun phrase, it can come either before or after the particle. If it is a longer noun phrase it comes after the particle. If it is a personal pronoun, it always comes before the particle.

Notes:

1. Many verbs can either be used as prepositional verbs or intransitively (i.e. without a preposition and with no prepositional object):

A nightingale was singing in the wood, and they stopped to **listen** (**to** it).
We tried to rescue a bird from the cat, but we didn't **succeed** (**in** doing so).
Similarly: advertise (for), agree (with), aim (at), apply (for), complain (of), consent (to), gaze (at), grumble (at), object (to), etc.

2. A number of phrasal verbs can also be followed by a preposition + prepositional object. These verbs are called **phrasal-prepositional verbs.** In such cases, verb and particle cannot be separated.

People should **stay away** (phrasal verb) **from** (preposition) **birds' nests** when there are eggs in them.
(**stay away from** = *phrasal-prepositional verb*; **birds' nests** = prepositional object)

Similarly: do away with s.th. *(abschaffen),* put up with s.th./s.o. *(ertragen),* look forward to s.th. *(sich freuen auf),* look down on s.o./s.th. *(herabsehen auf),* etc.

48 The Meaning of Prepositional and Phrasal Verbs

Farmers are always **talking about** the weather.
The harvest **was brought in** just in time.

Large fields **make for** a more economic use of machinery. (= lead to, tend to cause)
Two years ago he **set up** as a sheep farmer in Yorkshire. (= went into business)

There are only a few prepositional and phrasal verbs whose meanings are clear from the separate meanings of verb and preposition or particle.

Mostly the verb and the preposition or particle form a completely new unit with its own meaning. In such cases a dictionary must be consulted.

The passengers **took to** the lifeboats when the ship started to sink. (= got into ... quickly)
We've **taken to** windsurfing since living by the sea. (= started as a hobby)
Mark didn't **take to** his sailing instructor at all. (= get to like)

The treasurer has **gone off** with all our money. (= has run away with)
How did your interview **go off?** (= proceed)
The electricity **went off** during the storm. (= There was a black-out.)
The bomb **went off** without any warning. (= exploded)
It's so hot today the milk's **gone off.** (= that the milk has gone sour)
How's your headache? – It's **gone off** now, thank you. (= has disappeared)

Sometimes a prepositional verb has several quite different meanings, as for example *take to.*
Another example is:
go for a walk
go for a doctor (= fetch)
go for s.o. (with a knife) (= attack)

Quite often a phrasal verb has several meanings, as for example *go off.* New phrasal verbs and new meanings are continually coming into use.
Another example is:
turn out the light
turn out 50 washing machines a day (= produce)
turn out an unwelcome guest (= throw out)
turn out one's pockets (= empty)
turn out to watch the race (= come)
turn out (to be) a success (= prove to be)

49–51 Verbs with Two Objects

49 Sentence Patterns with a Direct and an Indirect Object

Many verbs may (or must) take an indirect object as well as a direct object. The direct object is generally a thing; the indirect object usually names the person who receives it, benefits from it, or suffers from it. These verbs fall into two main categories. (For the formation of the passive see **61.**)

	indirect object without a preposition	direct object		indirect object as prepositional object
1. The guide showed	the tourists	the sights of London.		
The guide showed		the sights of London	**to**	the tourists.
2. The guide described		the sights of London	**to**	the tourists.

1. Verbs which allow both kinds of indirect object:
These verbs can take an **indirect object without a preposition.** This type of indirect object always comes before the direct object.
The same verbs can also take an indirect object **with a preposition** (mostly *to*) before it. This indirect prepositional object comes after the direct object.
The most common verbs in this category are:

bring	lend	promise	show	
give	offer	read	throw	someone something/
grant	owe	sell	tell	something to someone
hand	pass	send	write	

2. Verbs which only allow an indirect *prepositional* object:
These verbs can only take an **indirect object with a preposition** (mostly *to*) before it. This indirect prepositional object usually – though not always – comes after the direct object. (For further details on its position see **50.2.**)
The most common verbs in this category are:

announce	admit	dictate	explain	propose	something to someone
address	describe	distribute	mention	say	

Notes:

1. Some of the verbs which can take both sorts of indirect object call for a preposition other than *to* with the prepositional object:

The tourist information office **found** the visitors an excellent hotel.
The tourist information office **found** an excellent hotel **for** the visitors.
Similarly: cook s.o. s.th./cook s.th. for s.o. — get s.o. s.th./get s.th. for s.o. — ask s.o. s.th/ask s.th. of s.o.
buy s.o. s.th./buy s.th. for s.o. — make s.o. s.th./make s.th. for s.o.

2. A number of verbs take an indirect prepositional object with *from*. In this case there is no 'prepositionless' alternative:

At the border some people tried to **conceal** their purchases **from** the customs officer.
Similarly: hide, steal, take, . . . s.th. from s.o.

50 The Position of the Direct and Indirect Object

1. Verbs which allow both kinds of indirect object

a) The waiter brought	**us each** indirect object	**a huge plate of salad.** direct object	
Mrs Brown bought	**choc-ices** direct object	for **all seven of the children.** indirect object	
b) Mother promised	**my little brother** indirect object	**a coke** direct object	if he would eat up his vegetables.
Would you mind passing	**the salt and pepper** direct object	to **Anne?** indirect object	She's been waiting for it.

The object which contains the most (or the most important) information usually comes second. (See also **6, 332.**)

a) This object is generally the longer of the two objects.
b) The shorter object can, however, come at the end if it contains the more important new information or if it needs to be emphasized, for example for contrast.

Notes:

The following rules apply to sentences in which the direct object is *it* or *them:*

1. If the indirect object is a noun phrase, this comes (normally with a preposition) in second place after *it* or *them:*

If you don't want your book, why don't you give **it** ***to your sister?***
And what about your tapes? – I've lent **them** ***to a friend of mine.***

2. a) If the indirect object is a pronoun, it also usually comes (with a preposition) after *it* or *them:*

Please lend me your notes. – I'm sorry, I can't lend **them** ***to you,*** I've already lent them to John.
Just fetch the newspaper and give **it** ***to me,*** will you please?

b) It can, however, come before or after *it/them* without a preposition. Usage varies from region to region:

Please lend me your notes. – I'm sorry, I can't lend ***you*** **them (them *you*),** I've already lent them to John.
Just fetch the newspaper and give **it *me* (*me* it),** will you please?

2. Verbs which allow only an indirect prepositional object:

In the first act a messenger on horseback announces **the hero's arrival** to **King Arthur and his knights.**
direct object — indirect object

The young warrior relates to **the King** **all the adventures he has had during his travels.**
indir. obj. — direct object

The stranger is made welcome and explains to **the Court** **his reasons for coming there to seek help.**
indir. obj. — direct object

With these verbs, the indirect prepositional object normally comes in second place. The direct object only comes in second place when it is much longer. The preposition is never dropped, not even when the indirect object comes first.

51 Other Sentence Patterns with Two Objects

The excavations may provide **archaeologists** with **further information about the Celts' way of life.**
direct object (someone) — prepositional object (something)

The mayor thanked for **their hard work** **all the young volunteers who had taken part in the dig.**
prepositional object — direct object

This group includes, for example:

accuse s.o. of s.th.	*beschuldigen*	inform s.o. of s.th.	*informieren*
assure s.o. of s.th.	*versichern*	provide s.o. with s.th.	*versorgen*
blame s.o. for s.th.	*tadeln*	remind s.o. of s.th.	*erinnern*
charge s.o. with s.th.	*beschuldigen*	reward s.o. with s.th.	*belohnen*
compare s.o. with s.o.	*vergleichen*	rob s.o. of s.th.	*berauben*
congratulate s.o. on s.th.	*beglückwünschen*	suspect s.o. of s.th.	*verdächtigen*
convince s.o. of s.th.	*überzeugen*	thank s.o. for s.th.	*danken*

Unlike the verbs dealt with in **49** and **50,** the verbs in this third group usually have a person as the direct object and a thing or abstract idea as the prepositional object. The direct object normally comes before the prepositional object. It only comes after the prepositional object when it is much longer.

Notes:

1. a) Certain verbal complexes consisting of verb + noun (formally, direct object) can be complemented by an indirect object of either kind:

Could you **do** my friend **a favour/a favour** for my friend?

Similarly: make s.o. an offer/make an offer to s.o., pay s.o. a visit/pay a visit to s.o., etc.

b) Some verbal complexes formed with *give* can only have a 'prepositionless' indirect object:

Please **give** me **a ring** tomorrow when the meeting is over. (= call me on the phone)

Similarly: give s.o. a kiss/a kick/a push/a shove/a shock, etc.

2. Another group of verbal complexes can only have an indirect prepositional object. This always comes after the direct object:

The drastic social welfare cuts **gave rise to** a wave of protests. (= caused)

Other examples are:

catch sight of	*erblicken*	make fun of	*sich lustig machen über*	take care of	*sorgen für*
give way to	*weichen*	make use of	*gebrauchen*	take no notice of	*nicht beachten*
lose sight of	*aus den Augen verlieren*	pay attention to	*achtgeben auf*	set foot on	*betreten*

52–53 Verbs with a Reflexive Object

52 Sentence Patterns

1. a) **Betty** hurt **herself** while skating. (direct object)
   b) Betty hurt her (a friend) with a skate.
2. a) **Roger** made **himself** a new sledge. (indirect object)
   b) Roger made him (his son) a new sledge.
3. a) On the ice rink **the older children** looked after **themselves.** (prepositional object)
   b) On the ice rink the older children looked after them (the younger children).

Many verbs can have a reflexive pronoun (sg. *-self*, pl. *-selves*) as the direct, indirect or prepositional object. This always refers back to the person or thing that is the subject (sentences 1a, 2a, 3a). It must not be confused with the corresponding personal pronoun, which usually refers to a noun other than the subject (sentences 1b, 2b, 3b).
As in German, the reflexive pronoun is normally unstressed (cf **87**.2).

Note:
The personal pronoun is used instead of the reflexive pronoun after the preposition in adverbials of place:
He put his bag **beside him** on the seat.
I hadn't enough money **on me** to pay for a taxi.

53 Verbs With and Without the Reflexive Pronoun

Why shouldn't the surgeon **pride himself** on his skill?
Similarly: absent oneself from (a meeting/ . . .), avail oneself of (an opportunity/ . . .)

Verbs which always take a reflexive pronoun are rare in English.

The doctor **prepared (herself)** to break the bad news to the girl's parents.
Similarly: dress (oneself), wash (o.s.), shave (o.s.), hide (o.s.), prove (o.s.) (to be), surrender (o.s.) to, yield (o.s.) to

A number of English verbs can be used either with or without a reflexive pronoun.

On the third day after the operation, the patient got up for the first time. He **washed himself** carefully with a soft cloth and tried **to dress himself.**
Go and **dress yourself** before you come down for breakfast.
Shaving every morning is rather a bore.
The young nurse **proved** to be very capable.

The reflexive pronoun is preferred when the speaker wants to describe an action more vividly or to indicate that it is carried out deliberately.
This explains why it is often used with the imperative of these verbs.
Conversely, the reflexive pronoun is less likely to be used when an action is performed routinely or without deliberation.

Just **fancy**, the old lady could not **remember** her husband's name! *(Stell* ***dir*** *nur* ***vor*** *. . .* ***sich*** *nicht* ***an*** *. . .* ***erinnern****.)*

Similarly:

approach	*s. nähern*	move	*s. bewegen*
change	*s. verändern*	recover	*s. erholen*
complain	*s. beklagen*	rely on	*s. verlassen auf*
imagine	*s. einbilden*	sit down	*s. setzen*
lie down	*s. hinlegen*	turn to	*s. wenden an*

Many verbs whose counterparts in German are reflexive, are not reflexive in English.

54–57 Verbs with Subject Complement and Verbs with Object Complement

54 Comparison of the Sentence Patterns

London is **the capital of the U. K.**
subject — subject complement

The traffic problem seems **insurmountable.**
subject — subject complement

The Tower remains **a tourist magnet.**
subject — subject complement

The verb *be* and a number of other verbs need to be complemented by something which describes a characteristic or a state of the subject. This is called the **subject complement.**
The subject complement is either a noun (phrase) or an adjective (phrase).

The Romans called **the city Londinium.**
object — object complement

Newspapers have made **Fleet Street famous.**
object — obj. complement

Most tourists think of **the Tower** as **a must.**
object — obj. complement

Another group of verbs have a direct or prepositional object, and in addition, an element which names or describes the object. This is called the **object complement.**
The object complement is either a noun (phrase) or an adjective (phrase). Some verbs call for a linking *as* before the object complement. (In German, *als, zu* or *für* are often used for such linking.)

Note:
Certain verbs can have a necessary adverbial instead of a subject complement or object complement:

Their son **was** ***a gifted mathematician.***	(subject complement)
Both their daughters **were** ***at college.***	(adverbial)
The teacher **kept** the pupils ***quiet.***	(object complement)
The games master **kept** the boys ***in school.***	(adverbial)

55 Verbs with Subject Complement (Linking Verbs)

These verbs are called linking verbs because they establish the connection between the subject and its complement. They fall mainly into the following categories:

1. Verbs which express a state of being or a position

be young/tall/a student/an engineer/...
come first/second/last/... (on a list)
lie asleep/helpless/hidden/open/exposed/...
stand alone/upright/still/firm/bewildered/...

The man **stood** upright before the judge.
The crime **lay** heavy on his conscience.

2. Verbs which express appearance (these verbs can have *to be* before the complement)

seem/appear (to be) sad/good/correct/absurd/friendly/disappointed/extravagant/...

After their return from the moon the astronauts **seemed (to be)** exhausted.
From the moon the earth **appears (to be)** very small.

3. Verbs which express the continuation of a state

keep quiet/cool/fit/fresh/warm/. . .	**stay** sober/single/hot/cold/cloudy/fine/. . .
remain silent/uncertain/a problem/. . .	

Even in the middle of the hurricane the seamen **kept** calm.
The weather will **remain** fine this week.

4. Verbs which express a process of change

become famous/angry(-ier)/worn/a habit/. . .	**go** blind/mad with rage/white with horror/bankrupt/dry/bad/. . .
come true/loose/open/apart/untied/undone/. . .	
fall asleep/ill/silent/a victim to/. . .	**grow** tired/old(er)/fat(ter)/loud(er)/desperate/. . .
get wet/tired/drunk/worse/cold(er)/. . .	**turn** nasty/pale/grey/Catholic/traitor/sour/. . .

After an hour in the car the baby **fell** asleep.
The weather **turned** very nasty after we had passed Leicester.

5. Verbs which express a sense impression (see also **56**)

look good/sad/ill/a fool/one's age/. . .	**sound** idiomatic/right/strange/a good idea/. . .
smell awful/bad/sweet/aromatic/nice/. . .	**taste** sour/sweet/bitter/strong/nice/delicious/horrible/. . .
feel soft/smooth/hard/rough/dry/sticky/. . .	

The hitchhikers **looked** very cold and miserable.
How fresh and clean the countryside **smells** after a shower.

Note:
There are also a number of intransitive verbs which can take a subject complement. These are verbs which express a transition to a different state (e.g. *wake up* = a change-over from being asleep to being awake).

He **woke up** happy. (He was happy when he woke up.)

Further examples are: **arrive** exhausted/. . .; **be born** rich/English/a princess/. . .; **marry** young; **return/come back/go away** a changed man/. . . .

56 Linking Verbs and Formally Identical Verbs with Object

The verb *smell, taste, look, sound* and *feel* can belong to two different categories. This determines whether they must be followed by an adjective (as the subject complement) or can be modified by an adverb:

Linking verbs with adjective	Formally identical verbs (with adverb)
Everything the competitors had cooked **smelt** and **tasted good**.	The judges first **smelt** the sauce before **tasting** it **carefully**.
Mr Brown's meat pie **looked** very **appetizing**.	The little girl **looked longingly** at the cakes.
This recipe **sounds** more **difficult** than it is.	The supervisor **sounded** the bell **impatiently** when the time was up.
Miss McNeill's rolls **feel** much **crisper** than anybody else's.	She **felt** the handle **cautiously** to see if it was hot.

As linking verbs they describe a characteristic of the subject and are therefore followed by an adjective as the subject complement.

When they have an object, they describe an activity, and so can be modified by an adverb of manner.

Note:
Intransitive verbs which express a transition to another state can also belong to these two different categories and can therefore be followed either by an adjective or an adverb:

Though very famous, the poet **died poor.**
(**he** was poor when he died)

The old man **died suddenly** of a heart attack.
(**his death** was sudden)

57 Verbs with Object Complement

These verbs fall mainly into two categories:

1. Verbs of activity which imply a result

appoint	s.o. (as/to be) chairman/...	**get**	s.th./s.o. ready/...
choose	s.o. as/to be representative/...	**keep**	s.o./s.th. quiet/...
christen	s.o. Peter/...	**make**	s.o./s.th. famous/...
crown	s.o. king/queen/emperor/...	**name**	s.o. Katherine/...
declare	s.o./s.th. a failure/...	**proclaim**	s.o. (to be) a traitor/...
elect	s.o. M.P./mayor/...	**render**	s.o./s.th. desperate/...

They **appointed** Mrs Smith chairman of the committee.
His behaviour **rendered** me speechless.

2. Verbs which express an opinion or supposition

With or without *to be:*

assume	s.o./s.th. (to be) wrong/a fraud/...	**presume**	s.o. (to be) innocent/...
believe	s.o./s.th. (to be) responsible for s.th./...	**suppose**	s.o./s.th. (to be) correct/...
consider	s.o./s.th. (to be) very important/...	**think**	s.o./s.th. very unfair/...
find	s.o./s.th. (to be) dull/amusing/a nuisance/...		

I **consider** Mr Miller **(to be)** a very efficient organizer.
Everybody **found** the meeting boring.

With *as* or *for:*

characterize	s.o./s.th. **as** amusing/...	**regard**	s.o./s.th. **as** reliable/promising/...
look upon	s.o./s.th. **as** a good choice/...	**take**	s.o./s.th. **for** granted/...
mistake	s.o./s.th. **for** s.o./s.th. else/...	**think of**	s.o./s.th. **as** the equivalent of .../...

The opinion poll showed that the older generation on the whole **look upon** the young **as** responsible members of society.
Nowadays we **take** the welfare state **for** granted.

Notes:
1. After *consider* and *find* the object + object complement construction can be used colloquially. Its use with the other verbs in the same sub-category (verbs with or without *to be*) sounds formal; in colloquial language *that*-clauses would be preferred:
We all **supposed that** our neighbour was a Conservative.

2. Another category of verbs which can take a direct object with an adjective as complement are verbs of preferring, disliking and wishing:
I **prefer** coffee weak. Some **like** it medium. Others **want** it very strong.

3. Object complements in active sentences become subject complements in the corresponding passive sentences:

They considered **Mr Smith** (dir. object) **an excellent speaker.** (object complement)

Mr Smith (subject) was considered **an excellent speaker.** (subject complement)

58 Passive and Active Voice to Express Different Perspectives

Passive sentences:	**The racing driver** subject: affected person	was pulled out of his wrecked car and rushed to hospital.
	One of the bystanders subject: recipient	was given first aid.
Corresponding active sentences:	**A fellow competitor**	pulled the racing driver out of his wrecked car.
	An ambulance	rushed him to hospital.
	Somebody subject: active agent	gave one of the bystanders first aid.

As the examples show, passive sentences differ from active sentences not only in their form, but also as regards their content. They present an action from a quite different viewpoint. In the passive sentence, the speaker chooses for the subject and starting-point of the sentence the person (or thing) that is affected by the action, or the person (or thing) that benefits from it or receives something. The agent (person or thing performing the action) does not need to be named.
In the corresponding active sentence, however, the agent must be named.

The office was broken into and vandalized last week. (agent unknown)
The new hospital was opened in 1980. (agent unimportant)

It follows that passive sentences are preferred when the agent is unknown or unimportant.

The racing driver was pulled out of his car **by a fellow competitor.**
One of the bystanders was given first aid **by an ambulance man.**
by-agent

In a passive sentence, the performer of the action can, however, be named **additionally,** in the form of a ***by*-agent.** This is a way of presenting the performer of an action as the most important piece of new information in the sentence.
(For the role of passive and active sentences in the structuring of information in texts, cf **6.**)

Notes:

1. For the passive verb forms see **178.**
2. The simple form of the passive can not only describe a process, but also the state which results from the process:
   The racing driver **was** very badly **injured** in the crash. (Process: *Er **wurde** verletzt*)
   The X-rays showed that he **was** very badly **injured.** (Resulting state: *Er **war** verletzt*)

The progressive form of the passive can only describe a process:
Would you wait for a moment. The X-rays **are being developed.** (*. . . **werden** gerade entwickelt.*)

59–62 Classes of Verbs and the Patterns of the Passive Sentence

As in the case of active sentences, the number of possible passive sentence patterns depends on the verb selected: what is decisive is what kinds of object the verb can take in an active sentence.

59 Passive Sentences with Verbs that Take a Direct Object

The circus was founded by the owner's father.
subject

The owner's father founded **the circus** in 1950.
dir. object

The subject of this kind of passive sentence corresponds to the direct object of the active sentence (cf **44**).

The elephants **were followed** into the ring by their trainer. *(Hinter den Elefanten kam . . ./Den Elefanten folgte . . .)*
The conjurer **is being assisted** by a member of the audience. *(Dem Zauberer assistiert . . .)*
The clowns especially **will be** vividly **remembered** by the children. *(Besonders an die Clowns werden sich . . . erinnern.)*

This way of forming the passive is possible in German too, but it is much more common in English. This is because there are many verbs in English which take a direct object whereas their German equivalents often take a different type of complementation (e.g. a dative object).

Note:
As in German, some verbs like *have, cost, weigh* cannot be made passive when they express a relationship. The passive is, however, possible with the verb *own*:

The renovation of the church **cost** over £20,000. (No passive possible.)
The local council **owns** most of these old houses. – The house **is owned** by the local council.

60 Passive Sentences with Verbs that Take a Prepositional Object

Economy measures are being talked about.
subject

They are talking about **economy measures.**
prepos. verb — prepositional object

The problem of public spending must **be looked into.** *(. . . muß untersucht werden.)*
New solutions **are being looked for.** *(Nach . . . wird gesucht./Man sucht nach . . .)*

Passive sentences with prepositional verbs are quite common. In this kind of passive sentence, the subject corresponds to the prepositional object of the comparable active sentence (cf **47**). The preposition keeps its position after the verb.

The corresponding German verb is often transitive; but if not, an impersonal passive construction can be used, or an active sentence with *man.*

Notes:
1. Phrasal-prepositional verbs (cf **47** Note 2) can also form this sentence pattern. Both particle and preposition keep their position after the verb:

Such extravagance cannot **be put up with** any longer. Expenses must **be cut down on.**

2. Nouns which are contained in adverbials (including adverbials of place) in an active sentence cannot normally be used as the subject of an equivalent passive sentence. If, however, the adverbial of place refers to something which is affected or altered by the action, a passive sentence is possible:

We live **in Munich.**	Several generations have lived **in this old house.**
(No passive possible.)	**This old house** has obviously been lived **in** by many generations.

61 Passive Sentences with Verbs that Take a Direct and an Indirect Object

In the case of verbs like *give, hand, show s.o. s.th./s.th. to s.o.* (which take a direct and indirect object with or without a preposition, cf **49**), two different passive sentence patterns are possible:

Sentence pattern 1 (very common)	Sentence pattern 2 (less common)
The foreign visitors were given a rousing welcome.	**A rousing welcome** was given ***to*** the foreign visitors.
subject	subject

We gave **the foreign visitors a rousing welcome.**
indirect object — direct object

Sentence pattern 1:
The subject of the passive sentence corresponds to the indirect object of the active sentence: it names the person or thing that receives something or benefits from it. As the receiver is usually a person, this is called the 'personal passive'.

Sentence pattern 2:
The subject of the passive sentence corresponds to the direct object of the active sentence: it usually refers to a thing. The indirect object is normally linked to the verb with *to.*

The exchange students **were shown** the sights of the town. *(Man zeigte den Austauschstudenten .../ Den Austauschstudenten wurden ... gezeigt.)* Their hosts **have been promised** a return visit. *(Man hat ihren Gastgebern ... versprochen.)*	The importance of such contacts **was explained** ***to*** everyone present. (One speaker explained *to* everyone present the importance of such contacts.) The many advantages of youth exchanges **had been described** ***to*** the delegates.

As the translations show, the passive sentence pattern 1 has no direct counterpart in German. Active sentences with *man* or impersonal passive constructions are used instead.

Verbs which only allow an indirect prepositional object (i.e. those which need *to* for linking such as *explain, describe s.th. to s.o.*, etc.), can only form passive sentence pattern 2.

Notes:

1. Verbs which need a preposition other than *to* for linking (cf **49** Notes 1 and 2) are usually restricted to passive sentence pattern 2:

   An excellent meal was cooked **for** us when we arrived.
   The whisky was well hidden **from** the customs.

2. In the case of verbal complexes such as *do s.o. a favour, make fun of s.o.*, it is usually the indirect object which is made the subject of a passive sentence because the direct object is felt to complete the meaning of the verb. In formal style though, the direct object is occasionally made the subject of a passive sentence, especially when the verbal complex is expanded – by an adjective, for example. Compare:

give s.o. a ring:	He was given a ring. (= He was called on the phone.)	(In this sense, no alternative.)
make s.o. an offer:	He was made an offer for his house.	An interesting offer was made to him.
take notice of s.th.:	Her new novel was taken notice of by the critics.	No particular notice was taken of his suggestion.

62 Passive Sentences with Verbs of Reporting, Opinion and Supposition

Stonehenge is said to be of pre-Celtic origin. subject Experts say that **Stonehenge** is of pre-Celtic origin.	This passive sentence pattern can be formed from the type of active sentence introduced by *People say that .../Experts believe that ...* The subject of the passive sentence is taken from the *that*-clause.
Its construction **is thought to have spanned** a period of over 1,000 years. *(Man glaubt, daß ...)* The stones **are believed to have been set up** for sun worship. *(Die Steine wurden vermutlich ...)* The Celts **are** popularly **supposed to have carried out** human sacrifices there. *(Es wird allgemein angenommen, daß ...)* 750,000 tourists **were reported to have visited** Stonehenge last year. *(... sollen Stonehenge ... besucht haben.)*	This sentence pattern is common in journalism: it gives the impression that a source is being quoted, without the need to name that source. In German, a similar effect can be achieved by the impersonal *man* together with a *daß*-clause, for example, or by the use of the auxiliary *sollen* (cf **233** Note 2) or adverbs like *angeblich, bekanntlich, vermutlich*.

Note:

Active sentences containing expressions like *People say that ...* and *Experts believe that ...* can be made into passive sentences by using the structure word *it* to introduce them. (This is, however, much less common than the sentence pattern described above.)

It has been said that Stonehenge is the finest Bronze Age monument in Europe.
It is thought that its construction spanned a period of over 1,000 years.

63–65 Further Sentence Patterns with Passive Meaning

63 1. The *get*-Passive

Samantha **got stung** by a bee while picking plums last weekend.
A wasp **has got caught** in the jam.
Don't go near the farmhouse, you might **get bitten** by the dog. *(... gebissen* ***werden.)***
After their first night camping out they **were** both badly **bitten** by mosquitoes. *(...* ***waren*** *... zerstochen.)*

Because of its passive meaning, the sentence pattern *get* + past participle is called the *get*-passive. It is mainly used colloquially, especially when the speaker wants to express that an event is unintended or unexpected. The *get*-passive, unlike the *be*-passive, can only describe a process and not a resulting state (cf **58** Note 2).

Note:
The *get*-passive sometimes has a causative as well as a passive meaning, i.e. it expresses the idea of someone causing something to be done:

He **got transferred** to a job nearer home so that he could spend more time with the children.
(Er ließ sich ... versetzen ...)

64 The *have*-Passive

The passengers **had** their tickets **examined** at the barrier. (The passengers' tickets were examined at the barrier.)
She **had** her handbag **stolen** on the train. (Her handbag was stolen on the train.)
The suitcase **had** its locks **forced open.** (The locks of the suitcase were forced open.)

The sentence pattern *have* + object + past participle can have two meanings:
In its **purely passive** meaning, the subject is the person (less often: the thing) that is affected by an action. This meaning can also be expressed by means of an ordinary passive sentence with *be.*

They **had** their luggage **sent on** in advance. *(Sie ließen ihr Gepäck vorausschicken.)*
He **had** his hair **cut** before setting off. *(Er ließ sich vor der Abreise die Haare schneiden.)*

This sentence pattern can also have a **causative** meaning. In this case the subject names the person who causes an action to take place. Instead of *have, get* can be used: *He got his hair cut.*

Note:
The following structures also have passive meaning:

become + past participle	His ideas eventually **became accepted.**
need + active gerund/*need* + passive infinitive	The law **needs changing/needs to be changed.**
Certain verbal complexes formed from *be* + adjective + infinitive (cf **268** Note 1)	The regulations **are** not **easy to understand.**

65 Verbs Active in Form but Passive in Meaning

The new Triumph **drives** very smoothly.
(... fährt sich sehr angenehm.)
These dresses **wash** easily and don't need to be ironed. *(... lassen sich leicht waschen ...)*
The window **won't open,** it must be jammed.
(... läßt sich nicht öffnen, ...)
Tickets for the play **are selling** well.
I don't want my picture taken, I don't **photograph** well. *(... ich bin nicht fotogen.)*

These are verbs of activity used intransitively in an active sentence pattern, and often modified by an adverb (*easily, well,* etc.). The construction has a passive meaning, however, because the subject of the sentence is not the person causing the action (e.g. the driver), as you would expect from the verb, but the affected thing (e.g. the car). In German, active sentences with the reflexive pronoun *sich* or *sich ... lassen* are often used instead.

Chapter 3: Nouns and Noun Phrases

66–68 Elements and Functions of Noun Phrases; Classes of Nouns (Summary)

66 Elements of the Noun Phrase

a very tasty **meal**

Alice likes **meat** but hates **vegetables.**

a meal, **the** cook, **that** dinner
my breakfast, **your** pudding
some pancakes, **several** eggs, **every** dish

some **good** cups, a **very old** glass
the plates **in the cupboard**
the person **who broke the teapot**
the girl **laying the table**

Sarah has bought herself a mixer.
She (= Sarah) doesn't need to borrow **ours** (= our mixer) any longer.
Is **this** (= this substance) salt or sugar?
Some (= some people) put ketchup on **everything** (= every dish).

The main element, or head, of a noun phrase is the noun. We distinguish between:

Simple noun phrases (i.e. without modification)
A simple noun phrase may sometimes be a noun used completely on its own, but in most cases it includes a determiner, e.g.
an article or a demonstrative determiner (cf **100–109**),
a possessive determiner (cf **96, 97**),
an indefinite determiner (cf **110–126**).

Noun phrases modified by attributes
A noun phrase can be modified by an attribute. This may be:
an adjective or adjective phrase (cf **129–130**),
a prepositional phrase (cf **140**),
a relative clause (cf **308–312**),
a non-finite construction (cf **257**).

Pronouns replacing noun phrases
Noun phrases can be replaced by pronouns, e.g.
personal pronouns (cf **82–85**),
possessive pronouns (cf **96, 99**),
demonstrative pronouns (cf **108–109**),
indefinite pronouns (cf **110–126**).

67 Functions and Case

Noun phrases can – either alone or in combination with prepositions – take on any function in a sentence except that of the predicate (cf **41**). They can also be used as an attribute in a superordinate noun phrase and can be part of a verbal complex (cf **140**.2 and **43**).
In strongly inflectional languages such as German or Latin, these functions are usually indicated by using special case forms (nominative, dative, etc.). In English, however, function is mainly indicated through word order. There is only a limited number of case forms:

The **policeman** stopped the **lorry driver.**
The **lorry driver** swore at the **policeman.**

The noun only has
- a **common case** for subject, object, and after prepositions,

At the **policeman's** signal the traffic started to move forward. (At **his** signal ...)

He swore at **him.**
Who swore at **whom**?
Whose car is this?
I apologized to the driver **whose** car I had damaged.

- a **possessive case** (also called *s*-genitive), which has the same function as the possessive determiner and can be replaced by it (cf **89**).

Some of the **pronouns,** however, have separate **subject and object forms** (cf **82**).
There is also a possessive, or genitive, form *whose,* which is used in questions and relative clauses.

68 Classes of Nouns

Nouns can be divided into different classes according to their meaning. These classes partly overlap. From the grammatical point of view, the most important distinctions are as follows:

Common nouns:	**This athlete** has **the ability** and **stamina** necessary to win **the race.** **Athletes** with **ability** and **stamina** have what it takes to win **races.**
Proper nouns:	**Larry Miller** wants to climb **Mt. Ida** in **the Rocky Mountains** this summer.

This distinction is important for the use of determiners (articles, demonstrative determiners, etc.): With **common nouns,** the determiner makes it clear who or what is meant. For instance, *this* denotes a definite, specific person or thing. If common nouns are used without a determiner, they refer to a general class of person or thing. (Cf **100.**)
Proper nouns are the names of particular persons or things. Most proper nouns are therefore used without a determiner, although there are a few exceptions which always have the definite article *the.* (Cf **107.**)

Countables:	**One house** *is* already finished. *It is* on show to the public.	**Two houses** *are* already finished. *They are* on show to the public.
Uncountables:	**This furniture** *looks* very modern. *Was it* very expensive?	**The surroundings** *are* beautiful. *They add* to the value of the house.

This distinction is important for number concord (agreement in number) between the subject and the predicate and between nouns, pronouns and determiners.
Countables are common nouns whose singular form refers to one example of a class of person or thing, and whose plural form refers to a number of such examples. (For plural forms cf **69–71.**)
Uncountables are nouns which do not allow a distinction in number. They therefore have **only one** form, whose meaning is either singular (the idea of an undifferentiated mass or entity) or plural. (For further details see **72–76.**)

Nouns denoting persons:	**He** is my **uncle**/a **bachelor**/an **actor**/...	(male)
	She is my **aunt**/a **spinster**/an **actress**/...	(female)
	He/She is a **teacher**/a **doctor**/...	(male **or** female)
Nouns denoting things:	Do you recognize this **melody/music**? – No, **it's** new to me.	

These are the two most important gender classes in English. This distinction determines one's choice of pronouns and determiners to replace a noun phrase (personal pronouns, possessive determiners, etc.). (For details see **77–81.**)

The Formation of Plurals

69 Plurals with *-s*

With most English nouns the plural is formed by adding *-(e)s* to the singular form.

idea	– ideas	[z]	ideal	– ideals	[z]
book	– books	[s]	root	– roots	[s]
class	– classes	[ɪz]	cause	– causes	[ɪz]
wish	– wishes	[ɪz]	garage	– garages	[ɪz]
switch	– switches	[ɪz]	bridge	– bridges	[ɪz]

Pronunciation:
[z] after a vowel or a voiced consonant
[s] after a voiceless consonant
[ɪz] after the sibilants [s, z, ʃ, ʒ, tʃ, dʒ] (always written *-es*, so sometimes an *e* has to be added.)
Note: house [haʊs] – houses [haʊzɪz]

city – cities [z] the Twenties
(**But:** the Kennedys, some lay-bys)

Compare: boy – boys, chimney – chimneys

Special cases:
Nouns ending in a consonant + *y* form their plural with *-ies.* (Exceptions: proper names and compounds with the adverbial particle *by.*)
After a vowel the *-y* is retained in the plural.

echo – echoes [z] hero – heroes
Similarly: embargoes, Negroes, potatoes, tomatoes, torpedoes, vetoes, etc.
But: kilos, radios, studios, discos, etc.
With optional *e:* buffalo(e)s, cargo(e)s, ghetto(e)s, Eskimo(e)s, flamingo(e)s, memento(e)s, motto(e)s, tornado(e)s, volcano(e)s, etc.

Some nouns ending in *-o* take the plural form *-oes.*

Most of these nouns take a regular plural form *-os.* Sometimes both spellings are possible: *-os* or *-oes.* (When in doubt consult a dictionary.)

thief [f] – thieves [vz], life – lives
(**Compare:** cliffs, hand-cuffs, etc.)
But: beliefs [fs], briefs, chiefs, handkerchiefs, proofs, reefs, roofs, safes
Two forms: dwarfs [fs]/dwarves [vs], hoofs/hooves, scarfs/scarves, wharfs/wharves

Nouns ending in *-f(e)* (but not *-ff*) normally form their plural with *-ves* [vz].
Some of them, however, retain the *f* [f] in the plural.

Dwarf, hoof, scarf and *wharf* can form their plural with either *-fs* or *-ves.*

path [θ] – paths [ðz], mouth [θ] – mouths [ðz]
Compare: deaths [θs], months [θs]
Either [ðz] **or** [θs]**:** baths, oaths, sheaths, truths, wreaths, youths
Note: clothes [kləʊ(ð)z] (= dresses, coats, etc.)
cloths [klɒθs] (= pieces of cloth)

With nouns ending in [θ] after a long vowel or a diphthong, the plural is usually pronounced [ðz]. But some of them have the alternative pronunciation [θs].

Note:
With numerals and abbreviations the plural *-s* is sometimes, for the sake of clarity, preceded by an apostrophe. With single letters the plural form is always *'s:*
Britain in the 80's (more commonly: in the 80s), three Liberal MP's (more commonly: MPs)
Dot your i's and cross your t's.

70 Other Plural Forms

With a number of nouns the plural is not formed by adding *-(e)s,* but in a different way:

foot – feet, goose – geese, tooth – teeth,
mouse – mice, louse – lice,
man – men, woman – women ['wɪmɪn]
Similarly: chairmen, Frenchwomen, etc.

- by changing the vowel of the stem
  This also applies to compounds formed with these nouns (cf **71**).

child – children, ox – oxen brother – brethren (in a religious context; otherwise: brothers)	• by adding *-(r)en* With *children* and *brethren* the vowel of the stem is also changed.
crisis [ɪs] – crises [i:z], larva – larvae [i:] stimulus – stimuli [aɪ], bacterium – bacteria [ɪə] series – series (singular and plural [i:z]) **But:** apparatus – apparatuses; albums, museums, kindergartens, and many others **Two forms:** indexes/indices ['ɪndɪsi:z] antennas [əz] (radio, TV, etc.)/antennae [i:] (of insects)	• by retaining the foreign plural form for words from other languages (especially Latin and Greek). But many loan words, particularly those in common use, form their plural with *-(e)s.* There are quite a few nouns which can take two forms, sometimes with a difference in meaning.
a Portuguese – five Portuguese **Similarly:** Swiss, Chinese, Japanese, etc. two aircraft/spacecraft/hovercraft a sheep – two sheep, a deer – some deer **Similarly:** grouse, fish, salmon, trout etc. (**But:** the fishes of the Mediterranean)	• by using the same form as in the singular for – nationalities ending in *-ese* and *Swiss,* – technical means of transport ending in *-craft,* – some birds and animals (frequently in a hunting context), including fish. (*Fish* also has the plural form *fishes;* this is usually used in the sense of "types of fish".)

Notes:

1. As in German, a number of nouns denoting measurements or quantities do not change in the plural:
   two **dozen** eggs; fifty **head** of cattle, twelve **foot** ten, ten **pound** fifty, etc.
2. The noun *penny* has a regular and an irregular plural form:
   ten **pennies** (= separate coins) – ten **pence** (= amount of money).

71 Plurals of Compound Nouns

mouse-**traps** (= traps for mice) horse**men** (= men on horseback) fathers-in-law, passers-by, lords spiritual **men**servants (= male servants) **women** teachers (= female teachers) (**Compare:** woman-haters = haters of women)	With these compound nouns it is the noun carrying the basic meaning which is pluralized. **But:** with compounds consisting of *man/woman* + a noun both elements are pluralized if *man/woman* indicates the sex of the person referred to by the second noun.
breakdowns, grown-ups, sit-ins, forget-me-nots, good-for-nothings, five-year-olds	If there is no noun carrying the basic meaning, *-s* is added to the end of the compound.

Note:

Some compounds tend to be used without consideration for the meaning of their individual elements. Plurals such as *spoonfuls, mouthfuls, handfuls* are, for example, commoner than the more logical form *spoonsful,* etc. And the words *general* and *martial* are now rarely regarded as adjectives in compounds; thus we find e.g.:

attorney generals (Generalstaatsanwälte), *governor-generals* (Generalgouverneure), *court-martials* (Kriegsgerichte) as well as: *attorneys general* etc.

In colloquial English we similarly find *father-in-laws, sister-in-laws,* etc., in addition to the more usual form *fathers-in-law,* etc.

72–76 Concord of Number between Nouns, Determiners, Pronouns and Verb Forms

72 Formal Concord and Notional Concord

The following are affected by concord, or agreement, of number:
- relations between nouns, determiners and pronouns
- the relation between subject and predicate (finite verb form).

Formal Concord

This **actor** *is* hopeless. *He keeps* forgetting *his* lines.	(*actor* → *this, is, he, keeps, his:* singular forms)
These **actors** *play their parts* extremely well.	(*actors* → *these, play, their, parts:* plural forms)

One uses the term **formal concord** when concord follows the form of the noun. This is the case with the majority of nouns in English, and with virtually all nouns in German.

Notional Concord

Amateur **dramatics** *is* her great passion. *It takes* up all her time.	(*dramatics:*	'plural' form ending in *-s* **but:** singular meaning → *is, it, takes.*)
The **cast** *were* roundly applauded for *their* marvellous performance.	(*cast:*	no plural ending, **but:** plural meaning → *were, their.*)

The term **notional concord** is used when concord does not follow the form of the noun but instead is determined by its meaning. Concord will then depend on whether the noun expresses the idea of an entity (singular meaning) or of 'plurality'.
Notional concord runs counter to a German native speaker's intuitive feeling for language, but in English more and more nouns are being treated in this way.

73 Formal Concord and Notional Concord with Uncountables

Most uncountables (nouns with only one number form) obey formal concord. But there are also many cases of notional concord.

1. Inflectionless form and singular meaning (formal concord)

Coal *is* formed from fossilized wood. **Similarly:** iron, oil, salt, butter, water, etc.	This group includes • the names of natural substances and materials
Machinery *has* largely replaced human labour in the mines. *(Maschinen . . .)* **Similarly:** garbage, luggage, hair, furniture, jewelry, cutlery *(Besteck)*, crockery *(Geschirr)*, etc.	• a number of collective nouns, many of which end in *-ry* (Their German equivalents are in some cases countables.)
This **information** *was* given to me by the National Coal Board. **Similarly:** advice, damage *(Schaden)*, progress, strength, confusion, knowledge, etc.	• many abstract nouns. (Their German equivalents are in some cases countables, e.g. *Informationen*.)

Note:
As in German, many nouns can be used either as countables or uncountables – the latter when they denote a natural substance or material:

A hot **coal** fell from the fire. (= a piece of coal) **Coal** *is* Newcastle's main industry.
So many **lambs** died in the cold spell that **lamb** *has* become very expensive.

Nouns denoting food or drink are often used as countables when they refer to individual types or portions:

The French are famous for their **cheeses** and their **wines.**
Two teas and **three coffees**, please.

With other uncountable nouns paraphrases are used to denote types, units or definite quantities:

a cheap **sort of** paper, a strange **kind of** love, a new **type of** plastic (material), an **article of** furniture, a useful **piece of** advice, two separate **items of** information, three **loaves of** bread, etc.

2. Nouns with plural form and plural meaning (formal concord)

Be careful, *these* **stairs** *are* slippery. *(Diese Treppe ist glatt.)* **Similarly:** surroundings, outskirts *(Stadtrandzone)*, contents *(Inhalt)*, wages *(Lohn)*, thanks, etc.	This group includes ● many concrete and abstract nouns referring to something that can be regarded as consisting of several parts. (Their equivalents in German are often singular.)
clothes *(Kleider)* – a garment *(ein Kleidungsstück)*; goods *(Waren)* – an article *(eine Ware, ein Artikel)*; particulars *(Einzelheiten)* – a detail, etc.	For some of these nouns there are countable nouns with similar meaning.
These **glasses** I'm wearing *darken* automatically. *(Diese Brille . . .)* All my **jeans** are dirty. **Similarly:** scissors, binoculars *(Fernglas)*, tights *(Strumpfhose)*, etc.	● 'doubles', i.e. nouns denoting objects consisting of two identical halves. Depending on the context, these nouns may denote one such object or more than one.
I don't think he owns more than **one pair of** trousers. **How many pairs of** pyjamas have you packed?	A paraphrase with *pair(s) of* is used if one wants to talk about the number of objects.

Notes:

1. *Barracks* (Ger. *Kaserne*) and *headquarters* can be used with both formal and notional concord:
   New **barracks** *are/A* new **barracks** *is* being built at the airport.
2. Some plural collective nouns and 'doubles' are identical with the plural forms of countable nouns, but there is a difference in meaning:
   Let's go to **the pictures.** (= to the cinema . . .) – Look at **these pictures.** (= paintings, drawings, photos, etc. . . .)

Similarly:						
	arms:	*Waffen – Arme*	looks:	*Aussehen – Blicke*	glasses:	*Brille – Gläser*
	minutes:	*Protokoll – Minuten*	spirits:	*Spirituosen, Laune – Geister*	scales:	*Waage – Skalen*
	pains:	*Sorgfalt – Schmerzen*			and others	

3. Nouns with plural form and singular meaning (notional concord)

Physics *is* the subject I like best. **Similarly:** mathematics, politics, economics, genetics, linguistics, dramatics etc.	In spite of their *s*-ending, the following have singular meaning: ● nouns ending in *-ics* which denote sciences and other specialist areas
Darts *is* often played in British pubs. *(Pfeilwerfen . . .)* **Similarly:** marbles *(Murmelspiel)*, billiards, dominoes, checkers/draughts [drɑːfts] *(Dame)*, etc.	● the names of some games
Shingles *is* a very painful disease of the nerves. *(Die Gürtelrose . . .)* **Similarly:** mumps, measles *(Masern)*, German measles *(Röteln)*	● certain diseases
Here *is* the **news.** *(Und nun die Nachrichten.)* **Note:** an interesting piece of news/news item *(eine interessante Nachricht)*	● *news* (the German equivalent is countable)

Note:
Nouns ending in *-ics* are also found with formal concord, though there is some difference in meaning:

His **mathematics** *are* almost non-existent. *(Seine Mathematikkenntnisse . . .)*
The **acoustics** of this hall *are* excellent. *(Die akustischen Verhältnisse . . .)*

4. No plural form, but plural meaning (notional concord)

The **police** *were* sent for immediately.
Similarly: clergy *(Geistlichkeit)*, gentry *(Landadel)*, people *(Leute;* **but:** *peoples = Völker)*, cattle *(Vieh)*, vermin *(Ungeziefer)*

The party consisted of twenty **people.**
The farmer owned *60* **cattle,** *several/many* of which had won prizes at the agricultural show.

Some nouns denoting groups of living beings have plural meaning, though they appear to be singular in form.

People and *cattle* are basically countable nouns with no corresponding singular form. They can be combined with numbers and words indicating expressions of indefinite number such as *many, several,* etc.

74 Formal Concord and Notional Concord with Countable Collective Nouns

Most nouns denoting groups of people have – in contrast to *police, clergy,* etc. (cf **73**.4) – normal singular and plural forms *(one team – two teams).*
In the plural they always have formal concord, whereas in the singular notional concord is also found:

The **government** *have* a major crisis on *their hands* but *they are* gradually getting things under control.
Brian's **family,** *who haven't* had a holiday for years, *are* enjoying *themselves* at *their* holiday camp. *They* love the company there.

The Kennedy **family,** *which has* played a prominent part in American politics for many years, *seems* to be dogged by ill luck. *It has* lost two of *its* members by assassination.

Notional concord is used if one is thinking of the individual members of a group rather than the group as a whole. Relative clauses are introduced by the relative pronoun *who,* which relates to persons (cf **78**). (But these nouns cannot be preceded by plural determiners such as *these* or by numbers.)

Formal concord is used if the group is seen as a whole. In this case the noun denotes not persons but a thing, so relative clauses are introduced by *which.*

Each **government** *has* tried *its* hand at solving this problem.

That **family** over there *is* having trouble putting up *their* tent. *They seem* to have picked the windiest spot on the camping site.

When the noun is the subject of a sentence and is preceded by a singular determiner such as *a, each, every, this, that,* the verb has to be in the singular.
Pronouns and determiners which follow later may, however, be in the plural. It is quite common to find such a change in perspective (and therefore in concord) in the middle of a sentence or text.

Similarly, with notional or formal concord:

cabinet, opposition, administration, jury,
company, firm, staff, class, school,
crew, club, band, choir, audience, crowd,
group, party, couple, tribe, clan, etc.

Notional concord is becoming increasingly common when referring to groups of people in all areas of public and private life, for example in
politics, administration, law,
business, education,
sports, music and many other cultural and social areas.

Note:
Notional concord is also commonly used with uncountable nouns such as *the public, the press* (Ger. *die Presse = Presseleute*) when one is thinking of a large number of individuals:

The press *were (was)* there in full force.

75 Notional Concord with Expressions of Quantity and Measure

A lot of/Lots of ***houses have*** been destroyed by the erupting volcano. (= many houses) There *was* **a lot/lots of** ***talk*** about diverting the path of the lava. (= much talk) **Half of** ***the villages*** *have* been evacuated; **the rest** *are* hoping to be spared. **A number of** ***experts*** *were* watching the scene from a safe distance. **Similarly:** plenty of, two thirds of, a good deal of, heaps of, the majority of, etc.	Expressions of quantity such as *a lot of, lots of* are treated as units, like *much* or *many.* The concord of the verb depends on the number of the noun which these expressions modify, and not on the (singular/ plural) form *lot* or *lots.* The same applies to many other expressions of quantity. (*A number of* and *the majority of* can only be used with nouns which have plural meaning and therefore always require a plural verb.)
Ten dollars *is* all I've got. *Another* **three miles** *brings* you to the main road. The last **two years** *has* been the best time of my life. I have put on *another* **two pounds** in weight.	Expressions of measure – amounts of money, distances, periods of time, etc. – are often seen as one unit, even if they contain numbers and are in the plural. They are therefore combined with singular verbs and even with singular determiners such as *another.*

76 Formal Concord and Notional Concord with Proper Names

Pat Walker *is* a taxi driver. **Detroit** *is* the automobile capital of America. **BP** *have/has* raised the price of petrol again.	Most proper names are singular in both form and meaning (formal concord). The names of companies, however, can, like collective nouns, have notional concord.
The Alps *form* a dividing line across Europe. In winter *they* often used to be impassable. **The Hebrides** ['hebrɪdi:z] *are* situated off the west coast of Scotland. **The Smiths** *have* moved to Cornwall.	Most proper names which are plural in form have formal concord, for instance the names of mountain ranges, groups of islands, or families.
The United Nations *was* founded in 1945. (= The United Nations Organization) **The United States** *is* the world's richest country.	*The United Nations, the United States* and *the Netherlands* are exceptions; they are seen as political entities with singular meaning (notional concord).

77–81 Gender and Gender Concord between Nouns, Pronouns and Determiners

77 Grammatical Gender and Biological Sex

The gender of English nouns is mainly determined by biological sex. A distinction is made between
- (male and female) persons and
- (sexless) things.

However, in the case of animals biological sex is often ignored. They are treated grammatically as things. Conversely, some inanimate objects and institutions are sometimes personified and treated grammatically as persons.

78 Pronouns and Determiners Indicating Gender (Summary)

Unlike in German, the gender of an English noun is not indicated by the article, but only by certain determiners and pronouns that replace the noun (gender concord). Some of these have different (masculine/feminine) forms for male and female persons. Others only distinguish between persons and things:

		For persons		For things
		male	female	
personal pronouns	singular	he, him	she, her	it
self-pronouns	singular	himself	herself	itself
possessive determiners and pronouns	singular	his	her, hers	its
		male **and** female		
relative pronouns	singular and plural	who		which
interrog. pronouns	singular and plural	who		what
genitive	singular and plural	usually *s*-genitive		usually *of*-phrase (cf **92–94**)
indefinite pronouns		someone/somebody, no one/nobody, etc.		something, nothing, etc.

79 Gender and Gender Concord when Referring to Persons

There are two types of noun referring to individual persons:

- Nouns which distinguish between male and female. These nouns usually consist of pairs of words with quite different forms (*boy – girl, husband – wife,* etc.). Nouns denoting a person's profession or nationality often consist of pairs of words ending in *-man/-woman* (*salesman – saleswoman, Frenchman – Frenchwoman,* etc.). With a few nouns, gender distinctions are made by the addition of special suffixes *(host – hostess, actor – actress, hero – heroine, widow – widower,* etc.).
- Nouns which are the same for both males and females.
  This is a very large group of nouns. It consists mainly of nouns denoting a person's profession or function (e.g. *doctor, servant, painter, listener, president*), but also includes nouns referring more generally to persons (e.g. *child, person, friend, stranger, neighbour*). The indefinite pronouns ending in *-body* and *-one* (*somebody, everyone,* etc.) can also be included here.

Only the second type poses a problem for gender concord:

The Prime Minister (= Mrs Thatcher) was cheered by **her** supporters. The **press secretary** shook **his** head.	If one is referring to a particular male or female person, the appropriate pronouns and determiners are used.
Is there **a doctor** in the house? If so, would **he or she** please come forward.	If one is not referring to a particular person, or if the sex of the person is not known, then both forms can be used together, e.g. *he or she.*
If a **thief** stole this brooch **he** would be disappointed, it's not real gold.	However, the masculine forms are often used in a general sense.
No **person** in **her** senses would have such valuable jewellery in a hotel bedroom.	But if a person is assumed to be female, the feminine forms are likely to be used.

Speak to any **employee** here and **they** will tell you the same sad story.
Nobody'd want to work in a place like that, would **they**?
It's time **somebody** put **their** foot down about the intolerable noise.

Most Oxbridge colleges are now open to **male** and **female students** alike.
There was a time when **women teachers** had to give up their jobs when they got married.
A **woman professor** is still something of a rarity.
Female politicians are few and far between.
(Politikerinnen sind dünn gesät.)
The number of **male nurses** is on the increase.

The use of *he or she* and *his or her* can seem rather clumsy, and the use of the masculine forms may cause misunderstanding. Consequently, the plural forms *they, their,* etc., which are neutral in gender, are becoming increasingly common, especially with the indefinite pronouns.

If a person's biological sex is particularly important for the context, then words like *man/woman, male/female* can be added to the noun. This is found, for instance, with women in professions which are regarded as typically male, and vice versa.

Notes:

1. In British English the expressions *boy-friend* and *girl-friend* imply a steady (sexual or romantic) relationship. Where the friendship is of a more general nature one uses the word *friend* for both sexes. A sex distinction can, however, be made indirectly by introducing personal pronouns or by giving the friend's name:
   I was out with **a friend.** I don't think you know **her.**
   I was out with **my friend Christine.**
2. The pronoun *it* can be used for *baby* and *child* if one is making a general reference:
   A **baby** can only express **its** anger by crying.
3. Since the use of some gender-distinguishing nouns can sometimes be considered sexist, they are increasingly being replaced by nouns which are neutral in gender, especially when they refer to indefinite or unknown persons:
   Cleaner wanted. (instead of *charwoman*) We must elect a **chairperson.** (instead of *chairman*)

80 Gender and Gender Concord when Referring to Animals

As with nouns referring to persons, there is a small group of nouns referring to animals which make sex distinctions (e.g. *cock – hen, bull – cow*) and a much larger group which are used for both sexes (e.g. *cat, dog, horse, fish, frog*). The choice of personal pronouns, possessive determiners, etc. is normally not determined by sex distinctions. More important is the speaker's attitude towards the animal in question:

Have you ever watched a **snake** swallowing **its** prey?
This **wasp** is getting on my nerves. **It** keeps flying round my head.
A **cat** will often find **its** way back home, however many miles **it** has to travel.
The **cow** had injured **its** leg.

If a speaker has no special relationship with an animal, then it is normal to use *it, its,* etc. This is the rule with lower animals. But it is also common with the higher mammals, no matter whether the animal's sex is known or not.

Bess is our best **cow. She** gives three gallons of milk a day.
Why don't you take the **dog** for a walk? **He**'s dying to go.
Look at that **elephant** – isn't **he** magnificent?
A **lioness** fighting for **her** cub couldn't have been fiercer.

If one has a special relationship with an animal and sees it as having a personality of its own, so to speak, one will use either *he* or *she*, depending on the sex of the animal. If the sex is not known, the tendency is to use *he*, particularly for large animals. Pets and other domestic animals, and even wild animals, are frequently referred to as *he* or *she*.

Notes:

1. The relative pronoun when referring to animals is almost always *which,* even if *he/she* etc. would be used:
   The white **rabbit, which** is Paul's favourite, added three more members to **her** family last week.
2. With nouns which refer to animals of both sexes, the sex can be made clear by using special words or additions to the nouns:
   a bull elephant, a she-bear, a tomcat (= a male cat), a billy-goat (a he-goat) – a nanny-goat (a she-goat)

81 Gender and Gender Concord when Referring to Things

For most nouns denoting things one uses *it* (*its*, etc.). Certain things and institutions are sometimes personified, in which case *she* is used instead of *it*. These include

She's really lovely, that **car** of yours.
The **flagship** Mary Rose, of **which** King Henry VIII was very proud, sank with all **her** crew before **she** ever set sail.

- ships and other means of transport or machines with which one has a special, personal relationship, e.g. one's own car.
  The appropriate relative pronoun, however, is *which*, not *who*.

Britain has divested **herself/itself** of most of **her/its** colonies.
With **her/its** teeming millions, **Asia** is faced with enormous problems.
Approaching **New York** by sea gives you the best impression of **her/its** unique skyline.

- countries, especially in literary style and when they are being seen as political and economic powers; this also applies to continents and cities.

Notes:

1. In poetic language, abstract concepts and natural phenomena are often personified:
   How soon hath **Time**, the subtle thief of youth
   Stolen on **his** wing my three and twentieth year! (John Milton)

   Slowly, silently, now the **moon**/Walks the night in **her** silver shoon. [= shoes]
   This way and that **she** peers and sees/Silver fruit upon silver trees. (Walter de la Mare)

Similarly: Death, Love, War = *he*; Nature, Peace, Liberty = *she*; the earth, the sea = *she*; the sun = *he*

2. The choice of pronouns and determiners with collective nouns such as *family* is subject both to number and gender concord. When referring to persons the nouns are replaced by *they* and *who*, and when referring to things, by *it* and *which*. For details see **74**.

82–85 Personal Pronouns

82 Forms

Most personal pronouns in English have – unlike nouns – both a subject and an object form. *One* is an indefinite, general personal pronoun.

Subject form:	I	you	he	she	it	we	you	they	one (Ger. *man*)
Object form:	me	you	him	her	it	us	you	them	one *(einen, einem)*

83 The Use of the Subject and Object Forms

Basically, the personal pronouns are used in the same way as the equivalent forms in German, that is, the subject form is used as the subject of a sentence and the object form is used as the object and after prepositions. (Compare: **They** are waiting for **us**.)
However, the object form is now being increasingly used instead of the subject form in certain constructions, especially when there is no finite verb after it.

I'm expecting my friends any minute. That'll be **them** now.
It's **me** who(m) she wanted to see in the play. (= She wanted to see **me**.)
But: It was *I* who asked her to come to the rehearsal. (= *I* asked her to come.)

The object form is preferred in colloquial English:

- as a subject complement after *be*
  This also applies to the '*it* cleft sentences' (cf **339–340**). But if the personal pronoun is the logical subject of the cleft sentence, then the subject form is normally used, even in colloquial speech.

Sarah is almost as tall as **him.** Are the University Players better than **us?**	● in comparisons with *as* and *than*
It's my sister who wants to play Lady Macbeth, not **me.** – Oh, no! Not **her** again!	● in short sentences where the personal pronoun is used on its own, i.e. without a finite verb form.
There has never been a more brilliant Shakespeare actor than **he.**	In all these cases, the subject form sounds formal.
The accident happened when the stage manager, his assistant and **I/me** were changing the scenery for the second act.	The object form is sometimes even found as part of the subject of a sentence, namely in combination with *and.* But even in colloquial English, the subject form is more common in such cases.

Notes:

1. In comparisons, the use of the object form can sometimes cause misunderstanding. In such cases it is better to use a clause of comparison (with an auxiliary verb or a main verb):
   Do you know her better than **him**? – Do you know her better than **he does**?
   – Do you know her better than **you know him**?
2. For special emphasis, a *self*-pronoun may sometimes be used instead of a personal pronoun:
   She told me her husband worked in the same office as **herself.**

84 *It* Used as a Structure Word

Like the German pronoun *es, it* can be used not only as a personal pronoun to replace a noun phrase, but also as a structure word with no real meaning.

Don't worry, **it** isn't a burglar; **it's** only me. *(Ich bin es nur.)* Do you know who that couple is? **It's** Jack and Mary O'Connor from Limerick. *(Es sind Jack und Mary . . .)*	*It* (+ *be*) is used like the German *es* when establishing the identity of persons or things. (*Be* is then always in the 3rd person singular.)
This is Mrs McCarthy. **She's** an old friend of ours.	If a person has already been named, then only *he* or *she* can be used.
It snowed last night, but **it** is already thawing again. **Similarly:** rain, hail, freeze, etc. (**But:** There was a flash of lightning/a clap of thunder. – *Es hat geblitzt/gedonnert.*)	With some verbs describing weather events, *it* is used as the formal subject when there is no real subject present (impersonal verbs).
It was cold and rainy yesterday. **It** is six o'clock. **It's** twenty miles to Cork from here.	The same applies with *be* when giving information about the temperature, time or distance, etc.
It must have been Patrick's twin brother that you saw. **It** was Tim and Kevin who suggested the trip.	In '*it* cleft sentences', *it* is the formal subject, standing for an element in the sentence that is emphasized (cf **339–340**).
It's not surprising that everyone got sunburnt on their first day in Greece. **It** seems total madness to lie in the sun all day. **It** was interesting watching the fishermen unloading their catch.	As a formal subject, *it* can also stand for a notional subject that follows later (a subordinate clause or non-finite construction). (Cf **257.1** Note, **263.2**, **263** Note 1.)
I don't *find* **it** surprising that everyone got sunburnt. I *consider* **it** foolish to lie in the sun all day. We *left* **it** to Eileen to book the ferry to Crete.	As a formal object – especially in sentence patterns containing an object + object complement – *it* stands for a following notional object (a subordinate clause or non-finite construction).
He didn't *think fit* to apologize for making us wait. Would she *prefer* to stay at the hotel? Do you *mind* if we leave our bags here? *(Macht es Ihnen etwas aus, . . . ?)*	However, *it* is not used with verbal complexes *(think fit, make sure, make plain)* or with most verbs which only have a direct object. (*Es* is often used here in German, though.)

Notes:

1. German *es* often has to be expressed with other constructions in English. Compare, for example:
   Has he arrived? – I suppose **so**./I don't know. *(Ich nehme **es** an./Ich weiß **es** nicht.)* (Cf **31–33**.)
   There were over fifty people present. *(**Es** waren über fünfzig Leute anwesend.)* (Cf **341–342**.)
   Smoking is not allowed here. *(**Es** ist nicht erlaubt, hier zu rauchen.)*
   More chairs were called for. *(**Es** wurden mehr Stühle verlangt.)*
   Somebody is knocking. *(**Es** klopft.)*
   I'm sorry I'm late. *(**Es** tut mir leid, daß ich mich verspätet habe.)*

2. *It* occurs as a formal object with no particular reference in certain fixed expressions, e.g.:

Hold **it**!	*Warte!*	to rough **it**	*primitiv/kümmerlich leben*
Hop **it**!	*Hau ab!*	to lord **it** over s.o.	*sich als Herr aufspielen*
Damn **it**!	*Verdammt!*	to have **it** out with s.o.	*die Sache endgültig bereinigen*

85 General Personal Pronouns (*one, you,* etc.)

One must always try to do **one's** best.
One ist as old as **one** feels.
One must make up **one's** mind about such things **oneself**.
One shouldn't let **oneself** be carried away by **one's** emotions.
You never can tell. *(Man kann nie wissen.)*
You're as old as **you** feel.

The general personal pronoun *one* (Ger. *man*) is used to refer generally to people. It is used in making generalizations in which the speaker is included.
One (one's, oneself) is used in formal style and also in clichéd expressions (proverbs, sayings, etc.). In colloquial English *you (your, yourself)* is generally used instead.

Someone has tried to smuggle a file into the terrorist's cell. *(Man/Jemand hat versucht . . .)*
They/People are expecting an amnesty to be issued soon. *(Man erwartet, . . .)*
They've cordoned off the area round the prison. (They = the police)
The area round the prison has been cordoned off.
An amnesty is expected to be issued soon.

If a speaker and the person spoken to are not meant to be included, the following can be used:

- *someone*, to refer to a single, unknown person;
- *they* or *people*, to refer to several unknown persons.
  (With *they*, one may also have a certain group of people in mind.)

In many cases, passive sentences can be used as an alternative to active sentences with *one, someone, they, people*.

Note:
In American English, the pronoun *one* is often used in combination with *his, himself* or *their, themselves* instead of *one's, oneself*.
One must always try to do **his/their** best.

86–88 *Self*-Pronouns and Reciprocal Pronouns

86 The Forms of the *self*-Pronouns

Singular forms:	myself	yourself	himself	herself	itself	oneself
Plural forms:	ourselves	yourselves	themselves			

The second syllable *(-self/-selves)* is almost always given greater stress than the first.

87 The Use of the *self*-Pronouns

The *self*-pronouns have two different functions: they are used as emphatic pronouns (Ger. *selbst*) and as reflexive pronouns (Ger. *mich, dich, sich* etc.).

1. *Self*-forms as emphatic pronouns

It was Turner's aim to reproduce light **itself** in his paintings. Rembrandt **himself** is thought to have worked on this painting. We inherited these pictures from a great-uncle. – Oh, I should have known you wouldn't buy pictures like these **yourselves.**

Emphatic *self*-pronouns serve to focus attention on a noun or pronoun (emphasis: cf **333.**1). They are always stressed. They can always be placed immediately after the focused word.
But if this word is the subject of the sentence, the emphatic pronoun usually stands at the end of the sentence.

Note:
Sometimes *self*-pronouns are used as alternatives to personal pronouns (subject or object form, cf **83**), especially after *as, than, like, except, but* (= except), *including, and, or:*

There was nobody at the exhibition *but* **myself** (but me).
His wife, *like* **himself,** was a talented painter.

2. *Self*-forms as reflexive pronouns

Mark and I helped **ourselves** to some drinks. *I* bought **myself** a sandwich and a coffee. Won't ***you*** treat **yourself** to another piece of cake? *(Nimm dir doch noch ein Stück Kuchen.)* Don't make such a pig of **yourself.** (= Don't eat so much.) Good-bye girls. Enjoy **yourselves.** Feeling sorry for **oneself/yourself** never does much good.

A reflexive pronoun is used as object if both subject and object refer to the same person or thing (cf **52–53**).
Such pronouns are generally not stressed (and should not be translated as *selbst*).
In imperative sentences the forms *yourself* (for one person) or *yourselves* (for more than one person) are used.
In non-finite constructions *oneself* or *yourself* are used as general reflexive pronouns (cf **85**).

Note:
Reflexive pronouns are only stressed (on the second syllable) if they also have an emphatic function. In such cases they normally express a contrast. In German this can be expressed by using a reflexive pronoun reinforced by *selbst*:

You ought to look after **your***self* – not me. *(Du sollst dich um* ***dich selbst*** *kümmern, . . .)*
He only thinks of **him***self*, he never considers his family. *(Er denkt nur an* ***sich selbst****, . . .)*

88 The Reciprocal Pronouns *each other/one another*

Unlike in German, the English reciprocal pronouns are not interchangeable with the plural reflexive pronouns (*ourselves,* etc.).

Reciprocal pronouns	Compare: Reflexive pronouns
The boxer and the novelist had never seen **each other** before the talk show. We should stop criticizing **one another.** We must all take part of the blame for our defeat.	After the match most members of the team went home to see **themselves** on TV. We bought **ourselves** a new TV just in time to watch the World Cup in colour.

Reciprocal pronouns are used to express a relationship of reciprocity, or mutual exchange, between two or more persons or things (Ger.: *einander – sich/uns/euch gegenseitig*). *Each other* is preferred when only two persons or things are concerned, and *one another* for more than two. Reflexive pronouns cannot be used in such cases since they do not denote an exchange between persons or things, but instead refer back to each individual or the group as a whole.

89 *S*-Genitive, *of*-Phrase and Possessive Determiners and Pronouns: a Comparison

	Noun head		
John's	moped		A noun can be modified by other nouns in the form of an *s*-genitive or an *of*-phrase, both having the same meaning. Nouns referring to persons are mainly used in the *s*-genitive form, whereas nouns referring to things occur mainly as an *of*-phrase (for details cf **90–94**).
the	wheels	**of the lorry**	
his	moped		The *s*-genitive and *the* + *of*-phrase can be replaced by possessive determiners (cf **96–97**).
its	wheels		
Our car is larger than		**the Browns'.** / **theirs.**	In some cases the *s*-genitive can be used without a noun head and then be replaced by a possessive pronoun.
Are you a friend		**of Mary's?** / **of hers?**	The double genitive (*of* + *s*-genitive) corresponds to a combination of *of* + possessive pronoun (for details cf **95** and **99**).

The *s*-genitive, the *of*-phrase and the possessive determiner can express a number of different relationships to the noun head:

Possession or belonging	**the Millers'** house	– **their** house	(They have a house.)
	the door **of the house**	– **its** door	(It has a door.)
Active agency or cause	**the architect's** plans	– **his** plans	(He made plans.)
	the effects **of the insulation**	– **its** effects	(It caused something.)
Fact of being affected by s.th.	**Pat's** appointment as designer	– **her** appointment	(Someone appointed her.)
	the demolition **of the building**	– **its** demolition	(Someone demolished it.)

The *s*-genitive and the *of*-phrase can also express other relationships, but here they cannot be replaced by possessive determiners. The *s*-genitive and the *of*-phrase can, for example, express:

Membership of a class	a **children's** book (a book for children, not for adults)
	two **hen's/hens'** eggs (two eggs laid by hens, not by ducks or geese)
A measure of time or distance	in **a week's** time, a **two hours'** stop, at a distance **of two miles**
Contents	a glass **of milk**, two pounds **of sugar**, a group **of students**

90–95 *S*-Genitive and *of*-Phrase

90 Formation and Position of the *s*-Genitive

Peter's dartboard – **my little brother's** toys
somebody's football – **everyone's** enjoyment

The *s*-genitive can be formed with nouns, noun phrases, and indefinite pronouns ending in *-body* and *-one*. It stands in front of the noun head.

the people next door's piano
somebody else's violin
Gilbert and Sullivan's operas (They wrote them together.)
(**But: Britten's** and **Elgar's** music: Each composed his own music.)

Noun phrases which are followed by attributes and nouns linked together by *and* can form a 'group genitive' by having the genitive ending added to the last word of the phrase.

the lady's [z] coat, Mr. Black's [s] hat the boss's [sɪz] suit, James's [zɪz] anorak	The genitive of words in the singular is formed by adding an apostrophe + *s* (pronounced [z], [s] or [ɪz] like the plural *-s*, cf **69**).
the ladies' [z] dresses, the Blacks' [s] coats the bosses' [sɪz] umbrellas	Plural forms ending in *-(e)s* only have an apostrophe added to them. (The pronunciation does not change.)
the children's [z] socks the men's [z] department	Other plural forms have an apostrophe + *s* added to them.

Notes:

1. Surnames ending in a vowel + voiceless *-s* (e.g. *Moss, Davis*) form the genitive in the same way as all other nouns ending in *-s:* singular: Mr Davis's dog, plural: the Davises' dog (both forms pronounced [sɪz]). In cases where the *-s* sounds like a plural or genitive *-s* (voiceless *s* after a consonant as in *Bates*, or a voiced *s* as in *Jones* or *Hayes*), there are some additional ways of writing and pronouncing the genitive:
   Singular: Mr Bates' [beits] cow. Plural: the Bates'/Bates's [beits/beitsɪz] cow.
2. Many foreign and historical proper names only have an apostrophe added to them:
   Socrates' ['sɒkrəti:z] philosophy, Guy Fawkes' [fɔ:ks] Day.

91 Formation and Position of the *of*-Phrase

the killing **of animals** the protection **of this threatened species** the cause **of (all) this**	The *of*-phrase can be formed with nouns, noun phrases and all pronouns, and normally comes immediately after the noun head.
The killing by a troop of hunters **of hundreds of baby seals** shocked the public. I regard **the protection**, by means of improved legislation, **of this threatened species** as absolutely essential.	In formal English the *of*-phrase can be separated from the noun head by inserting other words. To aid understanding, these inserted words are often – but not always – marked off by commas.

92 *S*-Genitive and *of*-Phrase when Referring to Persons

the director's desk, **Mr Green's** secretary, **Ms Cole's** letter to our Tokyo office	To express **possession, belonging** or **active agency,** nouns referring to persons usually occur as *s*-genitives. The *of*-phrase is only used
The reports **of our representative *stationed in Moscow*** are worth reading. (**But: Our man *in Moscow's*** reports are worth reading.)	● if the person in question is characterized by a lengthy attribute. (With short attributes after the noun the group genitive is more usual.)
It was terrible, he kept interrupting the speech **of the party chairman.** A huge crowd was awaiting the arrival **of the Prime Minister.** She knows the names **of all 650 M.P.s.**	● if the focus of the information is on the person, who is therefore best named at the end of the sentence (e.g. to express indignation, astonishment or admiration, etc.). (For the principles of end weight cf **6** and **332.**)
The influence **of his advisers** has often been overestimated. He can count on the support **of his friends.**	● with plural forms in spoken English, if they could otherwise be confused with singular *s*-genitive forms which sound the same.

Everybody was shocked at **Kennedy's** assassination.	If a person is **affected** by an action carried out by some other person, then either the *s*-genitive or the *of*-phrase can be used. The *of*-phrase is often preferred, e.g.:
He was accused of the murder **of his wife.** The witness examined the photos **of the suspects.** (= the photos showing the suspects, not belonging to or taken by them)	• if the focus is to be on the person affected; • if the *s*-genitive, which can also express a relationship of possession or active agency, could be misunderstood.

Note:
In some cases where a genitive is used in German, only an *of*-phrase is possible in English, for example, in *the sight of someone:*

I can't stand the sight **of that know-all.** *(Ich kann den Anblick dieses Besserwissers nicht ertragen.)*

93 *S*-Genitive and *of*-Phrases when Referring to Animals

Our dog's name is Rover. He is a sheepdog. Where is **Pussy's** basket? **The horse's** leg was broken, so it had to be shot.	Nouns referring to animals usually occur as *s*-genitives, especially in cases where the animal would be referred to as *he* or *she* (e.g. pets), but also when there is no special relationship between speaker and animal.
That's not a bird-cage. It's the cage **of our hamster Jonathan.**	But the *of*-phrase can also be used with all animals if one wants to achieve special emphasis.
Duck's eggs are larger than **hen's** eggs. *(Enteneier . . . Hühnereier.)* There is a **bird's** nest on our balcony. *(. . . ein Vogelnest . . . .)*	The one exception to this is in fixed expressions in which the *s*-genitive expresses membership of a class. (German uses compound nouns for this.)

94 *S*-Genitive and *of*-Phrase when Referring to Things

the end **of the road,** the roof **of the hut,** the sound **of music,** the history **of socialism**	Nouns denoting things (objects, abstract concepts, etc.) normally occur as *of*-phrases.
the university's president/the president **of the university** **London's** history/the history **of London** **the country's** problems/the problems **of the country**	Certain nouns denoting things can, however, also occur as *s*-genitives, since they are connected with people. This group includes nouns denoting • institutions, organizations, cities, nations and other forms of human community;
the novel's message/the message **of the novel** **the plan's** importance/the importance **of the plan**	• the products of human activity, especially mental activity;
the car's engine/the engine **of the car** **the train's** arrival/the arrival **of the train** **the volcano's** eruption/the eruption **of the volcano**	• machines, means of transport and natural phenomena which can be regarded as almost having a life of their own;
duty's call/the call **of duty** **nature's** wonders/the wonders **of nature**	• abstract concepts when they are personified (literary usage).
the crystal's structure/the structure **of the crystal.** **the tower's** height/the height **of the tower** **the lake's** surface/the surface **of the lake**	In some cases, the *s*-genitive may be used although no personification is intended, for example • when describing the characteristics and properties of a thing (its structure, shape, size, etc.);

yesterday's paper, **tomorrow's** programme, **last year's** fashion, **this week's** winner	• when expressing the idea that something belongs to a certain time or period (e.g. with *yesterday, today, tomorrow, last week,* etc.);
an **hour's** rest, a **fifteen minutes'** walk (or: a **fifteen-minute** walk) a **stone's** throw away, at **arm's** length (**But:** a distance **of ten miles**, a **twenty-mile** race)	• when indicating temporal duration. When expressing measures of distance or length, the *s*-genitive is only used in certain fixed expressions.

Notes:

1. The *s*-genitive with nouns denoting things is used quite widely in journalism; it is often preferred to the lengthier *of*-phrase in headlines, in order to save space:
   Firm's future uncertain

2. Apart from being used in expressions of length, such as *at arm's length,* the *s*-genitive is used in a number of other fixed expressions relating to human organs, parts of the body, etc.:
   to **one's heart's** content *(nach Herzenslust),* in **one's mind's** eye *(im Geiste, vor dem geistigen Auge),* to be at **one's wits'** end *(am Ende seiner Weisheit sein),* etc.

3. Certain types of proper nouns (when used as appositions) are linked to the corresponding common noun by *of,* for example the names of cities, counties, states and months:
   the city of York, the county of Devon, the State of Texas, the month of May
   (Exception: "In Dublin's fair city . . ." – Irish folksong)

95 The *s*-Genitive without a Noun Head and the Double Genitive

If you haven't got an *umbrella*, you can borrow **my sister's.** Whose muddy *shoes* are these? – They're **Mary's.**	The *s*-genitive can be used **without a noun head** in all cases where a possessive pronoun can be used instead (cf **99**): • to avoid repeating a noun which has already been mentioned
My grandfather's was a long and eventful *life.* (My grandfather had a long and eventful life.)	• to avoid anticipating a noun which follows the verb *be* (formal style).
Jenny spent most of her time at **her aunt's** *(house).* My mother asked me to go to **the baker's** *(shop).* **Madame Tussaud's** is in Baker Street.	In the case of people's homes, shops, businesses, and public buildings the noun head may be understood without being expressed.
I bought this at **Selfridges** (or: **Selfridge's**). (**Similarly: Harrods, Woolworths,** etc.)	(In the case of large stores, the *s* is sometimes added without an apostrophe, just like a plural *-s*).
Is that ***a*** novel **of Doris Lessing's** you're reading? I lent her ***some*** books **of George's** and ***two*** old paperbacks **of Brenda's.** ***Several*** friends **of the author's** were present at the reception. My great-grandparents were contemporaries **of James Joyce's.**	The **double genitive** is a combination of an *of+ s*-genitive and comes after the noun head. It is used with nouns denoting persons when there is a further meaning besides that of possession, belonging or active agency: • The double genitive is used after *a, some, any, several* or a number + a noun (and sometimes also after a noun without a determiner), to express the idea of something/someone being part of an indefinite quantity (partitive meaning).
Did you re-arrange all ***those*** books **of Peter's** this afternoon? I don't know why ***that*** novel **of Hemingway's** is so popular.	• It is also used after a demonstrative determiner + noun when expressing surprise, annoyance and other similar reactions.

Note:
Instead of the double genitive, the *of*-phrase (*of* + common case of the noun) is used with nouns referring to things, and also with nouns referring to persons when the person is affected by an action:

Some pages **of the book** were torn.
There's *a* photo **of the author** on the back cover.

96–99 Possessive Determiners and Pronouns

96 Forms

Possessive determiners	my car(s)	your . . .	his . . .	her . . .	its . . .	our . . .	your . . .	their . . .	one's . . .
Possessive pronouns	mine	yours	his	hers	–	ours	yours	theirs	–

97 The Use of the Possessive Determiners

Basically, the possessive determiners are used in English the same way as in German (cf **89**). There are only a few exceptions.

A tramp was leaning against a lamp post with **his** *hands* in **his** *pockets.*
The dog bared **its** *teeth* at the intruder.
Do you know how many people lose **their** *lives* in road accidents every year?
The lorry came so close that the cyclist lost **her** *balance.*

In English possessive determiners are used when referring to

- parts of the body and articles of clothing,
- abstract concepts such as *life, death, mind*, etc., when these are seen as related to individuals.

The wind blew in **their** *faces* when they opened the car window. *(. . . blies **ihnen** ins Gesicht.)*
Doesn't it get on **your** *nerves* having this traffic going past all day? *(Geht es **Ihnen** nicht auf **die** Nerven . . .?)*

In German the dative form of a personal or reflexive pronoun is often included, so that – unlike in English – no possessive determiner is needed to show who one is referring to.

Somebody caught **me** *by* **the** *sleeve.*
She was knocked *on* **the** *head* with a bottle.
Similarly: to hit s.o. in **the** eye, to seize s.o. by **the** throat, to lead/hold s.o. by **the** hand, to look s.o. in **the** face, etc.
(Also possible: to hit **someone's** eye, to hold **someone's** hand, etc.)

After certain activity verbs (especially verbs expressing sudden, violent contact), the definite article is all that is needed in English, as in German. In this case the person affected by the action is made the object of an active or the subject of a passive sentence, and the part of the body affected is introduced by a preposition (*by, on,* etc.).

98 Possessive Determiners Reinforced by *own*

To emphasize the notion or possession or belonging, possessive determiners can be reinforced by *own* as follows:

They built that log cabin with **their own** *hands.* *(. . . mit ihren eigenen Händen . . .)*
Martha not only bakes **her own** *bread* but even mills **her own** *flour. (. . . mahlt sogar ihr Mehl selbst.)*

- possessive determiner + *own* used **before** the noun: this construction usually corresponds in German to a possessive determiner + *eigen,* or sometimes a construction using *selbst.*

Do these *sheep* belong to the neighbouring farm?
No, they are **our own**. *(. . . unsere eigenen.)*

To avoid repeating a noun which has already been mentioned, the possessive determiner + *own* can be used without a noun.

Examples	Explanation
It's a common dream to possess *a piece of land* **of one's own.** *(... ein eigenes Stück Land ...)* They have *plenty of ideas* **of their own** for doing without complicated and wasteful technology. *(... viele eigene Ideen ...)* We could dig a well, and then we'd have *water* **of our own.** *(... eigenes Wasser.)*	● possessive determiner + *own* used as an *of*-phrase **after** the noun: this construction corresponds in German to *eigen* used without a possessive determiner. In this construction too, *own* can only be used together with a possessive determiner. It cannot follow an article or an expression of quantity, nor can it be used on its own in front of a noun.

99 The Use of Possessive Pronouns

Examples	Explanation
Their *ideas* on dress are different from **ours.** *(... anders als unsere/die unsrigen.)* Is that *anorak* **yours**? (Does it belong to you?) Whose *(gloves)* are those?/Whose are those *(gloves)*? – They're not **mine. Mine** are blue. (They don't belong to me. The blue ones belong to me.) **Ours** was a fateful *meeting.* (Our meeting was a fateful one.) **Theirs** was a stormy *relationship.*	Possessive pronouns (always used without an article) are substituted for nouns with possessive determiners, if the noun has already been mentioned or is implied. Possessive pronouns occur frequently as subject complements after the verb *be* (meaning *belong to*), for instance in answers to questions introduced by *whose* (cf **25**). In formal style they can also be used as the subject of the verb *be* and refer to a following noun.
The chief inspector's daughter is a very good friend **of mine.** *(... eine sehr gute Freundin von mir.)*	The construction *of* + possessive pronoun corresponds to the 'double genitive' (cf **89** and **95**).

100 Articles and Demonstrative Determiners and Pronouns (Summary)

Articles and demonstrative determiners and pronouns have a selective function, as can be seen from the following comparison with nouns used without a determiner.

Examples	Explanation
Bees make **honey** from **nectar.** Are you interested in **zoology**?	**Common nouns used without a determiner** refer to a class as a whole or something in general, without restriction.
There's ***a*** **spider** on the ceiling. Could you get me ***a*** **broom**?	**The indefinite article** refers either to a random example of a class, or to one which is new to the listener.
	The definite article and the demonstrative determiners refer to particular persons or things.
	The definite article is used
Did you take ***the*** **advice he gave you**? ***The*** **lady at the information desk** told me which number to ring.	● when an attribute, e.g. a defining relative clause or a prepositional phrase, makes it clear who or what one is talking about
The **boss** is away on business. How far is it to ***the*** **station**? Jupiter is the largest of ***the*** **nine planets.**	● when the frame of reference is clear; this may be quite narrow or very wide (one's place of work, a city, our solar system, etc.)
Let's call ***the*** **waiter.** I ordered a sirloin steak and a salad. ***The*** **steak** was rather tough	● when referring to persons or things which are present at the moment of speaking or have already been mentioned and are therefore known.

Do you know ***that* tall man** over there? We must get ***these* cards** sent off today. Pauline has developed a dreadful cold. ***This*** has upset all her plans.	**The demonstrative determiners** (and the demonstrative pronouns, which have the same form) always refer to persons, things or items of information which are present or have already been mentioned.
***The/This* winter** has been very mild. The weatherman was right. ***The/Those* snowfalls** caused havoc on the roads.	They therefore overlap to a certain extent with the definite article, but, as the term 'demonstrative determiner' implies, they serve to point to things much more explicitly.
If you could scrape the ice on ***this* side of the car,** I could do ***that* side.**	They are also used to distinguish between what is near and what is further away from the speaker.

Note:
With countable nouns in the singular, the definite article can also be used to refer generally to a whole class, particularly when classifying something in an abstract, scientific way. (In other areas they are used far less commonly in this sense than they are in German.)

The whale is a mammal. (= the species whale) But: **Women's** rights (= Die Rechte **der Frau**)
The adverb and its position. (= the part of speech called adverb)

The definite article is also used in a generalizing sense with musical instruments; this use is stylistically neutral:

She plays **the** piano/**the** guitar/etc. (*Sie spielt Klavier/Gitarre/*etc.)

101–103 The Indefinite Article

101 Forms

	unstressed forms:		stressed forms:	
before a (spoken) consonant:	**a** [ə]	**a** house, **a** European town	[eɪ]	I said *a* house, not *the* house.
before a (spoken) vowel:	**an** [ən]	**an** egg, **an** hour, **an** M.P.	[æn]	I said *an* egg, not *the* egg.

The indefinite article is normally unstressed. The stressed form is only used when making a contrast, speaking hesitantly or trying to speak very clearly.

Note:
The form *an* is only used before words beginning with an *h* if the *h* is silent. Some speakers do not pronounce the *h* before unstressed vowels and consequently use *an* (not *a*) before such words:

an hotel [ən əʊ'tel], *an historical novel,* etc.

(Such pronunciations are also found sometimes with speakers who otherwise do pronounce the *h* in such words.)

102 Position

We had **a** very varied week-end. article attribute noun	The indefinite article normally comes **before** the noun and its attributes. However, it comes **after**
What a magnificent view! **Many a** traveller must have rested here before. The chair-lift will be starting in **half an** hour.	• *what, such,* *many* (formal), *half*
Rarely have I seen **so impressive a** sight. This ist **too difficult a** climb for beginners.	• *so/as/too/how/however* + adjective (formal)
The tour was **quite a/rather a** strain. Our guide was **a quite/a rather** funny character. Or: . . . was **quite a/rather a** funny character.	• *quite, rather,* when not followed by an adjective. When there is a following adjective, the indefinite article may come before or after *quite* or *rather.*

Note:
Unlike in German, uncountable nouns following *what* and *such* are used without an article:
What disgraceful behaviour. *(Was für **ein** schändliches Verhalten.)*
We've never had **such** dreadful weather in July before. *(... so **ein** scheußliches Wetter.)*

103 Use

In English, as in German, the indefinite article refers either to any one single example of a class, or to one which the listener does not yet know about (cf **100**). Particularly in the first meaning, the indefinite article is used more frequently in English than in German.

1. The indefinite article used for members of a group

In contrast to German, the indefinite article is used in English when referring to a person as a member, or representative, of a particular group or class, e.g.

Ann works as **a waitress** *(... als Kellnerin).* Mr Mackenzie is **a Scot(sman).** And he is probably **a Presbyterian,** too. Churchill was **a Conservative.**	– a trade or profession – a nationality or an ethnic group – a religious group – a party or other political group.
Paul Gauguin *was* **a bank clerk** before he *became* **a painter:** (**But:** ... before he *turned* **painter.**) Picasso *died* **a millionaire.** *(... als Millionär.)* *As* **a social realist** the artist concentrated on depicting the working classes. His experience of war *made* him **a confirmed pacifist.**	The indefinite article is found in particular after linking verbs such as *be, become, remain* (but not after *turn*), and also after other verbs which take a subject complement (*die, wake up,* etc.), after *as* and after some verbs with object complements (cf **57**).
John F. Kennedy *was* **President** (of the USA) for only three years. Jim *was made* **captain** of the basket-ball team. The Democrats *nominated* Jane Byrne *as* **mayor.**	No article is used, however, when referring to functions and titles which are regarded as unique, i.e. where the person concerned is not seen as a representative of a group or class.

Notes:
1. Membership of a national, religious or political group can also be expressed by using an appropriate adjective, which sometimes has the same form as the noun:
He is **Irish (an Irishman)/Catholic (a Catholic)/socialist (a socialist).**

2. The indefinite article is found with other nouns too, when they are used as subject complements or preceded by *as*. (In German, no article is used in most of these cases.)
I*'m* **an optimist.** *(Ich bin Optimist).* He *woke up* **a happy man** *(... als glücklicher Mann.)*
Please accept this book *as* **a token of our appreciation.** *(... als Zeichen unserer Wertschätzung.)*

2. The indefinite article with expressions of quantity

This brandy costs only £2 **a** bottle. We paid 50 p **a** pound for these oranges. She drives to the supermarket once **a** week. My new car does 100 miles **an** hour.	The indefinite article is used with units of quantity, measurement and time in the sense of *per.* This reflects its original meaning as a number. *(**One** bottle costs £2.)*
I saw it at **a** glance. *(... auf einen Blick.)* **Similarly:** in **a** word *(mit einem Wort),* one at **a** time *(einer nach dem anderen),* etc.	This original meaning is even more obvious in certain idiomatic expressions in which *a* is used in the sense of *one single.*
There's **plenty of** time left. *(.. eine Menge Zeit.)* We did **part of** the shopping this morning. *(... einen Teil des ...)*	No article is used, however, before *plenty of* and *part of* (in contrast to their German equivalents).

Note:
The indefinite article is used in many idiomatic expressions in English, where their German equivalents have none, e.g.:

to have **a** good mind to do s.th.	*(gute Lust haben zu . . .)*	to take **a** fancy to s.o./s.th.	*(Gefallen finden an)*
to have **a** good knowledge of . . .	*(gute . . .-Kenntnisse haben)*	to take **a** seat	*(Platz nehmen)*
to be in **a** position to . . .	*(in der Lage sein)*	as **a** whole	*(als Ganzes)*
to be in **a** good temper	*(guter Laune sein)*	as **a** rule	*(in der Regel)*
to come to **an** end	*(zu Ende gehen)*	from **a** distance	*(aus der Ferne)*
to make **a** noise	*(Lärm machen)*	for **a** change	*(zur Abwechslung)*

104–107 The Definite Article

104 Forms and Position

		unstressed form:		stressed form:
before a (spoken) consonant:	[ðə]	**the** house, **the** USA	[ði:]	That's ***the*** solution.
before a (spoken) vowel:	[ðɪ]	**the** error, **the** hour	[ði:]	I said ***the*** error, not *an* error.

Use of the stressed and unstressed forms: The definite article is normally unstressed. The stressed form is only used when expressing an evaluation (e.g. *the solution = the ideal solution*) or a contrast, when speaking hesitantly or trying to speak very clearly.

Position: As in German, the definite article precedes the noun and its attributes:

the very large money box

However, it follows the expressions of quantity *all, both, half, double, twice, three/four/. . . times:*

all the gold coins, **both the** dollar bills, **half the** change, **double/twice the** amount

105 Common Nouns and Proper Nouns With and Without an Article: a Comparison with German

1. Common nouns

The definite article is used in English with common nouns only when referring to quite specific or definite persons or things. When referring to persons or things generally, without restriction, the noun is used on its own (cf **100**). This applies – in contrast to German – not only to countable nouns in the plural but also to uncountable nouns with singular meaning, e.g. abstract concepts. Compare the following:

- General concept:

Life (on this earth) is short. *(Das Leben . . .)*
Human life is short. *(Das menschliche Leben . . .)*

Books (with illustrations) are expensive.
Illustrated books are expensive.

- Particular examples:

"**The Life** *of Sir Winston Churchill*"
The life *our ancestors led* was hard.

The books *on the table* are John's.
The books *you lent me* are interesting.

As the first examples show, adjectives and other attributes are often not seen as restrictions but as forming a general concept together with the noun.
The definite article is only used if the attribute restricts the meaning of the noun to one particular case. In the case of abstract nouns, *of*-phrases and defining relative clauses have a restrictive effect on the meaning of the noun.

2. Proper nouns

Since proper nouns as such always refer to quite definite or specific persons or things, normally no determiner is needed to restrict the meaning.

- "An Illustrated History of **Medieval Scotland**"
  The castle dominated this view of **ancient Edinburgh.** *(... das alte Edinburg)*
  Old Jock McGregor was a great story-teller. *(Der alte Jock . . .)*

Most proper nouns are used in English without an article (for exceptions see **107**), even – unlike in German – when preceded by an adjective, if this adjective is not regarded as restrictive.

- The novel is set in **the Scotland** *of the Middle Ages.*
  The city had changed but it was still **the Edinburgh** *he loved.*
  Did you talk to **the** *old* **Mr McGregor** or **the** *young* **one?**

But with proper nouns too, *of*-phrases and defining relative clauses have a restrictive meaning, and so do adjectives which express a contrast (*old* contrasted with *young*), but most other adjectives do not.

106 Common Nouns Without an Article

Basically, common nouns are used without a definite article when referring to persons or things in a general sense.

This includes

- all uncountable nouns with singular meaning, in particular nouns denoting materials, and many abstract nouns (used without restrictive attributes, cf **105**.1)

Paper is becoming more and more expensive.
Her main subject was **English Literature.**
Similarly: socialism, Buddhism, old age *(das Alter),* industry, science, history, work, etc.

- *man* (Ger. *der Mensch*), *mankind/humankind* (Ger. *die Menschheit*) and other collective terms with a similarly broad meaning

The proper study of **mankind** is **man.** (Alexander Pope)
Similarly: posterity *(die Nachwelt),* society, youth, labour *(die Arbeiterschaft),* etc.

- institutions such as *school, church, university, hospital, prison,* when one is thinking of their function rather than anything concrete, such as a building

The injured man was taken to **hospital.**
Similarly: go to **town,** go to **bed.**
(**But: The school** stands by **the church.**
The town had 20,000 inhabitants.)

- *by* + means of transport
  (Here, too, it is the function that is meant and not a particular, concrete vehicle.)

We'll go to London **by bus.**
Similarly: by train/car/ship/plane/etc.
(**But: The bus/train/. . .** was crowded.)

- meals, when referring to them in a general sense and when one is not thinking of the food eaten at one particular meal

Lunch is at 12.30.
Similarly: breakfast, dinner, supper, tea, etc.
(**But: The dinner** last night was excellent.)

- times of the day in general, i.e. not of any particular day. (But after *in, during, in the course of,* nouns denoting times of the day are used with an article even in a more general sense.)

The party went on till **morning.**
(**But: The/That night** had been very cold.
He always comes **in the afternoon** and leaves **in the course of the evening.**)

Easter Monday is a public holiday. **May** is my favourite month. I met him **on Sunday** (= last Sunday). (**But:** That week I met him on **the Sunday.**) I'll see him **in June** (= next June). (**But: the September of** 1976)	● festivals, months and days of the week, when one is thinking of them as regular occurrences, but also when referring to the previous or following day or month. (Otherwise one uses the definite article.)

Note:
With the seasons, one can either use an article or omit it, without much change in meaning; an article is, however, preferred when referring to one specific time. The American *fall* is always used with the article:

We're going to Italy **in the spring.** (More rarely: . . . in spring.)
The woods are at their most beautiful **in (the) autumn.**
But only: . . . **in the fall.**

107 Proper Nouns With and Without an Article

Since proper nouns stand for something unique, they do not need to be further determined. Some of them are nevertheless used with the definite article, and this has to do with the history of the language. In most cases the nouns were originally common nouns which have never fully become proper nouns (in this respect). Here, one can only give a general guideline with regard to the use of the article; there are no hard and fast rules.

1. Proper nouns with a definite article

There are only a few groups of proper nouns with which the definite article is always used. These include

the Prince **of** Wales (**But:** Charles, Prince of Wales) **the** Isle **of** Man, **the** Cape **of** Good Hope, **the** Tower (**of** London), **the** City (**of** London), **the** House (**of** Commons)	● proper nouns consisting of a common noun and an *of*-phrase (including those where the *of*-phrase is commonly dropped);
the Browns, **the** Millers **the** Alps, **the** Falklands **the** Netherlands, **the** United States **The** United Nations was founded in 1945.	● proper nouns in the plural, especially surnames, the names of mountain ranges and groups of islands, some countries and institutions (even when the verb is used in the singular);
the Thames, **the** Suez Canal, **the** Mediterranean	● the names of rivers, canals, seas and oceans;
the Queen Mary, **the** Lusitania	● the names of ships.

2. Proper nouns without an article

Most other proper nouns are used without an article, even if they are formed with a common noun). These include (with some exceptions)

Earl Spencer is **Princess Diana**'s father. **Poor George** has cut his knee. **Old Dr Baxter** was our family doctor for years. **Dad** and **Uncle Ben** are twin brothers. **Similarly:** Mrs Williams, Colonel Brown, Lord Longford, Saint Joan *(die Heilige Johanna)*, etc.	● the names of persons (with or without a title) and nouns expressing family relationships which are used as names even when these are preceded by certain adjectives (but see Note 1)
St. Paul's Cathedral is not far from **London Bridge**, but quite a distance from **Oxford Circus.** **Fifth Avenue** runs alongside **Central Park.** **Similarly:** Victoria Station, Times Square, Green Park, Park Lane, Downing Street, Somerset House, etc.	● the names of streets, squares, bridges, parks and buildings, particularly when they consist of a proper noun plus a common noun. (**But:** ***the** Mall, **the** White House, **the** Empire State Building, **the** Post Office Tower* and some other names consisting only of common nouns and adjectives; ***the** Tate Gallery* and the names of other museums);

Chicago lies on **Lake Michigan.**
Similarly: (Latin) America, (northern) Italy, (beautiful) Yorkshire, Bavaria, Paris, Loch Ness, Ellis Island, Hudson Bay, Mount Everest, Snowdon, etc.

- the names of continents, countries, counties (or provinces, etc.), cities, towns, lakes, islands, bays, mountains (even when preceded by adjectives) **(exceptions: *the Matterhorn, the Zugspitze*** and others which are used with an article in the original language);

Is Spain a member of **NATO**? ['neitəʊ]
Similarly: UNESCO [ju:'neskəʊ], UNICEF ['ju:nisef], UNO ['ju:nəʊ], etc.

- the shortened names (of organizations, etc.) which consist of initials – when these are not spelled out but pronounced as one word.
(**But: *the UN*** [ju:'en], ***the EEC*** [i:i:'si:] etc.)

Notes:

1. With less commonly used combinations of an adjective + the name of a person the article is occasionally used even if the adjective has no contrastive function but is merely descriptive, e.g. *the unfortunate Bob, the clever Bertrand.* With very commonly used descriptive adjectives *(old, young, little, tiny, poor, dear, good)* the article is never used.

2. Proper nouns (without adjectives) are used with the stressed definite article when one wants to distinguish well-known personalities from other persons of the same name:
I was talking to Margaret Thatcher the other day. – You surely don't mean ***the*** [ði:] Margaret Thatcher?

108–109 Demonstrative Determiners and Pronouns

108 Differences in Meaning between *this/these* and *that/those*

English makes a much sharper distinction than German between the different demonstrative determiners and pronouns.

This/these

Are we taking all **these** boxes (here) onto the boat with us?
You've never been on **this** part of the river before, have you?
Fancy taking a rowing boat out on a stormy day like **this** (= today).

This/these are used to refer to something that is near to the speaker in terms of place or time (e.g. a present period of time).

The final briefing ended with **these** words: "Now **this** is what you must remember to do and in **this** order: Jump, count slowly to ten and pull the rip-cord."
At the air display a few weeks ago, he talked to some of the participants. **This** was what got him interested in flying. ...

By using *this/these,* a speaker can announce something that he is about to mention or describe in detail. *This* can, however, also be used to point back to something that has just been mentioned, especially when a speaker wants to say more about it.

That/those

Do move **those** oilskins (there), they're in the way.
Let's head for **that** little island over there.
Colin made himself a canoe in 1983. **That** summer he spent most of his time at the river.
Those speedboats ought to be banned.

That/those are used to refer to something more distant from the speaker (e.g. a past period of time). They can also express one's internal feeling of distance or detachment (dislike or contempt).

"Jump, count slowly to ten and pull the rip-cord – in **that** order. **That**'s all you have to remember." With **those** words the final briefing ended.
I'm not going to finance your crazy hobbies any more. And **that**'s **that**. *(Und damit basta.)*

By using *that/those,* a speaker can make a final comment on, or sum up, something that has just been said.
He can also use them to indicate that he regards a topic as finished and is not prepared to say anything more about it.

109 The Use of the Singular and Plural Forms

When did **this** information reach you?
That rumour has been circulating for a long time.
Have you read **this** (= this article)?
That's the same picture as the one in 'The Times'.

The singular forms *this* and *that* are used with nouns which have singular meaning (cf **72–76**). They precede the noun (as determiners) or are used alone (as pronouns).

Which is your *car*? **That one.**
I don't know which *pocket* I put the key in – **this one** or **that one.**

To avoid repeating a countable noun which has already been mentioned *this* and *that* are followed by the prop-word *one.*

A lorry was coming towards us, weaving from side to side. **This** was rather alarming, as you can imagine.
We were woken by a scream and the sound of breaking glass. "Whatever was **that**?" exclaimed Terry.

This and *that* may refer not just to a noun but to a larger unit, e.g. a sentence, or a situation perceived but not yet mentioned.

These knives need sharpening.
Could you hand me **those** scissors?

The plural forms *these* and *those* are used with nouns with plural meaning.

These are the best hammers we have. *(Dies sind...)*
Those weren't the correct measurements.

In contrast to German, *these* and *those* (never the singular forms *this/that*) are used with *be*+ subject complement in the plural.

Are those *screws* bigger than **these** (ones)?
If you don't like the brown *tiles,* what about **those** (ones) over there?

To avoid repeating a noun which has already been mentioned, *these* and *those* are normally used on their own, without the prop-word *ones.*

Notes:

1. *This/that* can also be found in sentences with a plural subject complement, if one is pointing to an event, not to persons or things. In this case *be* is also in the singular. (Compare the similar use of *it*: cf **84.**)
   (The door-bell is ringing.) Oh **that's** the Smiths, I expect. (that = the ringing of the bell)

2. *This/that/these*+ noun are generally not followed by defining relative clauses or other restrictive attributes. One uses *the*+ noun or *the*+ prop-word *one* instead. *Those* can, however, be followed by a restrictive attribute:
   There's the boy who fell in the water, but where's **the one** who rescued him?
   Which children saw the accident? – **The ones/those** on the bench over there.

110–113 Indefinite Determiners and Pronouns (Summary)

110 Grouped according to Meaning

Most of the so-called indefinite determiners and pronouns express ideas of (mainly indefinite) **quantity.**

Total quantity or its parts			Indefinite quantity	
all (the) children	**every/each** child	**no** child	**some** tea	**any** sandwiches
half (of) the girls	**any** day (you like)	**none** of the girls	(not) **much** time	**many** visitors
			little time	**few** friends
Consisting of two parts:			**a little** sugar	**a few** biscuits
both sides	**either** side	**neither** side	**enough** butter	**several** salads

111 Use as Determiners or Pronouns

We tried **every** *shop* in town but there was **no** *charcoal* to be had.
How much beer have we left? – **None** at all.

If you want **some** *matches,* I've got **some.**
Some *of the firewood* is wet.
Each *of the boys and girls* had a turn at looking after the fire.

Everybody expected **something** to happen, but **nothing** did.

Every and *no* can only be used as determiners (before nouns), *none* can only be used as a pronoun.

But all the other expressions of quantity listed in the above table can be used both as determiners and pronouns. As pronouns they usually refer to a previously mentioned noun or to a following *of*-phrase.

For *every, no, some* and *any* there are compounds with *-body, -one, -thing,* and these are used only as indefinite pronouns with no reference to a noun.

112 Use with Countables and Uncountables

When combining indefinite determiners with nouns, there are certain restrictions which have to be observed. The same applies to indefinite pronouns which refer to nouns. (But note: *either/neither verse – either/neither of the verses.*)

With countable nouns	in the singular	**every/each** word **either/neither** verse	
	in the plural	**several** passages **both** verses **many/few/a few** lines	**some/any** singers *(Ger. einige)* **some/any** jazz *(Ger. etwas)*
With uncountable nouns with singular meaning		**much/little/a little** applause	**all** pop songs **all** pop music **enough** records **enough** volume

113 Assertive, Non-Assertive and Negative Determiners and Pronouns

Many of the indefinite pronouns and determiners and some other expressions of indefinite quantity can be placed in one of the following three categories according to their meaning:

Assertive	Non-assertive	Negative
some and its compounds *a little, a few, several* *one (of the two)* *a good deal of, plenty of*, etc.	*any* and its compounds *either (of the two)* *much, many* (when used colloquially)	*no* and its compounds *none* *neither (of the two)* *little, few*
I've got **some** questions to ask. **One** of the opponents called the other a liar. We shall have **plenty of** time.	Have you **any** further questions? Did **either** of the opponents lose his temper? I don't have **much** free time.	**No** questions were asked. **Neither** of the opponents had *any* good arguments. She has very **little** time for *anything* but work.
Assertive pronouns, determiners and expressions of quantity indicate that a person or thing exists, or that something is true or valid for a person or thing. They therefore occur mainly in affirmative statements. (In formal style, *much* and *many* are also used with assertive meaning, whereas in colloquial style expressions such as *plenty of*, etc., are preferred. Cf **117.**)	Non-assertive pronouns and determiners leave it open whether a person or thing exists or whether something is true or valid for a person or thing. They are therefore commonly used in questions, for example. They also often occur in negated or restricted sentences, and here they have negative or restrictive (i.e. almost negative) meaning.	The meaning of negative pronouns and determiners is to negate completely or (in the case of *little* and *few*) almost completely that a person or thing exists or that something is true or valid for a person or thing. They can therefore also occur in combinations with non-assertive words like *any* and its compounds. (Cf also **20.**)

Notes:

1. Negative or restrictive meaning can also be created by using the following:

never:	She **never** paid ***much*** attention to ***any*** of the conventions.
without, un- (prefix):	**Un**troubled by ***any*** sense of duty, he went his way **without** regard to ***anyone*** else.
hardly, scarcely, seldom, rarely:	**Seldom** has ***anyone*** been treated so shabbily.
too:	I was **too** tired to take ***any/much*** interest in the proceedings. (= I was **so** tired that I **didn't** take any/much interest . . .)

2. Stressed *any* and its compounds and also *either* may be used to refer to one unspecified example from a quantity consisting of two *(either)* or more than two *(any)*. The meaning in this case is non-assertive. Although the context may, on the surface, appear to be assertive, the underlying idea is that no particular person or thing is meant. In affirmative statements they are therefore often used together with modal auxiliaries, which add an element of uncertainty:

   This could have happened to **any** of us.
   Both roads lead to Dundee, you can take **either.**

3. For the use of *either* with assertive meaning (Ger.: *jeder = der eine* ***und*** *der andere*) cf **123.**

114–115 *Some, any* and their Compounds

114 *Some, any:* their Referents and Compounds

He was given **some** *money* to buy sweets. *(Er bekam Geld/etwas Geld . . .)*
Are there **any** *chocolates* left? *(Sind noch Pralinen übrig?)*

Some or *any* + noun is used when referring to an indefinite, unspecified quantity or number. (No determiner is required here in German.)

You like *toffee,* don't you?
Did you put *baking-powder* in the cake?
Betty's got sticky *hands.*

If one is referring to a class as a whole, or if the quantity or number is self-evident, then *some* and *any* are not used.

I could lend you **some** *books* on the early days of the film industry if you want **any** (= books on the early days of the film industry).
Some *of this material* has not been published before.

Some and *any* are used with countable nouns in the plural and with uncountable nouns with singular meaning. They can also be followed by an *of*-phrase or refer to a noun which has already been mentioned, i.e. they can also be used as pronouns.

Some like it hot. *(Manche mögen's heiß.)*
"**Some** are born great, **some** achieve greatness . . ." (William Shakespeare).
Tell me **something** about your childhood.
Is there **anything** more you would like to know?
I can't think of **anyone** who would be interested in reading his memoirs.

Some can be used as a pronoun without reference to a noun to mean an indefinite number of people (particularly when expressing a contrast).
The pronouns *something, anything* are used for an indefinite thing, and *someone, somebody, anyone, anybody* for an indefinite person.

There are **some** [s(ə)m] good cafés in the town.
I've just made **some** [s(ə)m] tea. Would you like **some** [sʌm]?
Some ['sʌm] people say Brown's Café is the best, and ***some*** ['sʌm] say the Pantry, but if you want **some** [s(ə)m] nice home-made cakes, I would go to the Willow Tree.

When used as a determiner in front of a noun, *some* is normally unstressed (weak form: [s(ə)m]). When given greater emphasis (to express a contrast) and when used as a pronoun *some* is stressed (strong form: [sʌm]).

Notes:

1. *Some* [sʌm] can be used to refer to one unspecified person or thing:
   Some fool (or other) has put my telephone number in the ad.
   Some day you'll regret this.

When followed by an ordinal number, it means *approximately, about:*
   Some fifty people answered the advertisement.

2. *Some* and *any* can also be used to form compound adverbs.

Somewhere/anywhere are used to refer to an indefinite place, *somehow* refers to an indefinite manner, *somewhat* refers to an indefinite degree and *sometimes* to indefinite frequency:
   I put my glasses down **somewhere,** but now I can't find them **anywhere.**
   He **somehow** managed to lose his wallet.
   Her bag was **somewhat** old and worn.

115 The Use of the Assertive and Non-Assertive Forms

As shown in **113,** *some* and its compounds have assertive meaning, whereas *any* and its compounds have non-assertive meaning. It is therefore important to consider the type of sentence and the meaning of the context when using these words (cf **20, 22, 23**):

I need **some** advice.
I think there's **something** wrong with him.
Ask **somebody** to help you.

In **affirmative statements** with no negative or restrictive words one uses *some, someone,* etc. The same applies to affirmative imperative sentences.

Don't take **any** notice of him, he hasn't **any** idea what a good Western should be like.
The documentary was made *without* **any** hope of commercial success.
The film was very boring as *hardly* **anything** happened.
I *don't* know **any** of the actors playing in this film. (= **All** the actors are unknown to me.)

Just imagine, **somebody** in the film club hadn't heard of the Marx Brothers before.
I don't know **some** of the actors playing in the film. (= **Some** of the actors are unknown to me, but not all.)

In **negative statements** (and in negative imperatives) and also after negative or restrictive words one normally uses *any, anyone,* etc. (For the various negative and restrictive adverbs, determiners, etc. cf **113.4** + Note 1.)

With *any, anyone,* etc. the negation applies to the whole of a group or quantity.

However, *some, somebody,* etc. may be used in negated statements, particularly if they come before the negative word, but also in some cases when they come after it. Here, the negation applies only to part of the group or quantity in question.

Did he break **any** bones when he got knocked down?
Has **anyone** rung for an ambulance?
Is there **anything** we can do to help?
Have you got **some** sticking plaster handy?
(You have a first aid kit.)
Is **someone** doing **something** about getting help? (They must be by now.)
Would*n't* you like **some** brandy?

In ***yes/no* questions**, *any, anyone,* etc. are used if one does not know whether the answer will be affirmative or negative or if a negative answer seems more probable.
But if one expects or wishes to encourage an affirmative answer (e.g. in polite requests or offers), one uses *some,* etc.

This also applies to negative *yes/no* questions.

If he had **any** sense, he would take a taxi in weather like this. (But you know how stubborn he is.)
If **anything** goes wrong, I'll come over at once. (But I don't think there'll be any trouble.)
If, as you say, you need **some** exercise, why don't you walk home.
She'll certainly come unless **something** prevents her.

In **conditional clauses introduced by *if,*** one uses *any, anyone,* etc. if a condition seems untrue or improbable.

Some, etc. is used if the speaker thinks a condition is true or probable.
(In conditional clauses introduced by other conjunctions, such as *unless, provided that,* one almost always uses *some,* etc.)

Notes:

1 In affirmative questions introduced by interrogatives one normally uses *some* and its compounds, whereas in negative questions *any* and its compounds will be used; this is because the speaker has based the question on positive or negative assumptions:

What do you need **some** advice about? (I know you need some advice.)
Why didn't you tell **anybody** about your problem? (I know you didn't tell anybody.)

However, this may be reversed, depending on the meaning:

How can **anybody** be so stupid? (I didn't think anybody could be so stupid.)
Why don't you get **some** sleep. (You should get some sleep.)

2. When *any* is used not in the sense of an indefinite quantity but in the sense of 'any one, no matter which' (stressed *any*), it also occurs in affirmative sentences (cf **113** Note 2 and **125**).

3. *Any* can also be used as an adverb of degree to modify adverbs and adjectives, but only in a non-assertive context (negation, questions, etc.):

I can't go **any** further. Was the film **any** good?

116 *Much, many* and their Referents

Much and *many* can be used before a noun or an *of*-phrase or may refer to a noun which has already been mentioned.

Examples	Explanation
How **much** *time* have we left? – Not **much**.	*Much* (Ger. *viel*) only occurs with uncountable nouns with singular meaning.
We didn't do **much** today. **Much** was said, but **not much** was to the point.	It can be used without reference to a noun to denote an indefinite amount of something (Ger. *viel, vieles*).
Do **many** accidents happen at this crossing?	*Many* (Ger. *viele*) only occurs with countable nouns in the plural.
How **many** were injured in the coach crash? How **many** live on the new estate?	When used without a noun referent it means *many people.*

Note:
The comparative and superlative forms of both *much* and *many* are *more, most* (cf **137**).
Much (with uncountables) and *many* (with countables) can be put in front of the comparative form *more* (Ger. *mehr*) to reinforce it:

We have **much more** *free time* now. *(... viel mehr Freizeit.)*
They spent **many more** *days* there than they had intended. *(... viel mehr Tage ...)*

117 The Use of *much/many* and Comparable Expressions of Quantity

Examples	Explanation
Is there **much** unemployment in this area? The report hasn't **much** to offer in the way of encouragement. There aren't **many** jobs available around here.	Since *much* and *many* are non-assertive forms (cf **113**) they are used mainly in questions and negative statements.
The trade unions are often said to have **too much** power. **So many** long speeches were made that the delegates got restless. **How much** time gets wasted at meetings like this!	In affirmative statements they occur mainly after *too, so, as* and *very,* and they are used in exclamations after *how.*
The speaker earned **a lot of** applause. There was **plenty of** whispering going on. A **great deal of** what was said was nonsense. A **large number of** people left before the end.	Otherwise in affirmative sentences, in particular in colloquial language, the following substitute forms are used: *a lot (of), lots (of), plenty (of);* *a great/good deal (of)* (only for *much*); *a large number (of)* (only for *many*).
Much has been done to preserve our historical buildings. **Many** people contributed money to the fund.	In formal style, *much* and *many* are also used in affirmative statements without *too*, etc., especially in the subject position.

Notes:
1. *Enough* (Ger.: *genug, genügend*) can, like *much* and *many,* be used as a determiner or a pronoun. It is used with countable nouns in the plural and with uncountable nouns with singular meaning and can also be used without a noun referent:

There aren't **enough** *seats* available. – There's **enough** *room* for all of us.
That's **enough** from you. – **Enough** is **enough.**

2. *A lot, a great deal, much* and *enough* also occur as adverbs of degree (cf **147–149**):

We laughed **a lot/a great deal.** They didn't **much** like the show. The acting wasn't good **enough.**

118 *Little/a little, few/a few* and their Referents

Little, a little, few and *a few* can be used in front of an noun or an *of*-phrase or can refer to a noun which has already been mentioned.

There's **little** *hope* of finding any more survivors.
A little *water* was all the man asked for when they dug him out.
Little has been done to help the victims.
Everybody should contribute **a little** to the relief fund.

Little (Ger. *wenig*) and *a little* (Ger. *ein wenig*) only occur with uncountable nouns with singular meaning.

They can also be used as pronouns to refer to an indefinite amount of something, without reference to a previously mentioned noun.

Few *rivers* are as rich in history as the Nile.
My uncle has already been to Egypt **a few** *times.*
There are **few** (people) who are not fascinated by the mysteries of the pyramids.
A few found it too hot for any more sightseeing that day.

Few (Ger. *wenige*) and *a few* (Ger. *einige, ein paar*) only occur with countable nouns in the plural.
When used without reference to a noun they mean *few people/a few people.*

Notes:

1. *Several* (Ger.: *mehrere, verschiedene*), which means almost the same as *a few,* is also only used with countable nouns in the plural:
   They tried **several** approaches to the problem. **Several** (of them) proved unworkable.

2. The comparative and superlative forms of *little* are *less, least,* and those of *few* are *fewer, fewest* (cf **137**). In colloquial English, *less* is often used instead of *fewer:*
   The firm employs far **fewer/less** people than it used to.

119 Differences in Meaning between *little/few* and *a little/a few*

It's amazing *how* **little** it takes to shake the international money market.
There are *very* **few** economists who have specialized in this field.
The President showed **little** enthusiasm (**didn't** show **much** enthusiasm) for any of the Committee's suggestions.

Little and *few* used without the indefinite article belong in the category of the negative determiners and pronouns (cf **113**). They stress the idea that a number or quantity is very small (= almost none). In colloquial English they are common only when preceded by *too, as, so, very* and *how.* Otherwise, they are more typical of formal style; in informal style *not . . . much, not . . . many* are preferred.

I think we could do with **a little/some** fresh air.
In **a few** minutes the room was crammed with people.
A few more chairs were brought in.
Would you like to sit down **a little** while?

A little and *a few* denote a small indefinite quantity or number too, but from a more positive point of view: they stress the idea that something exists (= more than none). Like *some,* which has a similar meaning, they therefore occur mainly in assertive contexts (cf **115**).

Notes:

1. Since *little* and *few* have a restrictive meaning anyway, they are normally not further restricted by *only.* The equivalent of the German *nur wenig(e)* in English is *only a little/only a few* or *little/few* used on their own:
   There were **few/only a few** seats left vacant. *(. . . nur wenige Sitze . . .)*
   They allowed **little/only a little** time for each speaker. *(. . . nur wenig Zeit . . .)*

2. *Little* and *a little* are also used – with the same distinction of negative/positive meaning – as adverbs of degree (cf **147–149**).

120–121 *No, none, nobody, no one, nothing*

120 Referents of *no, none* and Compounds with *no*

He had **no** *plans* and **no** *idea* what to do next. I'll listen to **none** of your *nonsense.* What *justification* did she have for acting like that? – **None** at all.
"Nobody knows the trouble I've seen . . ." **No one** has a larger repertoire of negro spirituals than Mahalia Jackson. They've been playing **nothing** but that blues LP all day.

No (Ger. *kein*) is only used as a determiner, and *none* (Ger. *keiner*) only as a pronoun (preceding an *of*-phrase or referring back to an already mentioned noun).

Compounds with *no* occur as pronouns without reference to a noun:
- for persons *nobody, no one* (Ger. *niemand)*
- for things *nothing* (Ger. *nichts*).

Notes:

1. After *none* as a subject the predicate can always be in the singular. However, in colloquial usage the verb is often used in the plural, if the referent of *none* is a countable noun in the plural:
   None of the cafés we tried **was/were** open.
2. *None* can also be used as an adverb before *too* or *the* + comparative:
   The service in this restaurant is **none** *too fast. (. . . nicht allzu schnell.)*
   The food was **none** *the better* for being served on a silver platter. *(. . . auch nicht besser . . .)*

121 The Use of *no, none, nobody,* etc. and *not . . . any, not . . . anybody,* etc.

We recognized **no** landmarks for miles./We did**n't** recognize **any** landmarks for miles. There was **nothing**/There was**n't anything** to indicate whether we were on the right road. Dave has **no** sense of direction. We decided to take **none** of the usual routes. **No** previous experience with horse-drawn caravans is needed. Luckily, **no one** came to any harm when the horse bolted down the hill. How many people did you meet on the way? – **None.** Wasn't there anyone else staying there? – No, **no one.** We were the only guests.

No, none, nobody, etc. have virtually the same meaning as *not . . . any, not . . . anybody,* etc., but usually sound more formal.

In colloquial English they are only used
- when one wants to put special emphasis on the negative meaning
- if it is not possible to negate a preceding verb with *not.* This applies:
  - when the pronoun or determiner is in the subject position
  - in shortened sentences without a predicate.

In such cases *not . . . any,* etc. cannot be used.

122–123 *Both, either, neither*

122 *Both, either, neither* and their Referents

Both, either and *neither* refer to a group of two persons or things; they are therefore only used with countable nouns as referents. In this function they are always stressed.

Both *wheels* of the bicycle buckled under the impact of the crash. The two *cyclists,* who **both** had cuts and bruises, were signalling for help. **Both** *of the girls* were shaken and **both** were treated for shock. The police questioned the **two** witnesses. *(. . . die beiden/die zwei Zeugen.)*

Both implies that the two persons or things are dealt with together. As a determiner and as a pronoun, *both* therefore always has plural meaning. It is only used when the existence of a group of two has been previously mentioned or is already known.

If the number of persons or things has still to be mentioned, then *two* is used. (For the position of *both* cf **126**).

Is **either** *entrance* to the park open at night?
There were stone lions at **either** *end* of the bridge.
Neither *side* of the bridge had its railing intact.
Neither *of the two paths* down to the water looks very safe. I wouldn't advise you to take **either.**

Either implies that each of the two persons or things in the group is seen separately. The determiners *either* and *neither* therefore precede nouns in the singular.

When used as pronouns, they of course have plural noun referents.

Notes:

1. If *either* and *neither* are used as **determiners** of a subject (a noun in the singular), the predicate is always in the singular. But if they are used as **pronouns** in the subject position, then in colloquial English the predicate is often plural. (Cf **120** Note 1.):
   Neither *of the anglers* **has/have** moved for the last hour.
   Was/Were either *of the fish* big enough to eat?

2. *Both, either* and *neither* are also used in pair-word conjunctions, and here they are normally unstressed.
   I've got **both** a parcel **and** a letter to post. *(. . . sowohl . . . als auch . . .)*
   Give me **either** two 10 p stamps **or** one 20 p one. *(. . . entweder . . . oder . . .)*
   Neither the card from Paris **nor** the one from Reims ever arrived. *(Weder . . . noch . . .)*

3. For the use of *either, neither* as adverbs cf **150–151**. For the use of *neither* in shortened sentences cf **34.**

123 The Use of *neither* and *(not . . .) either*

Neither of the two stewardesses on board had flown to Tokyo before.
Which of the suitcases is yours? This one or that one? – **Neither.**
I **didn't** like **either** of the two meals offered.
Would **either** of these two flights fit in with a connection to Chicago?
(**But:** There used to be two planes leaving in the morning. Has **one** of them been cancelled?)
You can travel from **either** airport. It costs about the same.
Either of these two hotels will do. I'm sure they're equally comfortable.
The window seats on **either** side (= on both sides) of the plane were already taken.

The negative form *neither* is mainly used in the subject position or in shortened sentences without a predicate. Otherwise the form *not . . . either* (negated non-assertive form – cf **113** and **121**) is preferred in colloquial English.
In a non-assertive context, *either* is used in questions if the answer is open. (If one expects an affirmative answer, one uses *one of . . .* .)

Either is also used in affirmative statements, where it means *'one or the other of two, it does not matter which'.* (Cf **113** Note 2.)

Either may occasionally occur with the assertive meaning of *'each of the two'/'the one and the other'.*

Note:
Each is more commonly used than *either* in the sense of 'the one **and** the other'. *None of (the two)* can be used instead of *neither,* especially in colloquial style. (As subject it then often has a plural predicate; cf **120** Note 1.)
   On **each** side of the path, there were beautiful rosebushes.
   None of my two sisters are interested in gardening.

24–125 *Every, each, any, all (the)*

124 *Every, each, any, all:* their Referents and Compounds

1. *Every, each, any*

Every *town* and **every** *village* was decked with flags.
Everybody cheered and clapped.
Did **everything** go off as planned?

Every is only used as a determiner before countable nouns in the singular.
As pronouns one uses *everybody* or *everyone* for persons and *everything* for things.

Examples	Explanation
Each *child* came forward and was given a small present. **Each** *(of them)* was dressed in their Sunday best.	*Each* is used as a determiner with countable nouns in the singular and also as a pronoun before an *of*-phrase or with reference to a previously mentioned noun. (For the use of *each* **after** the referent cf **126.**)
Any *fool* knows what the capital of Australia is. Are these *leaflets* free? – Yes, you can take **any** *(of them)* you like. **Anybody** would be annoyed at having to fill in all these forms. You can ask me **anything** you like.	Stressed *any* is also used either as a determiner or as a pronoun preceding an *of*-phrase (less commonly on its own with reference to a previously mentioned noun). *Anybody, anyone* and *anything* occur as pronouns without a noun referent.

2. *All*

Examples	Explanation
All *attempts* to locate the wreck had ended in failure. Have they given up **all** *hope* of success? The divers were equipped with **all** *the latest devices.* **All** *of us* were thrilled by the idea of buried treasure.	*All* is normally used (like German *alle, alles*) with reference to a countable noun in the plural or an uncountable noun with singular meaning. It can be a determiner preceding the noun (or *the/this/my/* etc. + noun), or a pronoun preceding an *of*-phrase. (For the use of *all* immediately **after** the referent cf **126.**)
The *gold coins* were still in perfect condition. **All** *(of them)* had been carefully packed in a wooden chest.	*All* is seldom used on its own with reference to a previously mentioned noun. The noun is usually represented by a personal pronoun.
I don't want to get involved in any arguments. **All** I want is some peace and quiet. **All** he said was "No comment".	*All* can be used without any noun referent in front of relative clauses to mean *the only thing.*
He refuses to compromise. He wants **all** or nothing. **All**'s well that ends well. *(Ende gut, alles gut.)*	It is rarely used in the sense of *everything,* except in certain fixed expressions.
His resignation came as a shock to **all.** **Everybody** likes Pamela Wright. **All those** who worked with her couldn't help but admire her.	It is even less common to find *all* used (like Ger. *alle*) without a referent when speaking of people. Normally, one uses *everybody/everyone,* or – in front of relative clauses – *all those, all the people.*

Note:
All can also be used with certain countable nouns and proper nouns in the singular. When used before nouns referring to time (*day, night,* etc.) and before *my/his/. . .life, all* denotes a total duration. Used with the names of countries or cities, *all* refers to the whole area or territory or to its entire population. As with many other nouns with singular meaning, *the/my/ . . . whole* or *the whole of* can be used instead:

all day/afternoon . . .; **all the** time	**the whole (of the)** day/afternoon/time/. . .
all my life	**my whole** life/**the whole of** my life
all this trouble	**this whole** trouble/**the whole of** this trouble
all Scotland	**the whole of** Scotland

125 Differences in Meaning between *all/all the* and *every/each/any*

All, all the, every, each and stressed *any* refer to the whole of a quantity or number. The following table shows how their meanings are related:

	totality:	its parts:	random example:
unlimited quantity:	**all** meetings	**every** meeting	**any** meeting
limited quantity:	**all the** meetings	**each/every** meeting	**any** of the meetings

These determiners and pronouns are used as follows:

All ice will float on water. *(Alles Eis . . .)* **All** children like playing in the snow. *(Alle Kinder . . .)* **All the** ice (on the lake) has melted. *(Das ganze Eis . . .)* Not **all the** children living round here have learnt to skate. *(Nicht alle Kinder . . .)*	*All* without an article is used in general statements, e.g. about a substance or a class as a whole (cf **100**). *All the* refers to a limited quantity or number. This limitation (e.g. to a particular group of people) may be explicit or implicit. (Cf the use of the definite article: **100**.)
Every child likes ice-cream. *(Jedes Kind . . .)* **Everybody** has some favourite food. *(Jeder . . .)* I had less than six hours' sleep **every/each** night this week. Jane awoke **every/each** time the door banged. **Each** season has its own particular charm. Frank stays up for **every** late show on TV. We went to bed after midnight practically **every** night during the holidays.	*Every* and its compounds can (like *all* without an article) be used in general statements. Both *every* and *each* can occur in statements about a limited number. There is little difference in meaning, so that *every* and *each* are sometimes interchangeable. *Each* indicates that each individual person or thing is viewed separately. *Every,* like *all the,* implies that the individual persons or things are parts of a whole. So only *every,* and not *each,* can be used after *almost, nearly, practically.*
Open **any** newspaper and you'll find a picture of Tim Brandon with his climbing gear. Is there **any** book on the Antarctic you could recommend? **Anybody** could walk over the pack-ice. It just takes courage. I would have given **anything** if I had been chosen as a member of the expedition.	*Any* is used to refer to a random or unspecified example from a total number (Ger. *irgendeiner/jeder beliebige).* With this meaning, *any* (and its compounds) occurs most commonly in sentences containing modal auxiliaries or other elements which limit the validity of what is being said. (For the use of *any* to express quantity cf **114–115**.)

Notes:

1. In order to stress that one is thinking of the individual units without exception, *every single* or *every one of . . .* can be used. *Any* can also be reinforced by adding *one of:*

   Every single ticket/**Every one of** the tickets for the concert has been sold.
   The 15th, 18th, 20th – **any one of** those days would suit me.

(*Every one* and *any one* should not be confused with *everyone/anyone,* which can only refer to persons.)

2. In expressions of frequency containing cardinal or ordinal numbers one uses *every,* never *all* or *each:*

   The telephone has been ringing **every five minutes**. *(. . . alle fünf Minuten.)*
   Every other call/**Every second** call this afternoon was for you. *(Jeder zweite Anruf . . .)*

126 The Position of *all, both* and *each* in the Sentence

Since *all, both* and *each* generally speaking occupy the same positions in a phrase or sentence, they are here treated together. For further details on *all* and *each* cf **124–125** and on *both* cf **122–123**.

Both *finalists* in the tennis tournament were in fine shape. Why should I give up **all** *hope* of winning? **Each** *of the athletes* shook hands with the Queen.	*All, both* and *each* can – like other indefinite determiners and pronouns – be followed by a noun or an *of*-phrase.

The champion was bursting with self-confidence. He had won **both** *his last fights.* **All** *the competitors* taking part in the race were shocked at the accident.	*All* and *both* (but not *each*) can also be followed directly (without *of*) by an article, a demonstrative determiner or a possessive determiner + noun. (For the difference in meaning between *all* and *all the* cf **125.**)
We are **all** fond of card games. *Jane and Harry* **both** like playing chess. After the first ten moves *they* had **each** lost two pawns *(Bauern).* *We* had **all** been looking forward to watching the great champion in action.	If the referent is the **subject** of a sentence, *all, both* and *each* can also occur in the same position as a mid-position adverb, i.e. before a finite main verb (but after *be* as a main verb) or after the first auxiliary verb. (Cf **142.**)
There were two very strong Russian competitors, but the Canadian beat *them* **both.** His success pleased *us* **all.** (**But:** . . . pleased **all** *his friends.*)	If the referent is the **object:** ● *all* and *both* can follow a personal pronoun but not a noun phrase;
One judge gave *the German couples* **each** 5.8 points. (**But:** The reporter interviewed **each** *of the skaters.*)	● *each* can come after the referent if it is an indirect object, but not normally if it is a direct object.

Notes:

1. *Each* can be even further separated from its referent: it can follow a direct object if this contains an expression of quantity:
   The postcards cost 10 p **each.** He gave *the boys* two sandwiches **each.**

2. Like *all* and *both, half* can precede an *of*-phrase or be used in front of an article, demonstrative determiner or possessive determiner + noun:
   When I called, **half** *of the match* was over.
   He spends **half** *his free time* in front of the TV set.

127–128 The Prop-word *one/ones*

127 *One/ones* Replacing the Head of a Noun Phrase

Shall we buy a large **bottle** of retsina or a small **one**? *(. . . eine kleine?)*

These **olives** are not as good as the **ones** we had in Greece. *(. . . die, die wir . . . aßen.)*

In contrast to German, noun phrases in English cannot normally be used without their head (generally a noun). To avoid repeating a countable noun, the propword *one* (plural form *ones*) is used as a replacement.

Would you mind drinking **instant coffee**? We seem to have run out of **real coffee.**
Do you prefer **white coffee** or **black**?

An uncountable noun cannot be replaced by *one,* and so the noun usually has to be repeated. But if one is talking about common pairs of opposites (*black – white, hot – cold*, etc.) the noun may be omitted.

Notes:

1. Occasionally, *one(s)* can replace a noun which is understood implicitly:
   Isn't this a lovely photo of Mary and her **little ones**? (= children)
   Do you know **this one** (= this joke) – **the one** about the five-year-old who asked his mother . . .?

2. *One* can also replace an indefinite article + noun:
I bought a **book** of fairy-tales for Sammy and **one** (= a book) of nursery rhymes for Kitty.

3. To replace a noun in the *s*-genitive the genitive forms *one's* (singular) or *ones'* (plural) can be used:
The two **boys** didn't stop fighting until the smaller **one's** (= boy's) nose was bleeding.
The older **children** were throwing the younger **ones'** books around.

128 The Use of *one/ones*

Whether *one(s)* is used as a replacement for a countable noun or not depends on what kind of word **immediately** precedes it.

	***One(s)* has to be used after**
Which flowers would you like? – **The ones** over there in the window.	– *the*
This rosebush is the **only one** in my garden to have survived the winter.	– most adjectives
Are you going to have a wooden fence or a **wire one**?	– a noun used as an attribute
Both varieties of lily are good, but **this one** grows to a greater height than **that one.**	– *this* and *that* (cf **109**).
	***One(s)* can be omitted after**
What a lot of different apples! Let's try some of **these (ones)** and some of **those (ones).** (**But:** Give me a pound of **those in the shop window.**)	– *these* and *those* (it is normally omitted where there is a following attribute; cf **109, 109** Note 2)
I'll take some of these small oranges: **the larger (ones)** are not always **the juiciest (ones).** (**But:** Haven't you got **any smaller ones**?)	– *the* + a comparative or superlative (After a comparative without a determiner or with *a, some, any,* etc. *one/ones* has to be used.)
These grapes are **the first (ones)** we've had this year.	– *the* + an ordinal number
We've only got these two pineapples left. **Which (one)** will you take? – **Either (one)** will do.	– *which, either, neither, each, another.*
	***One(s)* is not used after**
How many pounds of strawberries did you pick? – **Five.**	– cardinal numbers
Are there any plums left on the tree? – Not **many,** but if you want **some,** I can get **a few** down.	– the expressions of quantity *many, few, a few, several, both, some, any, all*
Do these baskets belong to the farmer? – No, they're our **own.**	– *own* (cf **98**)
If our ladder is not long enough, I expect we can borrow **next door's.**	– an *s*-genitive (cf **95**)
Are these the peaches Sheila picked? – No, they're **mine.**	– a possessive determiner (here, a possessive pronoun is used instead; cf **99**).

Notes:

1. With traditional pairs of opposites the second adjective is used without a prop-word. With other pairs of opposites the prop word can often be omitted, too, e.g. after adjectives denoting colour:
the **Old World** and the **New**   the **right bank** (of the Thames) and the **left**
Would you like the **white note-paper** or the **blue**?

2. For the use of *one* after *every* and *any* see **125** Note 1.

Chapter 4: Adjectives and Adjective Phrases

129–130 The Adjective Phrase: Forms and Functions (Summary)

129 Adjectives and Adjective Phrases

The head of an adjective phrase is always the adjective itself.

The survivors of the shipwreck were **hungry** and **thirsty.**
The island seemed ***completely*** **uninhabited.**

It can stand alone without a modifier or complementation.
It can, however, be modified by an **adverb,** and/or have some form of **complementation** with it, e.g.:

The island is **famous** ***for its coral reef.***
We were **afraid** ***of being attacked by sharks.***
The sailors were **glad** ***to be rescued.***
It was **surprising** ***that the boat was undamaged.***

- a prepositional phrase
- a gerund construction
- an infinitive construction
- a subordinate clause.

130 Attributive and Predicative Use

Adjectives and adjective phrases can be used in two different ways:

a) attributively
(normally before a noun)

They had ***(unusually)*** **cold** weather.
(unusually = adverb; cold = adjective)

b) predicatively
(normally after a verb)

The weather remained	***(unusually)***	**cold.**	
Snow made the pass	***(almost)***	**impossible**	***to cross.***
	adverb	adjective	complementation

The following can be used attributively, i.e. as attribute to a noun:
- (adverb +) adjective

The following can be used predicatively, i.e. as subject or object complement (cf **54–57**):
- (adverb +) adjective
- (adverb +) adjective + complementation

Adjectives with complementation follow the noun: a special kind of predicative use

The farmers, (who were) **anxious** ***to get the harvest in on time,*** worked late into the night.

Adjectives with complementation cannot be used attributively **before** the noun (unlike in German: *die um eine rechtzeitige Ernte besorgten Bauern*). They must be placed after the noun. Formally speaking they are attributes of the noun, but can be regarded as shortened relative clauses in which they are used predicatively (as subject complements).

Notes:
1. Some adjectives ending in *-able/-ible* often follow the noun when this is preceded by a superlative, *only* or *every.* They then correspond to relative clauses (like adjectives with complementation):
He took the **earliest** plane **possible.** (... that was possible.)
Some adjectives ending in *-able/-ible* follow the noun when one means to refer to a particular, limited situation. Here, too, they correspond to a relative clause:
Here is a list of the duty-free goods (which are) **available** (on the plane).

2. Adjectives sometimes precede the noun while their complementations follow the noun. This happens when the adjective with its complementation expresses how well a certain purpose can be carried out:

Businessmen are often the most **difficult** passengers ***to please.***

Similarly: an **easy** book ***to read,*** a **safe** place ***for swimming,*** a **convenient** place ***for the meeting,*** etc.

Occasionally (especially in the language of advertising), a hyphenated combination of adjective + complementation is placed before the noun:

an easy-to-read book, an easy-to-cook meal, a ready-to-wear suit.

131–133 Adjectives Restricted in Use

131 Adjectives Used Only Attributively

His **chief** interests are oriental languages and philosophy. *(Seine hauptsächlichen Interessen . . .)*
Similarly: the **main** difference, a **mere** assumption, the **only** exception, etc.

Like their German equivalents, some English adjectives can only be used attributively and are always placed **before** the noun.

Linguistics **proper** does not concern itself with practical problems of language teaching.
The president **elect** stood up to speak.
Also:
Lords **Spiritual** and **Temporal** (religious and lay members of the British House of Lords), the Princess **Royal** (eldest daughter of the Queen / King), etc.

Proper in the sense of 'strictly so called, genuine' and *elect* (= elected but not yet in office) are also used only attributively, but are placed **after** the noun.
Some other adjectives of French origin also appear after the noun in fixed phrases relating to the law. (They are, however, placed before other nouns and can be used predicatively: *spiritual guidance, to be highly spiritual.)*

Notes:

1. *Next* and *last* can be placed attributively before or after the names of the days of the week:
   The talks are due to start **next** Tuesday / (on) Tuesday **next.**
   The meeting was held **last** Wednesday/(on) Wednesday **last.**

2. A noun can also have another noun placed before it as its attribute, e.g. the name of the material something is made of, or a place name:
   a **gold** bracelet, a **London** football club, etc.

3. Nouns can also occasionally have adverbs or prepositions as their attributes:
   the **up** train (train to London), the **down** train (train from London), the **then** government (government at that time), the **above** rules (as well as: the rules above).

132 Adjectives Used Only Predicatively

The house was **ablaze.** (attributive: a burning house)
The neighbours, (who were) **afraid** for their own safety, were out in the street. (attributive: fearful neighbours)
The old lady had been **alone** in her flat.
(attr.: the only person injured, the lone survivor)
The dog was still **alive** when dragged out of the fire. (attr.: a live animal, no living soul)

Some adjectives are only used predicatively. There often exist adjectives of similar meaning to these which can be used attributively before the noun.

Many of the adjectives which can only be used predicatively begin with the prefix *a-*, e.g.
ablaze, afloat, adrift, afraid, ashamed, averse, alone, alive, asleep, awake, aware, etc.

By two o'clock in the morning most of the remaining guests were rather **drunk.** (attr.: a drunken sailor)
I'd be quite **content** to stay at home tonight and read a book. (attr.: a contented guest)

In addition there are some others such as *drunk, content, well, unwell.*

133 Adjectives with Different Meanings in Predicative and Attributive Use

Some adjectives have several meanings, one of which only occurs predicatively and another only attributively (or sometimes both attributively **and** predicatively).

	Only predicatively		Only attributively	
ill	in ill health	My sister was very **ill** yesterday.	bad	**ill** manners, **ill** humour, **ill** luck, **ill** will
sick	*to be sick:* to have an upset stomach	He was **sick** after eating the fish.	in ill health	a **sick** man
fond	*to be fond of:* to like	I'm much too **fond of** cakes and chocolate.	tender, loving	**fond** love, **fond** looks, a **fond** mother
present	*to be present:* to attend, to be here / there	Miss Smith couldn't be **present** at the party.	existing now, being considered	the **present** situation / government, in the **present** case
	Only predicatively		**Attributively and predicatively**	
faint	dizzy, weak	When she saw the gun she felt **faint.**	low, weak, indistinct	a **faint** noise / light / smell Her voice grew **fainter and fainter.**
concerned	*to be concerned:* to take part, to be affected	Several known criminals were **concerned** in the raid. The jeweller **concerned** talked to a reporter.	worried	a **concerned** look I'm very **concerned** about his health.
involved	*to be involved:* to take part, to be affected	The three men **involved** in the shooting have been caught. Two innocent bystanders were **involved** in the struggle at the door.	complicated	an **involved** sentence The author's style is very **involved.**

Note:
In American English and in many other varieties of English, *sick* is also used predicatively to mean 'in ill health':
Several children are **sick** with the flu at the moment.

134–135 The Adjective Used as a Noun

In English, adjectives can only be used as nouns to a very limited extent. Other expressions must often be used for the German nominalized adjective.

134 The Adjective Used to Denote People

In German most adjectives describing a human quality or condition can be used as nouns to denote a whole class of people *(die Armen)* and to denote an individual person *(der/die Arme).* In English, however, the following rules must be observed:

1. A whole class: the + adjective

The blind often have a highly developed sense of touch.
The elderly form an ever-increasing percentage of the population.
"Give me **your tired, your poor,** your huddled masses yearning to breathe free . . ."
(Inscription, Statue of Liberty)
Only **the very wealthy** can afford servants.

When it comes to wine exports, **the English** are the best customers of **the French.**

The nominalized adjective can only denote a whole class of people. It is accompanied by the definite article or – occasionally – by a possessive determiner (cf the quotation).
In addition it can take attributes (cf *the very wealthy*).

The nominalized adjective has no plural *-s;* but when it is the subject, it needs a plural verb (concept of plurality).
Most nationality adjectives ending in *-sh* and *-ch* can also be used as nouns in this way (cf **361**).

2. Individual persons: adjective + noun

Somebody helped **the blind man** across the road to the bus.
The front seats were reserved for a group of **handicapped people.**
Next to me on the train sat **two Dutch ladies.**
Three Welshmen and **an Irishwoman** got talking.
A Spaniard started singing.

To denote one or several individual persons, a noun such as *woman, girl, man, boy, people* must follow the adjective.

This also applies to nationality adjectives ending in *-sh* and *-ch.* Some of these can also form compounds with *-man/-woman,* or a different noun altogether is used, e.g. *Spaniard* (cf **361**).

Notes:

1. A few nominalized adjectives (originally past participles) can also denote one or several individual persons. They occur in formal style (mainly in legal language):

   The deceased leaves a widow and two children. (The dead person . . .)
   Neither of **the deceased** has left a will. (. . . of the dead persons . . .)
   Similarly: the departed (the dead person), the accused, the undersigned

2. Some adjectives can be used as genuine nouns, i.e. they can be accompanied by an indefinite article and used in the plural:

   Many **whites** are unable to treat **a black** as **an equal.**
   There is a large proportion of **blacks** at our school.
   Similarly: a native, a female, a male, a mortal, a mute, a noble, a Red / a Green (in politics), etc.

135 The Adjective Used to Denote an Abstract Idea

For lovers of **the quaint and picturesque** Cornwall is the place to visit.
To me, Gothic cathedrals are the embodiment of **the sublime.**
To try to see the whole of England in a week is to attempt **the impossible.**

The nominalized adjective (used with the definite article) can only denote a **generalized** abstract concept. This use is mainly confined to formal English.

The most interesting thing about the town is its history. "I could tell you **many a strange thing** about that castle," said the old farmer. **What is most annoying** about such bus tours is that you haven't got a minute to yourself.

To denote a more **limited** abstract concept (limited by *about the town, about that castle,* for example) the adjective is either followed by a 'prop'-word like *thing,* or a relative clause introduced by *what* is used (cleft sentences, cf **339–340**).

Note:
For the use of the prop-word *one/ones* with adjectives *(an old book and a new one)* see **127–128**.

136–138 Comparative and Superlative Forms

136 Regular Forms

Most adjectives can form a comparison, i.e. there is – in addition to the basic form (e.g. *low, beautiful)* – a **comparative** form *(lower/more beautiful)* and a **superlative** form *(lowest/most beautiful).*

1. Forms with *-er/-est*

a) low	lower	lowest
Similarly: big, great, high, thick, thin, etc.		
b) narrow	narrow**er**	narrow**est**
Similarly: clever, simple, shallow, easy, etc.		

The following generally form their comparatives by adding *-er* and their superlatives by adding *-est* to the basic form:
a) adjectives of one syllable
b) adjectives of two syllables ending in *-er, -le, -ow, -y.*
For changes in spelling see **346**.

2. Forms with *more/most*

a) beautiful	**more** beautiful	**most** beautiful
Similarly: characteristic, important, etc.		
b) active	**more** active	**most** active
Similarly: basic, childish, savage, etc.		

The following generally form their comparatives and superlatives with *more/most*:
a) adjectives of three or more syllables
b) adjectives of two syllables not ending in *-er, -le, -ow, -y.*

Notes:
1. Some other adjectives of two syllables besides those ending in *-er, -le, -ow, -y* can also form their comparatives and superlatives with *-er/-est.* They include, above all, adjectives stressed on the second syllable:
The **severest** frost of the winter was recorded last night.
Similarly: complete, mature, polite [–'–]
The same applies to a few adjectives with stress on the first syllable: *common, pleasant, handsome.* ['––]

2. Adjectives of two syllables which form their comparatives and superlatives with *-er/-est,* still do so even when the prefix *in-* or *un-* is added and they then have three syllables:
friendlier – unfriendlier, politer – impoliter, etc.
All other adjectives of three syllables can only form their comparison with *more/most.*

3. Many adjectives of one or two syllables which form their comparatives and superlatives mainly with *-er/-est* can also take *more/most,* especially when they occur in predicative position before a subordinate clause introduced by *than:*
The sea was **calmer/more calm** than it had been for days.
The river is **shallower/more shallow** here than it is upstream.
But the following adjectives of one syllable take *-er/-est* only:
big, clean, far, fast, great, high, low, small, thick, thin, quick, wide, young, old.

137 Irregular Forms

Some adjectives and determiners have irregular comparative and superlative forms:

good well	better	best	much (money) many (coins)	more	most
bad ill	worse	worst	little (money)	less	least
little (in size)	smaller	smallest	Regular however: few (coins)	fewer	fewest

Note:
The German *die meisten* + noun corresponds in English to *most* + noun (without the definite article):
Most children love the snow, **most** adults less so. *(Die meisten Kinder . . .)*

138 Adjectives with Two Comparative or Superlative Forms

Some adjectives have more than one comparative or superlative form. Some of these words (e.g. *latter, last, next*) are no longer felt to be comparative forms by many speakers.

old older – elder oldest – eldest	My **elder** sister is a nurse. He was **the eldest** in a family of six. John is **older** than his brother. They live in the **oldest** house in the village.	*Elder* and *eldest* generally refer to members of a family. They can be used attributively or (after a definite article) predicatively. In other contexts *older/oldest* are used.
far farther – further farthest – furthest	Their cottage is the **farther/further** one of the two beyond the bridge, the **farthest/furthest** of all in fact. We made no **further** enquiries.	All forms can refer to distance. In a figurative sense, however (i.e. meaning 'in addition', 'other'), only *further* can be used.
near nearer – --- nearest – next	Our **nearest** neighbours lived a mile away. We must get out at the **next** stop.	*the nearest* (to a place) *the next* (in a sequence)
late later – latter latest – last	It was **later** than I thought. Of the two styles, Norman and Gothic, the **latter** predominates here. His **latest** book – we hope not his **last** – is on village inns.	*later* (in time) *the latter* (i.e. last mentioned in a sequence) *the latest* (i.e. newest, nearest in time) *the last* (i.e. end of a sequence).

Note:
Superlatives can be preceded by ordinal numbers, as in German:
Cricket is **the second most popular** sport in England. *(. . . der zweitbeliebteste . . .)*
Similarly: the second last/third last/ . . . word *(das zweitletzte/drittletzte/ . . . Wort)*
There are also such expressions as: the last but one/the last but two/ . . . (= the second last/ the third last/ . . .).

139 The Adjective in Comparisons

Examples	Explanation
No other means of public transport is **as fast as** the aeroplane.	● An **equal degree** is expressed by *as . . . (as)*
Travelling by train is **not as popular as** driving one's own car. Flying is **no longer so exciting as** it used to be. Trains are **less accident-prone than** cars.	● A **lesser degree** is expressed by *not as . . . (as)* *not so . . . (as)* *less . . . (than)*
The railway proved a **more efficient** form of transportation **than** the canals. At first the motor-car was **no faster/not any faster than** the horse.	● A **higher degree** is expressed by the **comparative** (+ *than*). The negative is generally formed with *no* or *not any*.
Aircraft can no longer go on getting **bigger and bigger.** Advances in flying techniques have become **more and more spectacular.**	● A **steady increase** (Ger. *immer* + comparative) is expressed by – **comparative** + *and* + **comparative** in the case of adjectives that take *-er/-est* – *more and more* in the case of adjectives that take *more/most.*
The greater the speed of a motor-vehicle, **the more uneconomical** (the less economical) it tends to be.	● A **proportional increase** (Ger. *je . . . desto . . .)* is expressed by *the* + **comparative** . . . *the* + **comparative.**
One of **the most important** achievements in the history of mankind was the invention of the wheel. The Concorde is **the fastest** passenger aircraft in the world.	● The **highest degree** is expressed by the **superlative.** Before a noun it is always preceded by a determiner, usually *the.*
Which plane is **(the) most comfortable?** (= more comfortable than all the others) Of all the ways of crossing the Channel by sea, the Hovercraft is **(the) quickest.** (= quicker than an ordinary ferry)	A superlative which stands alone, i.e. in predicative position and without a following attribute, can be used with or without *the* if a comparison between different persons or things is being made.
But: The Channel is **narrowest** between Dover and Calais. (= narrower than **it** is elsewhere)	If a comparison refers to one and the same person or thing, the superlative is always used without the definite article.

Note:
Most can also simply express a **very high degree.** To avoid any misunderstanding, the definite article is used with *most* meaning the **highest** degree:

This mountain pass is **most dangerous.**	(very dangerous / extremely dangerous)
This mountain pass is **the most dangerous.**	(more dangerous than all the others)

This does not apply to comparisons referring to one and the same person or thing:

Driving is **most dangerous** in bad winters.	(very dangerous / more dangerous than at other times)

Chapter 5: Adverbs and Adverbial Phrases

140–142 Functions, Meaning and Position in the Sentence (Summary)

140 Functions

1. Adverb

An adverb – which is always a single word – can have two different functions in a sentence: either it is an **adverbial,** i.e. it is itself a constituent part of the sentence (distinct from other constituent parts such as subject, predicate, etc.), or it is an **attribute** within one of these constituent parts of the sentence.

A fire has destroyed the forest **completely.** **Apparently** a camp-fire had got out of hand. **Besides,** there had been no rain for over two months.	● **As an adverbial** it can – modify the predicate and its complementation – modify the whole sentence – link sentences
Some holidaymakers had a **very** *narrow* escape. The flames spread **extremely** *quickly.* There was **quite** *an argument* over how to fight the fire. It's **only** *from the air* that you can get a clear picture of the situation.	● **As an attribute** it can modify – an adjective – another adverb – a noun phrase – a prepositional phrase

2. Adverbial phrase

By an adverbial phrase we mean a group of words which has the same functions as an adverb. It can be an **adverb phrase** made up of two adverbs. But usually it is a **prepositional phrase,** less often a **noun phrase,** neither of which need contain any adverb at all.

The trains run **fairly regularly.** **In addition,** they put on special excursions in the summer. He travels to Edinburgh **every other day.**	adverb phrase prepositional phrase noun phrase	as adverbials
How much is *a ticket* **to London?** *A holiday* **every year** is an absolute must for me.	prepositional phrase noun phrase	as attributes

Note:
Not only adverbs and adverbial phrases can occur as adverbials, but also subordinate clauses and non-finite constructions:

He visited his grandmother	frequently.	(adverb)
	on Saturday afternoons.	(prepositional phrase)
	whenever he came to York.	(adverbial clause)
	while staying in York.	(participle construction)

141 Adverbs and Adverbial Phrases Grouped according to Meaning

Adverbs and adverbial phrases can be grouped according to their meaning. The most important classes are:

Automation is **partly** responsible for unemployment.	– degree (cf **147**)
Machines can work more **efficiently** than humans.	– manner, method, means (cf **152**)
Undeniably, America has led the way in computerization.	– viewpoint or comment (cf **154**)
In Britain, many factories are now obsolete.	– place and direction (cf **156**)
The robot clanked noisily **across the room.**	
In 1913 the conveyor belt was introduced.	– time and frequency (cf **158**)
Planes are **often** flown by automatic pilot.	

Notes:

1. Some adverbs can belong to more than one class:

They treated her **roughly.**	(manner)
I earned **roughly** £3,000 a year.	(degree)
Our birch tree seeded itself **naturally.**	(manner)
Naturally, autumn ist the best time for planting.	(comment)

2. There are also a number of other classes of adverbs/adverbial phrases, such as:

– reason:	He daren't open the gate **because of the dog.**
– purpose:	I wouldn't do it **for love or money.**
– concession:	**In spite of/Despite their good intentions,** they failed miserably.
– condition:	Ring the bell **in case of an emergency.**

142 The Position of Adverbs and Adverbial Phrases

1. When used as adverbials

When adverbs function as adverbials (cf **140.**1) they can occur in three basic positions. Which position they have depends to a large extent on their meaning (cf **147–162**).

Front-position ↓	subject	(auxiliary) / main verb *be*	Mid-position ↓	main verb (+ dir. object) / subject complement	End-position ↓
Unfortunately	the town		**quickly**	doubled its population.	
	Immigration	will	**eventually**	stop.	
	They			need better housing	**immediately.**
	Overcrowding	is	**obviously**	a serious problem	**nowadays.**

Front-position means that the adverb comes before the subject.
In **mid-position** the adverb comes before the main verb in simple predicates, but mostly after *be* (even when this is a main verb cf *obviously* in the above example). When there is an auxiliary in the predicate, the adverb usually comes between the auxiliary and the main verb (cf *eventually*).
In **end-position** the adverb comes after the main verb and (if there is one) the direct object or the subject complement (cf *nowadays*). (Other types of complementation can however follow the adverb, e.g. an indirect object: *He had mentioned the problem repeatedly to the authorities.*)

Notes:

1. If there are several auxiliaries in the predicate, most adverbs in mid-position come after the first auxiliary:
   The first families *will* **soon** *be moving* into the new houses.

But adverbs of degree and manner come after the last auxiliary, as they are closely connected with the main verb (cf **148** and **153**):
   In ten years, this area *will have been* **completely** *ruined.*

2. Certain adverbs (especially adverbs of comment) can also come before the (first) auxiliary. In negative sentences it can happen that when an adverb is placed before the negative auxiliary it gives the sentence quite a different meaning from when it is placed after:

She **obviously** *must have been* very careless.
I **really** *can't understand* his behaviour. (= I can't understand his behaviour at all.)
I *can't* **really** *understand* his behaviour. (= I can't fully understand his behaviour.)

3. In the case of non-finite constructions (with infinitives, gerunds, participles) the adverb is either in end-position or before the non-finite verb form:

I saw him rounding the corner **hurriedly.** Do you remember her **suddenly** leaving the room?

In the case of the *to*-infinitive the adverb can either come before the *to* or after it (the latter is the so-called 'split infinitive'):

He vowed **never** *to enter* that house again. It was foolish of her *to* **stubbornly** *insist* on having the last word.

2. When used as attributes

When they are attributes, adverbs and adverbial phrases usually come either immediately before or immediately after the word or phrase they modify.

The illness left her **physically** *weak.*
The patient made **very** *good* progress.
But: His recovery was *slow* **enough.**

- Adverbs of viewpoint and degree (except for *enough*) usually come before.

My uncle **in Toronto** has invited me for Easter.
He came to see me after *his return* **from Chile.**
Our American trip **last year** was highly successful.

- Adverbs and adverbial phrases of place, direction and time usually come after.

3–146 Forms, Formation and Comparison of Adverbs

143 Forms and Formation

1. Adverbs of original form

They come **here seldom,** or at least not very **often.**
I've been looking for you **everywhere.**
He knew he would have to do it **now** or **never.**

In English (as in German) there are a number of adverbs which are not derived from adjectives. These are mainly adverbs of time and place.

2. Adverbs derived from adjectives by adding *-ly*

This is an **easy** song to learn. (adjective)
The words are **easily** remembered. (adverb)

Many adverbs are formed by adding *-ly* to adjectives.

He's **fanatic** about jazz.
He's been practising **fanatically.**

Adjectives ending in *-ic* form their adverbs by adding *-ally* (with the exception of *publicly*).

The band is too **loud.** *(. . . ist zu laut.)*
The choir sang **loudly.** *(. . . sang laut.)*

In German, adjectives and adverbs are identical in form.

Notes:

1. When adding *-ly*, note the following peculiarities in spelling and pronunciation (see also **346**):
   - With adjectives of more than one syllable the *-y* becomes *-i*: *happy* – *happily*
     (Adjectives of one syllable vary: *shy* – *shyly, dry* – *dryly/drily, gay* – *gaily.*)
   - *le* is dropped after a consonant: *simple* – *simply.* (But not after a vowel: *pale* – *palely.*)
   - Silent *-e* is dropped in the case of *due* – *duly, true* – *truly, whole* – *wholly.*
   - After a stressed syllable, *-ed* is pronounced as a syllable [ɪd]: *fixed* [fɪkst] – *fixedly* ['fɪksɪdlɪ]

2. Adjectives which already end in *-ly* and also *difficult* cannot add *-ly* to form adverbs. Paraphrases with *way, manner,* etc. are used instead (see however **143.**3 below):

friendly – in an friendly way, cowardly – like a coward, timely – in time, difficult – with difficulty

3. Adverbs can not only be formed from adjectives by adding *-ly*, but can also be derived from nouns and adjectives by adding *-wise, fashion, style*:

to fold s.th. lengthwise, to lay sticks crosswise, to walk clockwise round s.th., to arrange books fanwise,
to kiss Eskimo-fashion, to light a fire boy-scout fashion, to salute military style

(Words with *-wise* are always written as one word without a hyphen, words with *fashion* and *style* are either written as two words or with a hyphen.)

3. Adverbs with the same form as adjectives

A number of adverbs and adjectives have the same form and the same meaning.

Adverb	Adjective
The boss looks in **daily.**	The **daily** routine was beginning.
He got up **early.**	We had an **early** breakfast.
They'll most **likely** be late.	It's a **likely** explanation.
He disappeared **fast.**	He's made **fast** progress.

These include:
daily, hourly, weekly, monthly, quarterly (= 4 times a year), *yearly*, etc.; *early, likely, fast, long, far.* (For *slow, hard,* etc. as adverbs and adjectives, see **144.**)

Some adverbs and adjectives have the same form, but different meanings (or they correspond to different German words):

Adverb	Adjective
He ate **well.**	She is not **well.**
She spoke **ill** of us.	She is **ill.**
It's **still** dark.	It was a **still** evening.
Is it **only** six o'clock?	It was his **only** chance.

	adverb	adjective
well:	*gut*	*gesund*
ill:	*schlecht*	*krank*
still:	*(immer) noch*	*still*
only:	*erst, nur*	*einzig*

Note:
Enough, much and *little* can be used not only as adverbs, but also as determiners with nouns; *little* can also be used as an adjective:

adverb:	determiner:	adjective:
He earns well **enough.**	I have **enough** money.	
They're paid **much** better now.	They hadn't **much** capital.	
He **little** cares what other people earn.	There's **little** profit in it.	He has a **little** sweet shop in York.

144 Double Forms: Adverbs With and Without *-ly*

A number of adjectives have two adverb forms, one without a special ending (i.e. adjective and adverb are identical in form), and one with added *-ly.*

If I remember **right/rightly,** it's best to go **slow/slowly** just here.

The meaning of both adverbs is sometimes the same or nearly the same.

They worked **hard.**	*hart*
The scheme will **hardly** work.	*kaum*
That's not playing **fair.**	*fair*
It's **fairly** obvious.	*ziemlich*
He put his hands **deep** in his pockets.	*tief*
She **deeply** regretted her behaviour.	*zutiefst*
She's **pretty** clever at sewing.	*ziemlich*
The children are always **prettily** dressed.	*hübsch*

The meaning of both adverbs can, however, be quite different, as can be seen from the examples on the left.
Similarly:
high (hoch) – *highly* (höchst);
late (spät) – *lately* (in letzter Zeit);
most (äußerst) – *mostly* (vorwiegend);
etc.

That's **just** a mouse.	*nur*	Occasionally one of the two adverbs has several meanings.
He's **just** arrived.	*gerade*	
He was **justly** accused of fraud.	*zu Recht*	
They travelled far and **near.**	*nah*	
It's **nearly** midnight.	*beinahe, fast*	
The two girls are **nearly** related.	*nahe, eng*	

145 Comparative and Superlative Forms

The comparatives and superlatives of adverbs are formed in essentially the same way as those of adjectives (cf **136–138**).

soon / soon**er** / soon**est** early / earl**ier** / earl**iest** **Similarly:** long, fast, loud, hard, etc.		Adverbs of original form (i.e. not derived by adding *-ly*) form their comparatives with *-er* and their superlatives with *-est.*
quickly / **more** quickly / **most** quickly **Similarly:** easily, loudly, nervously, deeply, etc.		Adverbs derived from adjectives by adding *-ly* form their comparatives/superlatives with *more/most.*

well	better	best	badly/ill	worse	worst	The adverbs listed on the left have irregular (and sometimes two) comparative and/or superlative forms. These forms are identical with the corresponding adjectives or determiners. (See **138** for this and for the differences in meaning of the two forms.)
much	more	most	little	less	least	
far	farther	farthest	near	nearer	nearest	
	further	furthest			next	
late	later	latest				
		last				

146 Adverbs in Comparisons

In comparisons, the same structures are used with adverbs as with adjectives (cf **139**):

She whispered to me **as quietly as** she could.	• Equal degree: *as . . . (as)*
Human beings do **not** hear **as well as/so well as** bats or dogs. In old age our ears register high tones **less easily than** when we are young.	• Lesser degree: *not as . . . (as); not so . . . (as); less . . . (than)*
Sound travels **more rapidly** in water **than** in air. **Can't** the musicians play **any softer?** The professionals played **no better than** the amateurs.	• Higher degree: comparative (+ *than*) (negative mostly with *not . . . any* or *no*)
They shouted **louder and louder** to be heard over the noise. The echoes sounded **more and more faintly** across the valley.	• Steady increase: comparative + *and* + comparative or *more and more . . .*
The nearer he came **the more distinctly** he could hear the voices.	• Proportional increase: *the* + comparative . . . *the* + comparative
Who can sing **the loudest** and **the most powerfully** of everyone here? She speaks **fastest** when she is nervous.	• Highest degree: superlative (usually with *the*, except when the comparison refers to one and the same person or thing).

Note:
The phrase *none the* can be placed before the comparative to make the negation stronger:
She speaks French **none the better** for having lived in Paris for a year. *(. . . kein bißchen besser . . .)*

147 Meaning and Use

It's **quite** clear that the rebels are **fully** in command of the airport.
Life in the capital doesn't seem to be **in the least** affected.
Is there any news **at all** from the north of the country?

Adverbs of degree fall into the following categories:
- **intensifying adverbs,** e.g.
  very, completely, absolutely, quite (Ger. *ganz*), *so; in the least/at all* (in negative sentences and questions)

The village was **quite** badly damaged in the fighting and **almost** a quarter of the houses were destroyed.
In spite of everything I was **kind of** sorry to leave the country.

- **down-toning adverbs,** e.g.
  quite/rather (Ger. *ziemlich*), *almost, partly/in part, kind of/sort of* (colloquial, Ger. *irgendwie*)

The population has **hardly** any food in store for the winter.

- **restricting adverbs:**
  hardly/barely/scarcely/little (Ger. *kaum*).

The guerillas **badly need** medical supplies.
Similarly: entirely agree, completely forget, greatly admire, utterly deplore, deeply resent, perfectly understand, so want, etc.

Some intensifying adverbs of degree tend to be used in combination with particular verbs.

Notes:

1. The adverb *well* has intensifying meaning when it follows *may/might* or *can/could* in positive statements:
   It may/could **well** be that the conflict will be over by the summer.

2. *So* and *such* can be used to intensify an adjective standing before a noun in the following ways:
Such can be used with singular and plural nouns, *so* only with countable nouns in the singular (in formal style):
   I've never met **such** a brave girl/**such** brave girls.
   I've never seen **so** brave a girl. (For the position of the indefinite article see **102.**)
Such can also intensify a noun that has no adjective with it, if the noun expresses some sort of critical judgement. *Such* is less common when the noun is meant as a neutral description; *like this, like these,* etc. is then preferred:
   He's **such** a coward.
   In an emergency **like this,** one must be prepared for some inconveniences.

148 Position

When they are attributes, degree adverbs – with the exception of *enough* – come before the adjective or adverb/adverbial phrase they modify (cf **142.**2): ***very** good, **totally** beside the point;* but: *good **enough.***
When they are adverbials they occur in the following positions:

As your MP, I **wholly** sympathize with your objections to the scheme.
Residents' wishes were **all but** disregarded in this matter.
I **quite** like going to public meetings.
I'm sure you would have **greatly** admired her rhetoric.
The discussion afterwards might **almost** have ended in a fight.

Intensifying and **down-toning** adverbs of degree normally occur in **mid-position.**
With some of them, this is the only position possible e.g. *quite, rather, as good as, all but* (= *almost*), *almost, nearly, kind of, sort of.*
In sentences with several auxiliaries, these adverbs are usually placed after the **last** auxiliary. Only *almost* and *nearly* are often placed after the **first** auxiliary.

The publicity helped our plan **considerably.**
The new law has changed the situation **completely.**
Someone suggested forming a local action group, but no one cared **enough.**
The town centre has improved **a good deal** since they re-routed long-distance traffic.

Many of the others, especially the intensifying adverbs of degree, can also occur in **end-position.** *Enough* and the adverbial phrases *a little, a great deal, a good deal, a lot, by far, for sure, for certain,* etc., always take end-position, *a bit* and *at all* almost always.

She **barely** stopped herself from bursting out laughing.
You could **hardly** have expected him to be amused at finding his sleeves sewn up.

The **restricting adverbs** *(barely, hardly, scarcely, little)* usually take **mid-position** before the main verb (when there are several auxiliaries, after the first auxiliary).

Hardly had he gone back to bed when he heard the strange noise again.
Scarcely had she banged the door when she remembered that she had left the key inside.
They crept upstairs. **Little** did they expect to find the sight that met their eyes.

In formal English, however, they often occur in **front-position,** which makes their restrictive meaning more dramatic. In this case there is partial inversion (i.e. subject and first auxiliary change places, *do*-auxiliary necessary in simple tenses, cf **337**.3).

149 The Use of *very, much* and *very much*

Though his leg was **very** *painful,* he edged his way forward **very** *cautiously.*

Very is used to intensify adjectives and adverbs.

He couldn't *move* **(very) much** on the narrow ledge *(Felsvorsprung)* where he was lying.

Much and *very much* are used to intensify verbs. (*Very* cannot stand alone with verbs.)

The cold compresses don't seem to have helped **much,** my ankle is still swollen.
Did you hurt yourself **much** when you fell?
My leg was still a bit stiff, so I didn't enjoy the climb **much.** Or: . . . so I didn't **much** enjoy the climb.
We **much** admired him for risking his life in order to save the boy.
He **much** regretted having been so foolhardy.

Much is mainly restricted to negative sentences and questions, where it usually takes in end-position. With certain verbs expressing an emotional attitude (*enjoy, admire, regret, like, prefer,* etc.) mid-position is also possible.
With these verbs *much* can also be used in affirmative statements, but then only in mid-position.

The boys laughed **very much** at the jokes the bus driver told.
Peggy didn't talk **very much** on the way home.
We enjoyed our excursion to the seaside **very much.** Or: We **very much** enjoyed . . .

Very much is not restricted to particular kinds of sentences. It mostly occurs in end-position.

With the verbs expressing an emotional attitude it can also occur in mid-position.

Notes:

1. *Much* and *very much* are also used to intensify the comparatives of adjectives and adverbs:
   This is a **much** neater job.
   He worked **very much** more carefully at first.
2. *Very* is also used before some irregular superlatives like *first, last, best, worst* in the sense of *absolutely:*
   That was the **very first** basket I made.
3. *Very* can also be an attributive adjective and mostly corresponds to a German adverb such as *ganz, genau* etc.:
   Now start at the **very** beginning and tell me what happened. *(. . . ganz am Anfang . . .)*
   We were gossiping about Mr Blair. At that **very** moment his wife walked in. *(Genau in diesem Augenblick . . .)*
   He was enraged at the **very** idea of having to apologize. *(. . . schon beim bloßen Gedanken . . .)*

150–151 Focusing Adverbs

150 Meaning

The advertisements not **only** stress the machine's versatility but **also** emphasize its reliability.
This revolutionary technique was developed **exclusively** by our firm.
Housewives, **especially** those with young children, will welcome this time-saving idea.

The adverbs in this category focus attention on a word or phrase by, for example, establishing a comparison or some sort of limitation. They include: *also, too, as well, even, neither, nor, (not) either, only, merely, exclusively, chiefly, mainly, particularly, mostly,* etc.

151 Position

1. Focusing adverbs which are preferred in mid-position

One baker **only** delivers brown bread on Fridays.

- he only *delivers* it, he doesn't bake it
- only *brown bread,* not white bread
- only *on Fridays,* not more often.
- only *one baker* in town, not the others

Most focusing adverbs occur mainly in **mid-position.** They include for example *only, also, even, mainly, mostly, chiefly, merely, exclusively, especially, particularly.*
Theoretically they can refer to any part of the sentence or to an individual word (here, for example, *one* or *brown*).

You can **even** buy avocados *at the local shop* now.
He **especially** likes to go for a drink in the pub *before lunch.* (not *after* lunch)
People still **mainly** buy their meat in a butcher's shop rather than in a supermarket.

When speaking, a person makes it clear by stress (and intonation) what these adverbs are meant to refer to. (In our examples the syllable with the main stress is underlined.) In written texts it is usually clear from the context what the adverb refers to.

He takes a dip in the sea **even** *in winter.*
I swam **merely** *two lengths* today.
I enjoy swimming **only** *in warm water/in warm water* **only.**

To make it absolutely clear, however, these adverbs can also be placed immediately before the part of the sentence they modify (but see the note below). Some of them (especially *only, even, also*) can also come immediately after this part of the sentence.

Note:
If the subject is to be emphasized, only *even* can always be placed before it. In colloquial speech, *only* is not usually placed before the subject unless it expresses a restriction in number or amount. Normally other types of focusing constructions are preferred. Front-position is also avoided in the case of *mainly, chiefly,* etc.

Even *Bob* liked the play. – **Only** *twenty people* were present.
Peter was **the only one to** applaud. (Sounds more natural than: **Only** *Peter* applauded.)
It is mainly *children* **who** enjoy pantomimes.

Also as a focusing adverb cannot be placed before the subject, but can sometimes be placed immediately after it:
The puppet show, **also,** was a great success.

2. Focusing adverbs which cannot occur in mid-position

Andy asked Jill to go to the theatre, **too.**
I went to the cinema yesterday **as well.**

Peter, **too,** got tickets for the concert.
She told *Jim* **as well** about the film festival.

Too and *as well* mostly occur in **end-position** and can refer to any of the previous parts of the sentence, including the subject.
To make it absolutely clear, however, what they refer to they can be placed immediately **after** the appropriate part of the sentence.

Laura Gray's performance **alone** makes the play worth seeing.

Alone always comes immediately after the word or phrase it refers to.

I have no ear for music and I'm not interested in it **either.**
He can't sing. **Neither** can he play an instrument.
Bob's never been to the opera. **Nor** does he want to much.

Either (Ger. *auch* in negative and restrictive clauses) always takes **end-position.**
Neither and *nor* (Ger. *auch nicht*) always take **front-position** (with partial inversion, cf **337.3, 338.3**; for short sentences with *neither, nor* and *either* see **34**).

Adverbs and Adverbial Phrases of Manner, Method and Means

152 Meaning

These adverbs and adverbial phrases occur nearly always with verbs which express an activity or process (dynamic verbs). They fall into the following categories:

A fog-horn boomed **low, mournfully** and more and more **insistently.**
The ships were being **urgently** warned not to leave the harbour.
The storm **slowly** abated.

- **Adverbials of manner** describe – from the speaker's subjective point of view – how an action is carried out. They are mainly adverbs derived from adjectives which are capable of forming comparatives and superlatives.

I folded the letter **lengthwise.**
She kissed me on both cheeks **French-style.**
We shook hands each time we met, **German-fashion.**
He greeted them **in a friendly way.**
Aunt Eliza thought the children had behaved **in a disgraceful manner.**
The boys marched up and down **after the fashion of soldiers on parade.**

- **Adverbials of method** describe by means of a comparison with something else how an action is carried out. They include chiefly adverbs which are derived from nouns or adjectives by the addition of *-wise, fashion, style* (cf **143** Note 3), as well as prepositional phrases with *way, manner, style, fashion.*

He polished the paintwork **with a soft leather.**
They got the engine started **by means of much pushing from behind.**
Did you get your land-rover **through an advertisement?**
The braking distance of a vehicle can be worked out **mathematically.**

- **Adverbials of means** describe with what tools or other help an action is carried out. These adverbs are mainly prepositional phrases with *by (means of)* etc. (cf **174**) but also some adverbs with *-ly.*

153 Position

Before you set off, study the map **thoroughly.**
The ruined temple can't be reached **very easily.**
These statues must be handled **with great care.**

Adverbials of manner
These adverbials often occur in **end-position.** They must be placed there when they are necessary for a correct understanding of the whole sentence.

The trapper **desperately** looked round for a means of escape from the bear, which was now **steadily** advancing towards him.
It looked as though someone had been **wilfully** interfering with his traps.
The elk's footprints had been **completely** obliterated by a recent fall of snow.

Adverbs (not however prepositional phrases) occur in **mid-position** (always immediately before the main verb) when the most important information is conveyed by the verb with its complementation. The latter is then placed at the end of the sentence, where it carries particular weight.

Calmly and deliberately, the hunter raised his shotgun to his shoulder.
With great presence of mind, our guide took aim at the snake's head.

If the adverbial is 'to set the scene', as it were, for the whole of the following statement, it is placed in **front-position.** This also puts other parts of the sentence in emphatic end-position. (Cf **330** and **332.**)

Deal out the cards **clockwise.**
He won the game **with his two kings.**
You can only become a good bridge player **through practice.**

With more luck than skill, he managed to beat his opponent.
With the ace of trumps he might have won this game, **without it** he didn't have a chance.

Adverbials of method and means
These adverbs and adverbial phrases usually occur in **end-position,** never in mid-position.

It is less common to use them in **front-position** where they can have a 'scene-setting' function for the rest of the sentence or express a contrast.

Notes:
1. Some adverbs of manner describe the attitude or state of mind in which a person carries out an action. This is why they are often placed in front-position, i.e. next to the subject. They are usually separated from the rest of the sentence by a comma:

Resentfully, the two contestants glared at each other. (The two contestants were resentful.)

2. Some adverbs of manner such as *cordially, graciously, humbly, kindly* occur – when used in a stereotyped way – only in mid-position:

Would you **kindly** have your tickets ready?
You are **cordially** invited to attend our next meeting.

154–155 Adverbs of Viewpoint and Comment

154 Meaning

Adverbs which express a viewpoint or a comment generally modify the whole sentence. These adverbs express:

Not only **geographically** but also **psychologically** the British feel themselves to be islanders.
Similarly: morally, politically, technically, linguistically, etc.

- the aspect under which a speaker looks at something (e.g. from a *geographic* point of view)

Briefly, imports must be reduced, or else there will be disaster.
Similarly: frankly, bluntly, honestly, personally, in brief, in short, in general terms, etc.

- a speaker's characterization of his or her own words (e.g. their form)
(For the non-finite constructions like *to be honest, frankly speaking,* etc., see **298.**)

Naturally there must be sacrifices on all sides.
Next year will **probably** see an upward trend.
Similarly: (un)fortunately, typically, understandably, rightly, wrongly, strangely, perhaps, possibly, presumably, reportedly, evidently, obviously, apparently, surely, of course, etc.

- a speaker's personal opinion about something (e.g. how justified or likely something is).

Notes:
1. Adverbs of viewpoint ending in *-wise* (meaning: *with regard to/concerning*) are becoming more and more common colloquially, especially in American English:

Taxwise, business is in a much better position this year.

2. There is a strong tendency nowadays to use *hopefully* as an adverb of comment meaning *I/we hope* (Ger. *hoffentlich*), alongside its older use as an adverb of manner (Ger. *hoffnungsvoll*):

Hopefully, prices will remain stable for the rest of the year.
The journalists were waiting **hopefully** for a bulletin to be issued.

155 Position

Jim failed to keep his appointment. **Understandably** the dentist was annoyed.
I had my teeth checked up yesterday. **Fortunately** there was nothing wrong.
Apparently Betty needs to have her eyes tested.

Most adverbs of viewpoint and comment are preferred in **front-position**. This is a way of establishing one's point of view – usually following on from what has already been said – before making the actual statement.

The new cancer treatment, **understandably,** aroused a great deal of controversial feeling.
Would you, **in short,** be willing to help us with this project?
It is, **of course,** comforting to know that so many people care.
The response to the appeal was overwhelming, **to everyone's surprise.**

Many of these adverbs (and adverbial phrases) can also occur in various **mid-positions** or in **end-position**. Adverbs are then sometimes (adverbial phrases almost always) marked off by pauses in speaking or commas in writing to show that they are inserted or added comments.

Newton is **rightly** regarded as the father of modern science.
We shall **probably** be dealing with thermodynamics next term.
Similarly: wrongly, correctly, justly, possibly, presumably, reportedly, evidently, obviously apparently, surely

Some adverbs of subjective judgement mainly take **mid-position** without being marked off from the rest of the sentence by pauses or commas.

56–157 Adverbs and Adverbial Phrases of Place and Direction

156 Meaning

Is anybody sitting **there**?
Could you move your chair a bit **to the right**?
Similarly: here, inside, abroad, (at) home, down the road, by the river, round the house, etc.

Adverbials of place and direction include only a small number of adverbs; most of them are prepositional phrases (for prepositions see **164–170**).

Is Tim **back** yet? When did he come **back**?
Is anybody **in**? We followed him **in.**
A man was standing **behind the door.**
My button has fallen **behind the sofa.**

Most of them can be used for both place and direction.

Note:
At home always refers to place, while *home* refers mainly to direction. *Home* can also be used for place, however, especially after *be* (in American English after other verbs as well):
I met Chris on his way **home.** – Is Henry **(at) home**? – Mary's staying **(at) home** today.

157 Position

We stopped for a drink **at a roadside café.**
The children scrambled with difficulty **up the steep bank.**

Adverbials of place and direction normally occur in **end-position**.

From the top of the cliff the people below looked like midgets.
Hundreds of motorists are on their way to the coast. **There** they are hoping for a few hours' relaxation in the sun.

They can, however, occur in **front-position**, where they set the scene for the rest of the sentence, which contains the most important information (end-weight, cf **3, 6, 330, 332**).

Then they packed their bags and **off** they all went.
The door opened and **in** came a noisy, chattering crowd.

An adverbial of place or direction which is necessary to complete the sentence pattern has a dramatic effect when it is in front-position.

In the sky hung *a huge cloud of smoke.*
Out of the building staggered *a man with a small child in his arms.*
(**But compare:** Out of the building people *were staggering blindly.*)

The subject then comes at the end of the sentence (full inversion), if it is a noun or a noun phrase and the verb has no further complementation. The verb is always in the simple present or simple past tense.

He gathered all his courage and **down** *he* jumped.
The fire brigade should be here by now – ah, **there** *they* are.

If the subject is a pronoun, it keeps its position before the verb (no inversion).
(For details on the front-position of necessary adverbials of place and direction see **337–338.**)

Note:
If a direct object needs special emphasis (above all when it is rather long) and the adverbial of place or direction does not, the adverbial can come between the predicate and the direct object.

She found **in the drawer** her long-lost earring.
He took **from his pocket** a large leather-bound notebook.

158–159 Adverbs and Adverbial Phrases of Time and Frequency

158 Grouped according to Meaning

Adverbials of definite time I met him **yesterday.** She was born **in 1960.** **Adverbs:** yesterday, today, tomorrow, tonight **Adverbial phrases:** last night, this week, in 1960, on New Year's Eve, in summer, since Christmas, for two years, etc.	**Adverbials of definite frequency** The ferry leaves **hourly** in summer. He has done the crossing **three times.** **Adverbs:** daily, hourly, weekly, etc., once, twice **Adverbial phrases:** three times, four times, etc., every day, each time, every second week, every five minutes, once a month, etc.
Adverbials of indefinite time We were invited out **recently.** **Adverbs:** recently, lately, already, just, now, still, later, soon, once, etc. **Adverbial phrases:** once upon a time, one day, the other day, long ago, etc.	**Adverbials of indefinite frequency** I **sometimes** go there in the evening. **Adverbs:** never, ever, seldom, rarely, sometimes, usually, generally, often, always, etc. **Adverbial phrases:** as a rule, in general, for the most part, etc.

Note:
For the use of the assertive adverbs *already* and *sometimes* and the non-assertive adverbs *yet* and *ever* see **20, 22.**

159 Position

As regards their position, adverbials of definite time and frequency behave like adverbials of place and direction (cf **154**); adverbials of indefinite time and frequency, on the other hand, behave like adverbials of manner (cf **153**) and degree (cf **148**).

1. Adverbials of definite time and frequency

Examples	Explanation
A pageant will be presented in the market square **tomorrow.** A historic battle which was fought just outside the town **in 1643** is being commemorated. Will the performances take place **daily**?	These adverbials normally occur in **end-position.**
Twice the city was destroyed by fire and **twice** it was built up again. **During the time of Cromwell** the celebration of Christmas was forbidden.	If such an adverbial is in **front-position,** it usually serves to 'set the scene' (here, to establish the time) for the rest of the sentence (cf **330**).
Today it is accepted that the monarchy is subordinate to Parliament, but **in the 17th century** a civil war was fought over this issue.	In this position it can also express a contrast.
After eleven years as a republic, England gave Charles II a welcome more rapturous than any given to a monarch before.	An additional reason for front-position may be that another part of the sentence needs to come at the end, because of its length and the amount of information it contains.

Note:
Occasionally adverbials of definite time and frequency, like adverbials of place, occur in mid-position when the rest of the sentence is very long. This is especially the case with common adverbs such as *today, yesterday, everywhere, here, there:*
A spokesman for the Conservative Party **yesterday** denied rumours that the Minister of Transport was going to resign.
According to reports which are **everywhere** circulating, the Prime Minister is planning to call an election this year.

2. Adverbials of indefinite time and frequency

With these two categories a distinction must be made between adverbs and adverbial phrases.

Examples	Explanation
The Times **recently** published a very interesting article on the right to die. Two tragic cases have **just** shocked the nation's conscience. A legal battle is expected to be waged **shortly.**	**Adverbs of indefinite time** may always take **mid-position** (before the main verb or after the first auxiliary); most of them may also occur in **end-position** (but never *just* and rarely *still*).
He **sometimes** stops and speaks to me in the street. Do you **usually** park your car on this side of the road? – Yes, I **always** do. Do accidents happen here **frequently**?	**Adverbs of indefinite frequency** normally take **mid-position** (before the main verb or after the first auxiliary). Only a few of them may also occur in end-position (not possible in the case of *never, ever, always*).
Soon we'll be able to do our shopping in the new pedestrian zone. **Generally,** there isn't much through traffic here, and **never** are there any heavy lorries. **Seldom** have I driven through a narrower street.	**Both categories of adverbs** – with the exception of *just* – can occur in **front-position.** If *never, seldom, rarely, scarcely* are in front-position this causes partial inversion (i.e. subject and auxiliary change places, cf **337**.3 and **338**.3).

The other day I read a very interesting article about fairy tales. **Once upon a time** there lived a poor widow and her son Jack. One day ... **As a rule,** good triumphs over evil in such stories.	**Adverbial phrases** of indefinite time and frequency never occur in mid-position but always in **end** or **front-position.** Front-position is normal for *once upon a time* (opening words of a fairy tale), *as a rule, in general, for the most part.*

Note:
In negative sentences, *still* must be placed **before** the negative auxiliary, unlike *yet.* Note the difference in meaning between *still not* and *not yet*:

The Smiths said they would be here by eight, but they **still** haven't arrived. *(... immer noch nicht ...)*
Can I speak to Mr Miller? – Sorry, he hasn't arrived **yet.** *(... noch nicht ...)*

160 The Position of Several Adverbials at the End of a Sentence

When two or more adverbials come together at the end of a sentence – which often happens with adverbials of definite time and frequency, of place and direction and of manner – the order in which they appear is governed by the following principles:

	If none of the adverbials needs special emphasis, then the usual order is
The snow had melted **swiftly in the valleys with the coming of spring.**	– manner before place and time
The river curves **to the left at that point.**	– direction before place
There was activity **everywhere in nature after the long winter.**	– place or direction before time
The cows had to be got ready for milking **at six o'clock in the morning.**	– the more precise time before the more general.
Small clouds raced **across the sky all day in a never-ending succession.** (manner after place and time) A pair of thrushes are building a nest **this year in the branches of the old apple tree.** (place after time)	If an adverbial phrase is especially long or needs to be emphasized it can occasionally come at the end of the sentence even if this is not its usual position.

Note:
1. To avoid having three adverbials together at the end of a sentence, one of them is often placed in front-position:
Yesterday there was a keen wind blowing **strongly from the east.**

2. Unless they have special emphasis, adverbials of manner normally come before adverbials of direction. But in the case of phrasal verbs (cf **47–48**) they almost always come after the adverbial particle:
He went **quietly out into the garden.** – He went **out quietly.**

Linking Adverbs and Adverbial Phrases

161 Meaning and Use

In addition to adverbs and adverbial phrases which modify a word, a phrase or a sentence (cf **147–160**), there are also those which link sentences together and so are important for the structuring of texts. As a rule they establish a logical connection between the sentence they belong to and one or more preceding sentences. There are different types of logical connections:

Australia is famous for its great outdoors: **first(ly),** there are miles of unspoilt beaches, **second(ly)** there are vast areas of unexplored outback ...	**Sequence:** *first(ly), second(ly),* etc.; *first of all, next, then, last, finally,* etc.
Above all there is the climate, which lends itself to outdoor life. **In addition,** the Australians are warm and hospitable people.	**Addition, intensification:** *moreover, furthermore, above all, in addition, in fact, indeed, again,* etc.
There are many ways of exploring the country: **for example,** you can take a coach or a jeep, even a camel or a raft *(Floß)*. **In other words,** the choice is yours.	**Explanation, re-formulation:** *that is* (abbreviated to *i.e.*) *in other words, for example* (abbreviated to *e.g.*), *(or) rather,* etc.
Australia is one of the best places in the world for water sports such as swimming, surfing and sailing. **Similarly,** conditions for angling and big game fishing are ideal.	**Comparison:** *equally, similarly, in the same way, in/by comparison,* etc.
You may imagine that everything is very expensive. **On the contrary,** eating out, for instance, is surprisingly cheap.	**Contrast:** *in contrast, on the contrary, yet, (on the one hand) ... on the other hand,* etc.
Just as important, **however,** the quality of the food is superb. This, **at any rate,** is most visitors' opinion.	**Concession:** *however, though, after all, anyhow/anyway, at any rate, all the same, nevertheless,* etc.
If you have time and leisure enough, you can get there by sea in about six weeks; **otherwise** plenty of flights are available.	**Condition:** *otherwise/(or) else, in that case,* etc.
Domestic air routes are crowded in the holiday season, **so** it's best, **therefore,** to book in advance.	**Consequence:** *therefore, so, accordingly, consequently, thus, then,* etc.
All in all, Australia can offer you the experience of a lifetime.	**Summary:** *in sum, altogether, all in all, in conclusion,* etc.

162 Position

Marks and Spencer's is a chain store everyone knows. **After all,** there are branches all over Britain. Harrods is the most famous shop in London. **In fact,** it's one of the most famous in the world and **accordingly** it's on most tourists' shopping schedule.	Most of the linking adverbials usually occur in **front-position** (except for *though,* which never occurs in this position). They are normally marked off from the rest of the sentence which follows by a pause in speaking or a comma in writing.

It looks frightfully crowded but I'm going in **anyway.** You'd better wait out here, **however.**
Did you get what you wanted **then?** – No, I didn't. It was worth a try, **though.**

Among their real bargains were, **for example,** some lovely sheepskin jackets. She **therefore** rushed to the bank to cash a cheque. Alec, **however,** was less impressed by the quality.

End-position is also possible with the adverbs *anyhow, anyway, then* (Ger. 'also'), *after all* and (less commonly) *however.*
This is the usual position of *though.*

Some adverbs, such as *however, for example, therefore* also occur in **mid-position;** to show that they are insertions, they are often marked off by pauses in speaking and commas in writing.

Note:
If there are other adverbials at the beginning of the sentence, the linking adverbs generally take second place:
Last year, **on the other hand,** prices did not rise much.
In Britain, **moreover,** the rate of inflation is high.

163 Prepositions and Prepositional Phrases: Form, Meaning and Use (Summary)

Prepositions can be single words (*at, in,* etc.), compounds (*into, onto,* etc.), or combinations of several single words (*out of, by means of,* etc.). Together with the noun phrase which follows, they form a prepositional phrase (*in the house,* etc.). (For the function of prepositional phrases see **140.**)

1. Prepositions grouped according to meaning

Prepositions serve to express a relationship between different elements of the sentence. They can be classed in various groups, depending on the kind of relationship expressed. The most important groups are:

Sitting **on** a bench **in** the park, she saw an old friend coming **down** the path **towards** her.	space (place and direction) (cf **164–170**)
During the summer people like to eat outdoors.	time (cf **171–173**)
I refreshed myself **with** a cool drink.	manner and means (cf **174**)
Because of the heat, the swimming pools were packed.	reason and cause (cf **175**)
Let's stop **for** a rest under that tree.	purpose and intention (cf **176**)

2. Their use in concrete and figurative meanings

The majority of prepositions have a concrete spatial meaning, but can also be used figuratively, with the idea of space much weaker or totally absent.

The farmer is working **in** the field.	concrete idea of space
We are doing research **in** (the field of) biology.	weaker idea of space
After five years of hard work we are **in** despair.	hardly any idea of space

When used figuratively, a spatial preposition often moves into another class:

The track led right **through** the flooded fields.	space
Through the centuries the sea has gradually crept nearer.	time
Fertile land has been won **through** drainage of the marshes.	manner, means

In **164–170** the concrete meanings of the individual prepositions of place and direction are listed together with some typical figurative uses. Other figurative uses will be found in **171–176** with the prepositions of time, manner, etc.

Note:
For verbs, verbal complexes and abstract nouns which are closely connected to certain prepositions see **47–48, 269–272, 288–289.**

164–170 Prepositions Expressing Spatial Relationships

164 *In, into, out of*

These prepositions are connected with the idea of an enclosed two or three-dimensional space.

He lived **in** a small flat **in** a tower block. **Similarly:** (be/stay/. . .) in hospital, in bed, in the corner, etc. **Note:** **in** the street, **in** the sky, **in** a tree	*In* denotes position in relation to: – a space bounded on two or more sides
My uncle has a cottage **in** the mountains. **Similarly:** in London, in England, in the woods, etc. **Note:** **in** a field/meadow, **in** the picture, **in** the world	– a limited surface area (landscape, town, country, picture, etc.)
We sat **in** the shade of the old oak tree. **Similarly:** in the rain/sun/dark/light/heat/cold, etc.	– an environmental state (weather, etc.)
I thought you were **in** the oil business. **Similarly:** in politics/furniture/plastics/the law, etc.	– an occupation or field of activity
The company is **in** financial difficulties. **Similarly:** in danger/love/despair/tears/panic, etc.	– an abstract state
The starlet dived **into** the swimming pool. At the end, you see the hero riding **into** the sunset. My cousin Tom wants to go **into** show business. She burst **into** tears on being awarded an Oscar.	***Into*** is used like *in* for an enclosed space, a limited surface area, an environmental state, etc. but conveys the idea of direction or motion to within them.
I had to get **out of** the bath to answer the phone. He eats **out of** tins whenever his wife is away. I'll tell you as soon as he's **out of** the house. **Out of** sight is **out of** mind.	***Out of*** conveys the opposite idea – motion from an enclosed space, etc., or a position outside something (mostly the result of a motion).

Notes:

1. With certain verbs, such as *put, drip, drop, throw,* one uses *in* instead of *into* to express direction:
   She put the letter **in** her handbag and forgot about it.
2. *Within, inside* and *outside*, and in American English *inside of, outside of*, are also used as prepositions of place and direction. They emphasize the idea of an enclosed space or limited area more strongly:
   Please keep **within/inside (of)** the marked boundaries. *(. . . innerhalb . . .)*
   No one is allowed to come **inside (of)** this enclosure. *(. . . in . . . hinein . . .)*
   People were waiting **outside (of)** the gates. *(. . . vor den Toren.)*
   The children were sent **outside (of)** the house to play. *(. . . aus dem Haus/nach draußen . . .)*

165 *On (upon), onto, off*

These prepositions are connected chiefly with the idea of a surface and sometimes with the idea of a line.

Whose is that ball lying **on** the lawn? **Similarly:** on a chair, on the shelf, on the surface of the lake, on the water, on the continent, on page ten, etc. **Note:** be **on** a bus/train/plane (or other means of transport)	***On*** (formally ***upon***) denotes position in relation to – a horizontal surface (Ger. *auf*)
We must do something about that damp spot **on** the wall. **Similarly:** on the blackboard, on the ceiling, on the curtain, etc.	any other surface, not necessarily horizontal (Ger. *an*)
Her handbag was hanging **on** the door knob. **Similarly:** on her finger, on a hook, on a peg, on a nail, etc.	– an object serving as an attachment for something (Ger. *an*)

Gloucester lies **on** the River Severn, north of Bristol. **Similarly:** on the border, on the edge of a forest, on the road to London, on the shore, on the coast (**but: at** the seaside)	– a boundary line, e.g. a river, a street, frontier, side (Ger. *an*).
He has written an article **on** (about) the Scottish Highlands.	Figuratively, *on* is used for – subject matter (alternative: *about*)
No, I'm not here **on** business, I'm **on** holiday. **Similarly:** on leave, on strike, on a visit, on a trip, on fire, on sale, etc.	– a temporary situation or a process.
Put the book **on** the table please. **Similarly:** jump on the bus, hang a picture on the wall, put a ring on one's finger, go on strike, set on fire, etc.	***On*** can also be used for direction or motion in almost all these meanings: in its figurative meaning it can express the idea of beginning, causing (a situation), etc.
The rescuers climbed **onto** the roof. The injured man was lowered by rope **onto** a first-floor balcony.	***Onto*** is used to express direction or motion up or down to the surface of something.
Be careful you don't fall **off** the ladder. I can't get the lid **off** the pot of paint. She got **off** the bus at the town hall.	***Off*** is used for – direction or motion down from something (also from a means of transport)
Our village is somewhat **off** the beaten track. The islands are **off** the coast of Cornwall.	– position a short distance away from a boundary line
Jim has been **off** smoking for six months now. She's gone **off** ice-cream completely.	– the giving-up of a habit.

166 *At, from, to, towards, for*

These prepositions have to do with the idea of a point. Any dimensions, such as length, breadth and height, are disregarded – in contrast to *in, into, on,* etc. (cf **164–165**).

He stood waiting **at** the bus-stop for over an hour. **Similarly:** at the corner, at the door, at the baker's, at the end of the road, at the top of page 7, etc. The 9.45 flight to Seattle lands **at** Chicago and Denver as well. We could stop **at** Winchester for lunch.	***At*** denotes position in relation to a point. For this purpose many things can be seen as a point, e.g. – a place along a route or on a map
Both of the girls are **at** Cambridge University. **Similarly:** at one's office, at work, at school, at war with, at leisure, at rest, etc.	– a place of work or an activity
Water boils **at** 212 °F (100 °C), and freezes **at** 32 °F (0 °C).	– a degree on a scale.
Bob comes/is **from** New Zealand. I got the idea **from** Marion. He took a map **from** his pocket and pointed out the route. Could you get that atlas down **from** the top shelf?	***From*** is used for direction or motion away from something or someone. It can also mean *out of* or *off* something but is less precise than these. It is also used for
I think that saying is **from** the Bible. **Similarly:** quote from Shakespeare, paint from life, etc.	– a source or a model
Steel is made **from** iron. *(... wird aus Eisen gemacht.)* (**But:** This gate is made **of** iron. = *... besteht aus Eisen.*)	– the material something is made of.

The boy ran **to** his mother for protection.
The apples fell **to** the ground and rotted.
Please count **to** ten before opening your eyes.

When I saw them, they were walking **towards** town.
(= ... in the direction of the town.)
The old man just sat there looking **towards** the sea.

The children had already **left for** school. (= ... were already on their way to school.)
Is this the **train for** Leeds? (= ... that goes to Leeds?)
Similarly: make/set out/start, etc. for ...; the bus/the plane, etc. for ...; passengers for ...

They signed a petition objecting **to** the power station.
My attitude **towards/to** violence is clear.
The local people have a lot of sympathy **for** the demonstrators.
Similarly: reaction to, duty to, etc.; behaviour towards/to, feeling towards, etc.; taste for, preference for, etc. ...

To, towards, for are used for motion in the direction of something or someone.
To (like *into, onto*) implies that a destination is reached; it is also used figuratively in this way.

Towards leaves it open whether a destination is reached or not and emphasizes the idea of direction.

For expresses the intention of reaching a destination. It occurs chiefly after verbs denoting the beginning of a motion and in connection with means of transport.

To, towards and (more rarely) ***for*** are also used in connection with a state of mind or attitude.

Notes:

1. *At* can also be used for the direction or the target of an attack (both in a concrete and in a figurative sense):
   The boys were throwing stones **at** the ducks. *(... bewarfen ... mit Steinen./... warfen Steine nach ...)*
   I shouted **at** them to stop. *(Ich schrie sie an, sie sollten ...)*

2. *From* and *to* can also be used for position, given in terms of distance from a point; *for* can describe a movement or extent in terms of distance:
   A tanker is stranded about a mile **from** the coast. *(... von der Küste entfernt ...)*
   The nuclear power station is only a short distance **to** the south of the town. *(... südlich ...)*
   Similarly: to the north/left/right
   They marched **for** ten miles along the main road. **Similarly:** stretch/extend, etc. for ...

167 *Between, among*

These prepositions in their concrete meanings denote the position of something in relation to objects on either side or around it, or motion towards such a position.

The girl sat in the back of the car **between** her parents.
The helicopter landed **between** the two buildings.
Our farm is situated **between** the mountains and the sea.
Luxemburg lies **between** Germany, Belgium and France.

There's no public transport **between** the two villages.

Describe the relation **between** the three main characters.
The story is about the difference **between** appearance and reality.
Similarly: a distinction/quarrel/friendship/etc. between ...

The Indian settlement was well hidden **among** the trees.
She left the city to live **among** her own people.

Maria was **among** the first Indians to attend college.
(= ... was one of the first Indians who ...)

There is a lot of rivalry **among** the political representatives of the minorities.

Between denotes
- position in relation to two (or other **definite** number of) points, areas, etc.
- a linking together of various points
- an abstract relationship of two (or a definite number of) people or things.

Among denotes
- position in relation to an **indefinite** number of points
- membership of a group
- abstract relationships of the members of a group.

168 *Over, above, up – under, below, down*

These prepositions express differences in level or height. Contrasting pairs are *over – under, above – below,* and *up – down.* The difference between the (more precise) meaning of *over – under* and the (wider) meaning of *above – below* is roughly as follows:

over: vertically on a higher level	*above:* anywhere on a higher level
under: vertically on a lower level	*below:* anywhere on a lower level.

In more detail:

Over (above) the mantelpiece hung a portrait of the Queen. A flock of birds circled **over** (above) the castle.	*Over* means – vertically on a higher level than something (*above* includes this meaning as well)
It would be very difficult to climb **over** that fence. You'll have to use the stepping stones: there's no bridge **over** (across) the stream.	– from one side to the other. (When the object has a flat surface, *across* can often be used instead.) Figuratively it denotes
This tapestry is worth **over** a million dollars.	– a higher number
William I ruled **over** England from 1066–1087.	– power over someone or something.
They hid the documents **under** the floorboards. I found the book **under** a pile of old magazines.	*Under* denotes – a position vertically (or immediately next to something) on a lower level.
The cat crept **under** the blanket. (**Note:** He came out **from under** the blanket: . . . *unter der Decke hervor.*)	– the direction towards this position.
Under 30 people were present at the ceremony. The arts flourished **under** (the rule of) Elizabeth I.	Figuratively it is used with – numbers and power relationships (cf *over*)
The building is **under** repair at the moment. **Similarly:** under these conditions, under great difficulties, under the threat of, under the name of	– circumstances, processes and conditions.
A shark's fin rose **above** the surface of the water. The plane flew **above** the clouds. (**But:** fly **over** s.th. = *über etwas hinwegfliegen*)	*Above* denotes – a position anywhere on a higher level than something or the direction towards such a position (general difference in level)
I'll make a note of all expenses **above** (over) £5. **Similarly:** above average, above (over) the age of 15, etc.	– a higher position on a scale of numbers or measurements
That girl has ideas **above** her station. *(Stand, Rang)* His behaviour was **above** criticism. *(. . . über . . . erhaben.)* **Similarly:** above suspicion, above taking advice, etc.	– superiority (moral, in rank, etc.).
Parts of the marshes are **below** sea level. The temperature sank **below** freezing point. A lieutenant ranks **below** a general. It would be **below** his dignity to do the job himself.	*Below* denotes a position on a lower level than something (or the direction towards such a position), both in a concrete and figurative sense.
Look, there's a squirrel climbing **up** the tree. Halfway **up** the hill, they stopped for a rest.	*Up* denotes the direction to a higher level or a position on a higher level.
He ran **down** the stairs to answer the phone. They live **down** the road from us. *(. . . weiter unten . . .)*	*Down* denotes direction to a lower level or a position on a lower level.

Notes:

1. *Over* (often preceded by *all*) denotes a position or motion where contact is established with a whole area:
   Snow fell **over** the north of England yesterday. *(... im ganzen Norden/überall im Norden Englands.)*
   She travelled all **over** South America. *(Sie bereiste ganz Süd-Amerika.)*

2. *Underneath* and *beneath* are similar in meaning to *under* and *below*. *Beneath* is chiefly used in a figurative sense. (In its concrete meaning it sounds old-fashioned or literary.)
   He hid the bank notes **underneath** (under) the carpet.
   Such conduct is **beneath** (below) contempt.

169 *In front of, before – behind, after – beyond, past – beside, by, near*

These prepositions denote differences in position and distance in relation to a definite point (mostly viewed on a horizontal level). They can be used in adverbials of place and direction. The corresponding German prepositions are given for comparison.

I'm nervous about standing up to speak **in front of/before** all those people. Kate was sitting **in front of** me in the theatre. Your name should come **before** his in the list of performers. It's best to put quality **before** popular success.	***In front of/before:*** (Ger. *vor*) In concrete adverbials of place *in front of* is preferred. For a position in a sequence or on a scale of values only *before* can be used.
The bicycle shed is **behind** the school building. Joan is way **behind** Bridget in maths and science. All my friends were solidly **behind** me on the matter.	***behind:*** Like the corresponding German preposition *hinter*, this can also be used for a position on a scale of values or achievement, and to mean 'supporting'.
Two of us ran **after** the pickpocket. The police arrived ten minutes **after** the ambulance.	***after:*** Ger. *hinter ... her* or *nach* (in a sequence of time)
Beyond the house the ground rose steeply. He hit the golf-ball well **beyond** the hole. The cattle strayed **beyond** the boundaries of the park. How he can afford a horse is **beyond** my comprehension.	***beyond:*** Ger. *jenseits,* *über ... hinaus,* *auf die andere/auf der anderen Seite* This can also be used figuratively in the sense of 'surpass', 'be greater than'.
Several police cars rushed **past** the school this morning. The rectory is about 100 yards **past** the church.	***past:*** Ger. *an ... vorbei,* *hinter*
You can put your case in the corner **beside** the wardrobe. They rented a cottage **beside** Lake Windermere.	***beside:*** Ger. *neben* or (referring to an edge or boundary) *an*
We sat down **by** the stream to eat our sandwiches.	***by:*** Ger. *an, nahe bei*
Don't got too **near** the edge of the cliff.	***near:*** Ger. *nahe an/bei/zu*

170 *Along, (a)round, about – against, across, through*

These prepositions denote an arrangement or motion in relation to a line, a surface or an area. The corresponding German prepositions are given for comparison.

We were strolling **along** the road, admiring the scenery. Willow trees grew **along** the banks of the river.	***along*** (a line): Ger. *entlang*
Let's have a race **around** the park. There was a protective fence **round** each tree.	***round/around*** (a surface, an area): Ger. *(rings)um (... herum)*
Several rucksacks were lying **about** the hall of the youth hostel. He spends his summers travelling **about** Europe. I'm reading a book **about** (on) Captain Cook.	***about:*** (a surface or area): This conveys the idea of random arrangement or motion (Ger. *überall in ... herum).* It can also be used figuratively to refer to subject matter (Ger. *über*).

We leant our bicycles **against** the wall. The fight **against** pollution has only just begun. The majority is **against** us on the matter.	***against*** (a vertical surface): Like the German *gegen,* this can be used figuratively to refer to an attitude or action.
The little boy ran **across** (over) the road without looking. That's Mrs Carey, who lives **across** (over) the road from us.	***across*** (a surface): Ger. *über, auf der anderen Seite*
The footpath leads **through** a cornfield. He looked out **through** the window at the children playing. My grandmother has gone **through** difficult times.	***through*** (an enclosed space): Ger. *durch (... hindurch).* It can also be used figuratively to refer to an experience, etc.

171–173 Prepositions Expressing Time Relationships

171 *At, on, in*

None of these prepositions correspond to any one German preposition (e.g. *at* = Ger. *an, um, zu,* etc.) and so they are often used wrongly. Which one to use depends on the noun phrase that follows it.
Corresponding to their basic spatial meanings (cf **164–166**), *at* is used more in connection with a point in time, whereas *on* and above all *in* are used more for a period of time.

at six o'clock, **at** ten (minutes) to five, etc. **at** dawn, **at** sunrise, **at** sunset, **at** night, **at** midnight, **at** noon **at** Easter, **at** Christmas, **at** Whitsuntide *(Pfingsten)* **at** the moment *(jetzt),* **at** present *(zur Zeit),* **at** the beginning/end of (June/...), **at** the age of twenty, **at** all times, etc.	***At*** is used for – the exact time of day – certain more general times of day – some times of the year, especially church festivals – general points in time.
on a sunny day, **on** that day (**but: in** those days: *damals*) **on** Tuesday, **on** Sundays *(sonntags),* **on** weekdays **on** January 8th, **on** Saturday 1st August **on** Christmas Eve, **on** All Saints' Day, **on** Good Friday, etc. **on** that morning, **on** a sunny afternoon, **on** Friday night, **on** a dark winter evening in January, **on** the morning of June 28th, **on** the afternoon of that day (**but: in** the early/late morning of June 28th).	***On*** is used for – days in general – weekdays (also in the plural) – dates – public holidays with *Day/Eve,* etc. – general time – on a day which is specified in some way: by *that, a* + adj./noun, *the* + *of*-phrase (except when combined with *early/late*).
in the morning, at six o'clock **in** the evening, **in** the later afternoon **in** June, **in** mid-July, **in** spring, **in** high summer, etc. **in** (the year) 1910, **in** the mid-thirties, **in** the 20th century, **in** the age of Elizabeth I, **in** King John's reign, etc. **in** his youth, **in** old age, **in** her teens/thirties, etc., **in** the past, **in** the future, **in** the hour of danger, etc.	***In*** is used for – *the* + *morning/afternoon/evening* **without** further definition (except for *early/late*) – months, seasons – years, decades, centuries, eras – the different times of a person's life, *past* and *future* and other periods of time.

Notes:
1. *At night* refers in a general way to the hours of darkness, or their beginning; *in the night* means some particular time within this period:

At night the streets were always empty.	*(Nachts ...)*
He returned **at night.**	*(... bei Anbruch der Dunkelheit.)*
A loud noise woke me **in the night.**	*(... in der Nacht.)*

2. When they are contrasted in a general way, *night* and *day* can also be used with *by:*
We travelled **by night** and rested **by day.**

3. *In* can also be used to indicate a limited period of time (alternative: *within*) or a future point at the end of a period of time:
He learned French **in** two years. (or: . . . **within** two years.) The concert starts **in** an hour.

172 *Since, for, from, to, till, until, by*

These prepositions are used in connection with the beginning, duration or end of a period of time. Note that their usage is a lot more differentiated than that of their German equivalents. (For example, German *bis* can either mean *till* or *by.*)

I haven't seen her **since** my last birthday. *(. . . seit . . .)* She knew him very well, because she had been working with him **since** 1980.	***Since*** denotes the **beginning** of a period of time which stretches up to the present – or to a point of time in the past. It is used with the present perfect or past perfect (cf **191**, Note 1, **195.**1, **196**).
We've lived here **for** ten years now. *(. . . seit zehn Jahren/schon zehn Jahre lang.)* They had only known each other **for** five weeks when they got married. *(. . . seit fünf Wochen/fünf Wochen lang . . .)* Last time he was in prison **for** a year. This time it will be **for** five years at least.	***For*** denotes the **duration** of a period of time (the length of time is stated more or less precisely). This period of time can (as with *since*) stretch up to the present or to some particular point of time in the past. It can, however, belong altogether to the past or the future, without being related to any particular point in time. ***For*** can therefore be combined with all tenses (see also **195.**2).
I worked in a Brighton hotel **from** May **to/till/until** September. *(. . . von Mai bis September . . .)* We'll be in San Francisco **from** Tuesday **through** Friday. (= from Tuesday to Friday inclusive) **From** Monday **(on/onward)** there'll be new opening times. *(Ab Montag/Von Montag an . . .)* The match lasted **till/until** midnight. *(. . . bis . . .)* He stayed right **up to** the end of the match. **But:** It's three hours **to/till** the opening ceremony.	***From . . . to/until/till*** denote the **beginning** and **end** of a period of time. In American English *from . . . through,* is also used, with a similar (though more precise) meaning. If only the beginning of the period of time is mentioned, then *from* is used alone or with *. . . on/onward.* If only the end is mentioned, one uses *till, until,* or – to emphasize the length of time – *up to.* If it is a future event that marks the end of the period, one uses *to* or *till.*
Can you get that letter typed **by** three o'clock? *(. . . bis drei Uhr . . .?)* We started very early, and **by** noon we had reached Edinburgh. *(. . . bis zum Mittag . . .)*	***By*** denotes the **end** of a period of time (Ger. *bis spätestens*). It expresses the idea that at a certain point of time, something will have, is expected to have, or had already happened.

Note:
For can also denote a fixed or planned date: We have been invited **for** July 14th. *(. . . zum . . .)*

173 Other Prepositions Used in Time Adverbials

The following prepositions are used in more or less the same way as their German equivalents.

before/after Easter	*vor/nach*	**between** March and June	*zwischen*
But:		**towards** midnight	*gegen*
ten **to/past** nine	*zehn vor/nach neun*	**around** six o'clock	*um . . . herum*
an hour **ago**	*(jetzt) vor einer Stunde*	**during** the year 1980	*während*
two days **before**	*zwei Tage zuvor*	**through** the night	*. . . hindurch/über*
		throughout that day	*den ganzen . . . hindurch*
For *to/past* as used in telling the time see **368**, for the adverbs *ago/before* see **325–326.**		**over** the week end	*über*
		into the night/winter	*bis in . . . hinein*

174–176 Prepositions Expressing Other Relationships

174 Prepositions Used in Adverbials of Manner, Method and Means

By and *with* are the most widely used prepositions in this class. The others are more limited in their use.

	By is used with reference to
Ms Callaghan always somes to work **by** car. **Similarly:** by bus/train/plane/ship/air/sea/rail, etc.	– a means of transport (Ger. *mit*)
He informed me **by** letter of his decision to leave. **Similarly:** communicate by radio, send a message by telegram/telex, etc.	– a means of communication or a medium (Ger. *durch, über, per*)
I was told about the accident **by** a friend. Two skiers were killed **by** an avalanche yesterday.	– the agent in a passive sentence (the so-called *by*-agent, cf **58**).
	With (and its opposite *without*) can refer to
It's better to eat Chinese food **with** chopsticks. (Compare: I can't eat the rice **without** a fork.)	– an instrument or tool
Asians move **with** more grace than Europeans. (Compare: She poured the tea **without** much grace.) **Similarly:** fight with a sword, see s.th. with one's own eyes, explode with a bang, fight with courage, etc.	– a way of behaving, characteristic, etc.
	In is only used in certain fixed combinations, e.g. to refer to
The men at the bar were talking **in** Dutch *(... auf Holländisch.)* She answered **in** a low voice. *(... mit leiser Stimme.)* I never use a biro – I always write **in** ink. *(... mit Tinte.)* **Similarly:** paint in oil, speak in a whisper, write in block letters, etc.	– a language, way of speaking or writing, implement used in writing, etc.
The children were standing **in** a straight line. **Similarly:** in rows, in a circle, in single file *(im Gänsemarsch)*, etc.	– an arrangement of people or things.
	To express method and means, the following can also be used:
The survivors of the crash attracted attention **by means of** a fire.	– ***by means of*** (using s.th.) Ger. *mittels, durch*
He openened the door **with the aid of** a picklock.	– ***with the aid of*** (a thing) Ger. *mit Hilfe*
They got the car moving **with the help of** two boys.	– ***with the help of*** (a person) Ger. *mit Hilfe*

Note:
Through and *on* can also be used to express manner or means:

I got this job **through** a friend of my father's.	*through* (the agency of): Ger. *durch*
The seamen lived **on** nothing but fish.	*on* (a food, fuel, etc.): Ger. *von/mit*
The motor-boat runs **on** diesel.	

175 Prepositions Used in Adverbials of Reason and Cause

Because of is the most widely used preposition in this class, but there are a number of other prepositions which are more limited in their use. There are also a number of complex prepositions which are mainly restricted to formal language, and whose meaning is clear from the meaning of the individual words.

The airport was closed **because of** fog.	***Because of:*** Ger. *wegen*
She'll jump **for** joy when she hears the news. **Similarly:** for fun/love/fear/sorrow/grief, etc. I couldn't see anything **for** the mist. They praised the driver **for** her presence of mind. **Similarly:** blame/reward/punish/etc. s.o. for s.th.	***For*** can refer to – an emotion (Ger. *vor, aus*) – an obstacle (Ger. *wegen*) – an action or characteristic worthy of praise, blame, reward, etc. (Ger. *für, wegen*).
We were stiff **with** cold after waiting so long. You could see the girl was shaking **with** fear. **Similarly:** wet with rain, bright with joy, pale with anger, heavy with sleep, etc.; cry with rage, sing with joy, etc.	***With:*** is used after certain adjectives and verbs describing the cause of a state or of an emotional reaction (Ger. *vor, von*).
The delay arose **through** a misunderstanding. **Similarly:** fail through ignorance, through lack of experience, through mismanagement, etc.	***through*** (a shortcoming): Ger. *durch, wegen*
She has suffered **from** asthma all her life. **Similarly:** die from injuries, collapse from fatigue, from hunger; act from necessity, from cowardice, from conviction, etc.	***from*** (an illness, shortcoming or attitude): Ger. *an, aus, wegen*
She helped us **out of** the goodness of her heart. **Similarly:** out of kindness/fear/interest/curiosity, etc.	***out of*** (an attitude): Ger. *aus*
I recognized him **by** his flaming red hair. **Similarly:** know s.o. by their voice, see s.th. by s.o.'s face, etc.	***by*** (a mark of identity): Ger. *an*
My father retired early **due to** ill health. The murderer was acquitted **on grounds of** insanity. I had the contract changed **on the strength of** your advice. He has a lot of influence **by virtue of** his position.	***due to:*** ***on grounds of:*** ***on the strength of:*** ***by virtue of:*** } formal style: Ger. *aufgrund, wegen*

Note:
When *for* or *with* are followed by *all*, they have concessive meaning and correspond to the prepositions *in spite of, despite* (Ger. *trotz*):

For all my efforts/**Despite** (all) my efforts, I didn't succeed in making him change his mind.
With all his learning/**In spite of** (all) his learning, Peter can be remarkably stupid.

176 Prepositions used in Adverbials of Purpose, Intention and Aim

For is the most widely used preposition in this class – far more widely than German *für*. There are also some complex prepositions.

His secretary does all the work **for** him. She fought **for** women's rights in the late 19th century. They put guards at all the entrances **for** extra security.	***For:*** can be used with reference to a person, a cause (Ger. *für*) – a general aim or reason (Ger. *aus ... Gründen*)

Run **for** your life – there's a bomb in the building! They've got a machine **for** detecting firearms. **Further examples:** be destined/trained for s.th.; pray for peace, cry for help, fish for eels; go for a walk/swim/. . .; a knife for cutting meat, etc.
For the sake of peace, they agreed to compromise. The new machines have been introduced **for the purpose of** raising productivity. They bought some land **with a view to** starting a chicken-farm.

– a variety of specific aims and purposes (Ger. *um, nach, zum,* etc.) For the gerund after *for* see **296** Note 2.

for the sake of: Ger. *um . . . willen*
for the purpose of/with a view to + Gerund: Ger. *um . . . zu . . .,* *mit der Absicht . . . zu . . .*

Chapter 6: The Finite Verb Forms

-178 The Finite Forms of the Main Verb: their Function and Formation

177 Function

The finite form of the verb gives several kinds of information **at the same time:**

a) **Time relationships**

The workman **was mending** the roof.
He **had come** with his ladder earlier that morning
and **would** probably **finish** the job the next day.

The form *was mending* (past tense) is used to make it clear that one is talking about an action in past time.
The tenses in the second sentence are related to *was mending* as follows: *had come* (past perfect) refers to a time before this action, *would finish* (future-in-the-past) refers to a time after it. (For tense and time relationships see **179–180**)

b) **Aspect**

The workman **was mending** the roof.
He **removed** the old tiles, **laid** new ones and **fixed** them into place.

The form *was mending* (progressive form) presents the activity as being in progress at a particular moment (progressive aspect)
In contrast to this, *removed, laid* and *fixed* (simple form) describe a series of completed acts. (For the progressive aspect see **181–185**)

c) **Mood**

The workman **was mending** the roof.
I wish I **had** the money for more extensive repairs.

The form *was mending* is the indicative form of the verb, which presents the action as a fact.
The form *had* in the second sentence presents something not as a fact, but as an imagined possibility. This form is called the modal past, and corresponds to a subjunctive in German *(hätte).* (For the modal use of finite verb forms see **212–214**)

As our example *was mending* shows, when selecting finite verb forms in English you have to consider time relationships, aspect and mood. Finite verb forms are also dependent on person and number *(I, you, he . . . they),* and may be active or passive.
(For the passive see **58–65**)

178 Table of Forms

The following table shows how the indicative of regular verbs is formed, using as an example the verb *call*. In colour: simple form; in white: progressive form (continuous form).
For subjunctive forms see **213.1, 214.1**; for irregular verbs see **343**; for information on spelling see **346.**
The auxiliary verbs in compound tense forms are given in their full forms. For short forms (*I'm, he's, they'd,* etc.) see **219, 246, 252.**

		Active Forms:	Passive Forms:
Present Tense	(Simple)	I/you/we/they **call** he/she/it **calls**	I **am** he/she/it **is** we/you/they **are** } **called**
	(Progressive)	I **am** he/she/it **is** we/you/they **are** } **calling**	I **am** he/she/it **is** we/you/they **are** } **being called**
Past Tense		I/you/we/they he/she/it } **called**	I/he/she/it **was** we/you/they **were** } **called**
		I/he/she/it **was** we/you/they **were** } **calling**	I/he/she/it **was** we/you/they **were** } **being called**
Present Perfect		I/you/we/they **have** he/she/it **has** } **called**	I/you/... **have** he/... **has** } **been called**
		I/you/we/they **have** he/she/it **has** } **been calling**	–
Past Perfect		I/you/he/... **had called**	I/you/he/... **had been called**
		I/you/he/... **had been calling**	–
***will*-Future**		I/you/he/... **will call**	I/you/he/... **will be called**
		I/you/he/... **will be calling**	–
Future-in-the-Past (Conditional)		I/you/he/... **would call**	I/you/he/... **would be called**
		I/you/he/... **would be calling**	–
Future Perfect		I/... **will have called**	I/... **will have been called**
		I/... **will have been calling**	–
Future-Perfect-in-the-Past (Conditional Perfect)		I/... **would have called**	I/... **would have been called**
		I/... **would have been calling**	–

Notes:
1. In the first person singular and plural *(I, we)* of the future forms, some speakers from the South of England use *shall* and *should* instead of *will* and *would*.

2. As the gaps in the table show, the use of the progressive form in the passive is normally restricted to the present tense and the past tense. However, the progressive form is sometimes used in the other tenses if a speaker cannot think of an equivalent active construction:
You can't take that road, it **will be being repaired** from tomorrow on.

179 Present Tense Group and Past Tense Group

The two basic tenses in English are **present tense** and **past tense.** Any presentation of thought or action will be based on one of these two tenses. The other tenses are used to refer to a time before or after the time expressed by the present or past tense:

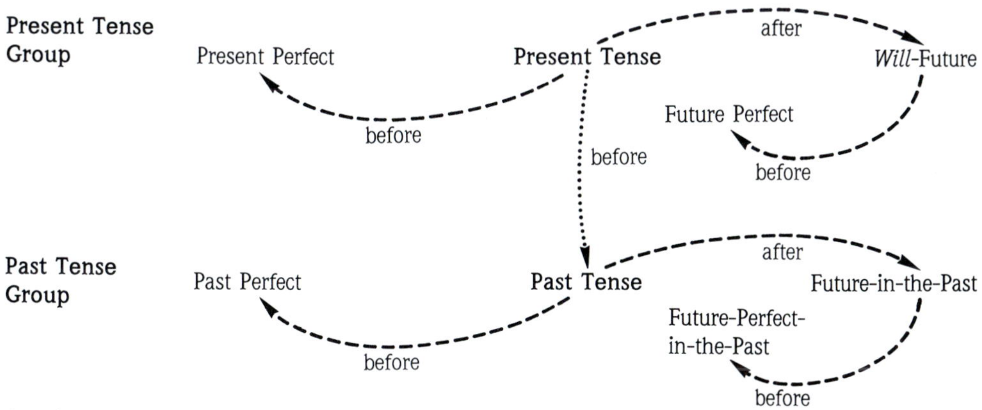

As this diagram shows, the present perfect and the *will*-future are related directly to the present tense, while the past perfect and the future-in-the-past are related directly to the past tense. The future perfect and the future-perfect-in-the-past, however, are related only indirectly to the present tense and past tense. The future perfect expresses 'time before' the *will*-future, the future-perfect-in-the-past expresses 'time before' the future-in-the-past (cf **207, 210**).

The diagram also shows that the past tense can express 'time before' in relation to the present tense. It is therefore often possible to change from one tense group to the other.

180 Use and Shifting of Tense Groups in Texts

- The tenses of the **present tense group** indicate that something is **related to present time.** One uses these tenses to describe what is the case or what is important at the time of speaking.
- The tenses of the **past tense group** indicate that no immediate relationship to present time is intended. These tenses are used to describe actions or events in **real past time** or in a fictitious past (e.g. in novels, fairy-tales, etc.).

In a connected text, the tenses of each group usually occur together with other tenses from the same group. However, there may be a shift from one group to the other if there is a change of focus from present time to past, or vice versa. This is often made explicit by the inclusion of time adverbials or other words indicating time. For example:

Zoo Talk
Chessington Zoo in Surrey **has** recently **had** a facelift and there **are** lots of improvements which **will benefit** not only the visitors but – much more important – the animals who **live** there. One **is** a Celebrity Bird Garden that **has** already **solved** a cockatoo's problem.

Present tense group:

has . . . had:	time before	A description of the present situation of the zoo
are:	**basic tense**	
will benefit:	time after	
live:	**basic tense**	
is:	**basic tense**	
has . . . solved:	time before	

During a frustrating winter in the quarantine quarters he **had preened** *(sich putzen)* so desperately – hoping he **would be joined** by a female – that he **had to** be put on tranquillizers so that his feathers **would stop** dropping out. Fortunately, before he **became** completely bald, he **was moved** to his new cage (with two female companions) in the bird garden, where he **has** now **grown** a healthy set of feathers again.
(From *The Observer Colour Magazine*, November 22, 1981)

Shift to the past tense group:

had preened:	time before	A description of past events *(During a frustrating winter . . .)*
would be joined:	time after	
had to:	**basic tense**	
would stop:	time after	
became:	see note below	
was moved:	**basic tense**	

Return to the present tense group:

has grown:	time before	Present situation (= he is now in good health)

Note:
In adverbial clauses of time, the idea of 'time before' or 'time after' is often already expressed by the conjunction (*when, before, after,* etc.). In such cases the basic tense is often used:

Time after: You'll have to have your eyes examined before you **take** your driving test.
(Only the present tense is possible here – cf **208–209**.)

Time before: After he **had been/was prescribed** glasses, he was able to see much better.
(Both the past perfect and the past tense are possible here – cf **197.2**.)

181–185 Progressive Form and Simple Form

181 Difference in Aspect

Progressive Form:

Look, Robert **is playing** tennis again.
He **has been playing** for two hours now.
He **was playing** last night when I passed the courts.

The progressive form presents an action (here: a game of tennis) as a process which

- is going on at a particular point in time (now, last night, etc.),
- is therefore not yet finished,
- is only of temporary duration.

This way of looking at things is called the **progressive aspect.** It is the principle on which the use of the progressive form is based in all tenses.

Simple Form:

Robert **plays** tennis.
He **has played** three matches today.
He **played** a double with his sister last night.

The simple form stresses a different aspect of an action, for example:

- an abilitiy or a habit, i.e. something that occurs repeatedly (sentence 1),
- a result (sentence 2),
- the fact that an action was completed (sentence 3).

How the simple form is to be interpreted depends on the tense used and the context.

For details of how to use the progressive form and the simple form see **186–197.**

Note:
The definition of the progressive aspect can be broadened to include:

a) a process that will continue although it is momentarily interrupted:
In a TV interview, the author said that he **was working** on a new novel.

b) something that happens repeatedly, if this situation is regarded as only temporary:
Peter **is doing** the cooking this week, because his wife is ill.

c) an action that is repeated over an unlimited stretch of time if it is always in progress at a certain moment:
Whenever I drop in, Mrs Smith **is baking** a cake.
Compare this with: Mrs Smith **bakes** a cake every week.

182 The Progressive Aspect and the Meaning of the Verb

All English verbs can be used in the simple form. But the progressive form can only be used with verbs whose meanings allow the progressive aspect (i.e. the idea of an action in progress and temporary duration). This type of verb meaning is called **dynamic.** Verb meanings which do not allow the progressive aspect (or do so only in special cases) and which therefore normally occur only in the simple form are called **stative.**

183 Verbs with Dynamic Meaning: Activity and Process Verbs

What's Bob **doing**? – He's **repairing** his motorbike. The petrol tank **is leaking.** It's **raining** hard now. **Similarly:** eat, work, talk, watch, listen, sleep, dream, sit (at the table); roll, float, drip, steam; snow, shine, etc.	This group includes: ● verbs which describe an intentional activity, and also verbs which describe other types of events in progress (e.g. 'activities' of inanimate objects, the weather, etc.)
It **was getting** dark. Hope **was fading** fast. **Similarly:** become (tired), grow (dark), go (blind); change, deteriorate (= become worse), darken, approach, disappear, dry (up), etc.	● verbs which describe a process of change. These verbs include those linking verbs which express the idea of 'becoming' (cf **55**.4) and some other (intransitive) verbs.

Note:
When verbs which denote activities of very short duration (e.g. *knock, clap, tap, nod*) are used in the progressive form, this usually expresses a series of repeated actions:

Somebody's **knocking** at the door like mad.

However, if the number of repetitions is stated, the simple form is used:

I **knocked** three times, but nobody heard me.

184 Verbs with Stative Meaning

1. Verbs of personal experience and attitude

These verbs describe a person's state of mind, a state that is not consciously brought about by that person. These verbs are therefore normally only used in the simple form. This group includes:

She **didn't feel** the cold, wrapped up as she was. I **could hear** footsteps crunching over the snow. **Similarly:** see, taste, smell, notice (Compare: He **was watching** TV/**listening to** the radio.)	● verbs of (passive) perception. With the exception of *notice* they are often used with *can*. (Verbs of active, intentional observation, on the other hand, are activity verbs.)
Now I **see** what you **mean.** **Similarly:** believe, think, feel, imagine, know, realize, understand, remember, forget, doubt, etc. (Compare: He **is meditating.**)	● verbs which express an opinion, supposition or knowledge. (Verbs describing active mental processes, however, are activity verbs.)
He **likes** peace and quiet. **Similarly:** love, prefer, approve of, dislike, hate, etc.	● verbs of emotional attitude (preference, aversion, etc.)
We **intend** to spend Sunday at home. **Similarly:** want, wish, hope, mean (to do), etc. (Compare: They **are planning** to go out.)	● verbs which express an intention or desire (except *plan*, which is an activity verb).

Notes:

1. The progressive form is used sometimes with verbs of passive sensory perception when a temporary state is being described (a), or when the perception is very intense or a person is only gradually becoming conscious of it (b):

   a) Grandma**'s not seeing** very well these days.

   b) (On the phone) Can you hear me? – Oh ... yes, now I**'m hearing** you.

2. Some verbs which express a desire or knowledge are occasionally used in the progressive form for intensification:

   I'm **hoping** to see her again. *(Ich hoffe sehr ...)*

   You **are forgetting** what I told you. *(Jetzt vergißt du aber ...)*

2. State and relation verbs

These verbs denote states, relationships or characteristics which (though they may be subject to change in reality) are not seen from the progressive aspect. This group includes:

His pulse **seemed** weaker and his voice **sounded** very faint. **Similarly:** exist, be, lie (= be situated); remain, stay, keep (fit); appear (correct); look (nice), sound (strange), smell (sweet), taste (bitter), feel (soft)	● verbs which express a state of being, an appearance, or a sense impression. This covers all linking verbs except those which describe a process of change (*become, grow,* etc.; cf **183**).
This rule **applies to** all of us. *(... betrifft uns alle.)* **Similarly:** have, own, possess, belong to, consist of, contain, imply, resemble; weigh (2 tons), measure (two inches), cost ($10)	● verbs which express a relationship (e.g. possession, belonging, measurement, etc.).

Notes:

1. Some of these state and relation verbs may occasionally be used in the progressive form if a temporary situation (a) or a process of change (b) is being described:

   a) The economy **is** not **looking** healthy these days.

   b) Petrol **is costing** more and more.

2. Verbs which express a position of rest, such as *lie* and *stand,* have dynamic meaning when the subject of the sentence is a person or a mobile object and their position is thus seen as temporary. Otherwise they have stative meaning:

   His clothes **were lying** on the floor. – London **lies** on the Thames.

185 Verbs with Dynamic and Stative Meaning

A number of verbs, many of them quite common, have several meanings, both dynamic and stative. Some typical examples are listed below:

	Stative meanings	Dynamic meanings
be	John's father **is** rich.	You **are being** too generous. (*be* = behave)
feel	Lambswool **feels** very soft. *(sich anfühlen)*	Wait, **I'm feeling for** the switch. *(tasten nach)*
guess	I **guess** you've heard this before. *(annehmen)*	You don't know this for certain, you **are** only **guessing.** *(herumraten)*
have	I **have** no time for you.	**Are** you **having** trouble with your car? (*have* = experience, undergo) When **are** we **having** breakfast? *(einnehmen)*
hear	I thought I **heard** somebody downstairs. *(hören)*	The case **was being** heard in the magistrate's court. *(vor Gericht anhören, untersuchen)*
look	Dad **looks** very tired tonight. *(aussehen)*	I waved to her, but she **wasn't looking.** *(her-/hinsehen)*
mind	I hope you **don't mind** waiting. *(etwas dagegen haben)*	Grandmother **was minding** the baby. *(aufpassen auf)*

see	We **saw** the Pope on our visit to Rome.	When I arrived, Alan **was seeing** his aunt to the door. *(begleiten)*
smell	These roses **smell** lovely. *(duften, riechen)* **Have** you ever **smelt** anything so awful? *(etwas riechen)*	Susan **has been smelling** all the perfumes in the shop to find the nicest one. *(an etwas riechen)*
taste	The potatoes **taste** very salty. *(schmecken)* I **tasted** garlic in the soup. *(etw. schmecken)*	The chef **was tasting** the salad dressing. *(kosten, abschmecken)*
think	I **think** he is wrong. *(glauben)*	Why don't you answer? – Sorry. I **was** just **thinking**. *(nachdenken)*

Notes:

1. Verbs which express physical sensation, such as *feel (sich fühlen), hurt, ache, itch,* etc, can be used in the progressive or the simple form without much difference in meaning:

   Is your head still **aching**? / **Does** your head still **ache**?

2. The progressive form of *be* only occurs with an adjective or noun which expresses a temporary characteristic (of a person's behaviour):

   John **is** a silly boy. – John **is being** silly (at the moment). But only: John **is** tall.
   He **is** a nuisance. – You **are being** an awful nuisance. But only: You **are** a good driver.

186–188 Simple Present and Present Progressive

186 Time, Tense and Aspect

Both present tense forms are used when talking about present time.

Present progressive: "Why **are** you **putting on** that jacket?"
"My other one **is being cleaned** at present."

By using the present progressive, one stresses that something is going on at the moment (i.e. at the moment of speaking or during a present period of time) and is limited in duration (progressive aspect, cf **181**). For verbs which allow this aspect (verbs with dynamic meaning) the present progressive is the proper tense form to describe present events.

Simple present: The earth **moves** round the sun.
On a clear night the sky **is lit up** by millions of stars.
I **believe** what I **see**.

One uses the simple present to express the idea that something happens or is the case without restricting this to the present moment or period of time. The simple present can therefore include past and future time, e.g. in statements that are permanently valid. For verbs which do not allow the progressive aspect (verbs with stative meaning) the simple present is the only possible present tense form.

Note:
For the use of the simple present and the present progressive to describe events in the future see **203, 204**.

187 The Use of the Simple Present

Light **travels** at a speed of 299,793 km/s.
Magnets **attract** iron.
Many metals **are corroded** by moist air.

The simple present is used
- to state facts which are seen as permanently valid, e.g. natural laws or typical characteristics.

Sheila **sings** beautifully.
What **does** Mr Durbin **do**? – He **teaches** music.
Sometimes the school orchestra **gives** a concert.
They always **play** "God Save the Queen" at the end.
Margaret never **listens to** classical music.

- to express abilities, what people do for a living, and other repeated actions. In such cases it is often combined with frequency adverbs such as *always, often, sometimes, rarely, never,* etc. (For the use of the present progressive with such adverbs see **188.**)

"Robinson Crusoe" **tells** the story of a sailor who **is shipwrecked** and **cast away** on an island and **stays** there for 28 years.
Prime Minister **Announces** Cabinet Changes

- as the basic tense when outlining the contents of a novel, film, etc., in book reviews, poetry interpretations, headlines, etc.

I **put** three matches into a test-tube. I **fasten** this to one side of the scales and **adjust** the balance by putting a weight on the other side. Now I **apply** heat to the test-tube and **wait** until the matches catch fire ... Now watch what **happens** to the scales ...

- in running commentaries on scientific experiments, sports events, conjuring tricks, etc. In such cases the speaker does not present each action as being in progress, but as a link in a chain of events.

In the evening, after the long day's work, the cowboys sat round the camp fire. Suddenly a horse **neighs** *(wiehert)* and **stamps** its feet. Before they **know** what is happening, they **are surrounded** by a band of silent Indians.

- as a 'dramatic' (or 'historic') present, to give a more vivid picture of past events.

I **hear** that you have got a new job, but I **forget** where.
He **says** he is going to leave the firm next year.
(**But:** He has got a new job. – So **I've heard.**)

- in expressions like *I hear/understand/forget, he says/tells me,* etc., when the information itself is more important than the already completed process of hearing, saying, etc.

Notes:

1. In sentences which start with *here, there* or an adverb of direction *(off, up, down,* etc.), the simple present of the verbs *go* and *come* is used to describe what is happening at the moment of speaking. (For word order see **157, 337.**2):
   Here **comes** the postman. – There **goes** the bell. – Off we **go**.

2. Certain verbs, e.g. *apologize, congratulate, declare, forbid, name, order, promise,* etc. denote an 'acting through words'. In the first person these verbs are used in the simple present and not in the present progressive, since it is by saying, for example, "I apologize" that a speaker actually carries out, or performs, the act in question (performative use):
   I **apologize** for being in such a hurry. – I **promise** to be more careful in future.

188 The Use of the Present Progressive

The present progressive is used

It's spring at last, and the trees **are bursting** into leaf.
The Jarvises **are gardening**: Mr Jarvis **is digging** the vegetable patch while Mrs Jarvis **is sowing** flower seeds.

- to describe processes that are taking place at the moment of speaking. There may be several things going on at the same time.

What do you need all those matches for? – **I'm making** a model windmill (at present).
Bob can't wait to get home. He's **working** on a huge jigsaw puzzle at the moment.

- to describe processes which the speaker knows have begun and are not yet finished, even if they are temporarily interrupted. In such cases, the present progressive is typically combined with adverbials such as *at the moment* or *at present.*

This summer the souvenir shops **are opening** on Sundays.
At the moment shopkeepers **are** not **doing** a very good trade.
This week we**'re offering** special bargains in all departments of our store.
This brand of tea **is selling** well.

You**'re** always **leaving** your things lying about.
I**'m** forever **tripping** over the lego bricks on the floor.
Mrs Winter **is** continually **knitting** things for her grandchildren.
My little sister **is** constantly **taking** her shoes off and **putting** them on again on the wrong feet.

- to describe habits, states or abilities that are limited to the present time and are therefore only of a temporary nature. It is up to the speaker to decide how far to extend the idea of 'present time'. Here, the present progressive is typically combined with adverbials such as *at present, these days, this summer,* etc.
- to express an emotional attitude towards habits or repeated actions. In this case the present progressive is used together with adverbs such as *always, forever, constantly, continually*, i.e. one is deliberately exaggerating in order to express annoyance, surprise or amusement. (In neutral statements and questions about frequency these adverbs are used with the simple form; cf **187**.)

189–190 Simple Past and Past Progressive

189 Time, Tense and Aspect

Simple past: George Bernard Shaw **was** not only a dramatist but also **wrote** numerous articles, essays and political pamphlets.
Past progressive: He **was** still **working** as a drama critic when his first play was performed.

Both of these past tense forms make it clear that something is seen as completely unrelated to present time (compare this with the use of the present perfect: **191, 194**). Verbs with stative meaning are normally only found in the simple past, but verbs with dynamic meaning are also found in the past progressive (cf **182**). The differences between the two forms are as follows:

- The simple past is used to describe past actions, events or states as accomplished facts.
- The past progressive emphasizes that an action or event was in progress at a particular moment in the past. In other words, the action or event had not yet been completed at that moment. The past progressive often describes something that was going on at a time when some new action or event took place. The past progressive supplies the **background**, the **new event** is introduced in the simple past form. (Background: *was working;* new event: *was performed.*)

Past progressive: Some people **were clapping**, some **were booing** and others **were getting** up to go.
Simple past: The curtain **rose** again, the actors **appeared** on stage, **bowed** and **filed off**.

A series of past progressive forms points out that several things were happening at the same time. To describe a number of things happening one after the other (a **chain of events**), the simple past forms are used.

Notes:

1. Past habits are generally expressed in the simple past or by using the auxiliary *used to* + infinitive (cf **239**). However, the past progressive is used to present a habit or action as temporary (cf **181** Note):
   My aunt **earned** her living in the theatre. She **used to act** in musical comedies.
   That particular year she **was playing** in "My Fair Lady".
2. For the modal use of the past tense (to express hypothetical wishes or conditions, etc.) see **212–218**.

190 The Use of Simple Past and Past Progressive in Texts

The past tense is the basic tense for all forms of narrative. Of the two forms, the simple past is the more frequent. The use of the past progressive is not always obligatory – the simple past can often be used instead (cf note below). The interaction between simple past and past progressive has, however, considerable stylistic importance in narrative texts:

- Simple past forms are used to present each new event in the narrative.
- In passages that do not carry the action forward, but merely describe situations or accompanying circumstances, the past progressive is often used (if the verb has dynamic meaning).

The use of the two forms is illustrated in the following example:

	Simple Past	Past Progressive
We **were standing** at the back of the main		background to "the lights **went on**"
hotel building (. . .) when the lights **went on** in	new event	
the kitchen half a dozen paces in front of us.		
Jackson **came** into the kitchen, slowly, alone.	new event	
He **did not know** he **was being watched.**	state (stative meaning)	background to "**came** into the kitchen"
I had never seen him other than polite and on		
guard; but now he **was** both angry and troubled	state (stative meaning)	
(. . .) His face **changed** – he **was looking**	new event	background to "**his face changed**" and "**we pressed** forward"
at something on the floor. We **pressed**	new event	
forward to see, (. . .)		
(From Doris Lessing, *The Golden Notebook*)		

Note:
The use of the past progressive is only obligatory if the simple past would have a different meaning, e.g. after a temporal clause starting with *when*:

When he got home, his wife **was making** some fresh tea.	(She had already started making tea before he got home.)
When he got home, his wife **made** some fresh tea.	(She didn't start making tea until he got home.)

191–193 Simple Present Perfect and Present Perfect Progressive

191 Time Relationships and Aspect

Both present perfect forms stress that an event or state is seen as related to present time, although it took place or began in the past. The present perfect can be related to present time in various ways. The following are some typical examples:

Resultative use: simple present perfect

Traffic out of London **has come** to a standstill. (= The streets are jammed with cars.) **I've been** to Torquay, but **I've** not **been** anywhere else in Devon. (= I know Torquay, but I don't know the rest of Devon.)	The process or action has already been completed, but at what time this happened is not important and is therefore not mentioned in the sentence. Instead, it is the **result** that is stressed. (The result can, for example, take the form of knowledge gained, or experience.) In such a context only the simple form is used, since it is the result and not the course of an action that the speaker is interested in.

Continuative use: simple present perfect and present perfect progressive

I've **been standing** in this queue since twelve o'clock. (= I came here at twelve and I'm still standing here.) *(Ich stehe schon seit 12 Uhr in dieser Schlange.)*	The action, process or state began in the past and extends up to the present time. Here the speaker is interested in **how long it has lasted so far,** and this duration is made clear by the inclusion of a time adverbial (cf Note 1). (In German, you would normally find the present tense to express a continuative meaning.)
The boys **have been singing** at the top of their voices all evening. They'll be hoarse tomorrow. Vivian **has sung** with the amateur musical society for over five years now.	Verbs with dynamic meaning are used in the present perfect progressive if one is referring to something that is still going on, and in the simple present perfect if one is describing a habitual activity.
She **has** always **liked** musical comedies as long as **I've known** her.	Verbs with stative meaning only occur in the simple form (cf **182–184**).

Notes:

1. The following time adverbials are used to indicate how long something has lasted so far:

- *since* + the point in time when something began: since two o'clock/since last year/since I met him, etc.
- *for* + a period of time (from the beginning up to now): for a week/for two months/for ages/for a long time, etc.
- other time adverbials describing 'time up to now': the whole day, all morning, all my life, etc.

2. *Just* is the only 'point-in-time' adverbial that can be combined with the present perfect. It expresses an immediate link with present time.

The box office **has just opened**.

For other time adverbials used with the present perfect see **195**.

3. For the present perfect used in temporal clauses to refer to the future see **208–209**.

192 The Simple Present Perfect with Resultative and Continuative Meaning

As shown in **191**, the simple present perfect can stress either a result or a period of time up to the present moment. These two ideas are not mutually exclusive. In many cases the simple present perfect may stress both a result and a period of time up to now.

Have you **finished** with the newspaper?
This week's colour magazine **hasn't been printed** due to an industrial dispute.
Has anyone **telephoned** about my advertisement *yet?*
How much of the crossword puzzle **have** you **solved** *so far?*
I **haven't seen** such a funny cartoon *for ages.*
There **has been** no great change in editorial policy *since the new editor took over.*
Has there **been** any more news about the train strike *since Saturday?*

1. In questions and negative statements

By using the present perfect a speaker may be asking about a **result** or stressing that a certain expected result has not come about.

At the same time one may also want to know whether something has happened **yet** (i.e. at some unspecified time up to now), or to point out that something has **not yet** happened. The idea of a period of time up to the present can be reinforced by adverbials such as *yet, so far, up to now.* As in the case of purely continuative use, the period of time may be indicated more precisely, e.g. with adverbials introduced by *since.*

I've **rung** *three times*, but nobody answered.
Every time we**'ve tried** to drop in on them, they**'ve** *always* **been** out.
Joan **has** *often* **asked** her friend Kate to stay the night, but she **has** *never* **been allowed** to.
They live next door to us, but **I've** hardly *ever* **spoken** to them.

She **hasn't written** *a single* letter *since she went away.*

2. In sentences with expressions of frequency
The simple present perfect combined with expressions of frequency always stresses both a result and a period of time up to now. It indicates that something has happened **several times so far** or has **not yet** happened at all. Such expressions include numbers, *every* (*day/time/*etc.), and adverbs such as *always, often, never, ever,* etc. (*Ever* only occurs in questions and negative or restrictive sentences; cf **20, 22.**)
Such sentences may also include adverbials or clauses which indicate the period of time in question.

193 The Use of the Present Perfect Progressive

Since the present perfect progressive stresses the duration and incompleteness of an action or event, it is used in contexts like the following:

It **has been raining** *for hours.* I hope it will clear up tomorrow.
Her cold seems to have got worse *since she got so wet yesterday.* She**'s been sneezing** and **coughing** more than usual.

- The action or event is still going on and the speaker assumes that it will continue into the future. It is either clearly stated how long it has been going on so far, or it is clear from the context.

There are puddles in front of the radiator where your coat **has been hanging** to dry.
I've just **been clearing** the snow from the path. A hot cup of tea is what I need now.
I've been admiring the snowy landscape outside. You must come and have a look.

- The action or event has in fact ended, but it has had (unintended) results (any intended results are not important here); or it may be that the speaker is still intensely affected by what has been happening.
There is usually no time adverbial indicating duration in these cases.

194–195 Present Perfect or Past Tense?

194 The Present-Related and the Past-Related Perspectives

Both the present perfect and the past tense can be used to describe a completed action or state. The choice of tense depends on how one views the action or state – in other words, on the speaker's perspective:

My sister **has bought** a moped. Now she can go to school on it.
I **haven't used** my bicycle *all winter* – the tyres are bound to need pumping up.

My sister **bought** a moped *last week.*
I **didn't pump up** my tyres *before we left* because I thought they were still O.K.

By using the present perfect a speaker makes clear that a past event is viewed **in relation to present time.** It is the result of the past event that is important. It is not stated when the event took place, nor is this relevant.
The speaker may at the same time be thinking of a period of time during which the event could have taken place, a period which extends up to the present. This period may then be explicitly mentioned (see *all winter* above).

If a speaker uses the past tense, this indicates that the past event is seen as **completely unrelated to present time.** The speaker focuses instead on the point or period in past time when the event took place. This is often indicated by a time adverbial or temporal clause, or made clear by the context.
(The event may have had results, but this is not what the speaker is interested in here.)

Note:
For the use of the present perfect to describe actions, events or states that continue into the present see **191, 193.**

195 The Choice of Tense and Expressions of Time

The perspective chosen by a speaker is always made clear by the tense chosen, and often, too, by the choice of time adverbial or other expression of time. The tense must always harmonize with the expression of time.

1. Time adverbials which allow only one perspective

Certain time adverbials cannot be used together with the past tense in British English; they are typically combined with the present perfect. (For American usage see the note to section 2 below.) On the other hand there are time adverbials that do not allow the present perfect, but are typical of the past tense. (Other tenses will not be considered here.)

Time adverbials with the present perfect	Time adverbials with the past tense
so far, up to now, up to the present moment *these three days/weeks . . .* (= in the last three days, etc.) *since yesterday/Christmas/May/. . .* Temporal clauses with *since (seit)*; *since when* in questions.	*yesterday, last year/month/. . .* *until recently* *two days/weeks/. . . ago* *the other day* (= a few days ago); *just now* (= just a moment ago) *before/after (last) Christmas; on Monday; in 1979* Temporal clauses with *when, while, before, after, once;* *when* in questions.

Note:
Within a temporal clause introduced by *since*, one can use either the present perfect (for actions, events and states that continue into present time) or the past tense (for those which began and ended in the past). In the main clause only the present perfect is found, never the past tense.

He **has been** a member of our club { since he **has been living** in this town. / since he **came** to this town. }

2. Time adverbials which allow two different perspectives

Certain time (and frequency) adverbials allow both the present perfect and the past tense. The choice of tense will then depend on any other time adverbials or indirect time information present in the context.

just	The taxi **has** ***just*** **arrived.** It's standing outside.	I **was** ***just*** **putting on** my coat *when the taxi arrived.*
already	Don't forget to close all the windows. – **I've** ***already*** **done** so.	*When we called for Tom,* he **was** ***already*** **waiting** at the front door.
yet	**Have** you **said** good-bye to Mary and Peter ***yet?***	The station restaurant **wasn't** open ***yet,*** but luckily we had some sandwiches left.
for + period of time	We are very excited. We **haven't been** abroad ***for four years.*** *(seit vier Jahren)*	*After her trip* she **talked** of nothing else ***for weeks.*** Now she's already planning the next trip.
recently	**Has** Jill **said** anything ***recently/(lately)*** about where she wants to go on holiday? (= in recent weeks)	I **got** some leaflets about Wales from the travel agency ***recently.*** (= the other day).
always	I'm feeling a bit nervous. **I've** ***always*** **been** afraid of flying. *(schon immer)*	*As a child* I ***always*** **got** car-sick. But now it doesn't bother me any more. *(immer)*
ever	**Have** you ***ever*** **travelled** on a jumbo jet? *(schon einmal)*	**Did** you ***ever*** **travel** by Greyhound *while you were in America? (einmal/jemals)*
never	I'd like to go to France in my summer holidays. **I've** ***never*** **been** there. *(noch nie)*	*During our holidays* we ***never*** **got up** before ten o'clock. *(nie)*
today	We **haven't had** many bookings ***today,*** but things usually improve in the late afternoon. (The day is not yet over for us.)	**Did** Mr Smith **ring** ***today*** to confirm his reservation? If not, it's too late. (The day is regarded as over.)
this week/ month/ etc.	**I've done** a lot of overtime ***this week,*** so I'm taking Friday off. (I've been busy up to the present moment.)	**I told** my boss about my holiday plans ***this week.*** (= some past time this week, e.g. on Monday)

Note:
In colloquial American English the past tense is often used in contexts where in British English the present perfect would be required:

Don't forget to close the windows. – I already **did** so.

3. Sentences without time adverbials

Even if there are no time adverbials in a sentence (or in a preceding sentence), the choice between present perfect and past tense is not arbitrary. A sentence may contain other words or phrases which indirectly refer to past time, and therefore call for the use of the past tense.
Compare the following:

Related to the present	Related to the past
We **have put** a man on the moon, but we **haven't been** able to solve our problems on Earth. (= so far) My father **has travelled** a lot. (= He knows a lot of foreign countries.) My suitcase **has been stolen.** (= I haven't got it any more, it's missing.)	Neil Armstrong **was** the ***first*** man on the moon. (= in 1969) My father **travelled** a lot ***as a young man.*** (= when he was a young man.) My suitcase **was stolen *on the train.*** (= when I was on the train.)

196–197 Simple Past Perfect and Past Perfect Progressive

196 Tense, Time and Aspect

Simple past perfect: When I returned I saw at once that the house **had been broken into.**
The man who was caught climbing over the wall **had been known** to the police for a long time.
Past perfect progressive: Cathy was now sure that the woman who **had been following** her the whole time was a detective.

The two past perfect forms only occur within the framework of the past tense group. They indicate that:

- an event or state came **before** some other event or state in past time (sentence 1). The simple form will be used here.
- an event or state had begun **before** a point in past time and continued up to this point (sentences 2 and 3). Verbs with stative meaning can only be used in the simple form. Verbs with dynamic meaning are used in the progressive form whenever the course and duration of an event are to be stressed.

Notes:
1. The past perfect expresses 'time before' in relation to an event or state in the past tense. 'Time before' a present perfect is expressed by a past tense:

I've **had** this car for two years. Before that I **had** a motorbike.

2. For the modal use of the past perfect (I wish I **had** never **seen** him) see **212, 214.**

197 The Use of Past Perfect and Past Tense

1. The past perfect in narrative: retrospection

At the bend of the road I *looked* back again (. . .); then I *turned* the corner, *passed* the village school, and *closed* that part of my life for ever.
It *was* a bright Sunday morning in early June, the right time to be leaving home. My three sisters and a brother **had** already **gone** before me, two other brothers **had** not yet **made up** their minds. They *were* still *sleeping* that morning but my mother **had got up** early and **cooked** me a heavy breakfast.

(. . .) They *were* from Hamburg, they *said*, and **had been** in Spain two years, **had circled** it twice and *were planning* to circle it again. They *called* themselves students, and *said* there *was* a large number in the country, playing instruments and living rough – partly for fun, and partly to get out of Germany: I *was* the first 'student' they**'d met** from England.
(Both passages from Laurie Lee, *As I Walked Out One Midsummer Morning*)

The past perfect can be used together with the past tense (as basic tense) in all forms of narrative (cf **179–180**).
If events are narrated in chronological order, the verbs will all be in the past tense (here: *looked, turned, passed, closed*).
In retrospective passages, where the narrator looks back to a previous time, this 'time before' will normally be expressed with past perfect forms. This is particularly important when there is a series of main clauses.

The past perfect has this same function in reported speech (as in this example) and in inner monologue (cf **321**).
(For further details on reported speech see **322–324**.)

2. Past perfect and past tense in temporal clauses

Before the lights went out, there **was** a tremendous thunderclap.
The barn caught fire after lightning **struck** it.
As soon as the rain **stopped**, the flood started to subside.

Before anyone could stop him, he **had jumped** out of the window.
As soon as she **had got rid of** her unwelcome visitor, she locked the door.

Conjunctions like *before, after, as soon as* themselves express a 'time before' relationship between a main clause and a subordinate clause, and the past perfect is generally not needed to make the relationship clear. In such cases the past tense is commonly used in both the main and the subordinate clause.
However, if there is special reason to stress that one event preceded another, e.g. if the result of the earlier event is important, then the past perfect will be used.

Note:
In a *when*-clause the past perfect only occurs if there is special reason to stress the idea of 'time before' an event in the main clause:

When the bride **arrived**, the organ started playing.
When the ring **had been found** at last, they went on with the wedding ceremony.

The event which happened first may instead be mentioned in the main clause, in which case the main clause verb must be in the past perfect:

When the bride arrived, the organ **had** already **started** playing.

198 Ways of Expressing Future Events

English has many more ways of expressing future events than German. There are often several ways of expressing the same idea. The form chosen depends on the speaker's intention or attitude.

Form (cf the table in **178**)	Speech intentions and use: Events under the control of the agent (usually the subject of the sentence)	Speech intentions and use: Events dependent on external circumstances
Will-future	I've run out of stamps. – I'**ll get** some for you, shall I?	It **will be** Christmas in a week. You **will like** the book I've bought you.
	Readiness, spontaneous decision	Prediction, supposition
Going to-future	Are you **going to have** a party on Boxing Day?	It's **going to snow** soon by the looks of it.
	Intention	Conclusion based on evidence
Present progressive	We'**re having** a goose for our Christmas dinner this year.	
	Personal plan or arrangement already fixed	
Simple present		What time **does** the church service **start** on Christmas Day?
		Official schedule, timetable
Future progressive	**Will** Mr Jones **be dressing up** as Santa Claus again and **handing out** presents?	
	Event expected as a matter of course (The question of what the event depends on is left open.)	

Note:
There are other ways of referring to future events, e.g.:

a) with verbal complexes like: — to refer to events seen as:

be about to + infinitive	imminent	The sun **is about to rise.**
be on the point of + gerund	imminent	The clock **is on the point of striking** six.
be bound to + infinitive	inevitable	The alarm **is bound to go off** and **wake** you.
be sure / certain to + infinitive	certain	You **are certain to hear** the church bells.
be (un)likely to + infinitive	probable / improbable	He'**s unlikely to oversleep.**

b) by using certain verbs or verbal complexes which express wishes or intentions, e.g.:

want, hope, expect, intend	+ *to* + infinitive	We **hope to go** skiing this year.
be expected, be supposed	+ *to* + infinitive	There'**s expected to be** frost tonight.

c) by using modal auxiliaries or some of their substitutes (cf **220**). — John **should / must / has to get** new skates.

199–200 The *Will*-Future

199 The *Will*-Future Expressing Prediction or Supposition

The State Opening of Parliament **will take** place on the 7th November.
Mounted police **will line** the route which the Queen **will take.**
Thousands of people **will cheer** when the procession goes past.
If everything goes according to plan, she'**ll pass** the gates at a quarter past two.
I'm sure we'**ll have** a good view from that street corner.
Some people **will** probably **camp out** all night.
The street entertainers **will** certainly **be** out in great numbers.

I hope (that) you'**ll enjoy** yourself.
I'm afraid (that) we'**ll have to** go now.

The *will*-future is used in predictions of future events or states, when they depend on external circumstances or certain conditions. (These circumstances or conditions are often expressed in temporal or conditional clauses. For tense in subordinate clauses see **208–209, 216.**)

Such predictions are based on the speaker's knowledge or experience. They can reflect varying degrees of confidence, from pure guesswork to absolute certainty. This can be made clear by the addition of *I suppose/expect/am sure/know; probably, certainly,* etc.)

The *will*-future is normally also used to refer to future events in *that*-clauses following verbs and verbal complexes denoting hopes or fears.

200 The *Will*-Future Expressing a Spontaneous Decision

Just a moment. I'**ll write** that down before I forget.
We'**ll let** you know as soon as we've fixed the date.
There goes the telephone. I'**ll answer** it, shall I?
John **will look up** the number for you in the telephone book.

The *will*-future can also be used to express a decision made at the moment of speaking, or the speaker's readiness to do something (usually in the first person). Here, *will* is commonly used in its short form *'ll.* (However, if one has already made up one's mind before speaking, the *going to*-future will be used; cf 201.)

Note:
In many cases there is no clear-cut distinction between the pure future and the modal use of the auxiliary *will* (cf **235–238**), particularly in the first person:

I **won't tell** anybody what you've just told me. (Either intention or prediction)

201–202 The *Going to*-Future

201 The *Going to*-Future Expressing Intention

We'**re going to clear out** the attic tomorrow and **get** rid of all those broken toys up there.
The Boy Scouts **are going to come** and collect unwanted books for their Bring-and-Buy sale next week.

The *going to* future expresses an intention that already exists at the moment of speaking (in contrast to *will,* which expresses a spontaneous decision, cf 200).

I'm not going to let you use the garage as a rubbish dump any longer.
I **was going to get** rid of my stamp collection, but I've changed my mind. (= I was intending to . . .)

In the first person it often expresses strong determination, expecially in the negative (cf *won't*, **236**).
If one no longer wishes to carry out one's former intentions, or is unable to do so, the *going to* form is used in the past tense.

202 The *Going to*-Future Expressing a Logical Conclusion

Look at those waves! It's **going to be** a very rough crossing, I'm afraid.
I fear Alan's **going to be** sick. His face is already turning green.
No one's **going to feel** like eating with the boat pitching up and down like this.

The *going to*-future indicates that available evidence has led the speaker to conclude that something is sure to happen. (However, predictions based on general knowledge or experience will be expressed with a *will*-future, cf **199**.)

Notes:
1. Since conditional *if*-clauses only express conditions, and not actual signs or evidence, the *will*-future – and not the *going to*-future – is normally used in the accompanying main clause:
   She'll **feel** better if she takes a tablet.

The *going to*-future can, however, be used to express a warning about the consequences of a person's behaviour:
   If you eat any more of those chocolates, you**'re going to be** sick/you'**ll be** sick.

2. The verb *go* can also be used with a *going to*-future. (However, this is avoided wherever possible, for stylistic reasons.)
   I'**m going to go** and lie down now.

203 The Present Progressive to Refer to Future Events

Have you heard? The Smiths **are leaving** the district next month and **are renting** a house in Scotland.
When **are** Dr Brown and Dr Mason **moving** into their new surgery?
The Taylors **are having** a housewarming party tonight. **Are** you **going**?

The flat **is being** completely **renovated** next month for the new tenants.
When **are** you **coming** to visit us again?

With activity and process verbs (especially verbs which express a transition to a different state, e.g. *come, go, leave,* etc), the present progressive can be used with future meaning to describe a plan or arrangement, normally one that has been made by the person named as subject of the sentence.
(In contrast to this, the *going to*-future is used when no definite arrangements or preparations have yet been made, cf **201**.)
To make clear that one is not referring to present time, the sentence normally includes an adverbial of future time, unless the time reference is clear from the context.

Note:
The present progressive can be used to describe planned or arranged future events even when the subject of the sentence is inanimate. In such cases, the active role played by a human agent is understood. Here, too, the future time reference must be made clear, e.g. with an adverbial:
   The sirens **are being tested** tomorrow.
   Fire drill **is taking place** on Tuesdays in future.

204 The Simple Present to Refer to Future Events

Easter Sunday **is** on March 29th this year.
School holidays **begin** on Thursday next week and **end** on September 7th.

Excursion to Blackpool on July 10th:
The coach **leaves** at 9 a.m. sharp and **arrives** in Blackpool at 11 a.m. approximately.
There **is** one stop on the way for refreshments.
Lunch **is** at 1 p.m. at the Bull Hotel, and the afternoon **is** at your own disposal.
The theatre performance **starts** at 8 p.m. and **ends** at 10.30 p.m., after which the coach **departs** promptly for home.

The simple present can be used with future meaning. But unlike the present tense in German, it is only used to describe future events or states which have been decided on or planned, usually by some outside authority. This form is, for instance, commonly found in references to the calendar, in programmes of events, business schedules, travel arrangements and timetables (and is therefore often called the 'timetable future').
In this case, too, the reference to future time must be clear from the context.

Notes:
1. In references to the calendar, the *will*-future is also possible (cf **199**):
   Easter Sunday **will be** on March 29th this year.
2. For the use of the simple present with future reference in temporal clauses see **208–209**, in *if*-clauses see **216**.

205–206 The Future Progressive

Only verbs with dynamic meaning occur in the future progressive. This form has two different uses.

205 The Future Progressive to Express the Progressive Aspect

This time next week we'**ll be lying** on the beach in Acapulco.
Who **will be keeping** an eye on your house when you're away?
When you get this card, I **shall** already **be heading** for home again.

The future progressive can be used to express the idea that an event (of temporary duration) will be in progress at a certain point in future time (cf **181**).
This point in time is usually stated explicitly, e.g. by a *when*-clause.

206 The Future Progressive for Neutral Predictions

The shops **will be closing** in half an hour.
John **will be meeting** us outside Selfridge's at 4 o'clock.
The sales **will be starting** after Christmas.
No matter how I try to plan things, I know I'**ll be buying** a lot of presents at the last minute as usual.

The future progressive can also be used to refer to future events which the speaker expects to take place as a matter of course. Unlike the *will*-future (**200**), the *going to*-future (**201**) and the present progressive (**203**), the future progressive tells us nothing about the attitude or role of the agent.

Will you **be seeing** Carol again when you go to Bristol next week?
Will you **be paying** in cash, madam, or by cheque?
Will anyone **be passing** the paper shop this afternoon?

This is why the future progressive is often used when making tactful inquiries about other people's intentions. Since this form focuses attention on a future course of events, and not on plans or intentions, a speaker can avoid giving the impression of curiosity or interference.

207 The Future Perfect

The future perfect expresses the idea of 'time before' in relation to a certain point in future time (cf **179**). The time relationship is often made clear by the use of time adverbials or temporal clauses with *by* or *by the time.*

By tomorrow evening we **shall have gathered** enough wood for our Guy Fawkes bonfire.
By midnight the fire **will have gone out** and everyone **will have gone** home.
In the year 2000 Guy Fawkes' Day **will have been celebrated** for nearly 400 years.

Dad **will have been lighting** fireworks for two hours on end by the time he's finished.

The simple future perfect usually expresses the idea that an event will have been completed by a certain time in the future (mainly resultative use).

It can also express that, by a certain point in future time, a state or event will have lasted or will have been going on for some time (continuative use).
In the case of verbs with dynamic meaning, the future perfect progressive is used to stress the idea of uninterrupted duration. (Cf the corresponding use of the present perfect and past perfect forms, **191**, **196**.)

208–209 Simple Present and Present Perfect in Subordinate Clauses Referring to the Future

208 Future Reference in Complex Sentences

The time relationship between two future actions or events is often expressed in a complex sentence consisting of a main clause and a subordinate temporal clause:

(1) When I **take** Peter to the station tonight, **I'll get** an evening paper.
(Compare: **I'll take** Peter to the station later on.)
(2) **I'll give** you the magazine as soon as **I've finished** with it.
(Compare: **I'll have finished** with the magazine in an hour or so.)

Since future time reference is expressed in the main clause, the subordinate clause contains
- the simple present, not the *will*-future (nor any other of the forms expressing future events) (sentence 1)
- the present perfect, not the future perfect (sentence 2).

Notes:
1. The simple present and not the *will*-future is used in other types of subordinate clause too, if the future time reference is clear from the main clause; e.g. in *that*-clauses and defining relative clauses:
Don't ring her before 3 o'clock. She'll just tell you that she **is** busy.
Let's phone from the first telephone box that we **see**.

2. For the use of tenses in conditional sentences see **216–218**.

209 The Choice of Present Perfect or Simple Present in Subordinate Clauses

You won't go before you**'ve looked** at our holiday snaps, will you?
When Roger **has fixed** the film projector up, we'll turn the lights out.
As soon as we **get** home, we'll get these pictures developed.
Sorting out these slides will keep me busy until the spring **comes.**
By the time he **finishes** in the dark room, it will be nearly midnight.

In subordinate clauses the present perfect is used to give emphasis to the idea of 'time before' in relation to a future action or event in the main clause (e.g. when the result of an action is important).
In other cases the simple present is used in subordinate clauses, since the time relationship between a main and a subordinate clause is already expressed in conjunctions like *as soon as, before, until, by the time.* (See also **197.2**. For complex sentences with *when*-clauses see the note to **197.2**.)

210–211 Future-in-the-Past and Future-Perfect-in-the-Past

210 Time Relationships within the Past Tense Group

The future-in-the-past and future-perfect-in-the-past express the same time relationships within the past tense group as the *will*-future and future perfect do within the present tense group (cf **179**).

(1) We **had** plenty of time.
(2) Our friends **wouldn't arrive** until eight.
(3) By then we **would** easily **have got** everything ready.
(Compare: We **have** plenty of time. Our friends **won't arrive** until eight. By then we'll easily **have got** everything ready.)

(1) Past tense:	the time when an action or event took place (basic tense)
(2) Future-in-the-past:	anticipation of a later time, a 'future as seen from the past'
(3) Future-perfect-in-the-past:	'time before' in relation to this anticipated 'future'

Note:
These two tense forms can also be called the conditional and the conditional perfect respectively, because of their modal use in main clauses which are superordinate to hypothetical conditional clauses (cf **217**):

If I were you, I **would not pat** strange dogs.
You **would** never **have been bitten** by that spaniel if you hadn't tried to run away.

211 Use

Trees, nothing but trees. He had no idea which way to go. He thought he **would try** going to the left this time. Darkness **would be falling** soon and he **would have been wandering about** lost for four hours.
He had not told anybody where he was going, so his absence **would** not **have been noticed** yet and no one **would be worrying** about him.

Since the future-in-the-past and future-perfect-in-the-past belong to the past tense group, they are mainly used in narrative, especially in reported speech and inner monologue (cf **321**, **322**).
The differences in aspect between the simple and the progressive form are the same as with the other tenses (see particularly **181**, **205**, **207**).

212 Ways of Expressing Modality (Summary)

In addition to the indicative, which is the mood for expressing 'reality' (i.e. for making statements or asking questions with factual content), the English finite verb has two moods for expressing 'modality' (i.e. non-factual content):

- the imperative for expressing commands or instructions;
- some remaining forms of the subjunctive for expressing things that are only imagined, desired or possible.

In most cases, however, modality is expressed by other means, e.g. by modal use of the past tense or the past perfect (as substitutes for subjunctive forms which no longer exist), by the conditional or by modal auxiliaries.

	Special forms of the verb to express modality	
Indicative	**Imperative**	**Subjunctive**
This **is** my opinion.	**Be** careful.	**Be** it right or wrong, it's our decision. **(Present subjunctive)**
James **was** right.		I wish she **weren't** so obstinate. **(Past subjunctive)**
What **comes** first?	**Come** over here.	I won't change my mind, **come** what may. **(Present subjunctive)**
	Other ways of expressing modality	
He **went** home yesterday.	**Modal past:**	It would be better, if he **went** now.
He **had gone** home the day before.	**Modal past perfect:**	If only you **had gone** sooner.
	Conditional:	I **would go** there, if I could.
	Conditional perfect:	I **would have gone** earlier, if I had been able to.
	Modal auxiliary + (perfect) infinitive:	We **could go** there some time. He **should have gone** two hours ago.

Note:
Certain verbs and adverbs have in themselves modal meaning, so that often no further indication of modality is necessary:

I **wish to see** her soon.	(main verb + infinitive)
I **hope** he **has arrived** by now.	(main verb + subordinate clause with an indicative form)
He **has probably arrived** by now.	(adverbial + indicative form)

213 The Present Subjunctive

1. Forms

. . . (that) I **come**/you **come**/he **come**/ . . .
. . . (that) he/she/it **have**/**run**/**do**/ . . .
. . . (that) I **be**/you **be**/he **be**/ . . .

The present subjunctive has always the same form as the infinitive (regardless of person and number). It therefore only differs from the present indicative in the third person singular, except for the verb *be*, where the form is always *be*.

2. Use of the present subjunctive and its paraphrase through modal auxiliaries

The present subjunctive occurs in the following types of clause:

a) in ***that*-clauses** after verbs and verbal complexes expressing a demand or a decision.

"We therefore *recommend* that the passenger **contact** the nearest airline office at least 72 hours prior to flight." (From an airline ticket)
The authorities *have decided* that a new runway **should be built.**
"Mr Begin *had requested* that I **autograph** the photos for his grandchildren (. . .) Susan *suggested* that she **go** and **get** the names of the grandchildren." (From Jimmy Carter, *Keeping Faith*)
"Heart specialists at Papworth Hospital, Cambridgeshire, *have urged* that the heart transplant programme there **be halted.**"
(From *The Observer*, August 29, 1982)

In British English the present subjunctive occurs mainly in a formal, official style of writing. The stylistically more neutral variant is *should* + infinitive (cf **234.**1).

In American English the present subjunctive is used more frequently and is not particularly formal.

However, this form is becoming more common in British English, e.g. in newspaper articles, news broadcasts, etc.

b) **in certain types of adverbial clause** (cf **317**).

In such cases, the use of the present subjunctive is generally characteristic of a more formal style, particularly in British English. The verb *be* is more commonly used in this form than other verbs.

We shall continue our endeavours, though the price **be/may be/is** high.
We welcome all contributions, whether they **be/are** large or small.

We desperately need money so that each of the children in our care **(can/will/may) be given** a start in life.
A bazaar was held in order that everyone **(could/would/should/might) have** a chance of contributing to the relief of hunger in the Third World.

The profits, if there **be / should be / are** any, go to charity.
Living conditions will be improved in this area unless there **be/should be/is** another serious drought.

- In **clauses of concession** either the present subjunctive, *may / might* + infintive or the indicative can be used, though there is a slight difference in meaning.
- In **clauses of purpose** there are the following alternatives:
  present subjunctive
  can / will / shall / may or *could / would / should / might* } + infinitive
- In **conditional clauses** expressing realistic conditions *should* + infinitive or the indicative are used more frequently than the present subjunctive (cf **216**, **210**).

Note:
In addition to being used in the above types of clauses, the present subjunctive also occurs in a number of set expressions:
a) in main clauses expressing wishes or curses (also: *may* + infinitive):
God **save** the Queen. – God **bless** you. – **Damn** you! – **May** you both **be** happy.
b) in clauses of concession which are not introduced with a conjunction:
We are going to leave tomorrow as planned, **come** what **may**. (. . . whatever happens.)
Be that as it may, there is nothing we can do about it now. (Even if this is so, . . .)
Like it or not, he will have to accept our decision. (Whether he likes it or not, . . .)

214 The *Were*-Subjunctive and the Modal Use of Past Tense and Past Perfect

1. Forms

Past subjunctive: (if) I/he/she/it **were** there/working/polite/...	In modern English only the verb *be* has a special past subjunctive form, and this only in the first and third person singular.
Modal past: (if) I/he/she/it **was** there/... (colloquial)	Colloquially, the past indicative form *was* is more usual.
(if) you/we/they **were** there/... (if) I/you/he/... **came/went/stopped/...**	In all other cases, the normal past tense forms are used to express modal (subjunctive) meanings.
Modal past perfect: (if) I/you/he/... **had come/gone/stopped/...**	The same applies for the past perfect forms of all verbs.

2. Use and time relationships

The *were*-subjunctive and the modal past tense and past perfect are used in a very similar way to the German imperfect subjunctive *(wäre, täte)* and pluperfect subjunctive *(wäre gewesen, hätte getan).* They occur

a) in hypothetical conditional clauses

If the youth club **were** nearer, I would go there more often. I couldn't have come if I **hadn't been given** a lift.	This is their most common use (cf **217**).

b) in adverbial clauses expressing a hypothetical comparison (after *as if, as though)*

He looks as if he **were** bored. Margaret sounded as though she really **meant** what she said.	The *were*-subjunctive and the modal past both refer to the same time as the tense used in the main clause.
She stared at me as though she **had** never **seen** me before.	The modal past perfect refers to 'time before'.

c) in clauses expressing a hypothetical wish (after *if only, I wish, I'd rather* and *it's time*)

If only he **didn't** always **talk** such nonsense. I wish I **knew** Mike and Alice better. It's high time we **went** home.	The *were*-subjunctive and the modal past after *if only* and *I wish* here express regret that something is not (at present) as the person in question would like it to be; after *it's time* these forms express a wish concerning a future action.
I'd rather Jenny **were** a bit more tactful. I'd rather you **told** me who you are going out with tonight.	After *I'd rather,* these forms may have either of these meanings.
I wish I **had been** friendlier to your cousin. If only I **hadn't opened** my big mouth. I'd rather you **hadn't told** me about their quarrel.	The modal past perfect (not possible after *it's time*) expresses regret about a previous situation or action.

Note:
If *I wish* and *if only* are used to express wishes regarding future actions, then they are followed by *would* + infinitive. The modal past cannot be used here:

I wish/If only she **would tell** me what is bothering her.

215 Conditional Sentences: Types of Condition in Conditional Clauses

Conditional sentences consist of a **main clause** and a **conditional subordinate clause.** The subordinate clause expresses a condition, and the main clause describes what follows from this condition, i.e. a consequence. There are two types of condition:

If the plane arrives on time, we shall just catch our train. **If the plane has arrived on time,** Pat will already be waiting for us.	1. **Realistic conditions,** that is, conditions which the speaker thinks either **can be fulfilled** or **have already been fulfilled.**
I should be very surprised **if the plane arrived on time.** **If I were a bird,** I'd fly to Africa in winter. **If the plane had arrived on time,** he would not have missed his connection.	2. **Hypothetical conditions,** i.e. conditions which ● in the view of the speaker **can only theoretically be fulfilled or cannot be fulfilled at all** (imagined conditions); ● the speaker considers (or knows) **not to have been fulfilled.**

The type of condition determines which tenses can be used in a conditional sentence.

Notes:

1. For the sequence of the clauses, the conjunctions which introduce conditional clauses and the use of commas in conditional sentences see **316, 317.4**.

2. Conditions may also be expressed with other types of clause or sentence, e.g. a sentence containing an imperative, or sometimes a relative clause:

Don't leave the door open or the cat will run out.	(If you leave the door open, the cat will run out.)
Anybody who heard them quarrel might have thought that they hated each other.	(If anybody had heard them quarrel, they might have thought . . .)

216–218 Combinations of Tenses in Conditional Sentences

Various combinations of tenses occur in conditional sentences, depending on the type of condition and the type of consequence which follows from it. In many cases there is a fixed sequence of tenses.

216 Realistic Conditions

1. Conditions which can be fulfilled:

Conditional clause	Main clause
Unless it **is raining** tomorrow,	we**'ll have** a barbecue in the garden.
If we **run out** of steaks,	we **might put** on some sausages as well.
If you **can spare** the time,	please **come** to our garden party tomorrow.
If you **put** some thyme on pork chops,	they **taste** delicious.
Present tense of main verbs or *can/must* + infinitive	*Will*-future (the commonest main clause form), modal auxiliary + infinitive, imperative, present tense

2. Conditions which have already been fulfilled:

Conditional clause	Main clause
If Jane **was knocked down** last week, If he only **had** the operation yesterday, If Kevin **has broken** his leg, If he **is** still in hospital, If Paul **has sprained** his ankle again,	she **can't have played** in the tennis match today. **don't expect** him to be feeling very lively yet. he **will be** in plaster for a long time. a visit **would cheer** him up. then it **was** definitely his own fault.
Past tense (but not the *were*-subjunctive), present perfect or present tense	Normally: modal auxiliary + infinitive, imperative or *will*-future; less common: other tenses

Note:
In conditional clauses *will* cannot be used to express a prediction *(will*-future). The modal auxiliary *will* can, however, be used to express the idea of willingness or insistence (cf **235, 236**):

We can set out before noon if you **will help** me load up the car. (= if you are willing to help me . . .)
If you ***will*** **carry** so much at once, you're bound to drop something. (= if you insist on carrying . . .)

217 Hypothetical Conditions

1. Conditions which cannot (or can only theoretically) be fulfilled:

Conditional clause	Main clause
If time travel **were** possible, If a man **killed** his grandmother, If the speed of light **could be exceeded,**	we **could go** back and change history. he **would destroy** his own existence. time travel **might me** possible after all.
Were-subjunctive, modal past or *could* + infinitive	Conditional or *could/might* + infinitive

Notes:
1. It is not possible to use the conditional form of the verb in the conditional clause. However, the form *would* + infinitive may be used to express willingness or a polite request:

It would be very nice if she **would lay** the table. (= if she were willing to . . .)
I should be very grateful if you **would help** me arrange these books. (=if you were kind enough to . . .)

2. With conditions which cannot (or can only theoretically) be fulfilled, the consequences expressed in the main clause usually relate to future or present time (see the above examples). But the speaker may wish to express consequences in past time, in which case the main clause will contain a conditional perfect or *could/might* + perfect infinitive:

If I **had** more money, I **would/might/could have bought** you that camera.

2. Conditions which have not been (and can no longer be) fulfilled:

Conditional clause	Main clause
If Angela **had left** in time, If I **had known** before, If Mark **hadn't had** his friend with him,	she **wouldn't have been** late for the theatre. I **could have got** you a cheap ticket. it **might have been** a very dull evening.
Modal past perfect	Conditional perfect or *could/might* + perfect infinitive

Note:
With conditions which have not been fulfilled, the consequences usually lie in past time as in the above examples. They may, however, lie in present or future time. In this case the main clause will contain a (simple) conditional or *could/might* + (simple) infinitve, and not the perfect forms:

If we **hadn't got caught** in that traffic jam, we **would/could/might be** home by now.

218 *Should* + Infinitive to Express Realistic and Hypothetical Conditions

Conditional clauses with *should* may express both realistic and hypothetical conditions. Note, however, that the use of *should* + infinitive presents a condition as somewhat **less likely** to be fulfilled than would be the case with other realistic conditional clauses, and as **less unlikely** than with other hypothetical conditional clauses. The main clause can contain various verb forms, depending on the type of condition expressed. The main combinations are:

Conditional clause	Main clause
In case there **should be** any difficulty,	just **sound** the alarm.
If anyone **should be behaving** suspiciously,	the store detective **will keep** an eye on him.
If all else **should fail,**	you **must threaten** to inform the police.
If a shop assistant **should have** any doubts,	she **might ask** to look in your bag.
If you **should be questioned,**	what **would** you **say**?
Should + infinitive	Imperative, *will*-future, modal auxiliary + infinitive, conditional

Notes:
1. Sometimes the present subjunctive can be used instead of *should* + infinitive to express realistic conditions (formal style; of **213**.1 b):

Unless it **be proved** that he is guilty, the accused may not be referred to as a criminal.

2. To express a hypothetical condition, *were to* can be used instead of *should:*

If I **were to be arrested,** I would immediately contact my lawyer.

Chapter 7: The Auxiliaries

219–222 Modal Auxiliaries: Forms, Syntactic Features, Speech Intentions (Summary)

219 Table of Forms

Affirmative forms				Negative forms		
Full forms	stressed	unstressed	Short forms	Full forms	Short forms	
can	[kæn]	[k(ə)n]	–	cannot	can't	[ɑː]
could	[kʊd]	[k(ə)d]	–	could not	couldn't	
may			–	may not	(mayn't) (rare)	
might			–	might not	mightn't	
will	[wɪl]	[w(ə)l]/[(ə)l]	'll [l]	will not	won't	[əʊ]
would	[wʊd]	[w(ə)d]/[(ə)d]	'd [d]	would not	wouldn't	
shall	[ʃæl]	[ʃ(ə)l]	('ll [l])	shall not	shan't	[ɑː]
should	[ʃʊd]	[ʃ(ə)d]	('d [d])	should not	shouldn't	
dare			–	dare not	daren't	
dared			–	dared not	–	
must	[mʌst]	[m(ə)s(t)]	–	must not	mustn't	[mʌsnt]
need			–	need not	needn't	
ought to			–	ought not to	oughtn't to	
used to			–	used not to	usedn't to	[juːsntə]

The use of full and short forms:
In colloquial speech, the short forms are preferred where they exist. The corresponding full forms are typical of formal style, e.g. in official speeches, documents, scholarly papers and business letters.
The affirmative short forms *('ll, 'd)*, however, cannot be used at the beginning of a sentence (in *yes/no* questions) or when they need to be stressed:

Will the train arrive on time? – I'm sure it **will**.

Pronunciation:
The **affirmative forms** (including the full forms) are normally **unstressed** because auxiliary verbs only supplement the main verb. Short vowels are usually weakened to [ə] or omitted (weak forms):

He **can** [kən]/[kn] leave now.

The auxiliaries are only stressed when there is special **emphasis** on them, e.g. in short answers (cf **29**, also **335**). Even the short vowels are then given their full value (strong forms):

Can he play the piano? – Yes, he **can** [kæn].

The **negative forms** (including their short forms) are always stressed and so never have weak vowels.

Note:
The short form *'d* stands not only for *would* and *should*, but also for *had*.
Compare: **I'd leave** now if I were you. = I **would/should leave** now if I were you.
I'd left when they arrived. = I **had** (already) **left** when they arrived.

220 Modal Auxiliaries and Time Relationships

In contrast to *have, be* and *do,* the modal auxiliaries are also called 'defective auxiliaries'. They have no infinitive and participle form, so not all tenses can be formed: only simple present and simple past tense forms exist.

1. Present tense forms

May Tina borrow the old Ford tonight?
– Certainly, if she **can** drive it.
My parents are very strict. I **daren't** ask them for the car.
I **needn't** fill up – the tank is still half full. But I **must** check the oil.
John **will** soon be old enough to take his driving test.
I **shall** buy a second-hand car as soon as I can afford it.

Can, may, will, shall, dare (not), must and *need (not)* are all present tense forms. They have no *-s* in the 3rd person singular.
These present tense forms can refer not only to present time but quite often to the future as well, especially when they are accompanied by the appropriate adverbials of time.
(For the *will*-future see **199–200.**)

2. Past tense forms

Could, might, should, would, ought to, dared (not) and *used to* are past tense forms. But not all of them actually refer to past time.

We **used** to go swimming a lot when we lived by the sea.
I never **dared** dive from the highboard when I was at school.

- Only *used to* and *dared (not)* always refer to the past.

Emily always loved horses and **could** ride at a very early age, but she **couldn't** persuade her father to buy her a pony.
The horse **wouldn't** jump the last fence despite his rider's efforts. (= refused to jump)
The horses **would** always be rewarded with a lump of sugar when they had done well.
(= used to be rewarded)

- *Could* and *would* only refer to the past when used with the following meanings:
  could (not): ability, inability, failure (cf **223, 224**).
  would (not): determination, habit (cf **236, 237**).

Could / Would you please help me to move these pot plants? *(Könntest / Würdest du . . .?)*
I think we **ought to / should** bring in the geraniums. There **might** be frost tonight. *(. . . wir sollten . . . Es könnte . . . Frost geben.)*

- *Could* and *would* in other meanings, and *might, should, ought to* are used in the same way as German subjunctive forms (*könnte, dürfte,* etc.), i.e. they express uncertainty, reservation or politeness.

My aunt asked me if I **could / would** help her to move the pot plants.
Dad suggested that we **ought to / should** bring in the geraniums. He was afraid there **might** be frost that night.

- In reported speech and in inner monologue, however, all these past tense forms can be used to refer to the past. (Cf **322**; for *must* and *need* see **324.**)

3. Substitutes

Mike's very practical – he **can** do all sorts of repairs around the house. But he **hasn't been able to** stop the tap from dripping yet.

You **may** go into the kitchen if the paint is dry. Frank **is allowed to** decorate his own room – why can't I?

For the missing tense forms, for the infinitive and participles of a modal auxiliary one has to use substitute expressions of similar meaning.

These substitutes can also be used as alternatives to the existing present (and past) tense forms of the modal auxiliaries, but there are certain differences in meaning (cf **227.**2, **229.**2, **232.**2).

221 Syntactic Features of the Modal Auxiliaries

1. Modal auxiliaries and the infinitive of the main verb

Sandra **can speak** French very well. *(... kann sehr gut Französisch.)*
My Italian has got very rusty. I really **must go** to Italy again next year. (*Ich muß ... nach Italien.*)
Professor Brien **must have had** a real gift for languages, otherwise he **could not have learnt** Chinese in such a short time.
I **should have brushed up** my Spanish before leaving for Mexico.

Modal auxiliaries can only be followed by an infinitive. They cannot be followed by a noun phrase or an adverbial of direction, as they can in German. The infinitive is used without *to* after the modal auxiliaries except in the case of *ought to* and *used to.*
All modal auxiliaries, except *used to* and *dare(d),* can be followed by the perfect infinitive when the speaker is referring to an event in the past.

The train is slowing down, so we **must be approaching** London now.
Dennis or his wife **may be waiting** for us on the platform.

The progressive infinitive is used when the speaker is referring to an action which is still taking place, but which will only last for a limited time.

2. The formation of questions and negatives

Can you lend me some money? – Yes, I **can.** I **can't** let you have much, though.
£2 **should** be enough, **shouldn't** it?
What do you mean, you have run out of money? You ***must*** have some left.

Questions and negatives of the modal auxiliaries are formed without the aid of the auxiliary *do.* Neither is *do* used in short answers, *yes/no* questions, question tags (cf **27**), or for emphasis (cf **335**).

Note:
For questions and negatives of *need* and *dare* (which can both be used either as auxiliaries or as main verbs) see **241–242.**
For questions and negatives of *used to* see **240.**

222 Modal Auxiliaries and Speech Intentions

Because ot their meanings, the modal auxiliaries are especially useful in expressing speech intentions of various sorts. They can be used

1. to influence a person's behaviour

Typical speech intentions of this kind are:

asking for s.th.	will / would	(cf **235**)	**Will / Would** you show us the broken lock, please?
	can / could	(cf **225**)	**Can/Could** you open this door? – **Can/Could** I come in?
	may / might	(cf **227**)	**May / Might** my assistant use your telephone?
allowing	can	(cf **225**)	You **can** use this room again now.
	may	(cf **227**)	You **may** phone your lawyer if you wish.
forbidding	can't	(cf **225**)	You **can't** talk to him yet, Inspector. He is too weak.
	may not	(cf **227**)	Mr Brown **may not** have any visitors yet.
	mustn't	(cf **227**)	He **mustn't** strain himself after the operation.
demanding,	must	(cf **229**)	You **must** tell us everything you noticed that night.
encouraging	should / ought to	(cf **232**)	You **should / ought to** have a burglar alarm put in.
conceding	needn't	(cf **229**)	You **needn't** lock the safe, there's nothing in it.
advising, warning,	should(n't) /		You **shouldn't** be so careless with your valuables.
reproaching	ought(n't) to	(cf **232**)	You **ought to** have informed the police at once.

Note:
When one is not trying to exert influence, but only wishes to state that something is necessary, allowed, etc., then the substitute expressions are generally used, and not the modal auxiliaries (cf **227**.2, **229**.2, **232**.2). In German, modal auxiliaries are used for both purposes:

The boss wants to see you. You **are to** come to his office at once. *(Sie **sollen** sofort . . .)*

2. to express a supposition

A statement like *This is true* presents something as a fact, by the use of the indicative form of a main verb (here: *is*). With the addition of a modal auxiliary *(This must/may . . . be true)* the validity of the statement is restricted in some way. The speaker then presents it as a personal supposition, which can be made stronger or weaker depending on the choice of modal auxiliary. If the sentence starts with *I am sure/I suppose/I guess,* etc. or an adverb like *certainly, surely, probably, perhaps,* the same effect is achieved.

certain	must	(cf **230**)	The door is locked. They **must** have gone out. (I'm sure they've gone out.)
	can't	(cf **226**)	This **can't** be the Smiths' car. They're on holiday. (This certainly isn't the Smiths' car.)
probable	will	(cf **238**)	Let's hurry. Mary **will** already be waiting for us. (Mary is probably already waiting for us.)
	should / ought to	(cf **233**)	Try again at two. He **should / ought to** be back by then. (I suppose he will be back by then.)
possible	may / might	(cf **228**)	I don't know where Mum is. She **may / might / could** be
	could	(cf **226**)	at our neighbours'. (Perhaps she is at our neighbours'.)

Note:
In questions, *can, could* and *would* can be used to express uncertainty or doubt (cf **226, 238**). Sentences with *I wonder if/where/what* can be used for this purpose as well:

What **can** he mean? (I wonder what he means.)

223–226 *Can/could*

Can and *could* express the idea of ability or possibility, like the German auxiliary *können*. They are used in the following ways:

223 *Can/could:* Ability and Inability

Rover has grown so much that he **can** now open the kitchen door with his paws.
Kittens **can't** see at all for the first eight days.
A few years ago we had a canary which **could** whistle "God save the Queen".
We acquired a parrot last year from an old lady who **couldn't** look after him any longer.
Dogs **can** readily be trained, and over the centuries man **has been able to** use them for many purposes.
Do you **know how to** milk a cow?

Can and *can't* denote an ability or inability which exists now or has always existed.

Could and *couldn't* denote an ability or inability which used to exist. It must be made clear by an adverbial of time or be evident from the context that past time is being referred to.
For the compound tenses, one uses the substitute expressions *be able to, be capable of* and *know how to.* (These can also be used in the simple present and past tenses.)

Note:
The 'ability' which is expressed by *can* and *could* can be the typical behaviour which arises from the nature or character of a person or thing:

Children **can** be very rough. *(... können ... sein/sind oft ...)*
My grandmother **could** spend hours in her rocking-chair, just staring out of the window.

For *will* and *would* to express typical behaviour see **237**.

224 *Can/could:* Success and Failure

You'll never get that bottle open with a knife.
– Oh, I will. I'm sure I **can** open it.
Sorry, I **can't** get the top off this jar.
I looked everywhere, but I **couldn't** find the cork-screw.
But compare:
She finally **succeeded in** unwrapping the parcel.
(She **could** unwrap it. = *Sie könnte ...*)
Nobody **will be able/has been able** to undo that knot.

Can, can't and *couldn't* can be used to denote ability combined with achievement (as opposed to a mere general ability): a person succeeds, does not succeed or did not succeed in carrying out a particular action.

The affirmative past tense form *could* cannot normally be used in this sense. It must be replaced by a substitute such as *be able to, succeed in* or *manage to.* These can also be used in the compound tenses.

225 *Can/could:* Request, Permission, Prohibition, etc.

This use results from the fact that *can* and *could* express a possibility. *Can* and *could* are less formal than *may* and *might* (cf **227**).

Can/Could you lend me your road atlas?
Can/Could I use your garage while you're away? – Oh yes, of course you can.

Can't/Couldn't he borrow somebody else's motor-bike – Jim's perhaps?

Questions with *can* and *could* meaning 'Is it/Would it be possible?' are used for informal requests (often as requests for permission to do something).
Questions with *can't* and *couldn't* meaning 'Isn't it/Wouldn't it be possible?' are often used for suggestions.
Could and *couldn't* sound politer than *can* and *can't.*

All right, your friend **can** ride my bike.
You **can / could** help me to mend the puncture.

You **can't** park here, but there is a car park round the corner.

Statements with *can* can be used to give permission or to make a demand. Statements with *could* can also express a demand.
Can't expresses prohibition, but it sounds less authoritarian than *mustn't* (cf **227**).

226 *Can/could:* Supposition

I've mislaid my banker's card. – **Can** it be in your other handbag?
Can I have left my cheque-book in the bank?
We **can't** possibly need to cash another cheque already!
The exchange rate **can't** have changed as much as that since yesterday.
The place looks very deserted. **Could** it be early closing day?
Could we have mistaken the opening times?
I wonder where Bill is. He **couldn't** be looking at the church – he hates churches.
That **could** be the old tea-shop the Browns were so enthusiastic about.
This inn **could** have been built in the 16th century, judging by the windows.

Since *can* and *could* express a possibility, they can also be used for suppositions. In this use they are often followed by the perfect infinitive.

Questions and negative statements with *can* mean 'Is it possible . . .?' / 'I don't think it is possible . . .'

Could can also be used in questions and negative statements, where it expresses greater uncertainty than *can* ('Might it be possible . . .?' / 'It is hardly possible . . .').

Could – like *may/must* (cf **228**) – can in addition be used in affirmative statements to mean 'It is possible . . .', 'It is perhaps true . . .'. (*Can* cannot be used in this way.)

227–228 *May/might* and *Mustn't*

May and *might* correspond in meaning to various German auxiliaries, mainly *dürfen* and *können*. For *nicht dürfen* the forms *may not* and *mustn't* are used in English.

227 *May/might – may not/mustn't:* Permission and Prohibition

1. Use of the auxiliaries

May we borrow your lawnmower, please? We can't get ours to start. – You **may** have it in an hour. I'll have finished with it then.
May the children pick some apples? – No, they **may not,** they aren't ripe yet.
You **mustn't** throw stones in the pond.

Might I suggest we have tea in the garden?
You **might** be more careful not to trample the flowerbeds, Tony.

The Carsons' children **have** never **been allowed to** climb trees.

May is used to ask for permission or to give permission.

May not is used for prohibition, mainly in answer to questions with *may*. Otherwise *mustn't* is preferred (cf **229** Note 1).

Questions with *might* sound very hesitant or polite.
Might in statements can express a demand, often with an undertone of annoyance or sarcasm.
May and *might* are more formal than *can* and *could* (cf **225**).
To express permission and prohibition in the missing tenses of *may* and *might*, one uses the substitute expression *be allowed to.*

2. Differences in meaning between *may/may not/mustn't* and their substitutes

Yes, you **may** ask your friends in, but you **may not** offer them any beer.
You **mustn't** drink more than one glass of wine.

May, may not and *mustn't* are used to permit or forbid something from a position of authority.

Pubs **are not allowed to** serve alcoholic drinks to under-eighteens.

If the speaker wants to leave open the question of who is responsible for permitting or forbidding something, then *be allowed to* is used, even in the present tense.

Patrons **may** park behind the inn.
Visitors **may not/are not permitted to** smoke in the hall.

May/may not can, however, be used for this purpose in formal style (e.g. in official notices), where *be permitted to* is the more usual substitute.

228 *May/might:* Supposition

Where's Bob? – I don't know. He **may** be upstairs or he **may** have gone out.
Anne **might** have put your bicycle pump somewhere, or she **might** at least know where it is.
We **may not/might not** be able to go to the village on our bikes, because it looks like rain.

May and *might* are used to express the possibility that something is the case or will be in the future. Combined with the perfect infinitive, they express the possibility that something was the case in the past.
The negative forms correspond to German *vielleicht nicht.*
Might suggests a lesser degree of probability than *may.*

Might/Could/Can I have left my umbrella in the car?

May in this meaning only occurs in statements. In the corresponding questions, one has to use *might, could* or *can* (cf **226**).

Notes:

1. *May/might* + infinitive also occur in various types of subordinate clauses as alternatives to other verb forms: e.g. in *that*-clauses after verbs and verbal complexes expressing possibility or fear, or in adverbial clauses of concession and purpose (cf **213.2** b):
   It is possible that we **may/will** move to Devon in a few months.
   They *feared* that there **might/would** be a drastic rise in the price of houses in the near future.
   Nobody is willing to live in the haunted house, however desperate they **may be/are** for accommodation.
   (... so verzweifelt die Leute auch nach Unterkunft suchen mögen/suchen.)
   Interest rates were reduced to 5 % so that people **might/would/should** be encouraged to take out mortgages. *(... damit die Leute ermutigt wurden, Hypotheken aufzunehmen.)*

2. *May* occurs as well – like German *mögen* – in set phrases of well-wishing, etc. (cf **213.2** b Note):
   May you both be happy. **May** the Lord bless and keep you.

Must and *Needn't*

English *must* corresponds to German *müssen* in the use of the affirmative forms, but there is a difference in the meaning of the negative forms:

must:	it is necessary **to do s.th.**	*müssen:*	it is **necessary** to do s.th.
mustn't:	it is necessary **not to do s.th.** (in German: *nicht dürfen*)	*nicht müssen:*	it is **not necessary** to do s.th. (in English: *needn't*)

229 *Must* and *Needn't:* Orders and Concessions

1. Use of the auxiliaries

You **must** go to the doctor if that cough doesn't clear up in a few days.
I **must** make an appointment to see the dentist about this aching tooth.
You **needn't** have your arm X-rayed – it's definitely not broken.

Since *must* denotes that something is necessary, it is often used for orders and exhortations.
I must expresses the speaker's intention to do something necessary.
Since *needn't* indicates that something is not necessary, it is often used for concessions: the person who *needn't* do something is free to decide whether to do it or not.

Joe **had to** be taken to hospital in an ambulance.
Patients who telephone the doctor's surgery first **won't have to** wait so long.
You'**ve got to** have an anti-tetanus injection at once.

Must and *needn't* only have present tense forms. *Have to* is the substitute most often used for the missing tenses. The form *have got to* is common in the present tense. (For *must* and *needn't* in reported speech see **324**.)

Note:
Although *must* and *mustn't* correspond to different auxiliaries in German, they express the same attitude on the part of the speaker:

You must	eat your vegetables.	exhortation to do s.th.
You mustn't	talk with your mouth full.	exhortation **not** to do s.th.
I must	go to the shop before it closes.	intention to do s.th.
I mustn't	spend too much.	intention **not** to do s.th.

2. Differences in meaning between *must/needn't* and their substitutes

When you are in London, you **must** find time to visit the British Museum.
You **needn't** go through all the departments, though.

Must and *needn't* express the speaker's personal conviction that something is or is not necessary.

At the entrance to the Museum you **have to** open your handbag for inspection.
You generally **don't have to** pay an entrance fee for admission to museums in Britain.
I'**ve got to** sit down for a moment, my feet are killing me.

Have (got) to and its negatives simply state that external circumstances or the orders of a third person make something necessary or not necessary. *Have got to* is preferred colloquially when one is not referring to a general necessity, but to a particular situation.

They **needn't have shown** us all those boring fossils. *(... hätten uns nicht ... brauchen.)*
We **didn't have to/didn't need to go** on the guided tour unless we wanted to. *(Wir brauchten nicht ... zu ...)*

Needn't have done denotes that something happened unnecessarily. *Didn't have to do/didn't need to do* (for *need* as main verb see **242**) denote that something was not necessary; whether it actually happened or not, is left open.

Note:
A necessity which is imposed by some outside authority or by circumstances can also be expressed by *be obliged to, be forced to* and *be compelled to:*
The employees **are obliged to** produce a doctor's certificate in case of illness.
She was **forced/compelled to** return to work because of financial difficulties.

230 *Must:* Supposition

I'm picking up our photos today, they **must** be ready now.
Something **must** have broken when I dropped my camera.

The light **can't/mustn't** have been very good when you took this snap.

Must can express a supposition: there are compelling reasons for supposing that something is the case. *Must* in this meaning can be followed by the perfect infinitive. (For *should* and *ought to* in a similar meaning see **233**.)
A supposition that something is not the case is expressed by *can't* (cf **226**), or sometimes by *mustn't*, which is not so strong as *can't*.

231–234 *Shall/should* and *Ought to*

Shall and *should* cannot always be used where German has the auxiliary *sollen;* for some of its meanings *be to* has to be used. On the other hand *should* is used where German has no auxiliaries at all. In many cases *ought to* has the same meaning as *should*.

231 *Shall:* Suggestions, Promises, Threats

Shall we go to the theatre tonight?
Shall I ring up and see if there are any tickets left?
The meal at the Devonshire Inn tonight **shall** be the best you've ever had.
You **shan't** have anything for your birthday if you don't behave.

Shall we/Shall I? (in question form) is used, like German *sollen*, to make a suggestion or to ask someone else what they want done.
Shall in statements in the 2nd or 3rd person expresses a promise or a threat, depending on the context. Sentences of this type tend to sound rather formal.
(For the use of *I/We shall* as a variant of the *will*-future see **178** Note 1.)

232 *Should/ought to:* Advice, Orders, Reproaches

1. Use of the auxiliaries

I suppose I **ought to/should** cut down on my beer intake, I'm getting so fat.
You **shouldn't** keep trying all those fancy diets.
You **ought to** be ashamed of yourself for staying in bed all morning.
He **ought to/should** have had more sense than to start jogging at his age.

Should and *ought to*, like German *sollte (eigentlich)*, both express an obligation. Both the affirmative and negative forms, therefore, are used for urgent advice, warnings or demands, often with a reproachful undertone (especially with *ought to*).
Should (not)/ought (not) to + perfect infinitive are used to criticize a past state or past behaviour.

2. Differences in meaning between *should/ought to* and *be to*

You really **ought to/should** go to see your son perform in the school play.
– I can't, **I'm to** chair an important meeting on Wednesday.
A representative from the Ministry **is to** visit the factory next week.

Should and *ought to* express the speaker's own feeling that there is an obligation to do something.
Be to is used when the obligation is imposed by someone or something else – for instance an outside authority, – or when it arises from a previous arrangement.

Everybody was very busy, because the firm's new show-room **were to** be opened to the public the next day.
The conference **was to be held/was to have been held** two weeks ago but had to be postponed.

Be to occurs both in present and past tense forms. *Was/were to* does not say whether the order or previously arranged plan was actually carried out or not. If it was obviously not carried out, *was/were to* + perfect infinitive can be used as well. Other forms of *be to* are not in use.

Notes:

1. *Was/were to* can also be used to mean that something was destined to take place later *(es sollte so kommen):*
   We would never have guessed it, but the new man **was to** become manager of the firm five years later. *(... sollte ... werden.)*

2. *Be expected to* and *be supposed to* can also express a demand made by a third person *(es wird erwartet):*
   I'm expected to contribute to the discussion. *(Ich soll zur Diskussion beitragen.)*
   I'm supposed to have all the facts and figures at my fingertips. *(Ich soll ... parat haben)*

233 *Should/ought to:* Supposition

The concert **ought to/should be** over at 10, so we'll be able to catch the last train.
Joan **ought to/should** have enjoyed the play, as her favourite actor was in it.

Should and *ought to* (sometimes with the perfect infinitive) express a supposition. They sound more cautious and less definite than *must* (cf **230**).

Notes:

1. *Should* (but not *ought to*) is also used with verbs like *say, think, hope, imagine* to soften their effect:
   With your detailed description of the way I **should say (hope/think/imagine)** they won't have any trouble getting here.

2. *Shall* cannot be used like German *sollen* to indicate that one's information comes from an unnamed source. For this purpose one uses phrases like *be said to, be reported to, be supposed to.* (Cf **62**; for *supposed to* see also **232** Note 2.)

234 *Should* in *That*-Clauses

1. *Should* after verbs and verbal complexes which express a demand or a decision

The law *requires* that all drivers **should carry** a valid driving licence.
The customs officer *ordered* that the car **should be** thoroughly searched.
It is important that a motorist **should have** a knowledge of first aid. *(Es ist wichtig, daß ... Kenntnisse ... hat.)*
After considering the report of the committee *it was decided* that the wearing of seatbelts **should be made** compulsory. *(... wurde beschlossen, daß das Tragen von Sicherheitsgurten zur Pflicht gemacht werden sollte).*
It was decided that the wearing of seatbelts **be made** compulsory.

Should occurs in *that*-clauses after verbs and verbal complexes expressing a demand or exhortation (*demand, order, insist, suggest,* etc.) or presenting something as being necessary, advisable or urgent (*require, be important/crucial/vital,* etc.). (In the corresponding German sentences the indicative of a main verb is used.)
Should can also occur after verbs and verbal complexes which express a decision: the decision to demand something (*decide, determine, reach the decision,* etc.). (In German, *sollen* is used in such sentences.)

As an alternative to *should,* the present subjunctive of the main verb can also be used (cf **213**.2 a).

2. *Should* after verbs and verbal complexes which express an emotional effect or evaluation

We *regret* that we **should have** no means of repaying your kindness to us. *I'm sorry* that you **should have been** unable to accept our invitation. Paul *was very surprised* that I **should remember** his birthday. *It is sad* that you **should not have** the opportunity to see your friends more often. *It is quite understandable* that Sandra **should prefer** to stay at home on a night like this. *(Es ist durchaus verständlich, daß Sandra es vorzieht...)* *What a pity* that she **has to** leave so early. *(Wie schade, daß sie so früh gehen muß.)*	*Should* (with either present or perfect infinitive) in the *that*-clause is used in formal style to make a statement sound more reserved or more polite. *Should* implies that the speaker's feeling or opinion about something has less to do with the actual fact than with the mere idea of it. *Should* occurs in this use mainly after verbal complexes with *be*, as for example *be sorry/delighted/surprised/shocked, it's sad/dreadful/understandable/surprising/a pity*, etc. Colloquially, it is more common to use the indicative of the verb in such *that*-clauses, as in German.

Notes:

1. It is often possible to use non-finite constructions (cf **260.1**, **268**) instead of *that*-clauses:
   It is important for tourists not to disturb the wildlife in this area.
2. *Should* also occurs in adverbial clauses of purpose (with *in order that* or *so that*) and in conditional clauses (cf **213.2** b, **218**):
   We had to keep Rover on a lead, in order that/so that he **shouldn't** be tempted to chase the lambs.
   If you **should** want to take a short cut over the fields, please keep to the footpath.

235–238 *Will/would*

Will and *would* have a wider range of meaning than German *wollen*: they include, for example, meanings which are covered by *werden* in German. Conversely, *wollen* cannot always be translated by *will/would*. (For the *will*-future see **199–200**, for the future-in-the-past see **210–211**).

235 *Will/would:* Willingness, Intentions, Requests, Wishes

Robin's going to the football match this afternoon. – I'll go with him if he doesn't mind. Father's watching the World Cup on TV. – We **won't** disturb him then. The police **are prepared to** bring in reinforcements if the crowd gets out of hand. Our local club **intends to** organize a trip to Wembley for the Cup Final. **Will you** please have your tickets ready? **Would you** keep this seat for me? **Won't you** join us for a celebration drink? **I'd like to** meet the captain of the team. **Would you like to/Do you want to** referee the next match?	Statements with *(I/we) will* express an intention or willingness which arises spontaneously, i.e. at the moment of speaking. Usually the short form *'ll* is used. This use can also be understood as the *will*-future (cf **200**). *Be prepared to* and *be willing to* can also express willingness to do something. *Intend to* always expresses an intention which has already been formed. Questions with *will (you)?* and the more polite form *would (you)?* generally express a request or a wish. *Won't (you)?* is an invitation. *Would like to, want to* and *wish to* (formal) also express or inquire about a wish.

236 *Will/would:* Determination

We **will** install the new machines, no matter what the trade unions say. In spite of the recession, the union **won't** accept any pay offer under 6 %. The manufacturers **wouldn't** pay for the parts damaged in transit. (= refused to pay) The management announced that they **would** dismiss the fifty workers as planned, in spite of protests. The firm **insisted on** closing their factory in Leeds. The strikers **were not willing** to negotiate.	*Will* (the stressed full form) and *won't* express that someone is determined to do (or not to do) something. *Wouldn't* in the sense of *refused to* is a genuine past tense and expresses a past decision not to do something. The affirmative form *would* can only refer to a past decision in reported speech and inner monologue (cf **322, 220**.2). The substitutes are *insist on (doing s.th.), be determined to (do s.th.);* in the negative *not be willing to, refuse to.*

Note:
Won't and *wouldn't* can also be used in connection with things, meaning something could not be done with the thing:
We pushed hard, but the car **wouldn't** budge. (= could not be moved)

237 *Will/would:* General Characteristic, Habit

A moving object **will** continue to move at the same speed until it meets with some resistance. (= always continues to move) Children ***will*** run after balls into the street. (= This is what you must expect.) When we were children we loved playing by the river. We **would (used to)** skim stones on the water, catch little fish, . . . (*skim, catch:* repeated activities) **But:** A tall tree **used to** stand next to the bridge, but it is gone now. (*stand:* here, permanent state)	*Will* can be used to point out a general characteristic or typical behaviour. *Will* is unstressed (although it always has its full form) in objective statements of this kind. When it is stressed, it expresses an emotional attitude (displeasure, amusement, resignation etc.) *Would* is a genuine past tense when used to describe a past habit. It occurs mainly in literary and poetic style. *Would* can only be used with activity and process verbs, unlike *used to*, which can also be used for a past state (cf **239**).

238 *Will/would:* Supposition

Was that the door bell? – Yes, **it'll** be the postman. He'll be bringing that registered letter I'm expecting. The telegram I sent this morning **will** have arrived by now. I suppose my aunt'll send me another book for Christmas this year. What a big parcel – **would** it be from Grandma?	*Will* (with either present or perfect infinitive) expresses a supposition for which no reasons need be given. It can therefore express varying degrees of probability, but always implies more certainty than *may, might* and *could* (cf **228, 226**). When the supposition refers to the future, it can also be understood as the *will*-future (cf **199**). The weaker form *would* can be used to express a guess, but this is more or less limited to questions.

239–240 *Used to*

Used to [ju:stə] differs from the other modal auxiliaries in having only a genuine past tense form with real reference to the past.

239 *Used to* Expressing a Former Habit or State

Is Jim still so athletic? When I knew him, he **used to** run two miles before breakfast every morning.
We **used to** go to the beach a lot as children, but now we hardly ever go.
This town **used to** be a quiet little fishing village before it became a tourist resort.
She **used to** believe that the sea air did her good, but she prefers the mountains now. *(Früher glaubte sie . . .)*

Used to, unlike *would* (cf **237**), can be used with all types of verbs (not only activity and process verbs) and is stylistically neutral. *Used to* often points out a contrast between the past and the present.

This is always the case when it is used with verbs expressing a state, a relation or an attitude (stative verbs).
Used to often corresponds to the German adverb *früher,* e.g. in sentences without an adverbial of time.

240 *Used to* in Negative Sentences and Questions

He	**never used to** **didn't use(d) to** **use(d)n't to** **used not to**	watch detective series

on TV, but now you can't drag him away from them.

Did you use(d) to **Used you to**	go to the theatre

a lot when you lived in London?

A common negation of *used to* is *never used to.* Otherwise the negative forms and questions are usually formed by using *did* (in American English almost always). The spelling varies between *use to* and *used to.* (The pronunciation [ju:stə] allows for both interpretations.)

In British English, *used to* can also (like the other modal auxiliaries) form its negative and questions without the *do*-auxiliary: *use(d)n't to/Used you/he/. . . to . . .?*

Note:
Used to + infinitive must not be confused with *be used to/get used to* + gerund, which can occur in all tenses. Compare:
When we lived in the country, I **used to** go for long walks. (= I often went for long walks)
Could you slow down a bit - **I'm not used to** walking so fast. (= I am not accustomed to it)
I expect that in time **I'll get used to** climbing hills again. (= I will become accustomed to it again)

241 *Need* and *Dare* as Auxiliaries

She **needn't** lay the table yet – dinner won't be ready for an hour. **Need** I peel any more potatoes? – No, you **needn't,** those are enough. You **needn't** have made so much coffee – I never drink more than one cup.	I **daren't** eat another piece of cake. I'm trying to lose weight. How **dare** she say I'm too fat? **Dare** I take the last sandwich? He **dared not** ask for some more jam, the waitress was already in a bad temper.

As auxiliaries, *need* and *dare* occur mostly in the negative forms and in questions (*dare* mainly in questions with *how*).
Like the other modal auxiliaries, they have no *-s* in the 3rd person singular; negatives and questions are formed without the aid of *do;* the infinitive which follows has no *to* (cf **221**.2).
Need can also be followed by the perfect infinitive *(needn't have done).*
The past tense form *dared* is rarer than the present tense form *dare.*

Notes:

1. The affirmative forms of the auxiliaries *need* and *dare* do occur in statements which contain a form of negation other than *not,* or a restriction (e.g. *never, no one,* etc.; *hardly, only,* etc.):
   No one without a genuine interest in the theatre **need** apply for the job.
   I **hardly dare** ask for higher wages.
2. For the use of *needn't* as the negation of *must,* see **229**.

242 *Need* and *Dare* as Main Verbs

1. *Need*

This pullover **needs to be washed** in cold water. **Do I need to take** a raincoat? He **doesn't need to buy** another suit, as he got himself a new one only last month. She **needs a new bikini,** she's only got one. His trousers **needed mending** after he fell off his bicycle. She **didn't need to try on** the sweater. She could see it was the right size. You **needn't have mended** this shirt, I'm not going to wear it any more. (= The work you did was not necessary.)

Need can be used as a main verb in all types of sentences. The 3rd person singular ends in *-s.*
Questions and negative forms are formed with the aid of *do.*
The main verb *need* can be complemented by an infinitive with *to,* a noun phrase or a gerund (cf **277**).

Need as a main verb occurs in all tenses, unlike the auxiliary *need.* Note that there is a considerable difference in meaning between the past tense form of the main verb *(didn't need to do)* and the auxiliary with perfect infinitive *(needn't have done,* cf **229**.2).

2. *Dare*

Peter would like to go camping with the older boys but he **doesn't dare (to) ask.** **Did** she really **dare (to)** bring her dog into the classroom? No member of the school team **has dared (to)** question the coach's authority yet.

Dare occurs, even as a main verb, mainly in negative sentences and questions, both formed with *do.*
It is followed by the infinitive with or without *to.*

243–245 *Do* as Auxiliary and Main Verb

243 Table of Forms

Finite forms:		full forms:	short forms:	Non-finite forms:	
Present tense:	I/you/we/they	**do (not)**	**don't**	Infinitive:	**do**
	he/she/it	**does (not)**	**doesn't**	Present participle:	**doing**
Past tense:	I/you/he/she/it/we/they	**did (not)**	**didn't**	Past participle:	**done**

244 *Do* as Auxiliary in Questions, Negative Sentences and Emphatic Sentences

Do you **play** the piano? – No, I **don't.**
Your brother plays an instrument, **doesn't** he?
– Oh yes, he plays the guitar, and so **do** I.
Normally I **don't** care for jazz, but I **do like** dixieland.
An analysis of the process of composition **does not** necessarily lead to a better understanding of music.

Do is used to form questions and negatives when the sentence contains no other auxiliary. It is also used in various types of short sentences and to put emphasis on a statement (emphatic *do*). (Cf **27, 29, 34, 335**)

The short negative forms are usually preferred to the full forms, which are mainly restricted to formal style.

245 *Do* as Main Verb

Where's Tony, what'**s** he **doing**? – He's mending his bike.
My brother and I always take turns to **do the washing-up.** *(... wechseln uns immer beim Geschirrspülen ab.)*
Betty **is doing** her room at the moment, but she'll be down in a minute. *(... macht gerade ihr Zimmer sauber ...)*
Do you really **do** the lawn twice a week? – No, I used to, but I **don't do** it so often any more.

As a main verb, *do* is one of the activity verbs (verbs with dynamic meaning).
It often combines with certain nouns to form verbal complexes, i.e. single units of meaning.

Like other activity verbs, *do* can be used in the progressive form.

Questions and negatives of the main verb *do* are formed with the aid of the *do*-auxiliary.

246–251 *Have* as Auxiliary and Main Verb

246 Table of forms

Finite forms:		full forms:	short forms:		
Present tense:	I/you/we/they	**have (not)**	I've/you've/ ... (not)	I/you/ ... **haven't**	
	he/she/it	**has (not)**	He's/she's/it's (not)	he/she/it **hasn't**	
Past tense:	I/you/he/she/it/we/they	**had (not)**	I'd/you'd/ ... (not)	I/you/ ... **hadn't**	
Non-finite forms:	Infinitive: **have**	Present participle: **having**		Past participle: **had**	

The short forms are generally used when *have* is an auxiliary, especially in the phrase *have got*. In formal style the full forms are preferred.

247 *Have* as an Auxiliary in Compound Tenses

I've been to France twice this year.
I **had hoped** to go to Paris last year, but I couldn't.
Have you ever **been** to Spain? – No, **I haven't.**

Have is used with a past participle to form the perfect tenses (cf **178**). As with all the auxiliaries, questions and negatives are formed without the aid of *do*.

248 *Have to*

Do you **have to** finish that essay today?
No, I **don't have to** hand it in till next Wednesday.

Have to needs the *do*-auxiliary in questions and negatives, etc.
(For *have to* and *must/needn't* see **229**.2.)

249 *Have something done*

Your hair looks nice. Where **did** you **have it done**?
I **didn't have these trousers cleaned,** I washed them in the machine.

Here, *have* means 'to cause something to be done'. In this meaning it needs the *do*-auxiliary to form questions, negatives, etc. (See also **284**. For the same construction with a passive meaning see **64**.)

250 *Have/have got* (= possess)

Have you enough wool to finish your pullover? – No, I **haven't.**
She **hadn't** any interest in needlework when she was young.
Have they still **got** that material at the shop? – I don't know. But if they **haven't got** it any more, they can order it.

Do you **have** any buttons like this one? – Sorry we **don't have** that colour.
I **have** much less time for knitting these days than I used to.

When *have* means 'to possess a thing or a characteristic' its questions and negatives can be formed without the *do*-auxiliary in British English.

In colloquial British speech, *have got* is preferred when referring to the present. Since this is actually a present perfect form, *do* is not needed to form its questions and negatives.
In American English, the questions and negatives, etc. of *have* are usually formed with *do*.
As *have* in this meaning describes a relation and not an activity (stative meaning), it only occurs in the simple form (cf **184**.2).

251 *Have* in Verbal Complexes

He couldn't answer the telephone because he **was having a shower.**
Did you **have a nice walk?**
I **didn't have breakfast** this morning, so I'm starving!

Have can combine with a number of nouns to form verbal complexes, which are then used like activity verbs. In such verbal complexes, *have* can therefore form the progressive tenses.
In the simple tenses the *do*-auxiliary is used to form questions and negatives, etc.

252 Table of Forms

Finite forms:		**full forms:**		**short forms:**		
Present tense:	I	**am**	**(not)**	I'**m (not)**		–
	you/we/they	**are**	**(not)**	you'**re**/we'**re**/they'**re (not)**	you/we/they	**aren't**
	he/she/it	**is**	**(not)**	he'**s**/she'**s**/it'**s (not)**	he/she/it	**isn't**
Past tense:	I/he/she/it	**was**	**(not)**	–	I/he/she/it	**wasn't**
	you/we/they	**were**	**(not)**	–	you/we/they	**weren't**
Non-finite Forms:	Infinitive: **be**		Present participle: **being**		Past participle: **been**	

The use of short and full forms depends only on the level of style (cf **219**), and not on whether *be* is an auxiliary or a main verb.
In negative questions *aren't [a:nt] I?* is used as the short form of *am I not?* In negative statements there is no accepted alternative short form to *I'm not.*

Note:
The short form *ain't* [eɪnt] (in *I ain't/ain't I?* for *I'm not/aren't I?*) is regarded as sub-standard (cf **10**). *Ain't* is also used for *aren't, isn't, haven't, hasn't:*

Ain't she sweet? (= **Isn't** she sweet?)
Ain't got no cigarettes. (= **I haven't** got any cigarettes.)

253 *Be* as Auxiliary in Compound Tenses

They'**re building** some new houses in our road.
The street **is being widened.**
That fence **was put up** last year.

Be is used with the present participle of another verb to form the progressive tenses. It is used with the past participle of another verb to form the passive (cf **178**).

254 *Be to*

The wedding **is to** take place in March.
(... soll ... stattfinden.)
The club members **were to** meet in May but the date has now been changed. *(... sollten ...)*

When *be* is followed by *to* and an infinitive, it usually expresses the idea that an event has been arranged, either by agreement or as ordered by a third person or an authority (cf **232**.2)

255 *Be* as a Linking Verb

He **is** { a doctor. / always busy. / often away from home. }
Is his wife a doctor, too? – No, she **isn't.** She **is** a teacher.

When *be* is followed by a subject complement (noun, adjective, etc.) or a necessary adverbial (cf **54, 55.**1), it is a linking verb, and as such, a main verb. But in spite of this, questions and negative statements are always formed without *do.*

As a linking verb, *be* can have the following meanings:

1. *Be* expressing a state, relation or characteristic

Sheila **is** very musical.
She **was** Mr Benn's best pupil.

In this meaning *be* can only be used in the simple form, like the other state and relation verbs (cf **182**, **184**.2).

2. *Be* expressing a way of behaving

You**'re being** very stubborn. Maybe your parents are right to want you to continue with your piano lessons.
I wish our neighbour would stop practising the trumpet. He**'s being** a terrible nuisance.

Combined with certain adjectives and nouns, *be* can mean 'to behave in a certain way (at the moment)'. In this sense it can be classed as an activity verb and can therefore occur in progressive tenses (cf **185**).

Be sensible. Don't waste all your money on records.
Don't be such a tyrant.
Do be careful with the tape-recorder. It was very expensive.

The imperative of *be* can also be used in this sense (cf **35**).
The negative imperative is formed with *do*.
The affirmative imperative can be made emphatic with *do*.

Note:
The imperative of *be* can sometimes be combined with an adverbial of place:
Be there in time. – **Be back** at ten.

Chapter 8: Non-Finite Constructions

256–258 Infinitive, Gerund, Participles: Forms, Functions, Meanings (Summary)

256 Forms

The infinitive, the gerund and the participles are called non-finite forms. They can be formed from all verbs except the modal auxiliaries. Unlike the finite forms of the verb, they contain no information about person (*I, you, he,* etc.) or number (singular, plural). They do, however, have various active and passive forms.

Active forms	Passive forms	
(to) **count** the votes (to) **be counting** (to) **have counted** (to) **have been counting**	(to) **be counted** (to) **have been counted**	1. Infinitive ◄ Progressive infinitive ◄ Perfect infinitive ◄ Perfect progressive infinitive
counting the votes **having counted** **having been counting**	**being counted** **having been counted**	2. *-ing* forms: either gerunds or present participles, according to their function ◄ Perfect forms ◄ Perfect progressive form
	the votes already **counted** a **written** constitution	3. *Past participle* ◄ (For the irregular forms see **343.**)

As the above examples show, non-finite verb forms can have the same types of complementation as finite verbs – e.g. an object (cf: They counted **the votes**), or be modified by an adverbial (cf: The votes had **already** been counted). (For non-finite constructions with notional subjects of their own, see **259–262.**)

Note:
Non-finite constructions are negated by placing *not* in front of them (cf **19** Note 3):
We must be careful **not to count** the spoiled votes.

257 Functions

Whereas finite forms of the verb always form the predicate of a sentence, constructions with infinitive/gerund/participle + complementation have other functions. (In referring to such constructions we shall mainly use the briefer terms infinitive/gerund/participle.)

1. Infinitive and gerund

The infinitive and the gerund contain characteristics of both verb and noun. Like nouns, they can occur in the following functions: subject, complementation to the finite verb or verbal complex, attribute to a noun. In addition they can also function as adverbials.
The gerund – but not the infinitive – can take a preposition in front of it, just like a noun.

Example	Form	Function
To err is human.	Infinitive	as subject
Forecasting the future is always risky.	Gerund	as subject
I don't *want* **to know what is in store for me.**	Infinitive	complementing a verb
My mother *enjoys* **reading her horoscope.**	Gerund	complementing a verb
I don't *believe in* **consulting the stars.**	Prep. + gerund	complementing a verb
My friend *was afraid* **to walk under the ladder.**	Infinitive	complementing a verbal complex (formally: complementing the adjective)
Mary *was uneasy about* **travelling on the 13th.**	Prep. + gerund	complementing a verbal complex (formally: complementing the adjective)
You could hang up a horseshoe **to bring good luck.**	Infinitive	as adverbial
In spite of **wearing my lucky charm,** I lost the match.	Prep. + gerund	as adverbial
The last room **to be occupied** is always No 13. He ignored *the gypsy's advice* **not to wear red.**	Infinitive	as attribute to a noun
The fear of **seeing black cats** is widespread.	Prep. + gerund	as attribute to a noun

Note:
The gerund is much more commonly found as the subject at the beginning of a sentence than the infinitive. But the infinitive often occurs as the notional subject of sentences with introductory *it:*

Subject	Notional subject
Forecasting the future is always risky.	
It is always risky	**to forecast the future.**

2. *Present* and *past participle*

The present and the past participle contain characteristics of both verb and adjective. Like adjectives, they can occur as a complementation to the finite verb and as an attribute to a noun. They also occur as adverbials.

Example	Form	Function
They *sat* **talking** round the fire.	Present participle	complementing a verb
The cheese biscuits *remained* **untouched.**	Past participle	complementing a verb
Bill opened a bottle of **sparkling** *wine.* *The guests* **living nearby** came last.	Present participle	as attribute to a noun
There was **boiled** *rice* to go with the curry. *The sherry* **served before the meal** made Jim tipsy.	Past participle	as attribute to a noun
Reaching for the sugar, I knocked over a glass.	Present participle	as adverbial
Settled comfortably in their chairs, the visitors relaxed.	Past participle	as adverbial

258 Meanings

Although infinitive, gerund and participle can have similar functions (e.g. complementing a verb, as adverbial) they are not interchangeable, as each of these constructions expresses a different idea.

1. Meanings of infinitive and gerund

The difference in meaning between the infinitive and the gerund can be seen most clearly by comparing the following examples:

We told him **to turn off the lights.**
("You **must turn off the lights.**")
The **infinitive,** unlike the gerund, often has a **modal meaning,** i.e. it expresses the idea that something ought to take place or might be the case – like sentences with modal auxiliaries.

He remembered **turning off the lights.**
(Fact: **He had turned off the lights.**)
The **gerund** often has a more **factual meaning** as compared with the infinitive, i.e. it implies that an action or a state is regarded as a fact.

The modal meaning of the infinitive and the factual meaning of the gerund can help to explain how they are used:

(1) The team are hoping **to produce a more powerful vaccine soon.**	(1) Researchers are engaged **in developing new methods of treating typhoid.**
(2) The doctor gave me some advice on **how to avoid infections while in Mexico.**	(2) **On arriving home from New Guinea** he was rushed to hospital.
(3) The safest dish **to choose** would be the chili con carne.	(3) He regretted **eating (having eaten) some unwashed fruit.**
(4) Drink your tea. You need lots of liquid **to combat the effects of the heat.**	(4) She is very good **at cooking southern Indian dishes.**
(5) **To go on a safari in Africa and to bring home lots of trophies** was his one great ambition in life.	(5) **Watching films about wild animals** is nothing like **seeing them in their natural surroundings.**
(6) He seems **to have recovered from his malaria.**	(6) Some people are terrified **of travelling by plane.**
(7) She is considered **to be an expert on Indian temples.**	(7) I always enjoy **seeing new places.**

Sentences (1)–(5):
The infinitive indicates that a particular action has yet to be carried out; up to now there is no more than the intention, wish or aim to carry it out.
Sentences (6)–(7):
The infinitive implies that something is looked on as probable or possible, and not as a plain fact.

Sentences (1)–(3):
The gerund indicates that the action is actually being carried out or has been carried out.
Sentences (4)–(7):
The gerund here presents something as given, i.e. its existence is taken for granted. The rest of the sentence makes a general statement about it (e.g. some sort of characterization, a comparison, an attitude to it).

2. Meanings of present participle and past participle

The meanings of the participles can best be understood by comparing them with finite verb forms (progressive form, passive and perfect forms):

(1) We watched **the procession crossing the bridge.**	(1) **Pulled by four horses,** the brewers' cart moved slowly forward.
(2) **Walking in the middle of the road,** a man was nearly run over.	(2) The flags **waved by the children** added to the colourful scene.
(3) **Not knowing how long we would have to wait,** we had taken thermos flasks with us.	(3) **Frightened by the noise,** one of the horses got out of control. (Having been frightened . . .)

Sentences (1)–(2):
The present participle of verbs with dynamic meaning (activity and process verbs) can, like the progressive form, describe the course of an action. It may be in progress at the same time as another (1), or be still taking place when another action starts.
Sentence (3):
The present participle can also be formed from verbs with stative meaning which do not occur in the progressive form. In this case the present participle usually gives the reason for an action (causal meaning).

The past participle can be compared with the passive form of the finite verb as it presents an event from the passive point of view.
Sentences (1)–(2):
It can indicate that an action takes place at the same time as another one.
Sentence (3):
Like the present perfect and past perfect it can also indicate that an action took place before another one and brought about a certain result (in this meaning, the passive perfect form of the present participle can be used). Usually the past participle has causal meaning as well.

259 Non-Finite Constructions compared with Subordinate Clauses

Infinitive, gerund and participle constructions are comparable to subordinate clauses as, like them, they are embedded in a superordinate clause (cf **302**).
The comparison with subordinate clauses is particularly useful to explain those non-finite constructions that have their own notional subjects. The example below compares a *that*-clause with an infinitive construction (after *expect* either construction is possible):

(same subject)

Sub. clause	Peter	expected that	he	would arrive at six o'clock.
Infinitive	Peter	expected		**to arrive at six o'clock.**
Sub. clause	He	expected that	they (his parents)	would arrive at six o'clock.
Infinitive	He	expected	**them** (his parents)	**to arrive at six o'clock.**

Notional subject of the infinitive construction

The subordinate clause can have the same subject as the main clause. In the corresponding infinitive construction the subject is omitted.
The subordinate clause can also have a different subject from the main clause. In this case the corresponding infinitive construction has its own (notional) subject. Personal pronouns are put in the object case (*them;* hence the term 'object + infinitive construction').

Mark wanted	**his sister**	to play	the saxophone.	Infinitive
They hated	**her**	playing	the saxophone.	Gerund
We watched	**her**	playing	the saxophone.	Participle

(Infinitive, Gerund, Participle: with notional subject)

Not only infinitive constructions, but also gerund and participle constructions can have their own (notional) subjects. In German a subordinate clause often has to be used *(wollte, daß . . . ; haßte es, wenn . . .)* where in English a non-finite construction is usual – or even the only way of saying something (e.g. after *want*)

Note:
Instead of a personal notional subject, non-finite constructions can have the structure words *it* or *there* as subject:
I want **it to be understood** that I will not tolerate this situation much longer.
He complained about **there being** too much noise.

260 The *for* + Infinitive Construction

We are using this term to denote the construction formed from *for* + noun phrase + infinitive. To understand this widely-used construction it is important to realize that *for* cannot usually be regarded as a preposition comparable to German *für*. *For* is often a structure word showing that the following noun phrase is the subject of the infinitive construction.
The *for* + infinitive construction mostly corresponds to a German subordinate clause (often a *daß*-clause):

	structure word	notional subject	
We were anxious	**for**	***them*** (the painters)	**to finish the job quickly.**

infinitive construction

(Wir wünschten dringend, daß sie die Arbeit schnell erledigen würden.)

The *for* + infinitive construction is used chiefly in the following ways:

1. as complementation

They've arranged **for *the electricians* to come next week.** *(Sie haben es so eingerichtet/abgesprochen, daß die Elektriker nächste Woche kommen.)*
I'm keen **for *John* to have a look at the washing machine tonight.** *(Mir liegt sehr daran, daß John sich ... die Waschmaschine anschaut.)*
It's important **for *the instructions* to be clear and simple.** *(Es ist wichtig, daß die Gebrauchsanweisung klar und einfach ist.)*
It was impossible **for *the vacuum-cleaner* to be repaired.** *(Es war unmöglich, den Staubsauger zu reparieren.)*
It was not easy **for *him* to put up the shelves without the aid of an electric drill.** *(Es war nicht leicht für ihn/Es fiel ihm nicht leicht ...).*
It was unimaginable **for *her* to live without the comforts of civilization.**
Either: *Es war ihr/für sie (selbst) unvorstellbar, ohne die Annehmlichkeiten ... zu leben.*
Or: *Es war (für andere) unvorstellbar, daß sie ohne ... leben könnte.*

- after certain verbs: *arrange for, provide for, wait for, ask for, long for, can't bear*
- after certain verbal complexes with personal subjects: *be eager, be anxious, be keen* (cf **264**)
- after verbal complexes starting with the structure word *it,* such as *it's hard/good/bad/sad/impossible/important,* etc. (cf **268**). When the notional subject of the infinitive is a thing, then *for* is merely a structure word and cannot be translated by *für.*

  When the notional subject is a person, it may be possible to translate *for* by *für.*

  In some cases a sentence can be understood in two different ways.

Notes:

1. In the case of verbal complexes starting with the structure word *it,* the *for* + infinitive construction is the notional subject of the superordinate clause. It can, therefore, be made the real subject at the beginning of a sentence. This position makes the sentence sound formal and is only used when the verbal complex is especially emphasized.
   It is most unusual **for that road to be flooded.** *(Es ist sehr ungewöhnlich, daß diese Straße überflutet wird.)*
   For that road to be flooded is most unusual. *(Daß diese Straße überflutet wird, ist sehr ungewöhnlich.)*

2. The *for* + infinitive construction can also be used with verbs followed by a direct object and an adjective as object complement, e.g. *make s.th. impossible/necessary/etc.:*
   The bad weather made it impossible **for the bridge to be finished in time.**

2. as an adverbial (to express purpose or result) (cf **296–297**)

Let's tape this programme **for *Sue* to watch later.** (... so that Sue can watch it later.)
Leave the door open **for *us* to hear the telephone.**
Breakfast TV is *too early* **for *me* to enjoy.** (... so early that I can't enjoy it.)
The speaker talked *too fast* **for *the viewers* to follow.**
The sound wasn't *clear enough* **for *me* to hear properly.**

- after many activity verbs;
- after *too* + adjective (or adverb) and after adjective (or adverb) + *enough.*

3. as an attribute to a noun (to express purpose, obligation or possibility) (cf 300.1)

She made some sandwiches **for *them* to eat on the journey.** (= which they could eat on . . .) *(Sie machte ihnen ein paar belegte Brote für die Reise.)*
There was no other person nearby **for *us* to ask.** *(. . ., die wir hätten fragen können.)*
Have you a timetable **for *me* to look up the time of the train in?** *(Haben Sie einen Fahrplan? Ich würde gern . . .)*

The *for* + infinitive construction in this case corresponds to a relative clause with a modal auxiliary. It is very often used after *there is*, after *have* and after other verbs which express that something is available.
In German various other constructions have to be used. They are usually less precise, and their exact meaning can only be understood from the context.

Note:
The *for* + infinitive construction also occurs after certain abstract nouns where it often corresponds to a *that*-clause (cf **288**):
The necessity **for him to earn some money** was impressed upon him.
(The necessity that he should earn some money . . .)

261 Gerund Constructions with Notional Subjects of their Own

A gerund construction can also have its own notional subject after certain verbs, verbal complexes and nouns, and when functioning as an adverbial. (Cf **269–272, 288, 292.**2)

Would you mind ***your son* helping me with this case?**
She kept hold of the old man's arm for fear of ***him* falling again.**
The family were overjoyed at ***Ted's* having been awarded a medal for life-saving.**

I appreciate ***your* coming to the rescue so quickly.**
In spite of *their* taking great care, the ladder slipped on the muddy ground.

If the notional subject is a noun, it is normally in the common case (cf **67**).
For pronouns, the object forms are used (cf **82**).

In formal style the notional subject can take the form of the *s*-genitive (possessive case), but only for a person (or occasionally an animal).
Instead of the object forms of personal pronouns, the possessive determiner can be used. This does not sound as formal as the *s*-genitive.

262 Absolute Participle Constructions

***His wife* being so fond of jewelry,** he brought her a necklace from India. *(Da seine Frau so gerne Schmuck trug, ...)*
With *Joan* being so knowledgeable about old silver, she's not likely to be swindled. *(Joan weiß so viel über altes Silber. Sie wird . . .)*
With *the old panelling* so beautifully restored, they should get a good price for their house. *(Nachdem die alte Täfelung so schön restauriert ist, ...)*
Antique furniture is selling well, **with Chippendale fetching the highest prices.** *(. . ., wobei Chippendale die höchsten Preise erzielt.)*

Of all the participle constructions with their own notional subjects, those used as adverbials are of particular interest.
They are called absolute participle constructions and are often introduced by the structure word *with* (which must never be translated by *mit*).
An absolute participle construction usually corresponds to a main clause or a subordinate adverbial clause in German (for details see **294**).
(For the participle with its own notional subject after verbs of perception and observation see **281–282.**)

Note:
Infinitive constructions and verbless subordinate clauses are also occasionally introduced by the structure word *with* + notional subject. Like absolute participles, such constructions have adverbial function:

With George to advise her, she felt confident that the new shop would be a success.
With old books so much in demand, his business is doing well.

263 Non-Finite Constructions after Verbs and Verbal Complexes: Formal Criteria

Whether it is correct to use an infinitive, a gerund or a participle depends partly on formal criteria and partly on the meaning of the different constructions themselves. The following paragraph lists the formal criteria; for meaning see **264–286.** A dictionary will give more detailed information in individual cases.

1. Non-finite constructions after verbs

They *wanted*	**to sell**	me a very expensive ring.	Verb + infinitive
He *considered*	**buying**	the diamond necklace.	Verb + gerund
The pearls *lay*	**gleaming**	in the box.	Verb + present participle/past participle
	scattered	all over the floor.	

When a verb is immediately followed by a non-finite construction, this can be an infinitive, a gerund or (occasionally) a present or past participle. The verb itself usually determines which is to be used (cf **264–286**).

He *dreamt of*	**finding**	gold one day.	Verb with preposition + gerund
No one *would object to*	**inheriting**	a gold mine.	

(Compare: They *objected to* his crazy ideas: verb with preposition + noun phrase)

Prepositional verbs (i.e. verbs always combined with a preposition) always take a gerund. Note that *to* can be a preposition after this type of verb and then must not be confused with the *to* of the infinitive: *to* takes a gerund after it when it would also be possible to use a noun phrase in the same position.

2. Non-finite constructions after verbal complexes

He *is unable*	**to tell**	real furs from fakes.	Verbal complex + infinitive
Sheila *is fond of*	**wearing**	spectacular hats.	Verbal complex with preposition + gerund
She is *used to*	**getting**	expensive presents.	

After a verbal complex with a personal subject, no preposition is used before a following infinitive, but there is always one before a gerund. (Note that *to* can be a preposition here as well, e.g. *be used to, be accustomed to (doing) s.th.*) The verbal complex itself determines which construction is to be used (cf **264–278**).

It was difficult	**to fasten**	the bracelet.	*It* + verbal complex + infinitive (common)
It's interesting	**to watch**	the goldsmith at work.	
It's not worth	**repairing**	this watch.	*It* + verbal complex + gerund (rare)
There's no	**knowing**	what the price will be.	*There is no* + gerund

Verbal complexes introduced by the structure word *it* generally take the infinitive. This then functions as notional subject of the sentence (cf **257.1** Note)
The gerund occurs after *it's no use, it's no good, it's worthwhile, it's (not) worth* as well as after *there is no.*

Notes:
1. Colloquially, a gerund can be used after several other verbal complexes starting with *it* which would normally take an infinitive, e.g. *it's a pleasure, it's nice:*

It was nice **meeting** you. It's been a pleasure **talking** to you.

2. In infinitive constructions following a verb or verbal complex, the *to*-infinitive is generally used. Some verbs of causing and allowing, however, (**283–286**) and verbs of perception and observation (**281–282**) are followed by the bare infinitive (i.e. without *to*). *Help* can be followed by an infinitive with or without *to*:

She helped him **(to) write** his thank-you letter.

The modal auxiliaries and the expressions *had better, would sooner, would rather, cannot but* are also followed by the bare infinitive without *to*:

We'd better **send** the Browns a Christmas card this year.

3. The *-ing* form after verbs and verbal complexes is called the gerund if it functions as a direct object (i.e. if a noun phrase could be used as a direct object in its place), or if there is a preposition before it. If the *-ing* form functions as a subject complement or object complement, it is regarded as a present participle. There are however a number of border-line cases where it is hard to tell which is which. Compare:

He is busy	**reading**	his mail.	He is busy	**with** his mail.
She went on	**working**.		She went on	**with** her work.
They kept (on)	**asking**	questions.		

These cases are dealt with in **269** and **276** under the heading of *Gerund* as, from the point of view of their meaning, the verbs in question belong with the other verbs and verbal complexes which take a gerund.

64–268 Verbs and Verbal Complexes with the Infinitive

The most important verbs and verbal complexes which are followed by the infinitive can be classed into five groups. Four of these groups (**264–267**) consist of verbs and verbal complexes of similar meaning. They take the infinitive mainly because of its modal meaning (cf **258**.1).

The fifth group consists of verbal complexes of various meanings. They are followed by the infinitive mainly for formal reasons (e.g. the *it*-construction). (Cf **263.2**.)

264 Verbs and Verbal Complexes Expressing Intention, Willingness or Wishes

We plan to leave tomorrow. He is willing to go with you.	I want (him) to stay at home I am anxious (for her) not to be late.
plan to do s.th. **Similarly:** intend, mean (= intend), threaten, offer, refuse, decline (= refuse), decide, determine, hope, attempt, try	**want (s.o.) to do s.th.** **Similarly:** wish, expect, would like/love/prefer/hate
be willing to do s.th. **Similarly:** be ready, be prepared, be inclined, be interested, be afraid	**be anxious (for s.o.) to do s.th.** **Similarly:** be eager, be keen

(For the use of the gerund after *like, love, prefer, hate, be keen, be interested, be afraid* see **273**, for *try* see **274**.)

The infinitive is used here because it describes an action which has yet to be carried out. In some cases the infinitive can have its own notional subject. This is preceded by *for* in the case of the verbal complexes (cf **259, 260**).

265 Verbs Expressing Advice, Exhortation, Causing and Allowing

My friends told **me** to catch the number 9 bus. → I was told to catch the number 9 bus.

tell s.o. to do s.th.
Similarly: advise, recommend, ask, beg, persuade, encourage, remind, press, urge, command, direct, require, order, cause, force, allow, permit, forbid, warn
(**Note:** warn s.o. **to do** s.th.: *jdn. ermahnen, etw. zu tun,* warn s.o. **not do do** s.th.: *jdn. davor warnen, etw. zu tun.*)
Also: let s.o. do s.th. (rarely in the passive), make s.o. do s.th.

(For the use of the gerund after *advise, recommend, encourage, urge, allow, permit, forbid* see **275**.
For the verbs of causing and allowing *cause, force, make, let, allow, permit* see **283, 285.**)

As with the verbs in the previous group, the action has yet to be carried out. In active sentences the verbs are always accompanied by an object (which is at the same time notional subject of the infinitive construction). The object denotes the person who is to carry out the action. In passive sentences this person is made the subject of the whole sentence.

266 Verbs Expressing an Opinion or Supposition

We think him to be the best man for the job. (formal)
He is thought to be the best man for the job. (less formal)

Compare: We think (that) he is the best man for the job. (neutral)

think s.o./s.th. to be s.th.
Similarly: believe, consider, suppose, imagine, judge, find, know, understand *(halten für, wissen),* admit *(zugeben)*

The infinitive is used here because something is presented not objectively as a fact but as a personal opinion. After the active forms of these verbs, the infinitive (usually only *to be* is possible) has to have its own notional subject. This construction sounds very formal; in colloquial speech, *that*-clauses are preferred. The corresponding passive construction with the infinitive does not sound quite so formal.

Note:
After most of these verbs *to be* can be dropped, giving the sentence pattern with object + object complement (cf **54, 57**).

267 Verbs and Verbal Complexes Expressing a Degree of Probability

We seem to have run out of money.
Is Jimmy likely to have some change?

Compare: It seems that we have run out of money.
Is it likely that Jimmy will have some change?

s.o. / s.th.	**seems / is likely**	**to do/to be doing/to have done s.th. / to be/to have been/etc.**

Similarly: appear, be unlikely, be sure, be certain

As with the previous group of verbs (**266**), something is not being presented here as a fact. Rather, the speaker is judging a situation subjectively.
These verbs and verbal complexes can only be followed by the infinitive if the sentence has a 'personal' subject (person or thing). The alternative is a construction with the structure word *it* as formal subject followed by a *that*-clause.

Note:
The infinitive is also used after *happen* and *chance.* Although a fact is being stated, it is the unexpectedness of the event that is being stressed:

I happened/chanced to meet her on the bus. (Also: It happened/chanced that I met her on the bus.)

268 Verbal Complexes with the Structure Word *it* (Various Meanings)

It was hard to forgive her for that remark. Is it safe for us to interrupt Dad when he's watching the Cup Final?
it is hard (for s.o.) to do s.th. **Also** other verbal complexes which establish how easy or difficult an action is: it is easy/simple/difficult/safe/dangerous/convenient/etc.
It is unusual to bring flowers when you visit someone in England. It is quite normal for the neighbours to drop in unannounced.
it is unusual (for s.o.) to do s.th. **Also** other verbal complexes which establish how frequently something happens: it is usual/normal/common/the custom/rare/etc. (Comparable expressions: there is a tendency (for s.o.) to do s.th./the tendency is (for s.o.) to do s.th.)
It is important (for us) to keep on good terms with Aunt Gertrude.
it is important (for s.o.) to do s.th. **Also** other verbal complexes which establish how urgently something should be carried out: it is necessary/crucial/essential/advisable/preferable/urgent/etc.
It would be awful to lose contact with the Kellys altogether. It must have been disappointing for you to have missed meeting your cousin from Australia.
it is awful (for s.o.) to do s.th. **Also** other verbal complexes which describe the emotional effect of something: it is sad/dreadful/surprising/shocking/disappointing/annoying/a pity/a pleasure/etc.
It was foolish to lose your temper over it. It would be sensible of you to apologize.
it is foolish (of s.o.) to do s.th. **Also** other verbal complexes which express a judgement (praise or criticism). it is sensible/clever/crazy/right/wrong/brave/generous/strange/etc.

These verbs are followed by the infinitive chiefly because they are formed with the structure word *it* (cf 263.2). The infinitive can, in almost all cases, be expanded to the *for* + infinitive construction, with the exception of the last group (verbal complexes expressing a judgement). In this group the notional subject of the infinitive (the person who is judged) is usually introduced by *of* (cf Ger. *von*).

Notes:
1. A number of these verbal complexes can also be constructed with an ordinary ('personal') subject and an infinitive. Compare:

The argument was difficult to follow.	It was difficult to follow the argument.

(The same applies to the other verbal complexes which express how easy or difficult an action is.)

You were right to demand an explanation.	It was right of you to demand an explanation.

(The same applies to many other verbal complexes which express a judgement.)

2. Some verbal complexes with the structure word *it* can also take *that*-clauses (for the finite verb forms in these *that*-clauses see **213.**2 a, **234**, **305.**2). Compare:

It is important that some member of the family (should) attend the funeral.
It is important for some member of the family to attend the funeral.

It was a pity that she missed/should have missed her sister's wedding.
It was a pity for her to have missed her sister's wedding.

269–272 Verbs and Verbal Complexes with the Gerund

The most important verbs and verbal complexes which can be followed by the gerund are classed below in four groups according to their meaning. Included are not only those verbs and verbal complexes which are followed immediately by the gerund, but also those which are linked to the gerund by a preposition. A preposition can, of course, only be followed by a gerund, but this is not merely a formal rule: meaning is also relevant. After all the verbs and verbal complexes in these groups, the gerund is used to present something which is seen as already existing in some form (factual meaning: cf **258.**1).

269 Verbs and Verbal Complexes Expressing one's Occupation with Something

1. Occupation in a general sense

When her right arm was in plaster, Pauline practised writing with her left hand.
Do you know anybody who specializes in interpreting handwriting?
My cousin Vera is engaged in studying Egyptian hieroglyphics.
The boys were busy copying out the words of the song.

practise doing s.th.	**Similarly:** try (cf **274**)
specialize in doing s.th.	**Similarly:** concentrate on
be engaged in doing s.th.	**Similarly:** be occupied with, be concerned with, take part in
be busy doing s.th. (cf **263**, Note 3)	

2. Mental occupation

Joe's considering taking up fishing.	I can't imagine him sitting still for hours. The angler was aware of a fish biting.
consider doing s.th.	**imagine (s.o.) doing s.th.** **Similarly:** fancy (= imagine), remember (s.th. in the past)
think of doing s.th.	**dream of (s.o.) doing s.th.** **be aware of (s.o.) doing s.th.** **Similarly:** be conscious/unconscious of, pay attention to

Here, the gerund generally describes an action which is just taking place or has already taken place. After verbs such as *consider, imagine,* etc., it describes something that is imagined as taking place, e.g. one sees oneself already doing something. This is why – in contrast to verbs such as *plan, intend, hope,* etc. (cf **264**) – the gerund and not the infinitive is used.
Some of these verbs can have a gerund with its own notional subject.

Note:
Verbal complexes such as *be good/bad at* describe how well or badly someone can do something – having, of course, already done it a number of times. Consequently these verbal complexes are also followed by the gerund:

He's not very good at doing sums, but he's excellent at spelling.

Similarly: be outstanding in/famous for; be capable of/experienced in/an expert in/efficient in/knowledgeable about; be terrible at/hopeless at, etc.

270 Verbs Expressing Avoidance or Prevention

He always avoids drinking before driving. Please refrain from smoking.	It's only vanity that keeps me from over-eating.
avoid doing s.th. **Similarly:** escape, resist, delay, postpone, put off	**keep s.o. from doing s.th.** **Similarly:** prevent, dissuade, discourage, protect, save
refrain from doing s.th.	

If one wants to avoid or prevent something, one assumes the existence of something which is to be avoided. The gerund is therefore used because of its factual meaning.

Note:
In the case of *risk* one assumes the existence of something which is in itself undesirable or which could have undesirable consequences. It is therefore followed by the gerund:

The children risked being caught shoplifting.
She risked leaving the car window open.

271 Verbs and Verbal Complexes Expressing an Emotional Reaction or Attitude

1. Activity verbs describing an emotional reaction

Most people enjoy travelling to foreign countries.
Didn't you boast of being able to speak French fluently?
I'm not worrying about us making ourselves understood in Norway.
We thanked the waiter for so patiently explaining the items on the Chinese menu to us.

enjoy doing s.th.	**Similarly:** regret doing s.th. (in the past)
boast of (s.o.) doing s.th.	**Similarly:** complain of, object to, worry about
praise s.o. for doing s.th.	**Similarly:** blame s.o./pity s.o. for doing s.th.

2. Verbs and verbal complexes describing an attitude of liking or disliking

I like playing the piano.
Are you fond of going to concerts?
Do you mind me practising the violin this afternoon?
Mum didn't approve of me giving up music lessons.

like (s.o.) doing s.th.	**Similarly:** love, appreciate, prefer, favour, (don't) mind, hate, dislike, detest, resent, cannot stand, cannot bear
approve of (s.o.) doing s.th.	**Similarly:** disapprove of
be fond of (s.o.) doing s.th.	**Similarly:** be keen on, be interested in, take an interest in, be enthusiastic about, be crazy about, be opposed to, be afraid of

(For the infinitive after *like, love, prefer, be keen*, etc. in the sense of *want*, see **264** and **273**.)

3. Verbal complexes with a personal subject describing an emotional effect

We were surprised at her choosing to study the flute and not the piano.

be surprised at (s.o.) doing s.th.	**Similarly:** be glad about, be proud of, be ashamed of, be disappointed at/about, be amazed at, be astonished at, etc.

(For the construction *be surprised/glad to hear that s.o. has done s.th.* see **278**.)

The gerund is used here for something which sets off a personal reaction or a feeling. The existence of what it refers to is taken for granted as a personal or general experience.

272 Verbs and Verbal Complexes Expressing or Establishing a Relationship

My duties at the Duponts' place included cooking and baby-sitting.
Being an au pair girl can amount to being treated like a servant.
You can't compare working in a foreign country with going there as a tourist.

include doing s.th.
Similarly: involve *(zur Folge/zur Bedingung haben)*, mean *(bedeuten)*

amount to doing s.th. *(auf etwas hinauslaufen)*
Similarly: depend on, refer to *(sich beziehen/anspielen auf)*, apply to *(zutreffen auf, gelten für)*, differ from, be different from

compare doing s.th. with doing s.th.
Similarly: confuse ... with, combine ... with, distinguish ... from

In this group a relationship (such as belonging, comparison, difference, etc.) is established between two actions, states, etc. The gerund is used because what it refers to is known to exist in some form.

Note:
Occasionally the gerund in this group has its own notional subject:
This job would involve **my** living out in the country.

273–278 Verbs and Verbal Complexes with the Infinitive or the Gerund

273 *Like, love, prefer, hate, be keen, be interested*

Would you *like* **to have** supper with us?
I'*d love* **to stay** longer, but I'm afraid I must be getting home.
I *hate* **to mention** it, but there's a caterpillar *(Raupe)* in the salad.
I'*m* rather *keen* **to try** this interesting-looking vegetable. *(Ich würde gern ... ausprobieren.)*
They *like* **to eat** out on Sundays.
He *hates* **to leave** anything on his plate.

The infinitive is used to express a wish for something to happen in a particular case (modal meaning). It must therefore be used in combinations of *should/would* + *like/love/prefer.*
Like, love, hate and *prefer* + infinitive can also denote habitual behaviour (due to some preference or dislike).

Do you *like* **cooking?**
Bill *loves* **trying out** exotic recipes.

No one *hates* **peeling** potatoes more than I do.

Our friends *are* very *keen* **on buying** their food at health shops. *(... kaufen ... gern ...)*
More and more people *are becoming interested* **in growing** their own vegetables.

The gerund is used to express a general preference or dislike. The action or state concerned is taken for granted as something generally known to exist (factual meaning).
The verbal complexes *be keen* and *be interested* take a preposition before the gerund.

Note:
Be afraid can be followed either by the infinitive or *of* + gerund. The infinitive denotes a particular action which has not yet been carried out and which one fears.
The gerund denotes either a generally known activity, which one fears, or an imagined consequence over which one has no control.
To sum up: the infinitive can only be used for something which can be carried out deliberately; the gerund can also be used for something which may happen to a person:

I'm afraid to ski down that steep slope.

I'm afraid of skiing.
I'm afraid of breaking my leg.

274 *Remember, regret, forget* and *try*

I must *remember* **to set** the alarm for six thirty tomorrow. Don't *forget* **to put** your clocks back an hour tonight. We *regret* **to tell** you that your application has come too late to be considered. He *tried* **to repair** his watch himself and made a mess of it.	The alarm didn't go off although he clearly *remembered* **setting** it/**having set** it. He *forgot* **having made** this early appointment and kept me waiting for half an hour. You'll *regret* **not making** more effort to be punctual. If you want your electric clock to work, *try* **putting in** a battery.

The infinitive is used here for an intended action, i.e. one which has not yet been carried out (modal meaning).

The gerund with *remember, forget* and *regret* describes an action that has already taken place (the perfect form is also possible).
The gerund with *try* denotes a well-known method or a skill which a person already possesses (factual meaning).

275 *Advise, recommend, encourage, urge, allow, permit, forbid*

Mary *advised* her mother **to buy** the red off-the-shoulder dress. The shop assistant *recommended* him **to wash** the jeans separately the first few times. The store only *allows* you **to try** on three garments at one time.	Doctors *advise* **wearing** natural fibres such as cotton in summer. Most manufacturers *recommend* **washing** knitwear by hand. Many shops don't *permit* **smoking** on the premises. *(in den Geschäftsräumen)*

The infinitive is used when someone advises, allows or forbids a person to do something in a particular case. The person who is being advised etc. always has to be named, so active sentences with this construction must contain an object (= notional subject of the infinitive).

The gerund is used when someone advises, allows or forbids something in general. Those who are being advised, etc. are not named, so the gerund construction cannot have a notional subject.

Note:
After *suggest* and *how about/what about* one can only use a gerund, never an infinitive:
Last season the fashion articles all suggested mixing green and navy blue.
How about/What about dyeing that T-shirt purple?

276 Verbs Expressing Beginning, Continuation or Ending

1. *Begin, start, continue, cease*

The boat *started* **to sink**. They *began* **to realize** the danger they were in.	The boat *started* **sinking**. The crew *began* **distributing** life-jackets.

begin to do s.th. – begin doing s.th.
Similarly: start, continue, cease

These verbs can take either the infinitive or the gerund. There is no difference in meaning. However, when they are followed by verbs with stative meaning (*realize, understand, like,* etc.), these normally come in infinitive form.

2. *Go on, stop, quit, finish, give up, leave off*

First she read the business pages, then she *went on* **to study** the job advertisements. On the way home from the factory he *stopped* **to buy** a newspaper. You must *finish* (those letters) quickly (in order) **to be** in time for the post. She *quit* (her job) **to have** more time for her family.	Mary and I *went on* **arguing** about the causes of unemployment all the evening. He *stopped* **reading** the paper when the boss came in. Have you *finished* **sorting** the mail? Do *quit* **grumbling** and get on with your work.
go on to do s.th. (= do s.th. next) **stop to do s.th.** (= stop one activity in order to do s.th. else) (Occasionally after: quit, finish, give up, leave off)	**go on doing s.th.** (= continue doing s.th.) **stop doing s.th.** (= cease doing s.th.) **Similarly:** quit, finish, give up, leave off

The infinitive is used here for an action which is planned but has yet to be carried out (modal meaning).
After *go on* it denotes the next step in a sequence of actions.
After *stop* it denotes the purpose for which another action or activity is brought to an end.
The infinitive occurs occasionally after *quit, finish, give up* and *leave off* in a similar function. i.e. as an adverbial of purpose.

The gerund here describes the action itself which is already taking place and which is either continued or brought to an end (factual meaning).

Note:
Go on doing s.th. is on the border between the gerund and the present participle (cf **263** Note 3). The same applies to *keep (on)/carry on doing s.th.*, which can only be constructed with *-ing* forms.

277 Verbs Expressing Necessity: *need, want, require, deserve*

That question *needs* **to be gone into** thoroughly.	That question *needs* **going into** thoroughly.
s.th. needs to be done – s.th. needs doing **Similarly:** want, require, deserve	

After these verbs the gerund has (in spite of its active form) the same passive meaning as the passive infinitive.

Notes:
1. When used to express necessity, *remain* and *be* are followed by the passive infinitive. (Similar German sentences have the active infinitive.) The gerund cannot be used.
All that *remains* **to be decided** is the price of the article. *(Alles was noch zu entscheiden bleibt . . .)*
Such matters *are* always **to be handled** very carefully. *(. . . sind . . . zu behandeln.)*

2. *There is* + noun (more rarely *there remains* + noun) may also be followed by the active infinitive. It expresses an active perspective, like the construction with personal subject + *have* + noun + infinitive:
There is a problem (for us) **to solve.** (There is a problem which we have to solve.)
We have a problem **to solve.**

278 Verbal Complexes Expressing an Emotional Effect

I was angry to find that I wasn't invited to take part in the discussion. We were surprised to hear that he had left the Labour Party. (Or: We were surprised to hear about his decision/to hear the news.)	I was angry about not being invited to take part in the discussion. We were surprised at his having left the Labour Party.

be angry to hear/see/find that s.th. is the case – be angry about s.th. being the case
Similarly: be surprised (at), be glad (about), be sorry (about), be alarmed (at), be shocked (at), be delighted (at), be relieved (at), be excited (at), be worried (at), etc.

These verbal complexes always have a personal subject and often consist of *be* and an adjective which is originally the past participle of a verb. They can take the following non-finite constructions:

- infinitive of a verb of perception *(see/hear/find)* + *that*-clause, prepositional phrase or noun phrase. This construction is stylistically neutral and is preferred in colloquial speech.
- preposition + gerund (with or without its own notional subject). This construction sounds rather formal.

Note:
For the infinitive after verbal complexes with the structure word *it* (*it is surprising/alarming,* etc.) see **268**.

279–280 Verbs followed by a Participle as Subject Complement

279 Verbs describing a Position

We sat waiting for the rain to stop. *(Wir saßen und warteten darauf, daß ... aufhörte.)* They remained standing by the window. *(Sie blieben am Fenster stehen.)*	He lay stretched out on the bed. *(Er lag auf dem Bett ausgestreckt.)* Please remain seated. *(Bitte bleiben Sie sitzen.)*

sit talking/reading/wondering/.../bent over a book/... **stand** waiting/watching/waving/.../confused/... **lie** dying *(im Sterben liegen)*/gasping/.../exhausted/...	**remain** sitting/standing/.../seated/... **stay** floating/drifting/.../fixed to the wall/...

After these verbs, the present participle indicates that the action is taking place at the same time. In German two verbs linked by *und* are often used to express this idea *(... saßen und warteten ...).* The past participle describes the result of a previous action.

280 Verbs describing a Movement (Arriving, Leaving)

He came running along the platform. *(Er kam ... gelaufen.)* They arrived panting for breath. *(Sie kamen nach Atem ringend an.)*	We left rested and refreshed after our two hours' stop. *(Wir gingen ... ausgeruht und erfrischt weg.)* Did they arrive very worn out by the journey? *(Kamen sie sehr erschöpft ... an?)*

come/arrive/return/leave/go (away) running/hopping/stumbling/.../injured/excited/...

Both participles describe how the movement in question is carried out. The present participle describes an action taking place at the same time as the movement; the past participle expresses the result of a previous action.

281–282 Infinitive and Participle after Verbs of Perception and Observation

Verbs of perception *(see, hear, feel, smell, notice, find)* and observation *(watch, observe)* are followed by various non-finite constructions. The choice is regulated to some extent by the different meanings of the infinitive, present participle and past participle. (See also **282** Notes for certain restrictions.)

281 Structures

The caretaker *saw* him **open** the window.	A neighbour *saw* him **knocking** at the door.
He *was seen* **to open** the window.	He *was seen* **knocking** at the door.
Did you *hear* someone **bang** the door? The little boy *watched* the man **shut** the gate.	We *watched* the piano **being carried** upstairs. The key *was found* **hidden** under the mat.

The infinitive can be used after active or passive forms of verbs of perception and observation.
The infinitive has no *to* after active forms, but after passive forms the *to*-infinitive is used. The infinitive itself can only be used in its active form.

Both the present and the past participle can be used after the active and passive forms of these verbs.
The present participle itself can either be in the active form *(knocking)* or in the passive form *(being carried)*.
The past participle only has one (passive) form.

282 Differences in Meaning between the Infinitive and the Present Participle

There are differences in aspect between the infinitive and the present participle which are similar to those between the simple form and the progressive form of the finite verb (cf **181**).

We *saw* the ambassador **arrive** in a limousine. (Cf: The ambassador **arrived** in a limousine.) *Did* you *hear* the bomb **go off**? The witness *saw* a man in a grey raincoat **place** a parcel near a pillar and **walk** out of the building.	We *watched* the V.I.P.s **arriving** at the Town Hall. (Cf: The V.I.P.s **were arriving** at the Town Hall.) We *could hear* the crowd **shouting** anti-war slogans all the time. They *found* a group of people **sitting** on the steps, **blocking** the entrance.

The infinitive indicates that an action or event is being regarded **as a whole**, with its result included.

It is mainly used for single, short actions or for a chain of events.

The present participle indicates that an action or event is regarded as a **process** which is taking place (progressive aspect).
It is used mainly when an action lasts a certain length of time, keeps being repeated, leads to no particular result (e.g. with verbs which describe a position) or takes place at the same time as something else.

Notes:

1. Because of its meaning, the infinitive is not used after *find* (= Ger. *vorfinden*) and *smell* (one would hardly perceive the whole of an event through one's sense of smell).

2. The past participle only occurs after verbs of perception (mainly *see, hear* and *find*). It describes from the passive perspective

- the result of a previous process

We **found** his bicycle **chained** to a fence.
(Cf: He **had chained** his bicycle to a fence.)

- a process taking place at the same time as it is perceived. The passive form of the present participle is possible here too, but this stresses the progressive aspect (cf **181**).

I **heard** my name **shouted** from the other side of the street.
(Cf: Someone **shouted** my name from the other side . . .)
I **heard** my name **being shouted** again and again.
(Cf: Someone **was shouting** my name again and again.)

283–286 Infinitive and Participle after Verbs of Causing and Allowing

The various meanings of the German verb *lassen* are expressed by a number of different English verbs and non-finite constructions.
The main meanings are:

283 Causing Someone to Do Something

They **make** the factory workers **keep** their hair tied back for safety. *(Aus Sicherheitsgründen läßt man . . . die Haare zurückgebunden tragen.)*
The officials **had** us **put on** safety helmets before going down the mine. *(. . . ließen uns Schutzhelme aufsetzen . . .)*
They **were made to wear** protective clothing. *(Man ließ sie/Sie mußten Schutzkleidung tragen.)*

In this causative meaning, the following verbs are used:

- **make** / **have** } **s.o. do s.th.** (infinitive **without** *to*)

Make can also occur in the passive form; it then takes the infinitive **with** *to.*
Have+infinitive is not possible in passive sentences.

The strike at the airport **caused** me **to cancel** my trip. *(. . . veranlaßte mich . . .)*
I **got** the travel agency **to change** my booking. *(Ich brachte das Reisebüro dazu . . .)*
You **can be compelled to open** all your bags at the customs. *(Man kann gezwungen werden . . .)*
People **were forced to wait** for hours before they were able to get their luggage. *(. . . waren gezwungen . . ./mußten stundenlang warten . . .)*
I **was caused to cancel** my trip because of the airport strike.

- **cause** / **get** / **force** / **compel** } **s.o. to do s.th.** (infinitive **with** *to*)

The passive forms *be forced/compelled to do s.th.* can be used as substitutes for the modal auxiliary *must* expressing necessity (cf **229**).

Cause can also occur in the passive, but not *get* + infinitive.

284 Causing Something to be Done

The gallery **had** their Rembrandt **cleaned** and **restored**. *(. . . ließ ihren Rembrandt reinigen und restaurieren.)*
We're **going to have** this bronze statue **valued**.
You'll **have** your Chippendale chairs **insured**, won't you? *(Sie werden . . . versichern lassen . . .?)*
You **must get** that Wedgewood vase **mended** professionally. *(. . . reparieren lassen.)*

In this second causative meaning (where the action itself is more important than the person carrying it out), one normally uses:

have / **get** (colloquial) } **s.th. done** (past participle)

(For the purely passive meaning of the construction with *have* see **64**.)

Note:
The construction *have s.th. done* must not be confused with the present or past perfect. It is important to place the object and past participle in the right position:

They **had** burglar alarms **installed** in all rooms. *(Sie ließen . . . Alarmanlagen installieren.)*
They **had installed** burglar alarms in all rooms. *(Sie hatten . . . Alarmanlagen installiert.)*

285 Allowing

They **let** him **do** just as he liked.
(Sie ließen ihn machen, was er wollte.)
Her parents **will never allow** her **to go** to India on her own.
The Russian authorities **don't permit** you **to take** photos of bridges and railways.
Non-believers **are not permitted to enter** this Hindu temple. *(Ungläubigen ist es nicht gestattet . . ./Ungläubige dürfen . . . nicht betreten.)*

To express this meaning one uses the following verbs:

- **let** — **s.o. do s.th.** (inf. without *to*)
- **allow** / **permit** (formal) — **s.o. to do s.th.** (inf. with *to*)

The passive forms *be allowed/permitted to do s.th.* can be used as substitutes for *may* expressing permission (cf **227**).

Note:
To express the idea of 'not allowing' one can also use the construction *not + have s.o. doing s.th.* (present participle):

I can't **have you taking** photos in the church. *(Ich kann es nicht zulassen/dulden, daß . . .)*

286 Preserving a Situation Unchanged

She **left** us **puzzling** over what she meant.
(Sie ließ uns im Unklaren darüber, was sie meinte.)
He **kept** the press **waiting** for half an hour.
(Er ließ . . . warten.)
The country **was kept guessing** as to his real intentions. *(. . . wurde im Unklaren über . . . gelassen.)*
He **was left unmoved** by the attacks on his political credibility. *(. . . blieb unberührt . . .)*
She **kept** her eyes **fixed** on the speaker.

In this sense the following verbs are found:

leave / **keep** — **s.o. doing s.th.** (present participle)

Leave usually implies that the resulting situation is unintentional. *Keep*, on the other hand, may imply an intentional effect. Both verbs can occur in the passive.

A past participle can also be used after these verbs to express the idea of an unchanged situation.

Note:
German *lassen* can also correspond to a number of single verbs which are either causative-transitive or have a passive meaning (cf **45**, **65**):

The men **had** all **grown** beards during the expedition. *(. . . hatten sich . . . einen Bart wachsen lassen.)*
This camp-bed **folds up** very small. *(. . . läßt sich . . . zusammenfalten.)*

287 Verbs and Verbal Complexes plus Non-Finite Constructions where Adverbs are Used in German

A number of verbs and verbal complexes plus non-finite constructions correspond more or less to the meanings of German verb + adverb combinations. Some typical examples:

She **is fond of** meeting people. *(Sie lernt gern Leute kennen.)*	like/love/be fond of/prefer/hate/ dislike doing s.th. (would) like/love/prefer/hate to do s.th.	*etw. gern/lieber/nicht gern tun*

You**'re sure to** enjoy the picnic. *(Du wirst ... bestimmt genießen.)*	be sure/be certain/be likely to do s.th. appear/seem to do s.th.	*etw. sicher/wahrscheinlich/anscheinend tun*
I **happened to** meet him on the bus. *(Ich traf ihn zufällig ...)*	happen/chance to do s.th.	*etw. zufällig tun*
They **were quick to** answer our letter. *(Sie beantworteten ... schnell.)*	be quick/slow/prompt to do s.th.	*etw. schnell/langsam/sofort tun*
Sue Martin **kept** calling me names. *(... beschimpfte mich andauernd.)*	keep (on)/go on doing s.th. continue doing s.th./to do s.th.	*etw. andauernd/weiterhin tun*
Granny **used to** have many friends. *(Oma hatte früher viele Freunde.)*	I used to do s.th.	*ich tat früher etwas*

Notes:

1. *Fail to do s.th.* and *miss doing s.th.* often correspond simply to negative sentences in German:
   I failed to meet him. *(Ich traf ihn nicht.)*
   He missed seeing that film. *(Er hat diesen Film nicht gesehen.)*

2. Some German adverbs correspond to verbs and verbal complexes plus *that*-clauses:
   I**'m afraid** (that) I can't come. *(Ich kann **leider** nicht kommen.)*

288–289 Infinitive and Gerund after Abstract Nouns

288 Structures

The decision *to close the factory* was not taken lightly.
Have you heard about **the plan** *for the firm to be nationalized?*
(Compare: ... the plan that the firm should be nationalized?)

- noun + infinitive (also with *for* + notional subject)

Their reasons *for dismissing so many employees* are obvious.
They underrated **the danger** *of automation destroying jobs.*
(Compare: ... the danger that automation would/might destroy jobs.)

- noun + prep. + gerund (also with notional subject)

The infinitive and the gerund can occur as attributes to an abstract noun.

- The infinitive is always used with *to*. It can sometimes be expanded by a notional subject introduced by *for*.
- The gerund is always preceded by a preposition. It can sometimes have a notional subject of its own.

The infinitive and the gerund in this function can often be replaced by *that*-clauses. (See however the infinitive and participle corresponding to relative clauses in **300–301**.)
Which construction is used depends on the individual noun, not, however, on its position or function in the sentence.

289 The Choice of Infinitive or Gerund and the Meaning of the Noun

Many abstract nouns are formed from verbs and adjectives, or related to them. Thus they can usually be followed by the same constructions as the corresponding verbs or verbal complexes formed with *be* + adjective.

1. Infinitive

The Minister's willingness to take the blame was respected by all.
Will he accept their advice to resign?

(s.o.'s) **willingness to do s.th.** (cf **to be willing to do s.th.**)
Similarly: eagerness, inclination, plan, wish, agreement, attempt, etc.
(s.o.'s) **advice to do s.th.** (cf **to advise s.o. to do s.th.**)
Similarly: order, command, permission, etc.

The infinitive occurs mainly after nouns which express:

- intention, willingness, or a wish
- advice, exhortation, causing or allowing.

In all these cases the infinitive construction describes an action which has not yet been carried out (modal meaning).

2. Gerund

Though glad at the success of her play, she can't get over her dislike of being interviewed.
Her habit of asking tactless questions made Jane very unpopular.

(s.o.'s) **dislike of doing s.th.**
Similarly: love of, hate of, preference for, doubt about, fear of, worry about, etc.
(the) **habit of doing s.th.**
Similarly: method of, question of, problem of, etc.

The gerund can occur after nouns which

- express an emotional reaction or attitude to something
- refer to something in a general way.

We have no objection to your taking a holiday job.

objection to (s.o.) doing s.th.
(cf **to object to (s.o.) doing s.th.**)
Similarly: surprise at, interest in, etc.
(cf to be surprised at/be interested in ...)

If a preposition is necessary between the verb/verbal complex and the gerund, the same preposition is normally used between the corresponding noun and gerund.

3. Infinitive or Gerund

He had no chance to express his opinion on the matter.
Is there no chance of their altering their decision?

(a) **chance to do s.th./of doing s.th.**
Similarly: opportunity (of), desire (of), hesitation (in), intention (of), reason (for), idea (of), pleasure (at/in), etc.

Many nouns, however – unlike the corresponding verbs/verbal complexes – can be followed by the infinitive or by a preposition + gerund without much difference in meaning.
Information on individual words will be found in dictionaries.

290–291 Infinitive Constructions with Interrogatives

290 Structures

		Infinitive construction			
The boys	wondered / were not sure / had no idea / discussed the question	how		to	get better results.
		whom		to	turn to for advice.
		whether		to	leave school or stay on.
		how	they	might	get better results.
		whom	they	could	turn to for advice.
		whether/if	they	should	leave school or stay on.
		Indirect question			

Infinitive constructions which start with an interrogative or the conjunction *whether* (never *if*), correspond to indirect questions with modal auxiliaries (usually those that have the same subject as the main clause).
They occur after verbs (*wonder, ask,* etc.) and verbal complexes (*not be sure, have no idea,* etc.) and also as attributes to abstract nouns (*question, problem,* etc.).

Notes:

1. Infinitive constructions with interrogatives or *whether* can also follow prepositions after verbs (prepositional verbs), verbal complexes and nouns. Sometimes the preposition can be dropped, as with indirect questions (cf **307**.2):
   The group **agreed on** when to meet next time.
   We were **doubtful (about)** what to do next.
   The **problem/question (of)** how to deal with the matter was put to the vote.

2. The infinitive construction with *how* also occurs after *know, learn, teach* and *show. How* can be dropped after *learn* and *teach* but not after *know* and *show.*
   Do you **know how to** play cricket? Can you **show me how to** play the game? (*how* necessary)
   During the holidays many children **learned (how) to swim,** whereas the older ones **were taught (how) to** sail. (*how* not necessary)

291 Meaning and Use

We didn't know what to do with all those black berries.
(either: We didn't know what we **should** do ...
or: We didn't know what we **could** do ...)

The question of how to protect rare plants was raised at the meeting.
(either: how rare plants **should** be protected ...
or: how rare plants **could** be protected ...)

He told us where to find the nicest mushrooms.
(only: ... where we **could** find ...)

Because of its modal meaning (cf **258**), the infinitive combined with an interrogative can express either obligation or possibility. When it is unimportant or self-evident which of these modal meanings is intended, the shorter, more elegant infinitive construction is preferred to the more precise indirect question.

Participle and Gerund Constructions as Adverbials

292 Structures

1. Participle constructions as adverbials

Adverbial participle constructions can be formed with both present participle and past participle. They are comparable to subordinate adverbial clauses. One must distinguish between:

- **related participle constructions**

Looking out over the calm sea, he began to dream. (While **he** looked out over the calm sea, **he** began to dream.) same subject	Related participle constructions refer to the subject of the whole sentence: comparable subordinate clauses have the same subject as the main clause.
Always take along your raincoat **when** going for a walk in Ireland. (... when you go for a walk in Ireland.) **Though** signposted, the mountain trail was not easy to follow. (Though it was signposted, ...)	Related participle constructions can be introduced by **conjunctions** in the same way as subordinate adverbial clauses.

- **absolute participle constructions**

The sun having come out, they decided to go for a walk. (As **the sun** had come out, **they** decided to go for a walk.) different subjects	Absolute participle constructions have notional subjects of their own: comparable subordinate clauses do not have the same subject as the main clause.
With temperatures reaching the eighties yesterday, the ice-cream sellers did a roaring trade.	Absolute participle constructions are often introduced by *with* (cf **262**, **294**).

2. Gerund constructions as adverbials

Gerund constructions can only function as adverbials when they have a preposition in front of them. They are also comparable to adverbial clauses.

In spite of being warned, she risked skating on the thin ice. (Though **she** was warned, **she** risked skating on the thin ice.) same subject	Adverbial gerund constructions normally refer to the subject of the whole sentence.
She walked very carefully **because of** the path being slippery. (**She** walked very carefully because **the path** was slippery.) different subjects	But occasionally the gerund construction has its own notional subject.

Notes:

1. Participle constructions without their own notional subjects are understood by the listener or reader to refer to the subject of the whole sentence. Humorous misunderstandings can arise when the (intended) subject of the participle construction is different from that of the whole sentence, but is not named (so-called 'dangling participles'):

   Before launching the 'Queen Anne', the duchess gave a little speech. Then, after breaking a bottle of champagne over the bow of the ship, she slid majestically into the water.

Sometimes it is stylistically acceptable not to name the subject of the participle construction, for instance, when the formal subject of the sentence is *it* or *there* and the notional subject of the participle is therefore obvious:

   Seeing so many men searching for a job, **it** became very obvious that things were building up to a crisis. (As you/one/people could see so many men ...)

'Dangling participles' are also often used as inserted comments, conjunctions and – more rarely – as prepositions (cf **298–299**).

2. Adverbial participle and gerund constructions can come either before or after the main clause. Participle constructions can also come after the subject, i.e. in the middle of a sentence. In this case they can be regarded as corresponding to non-defining relative clauses (cf **301.2**).

Soon becoming bored, the girls started to talk among themselves.
The girls, soon becoming bored, started to talk among themselves.

293 Related Participle Constructions

Adverbial participle constructions are shorter and sound stylistically more polished than adverbial clauses. They therefore often occur in formal style. They are sometimes used with conjunctions, sometimes not.

1. Without conjunctions

When they are used without conjunctions, these participle constructions are not so fixed in their meaning as comparable subordinate clauses. They are used mainly for:

Passing the factory, we saw that the old chimney had been demolished.
(When we passed the factory, we saw . . .)

Having set the fuse for blowing up the bridge, the men retired to a safe distance.
(When they had set the fuse . . .)

- Time
  To express the idea of something happening at the same time as something else, one uses the present participle – mainly of dynamic verbs, as these can describe actions that take time.
  To express the idea of something happening before something else, one uses the perfect form of the present participle.

Having become unsafe, the tower had to be closed to the public. (As it had become unsafe . . .)
Known for its historic windmills, the island attracts thousands of tourists every year. (As it is known for . . .)

- Reason
  The present participle and the past participle of all verbs can have this meaning. The participles of stative verbs almost always have to be understood in this way.

The passengers gathered on deck as they passed the headland, **photographing, filming** and **admiring** the scenery. *(Die Passagiere versammelten sich an Deck. Sie photographierten, filmten . . .)*
Escorted by many small boats, the ship entered the harbour. *(Von vielen kleinen Booten begleitet, lief das Schiff in den Hafen ein.)*

- Accompanying circumstances
  It is mainly the present participle and past participle of dynamic verbs that are used with this meaning. (They can correspond to participle constructions in German, but also to main clauses with *und* or subordinate clauses with *indem* and *wobei.*)

Living by the sea, I got used to the ceaseless sound of the waves, which at first I had found irritating. (= When I lived . . . or: Because I lived . . .)

Often these meanings overlap (time and reason, for instance, can be present together) so that more than one translation is possible.

Protected by a dam, the village would not have been flooded by the spring tide. (If it had been protected by a dam, . . .)
Looking through a telescope, you can see the opposite coast line. (If you look . . .)
Badly **battered** by the storm, the fishing boats nevertheless all reached the harbour safely. (Though they were badly battered . . .)

Participle constructions without a conjunction can have other meanings as well. In certain contexts they can, for example, express condition, means, or concession.

2. With conjunctions

Participle constructions are introduced by conjunctions when the meaning needs to be made absolutely clear. The following conjunctions are used:

After presenting the case for the defence, the lawyer sat down.
Once arrested, a person must be charged with an offence within 24 hours. *(Sobald . . .)*
Though struggling desperately, the suspected thief was eventually overpowered.
The accused looked nervous when the jury returned, **as if expecting** the worst.
When cross-examined, the witness became confused.
Though found guilty by the court, the prisoner still protested his innocence.

- with the present participle:
  after, before
- with the past participle:
  once, as soon as
- with both participles:
  when, while, (al)though, if, even if, as if, since (= 'seit'), *till, until*

The conjunctions of reason *(because, as/since)* are hardly ever combined with participle constructions. As shown above (Section 1), causal meaning is usually expressed by the participle itself without any conjunction.

Notes:

1. To express reason, one can also use a combination of participle with *as* + personal pronoun + auxiliary:
   The trial, **publicized as it was** in the press, aroused great national interest.
   Adhering as they do to conservative ideals, most of the villagers were shocked at the judge's mild verdict.
2. Sometimes a conjunction can be necessary to avoid a misunderstanding:
   Clare noticed an odd-looking man **entering** the courtroom. (= **The man** was entering the courtroom. Cf **281**)
   Clare noticed an odd-looking man **when entering** the courtroom. (= **Clare** was entering the courtroom.)

294 Absolute Participle Constructions

The explorers suddenly found themselves in a vast cavern, **their lamps casting** strange shadows. *(. . . Ihre Lampen warfen . . .)*
Many caves have been made accessible to the public, **some of them** even **being equipped** with electric light. *(. . ., wobei einige sogar . . .)*

Absolute participle constructions mainly express the **circumstances** accompanying an action; in German their meanings would normally be expressed by main clauses or subordinate adverbial clauses introduced by *wobei* or *indem.*

Their existence discovered in 1940, the cave paintings at Lascaux became a sensation in the art world. *(Als ihre Existenz 1940 entdeckt wurde, . . .)*
Stalactites and stalagmites are generally very old, **their formation having taken** centuries. (. . . *Ihre Entstehung dauerte . . ./. . . da ihre . . .)*

They can also be used as expressions of **time and reason** and then correspond to German subordinate clauses with *als, wenn, da, weil,* etc.

With a fall of rock blocking their way, the team had to turn back. *(Da . . .)*
The cave was pitch dark, **with bats flying** all around. *(. . ., und Fledermäuse . . .)*

Absolute participle constructions which are not introduced by *with* are typical of a formal, elevated style in written English.

The *with* + participle construction, however, is found on all stylistic levels and is very common in colloquial English.

295 Gerund Constructions as Adverbials

The meaning of adverbial gerund constructions depends on the preposition they follow. They can be divided into two groups:

On hearing the crash Mrs Brown rushed out into the street. (When she heard ...)
Tom got a bruised knee **from falling off** his bicycle. (... because/when he fell off ...)
In case of the neighbours **complaining,** the boys can always go elsewhere to play football. (In case the neighbours complain, ...)
In spite of being told to take care, Fred kicked the ball through Mrs Black's window. (Although he was told to take care, ... *Obwohl er ermahnt wurde .../Trotz der Ermahnung ...)*

- Meanings which can also be expressed by adverbial clauses, e.g. expressions of
  - time *(on, since, after, before)*
  - reason *(because of, from, for)*
  - condition *(in case of)*
  - concession *(in spite of, despite).*

  Gerund constructions sound more formal (except those with *from* and *for*) than the corresponding adverbial clauses.
  They correspond to German adverbial clauses, or occasionally expressions with nouns.

Instead of helping to mow the lawn, she went out on her roller skates. *(Statt ... zu ...)*
Apart from going for a stroll now and then, Grandpa never takes any exercise. *(Abgesehen davon, daß ...)*
By doing an hour's jogging a day she keeps very fit. *(Indem/Dadurch daß ...)*
He did a good thing **in joining** that sports club. *(Er tat gut daran, ... beizutreten.)*

- Meanings which in English cannot be expressed by adverbial clauses. These include gerund constructions *with instead of, apart from, without, by* and *in.*
  These constructions are common on all stylistic levels. They correspond to German infinitive constructions or subordinate clauses.

Note:
As *since, after* and *before* may be either prepositions or conjunctions, an *-ing* form following them may therefore be understood either as a gerund or as a present participle. Compare:
before his arrival (preposition + noun), before he arrived (conjunction + adverbial clause)
before arriving (**either:** preposition + gerund **or:** conjunction + present participle).

296–297 Infinitive Constructions as Adverbials of Purpose and Result

Because of its modal meaning, the infinitive lends itself to expressing what is intended and not yet carried out (cf **258.1**). This is why it is also found as an adverbial of purpose or result (in such cases, always with *to*).

296 As Adverbial of Purpose

A large crowd was waiting outside the theatre **to catch sight of** the rock group.
A way was cleared **for the film star to reach** the hotel entrance.
The famous dancer posed at the top of the steps **in order to give** the photographers a chance to get their pictures.
So as not to face the press the manager of the group slipped out the back way.

Normally, the *to-* infinitive alone (sometimes with *for* + notional subject, cf **260.2**) is enough to express the idea of purpose.

If the idea of purpose is to be especially emphasized, or if the infinitive is negated, *in order* or *so as* is placed before it.
(For adverbial clauses of purpose see **317.7.**)

Notes:

1. An infinitive can also come after the conjunction *as if*. This construction expresses comparison and intention at the same time:

He opened his mouth **as if to speak,** but the words wouldn't come. (... as if he wanted to speak ...)

2. Gerund constructions, too, can be used to express purpose. They are preferred when the purpose is to be given briefly in general terms.
The infinitive is preferred, on the other hand, when the purpose is more precisely defined – e.g. by a longish object:

This machine has been designed **for cutting cloth.**
This machine has been designed **to provide maximum protection for the operator.**

297 As Adverbial of Result

The book was ***too exciting*** **to put down.**
Some scenes were described ***realistically enough*** **to send** cold shudders down one's spine.
Aren't those comics ***too childish*** **for you to be reading?**

Would you be ***so kind as*** **to pass** me that magazine next to you?
The novel is not ***such a masterpiece as*** **to deserve** all that praise.

The following constructions are used to express result:
- *too* + adjective/adverb + infinitive
- adjective/adverb + *enough* + infinitive.

Here, too, the infinitive can have a notional subject introduced by *for* (cf **260**.2).

In formal style there are also the constructions:
- *so* + adjective/adverb + *as* + infinitive
- *such (a)* + noun + *as* + infinitive.

Note:
Sometimes the infinitive (as in German) expresses a (usually unpleasant) sequence of events and corresponds then to a main clause with *and* or *but*:

They arrived home **to find** slogans smeared on the wall. (... and found ...)
He complained to the police, **only to be told** they could do nothing about it. (... but was only told ...)

298–299 Infinitive and Participle Constructions as Comments and Sentence Links

298 Used as Adverbials

To be honest,
Honestly speaking,
(Cf: Honestly)
} I wouldn't recommend that record-player.

To start with,
(Cf: Firstly)
} it's far too expensive.

Mainly comments:
to be honest, to be frank, to tell the truth, to speak plainly, to be sure, honestly speaking, generally speaking, roughly speaking, strictly speaking, properly speaking

Mainly links:
to start with, to begin with, to be brief, to sum up, to conclude

Infinitive and participle constructions correspond here to adverbials of comment (*honestly, frankly, certainly,* etc.) and linking adverbials (*firstly, lastly, finally,* etc.).

In formal terms, they are so-called 'dangling' infinitive and participle constructions (cf **292** Note 1). They have no notional subject of their own, but are always meant to refer to the speaker (regardless of who or what is named as the subject of the whole sentence). They are marked off from the rest of the sentence by pauses in speaking and commas in writing. (For their use in text cohesion see **329, 331** Note 2.)

Note:
The expressions *to start with/to begin with* can lead to misunderstanding if – as often happens – they are not marked off from the rest of the sentence by a comma. Note that the preposition *with* belongs to the infinitive and not to what follows:

We'll have to set out early. **To start with** the trip will take us at least two hours. And then ...
(= Firstly, the trip will take us ...)

299 Used as Conjunctions

Supposing (that) you do get the job, will you be earning more money than you do now?
(If you do get ...)
Granted that money isn't everything, it still helps. (Even if money ...)
Similarly:
assuming/presuming/providing (that)
considering/seeing (that), given that, etc.

A number of 'dangling' participles can also be used as conjunctions, often combined with *that*. Many of them introduce conditional clauses.

Note:
Certain participles, chiefly in formal style, are used like prepositions before noun phrases:

It was very generous of him, **considering** his usual attitude to parting with his money.
(... when you consider ...)
Similarly: concerning, excepting, given, including, owing to, according to, etc.

300–301 Participle and Infinitive Constructions Corresponding to Relative Clauses

300 Structures

Participles and infinitives can occur as attributes to noun phrases and so correspond to relative clauses. (For another type of non-finite attribute see **288**.)

1. Participle constructions

The girl	**wearing** the red coat	has just dropped her glove.
Compare: The girl	who is wearing the red coat ▲ subject (in an active relative clause)	has just dropped her glove.
The scarf	**found** on the floor	belonged to a customer.
Compare: The scarf	which was found on the floor ▲ subject (in a passive relative clause)	belonged to a customer.

In this function participle constructions correspond to relative clauses in which the relative pronoun is the subject.
The present participle replaces an active relative clause, the past participle a passive one. For restrictions in meaning see **301.1**.

2. Infinitive constructions

The first Englishman		**to sail** round the world	was Sir Francis Drake.
Cf: The first Englishman	who ▲ subject	sailed round the world	was Sir Francis Drake.
1492 is a date		**to remember.**	
Cf: 1492 is a date	(which) you ▲ object	should remember.	

These infinitive constructions are of two types:

- The relative pronoun in the corresponding relative clause is the **subject** (as with the participle construction above).
  This type is only possible after noun phrases with the definite article and one of the following (restrictive) words:
  – a superlative (*the best, biggest,* etc.) or *the only*
  – an ordinal number or other numerical expression (*the first, the last, the few,* etc.)
- The relative pronoun in the corresponding relative clause is the **object** (or has been dropped). The relative clause must contain a modal auxiliary as well (mostly *should*). The infinitive expresses here an obligation or possibility (for its modal meaning see **258.1**).

Notes:

1. Superlatives, ordinal numbers and numerical expressions like *the few* can stand alone without a following noun. *Only,* on the other hand, must be followed by the prop-word *one / ones* if the noun is dropped:
   Mary is always **the last** to arrive. But she's not **the only one** to be unpunctual.
2. Infinitive constructions of the second type *(a date to remember)* can be expanded by *for*+ notional subject:
   A date for schoolchildren to remember is 1492. (. . . which schoolchildren should remember.)

301 Non-Finite Constructions as Defining or Non-Defining Attributes

As with relative clauses, some non-finite attributes are defining and some non-defining. The infinitive constructions in **300.2** almost all correspond to defining relative clauses. The difference is only important therefore with participle constructions.

1. Participle constructions as defining attributes

In this function, participle constructions are not marked off from the rest of the sentence by commas in writing, nor by pauses in speaking. They occur on all stylistic levels.

The family **eating at the next table** seem to be Japanese. (The family who are eating at the next table . . .)
I asked the waitress **serving us** for some salt, but she brought us some pepper instead. (. . . the waitress who was serving us . . .)

The present participle expresses the idea of something taking place at the same time as something else; in the case of dynamic verbs (cf **182–185**), this means that an action is seen as being in progress. Present participle constructions can therefore always replace relative clauses with present or past progressive and are usually preferred to relative clauses in the middle of a sentence.

People working/who work in restaurants usually have to put up with irregular hours.
(**But only:** I got this information from the woman **who works next to me in the factory.**)
Anyone **wanting/who wants to be sure of a place** should book in advance.
(**But only:** Did I tell you about that rich aunt of mine **who wants** to take us to the Ritz tonight?)

Present participle constructions can also occasionally be used as an alternative to relative clauses containing simple present or simple past tenses, but only with reference to an indefinite or unknown person or thing. For particular, known people or things, relative clauses are used. (In case of doubt, it is safer to use a relative clause.)

The pub (which is) **frequented by everybody round here** is the Black Bull. (**But only:** You mean the pub **which is being renovated.**)
The beer glasses (which had been) **broken in the fight** had to be paid for. (**But only:** The darts match **which will be played tonight** is the most important of the season.)

Past participle constructions can replace relative clauses containing a variety of tenses – but not progressive or future forms.
Where they are possible as alternatives, past participle constructions are generally preferred to the longer relative clauses.

Note:
The present participles of certain verbs expressing a relationship (i.e. those always occurring in the simple tenses) can be used to refer to **particular** things (e.g. after *the* + noun): among these verbs are *belong to, consist of, face* (= be opposite), *lead* (expressing a spatial relationship):

She went through **the door leading** (which leads) **into the yard.**
She lives in **the flat facing** (which faces) **the park.**

2. Participle constructions as non-defining attributes

The night, **now drawing on quickly,** made her long for the warmth of home.
The moon, **partly covered by clouds,** cast a feeble light.
My father, **suffering from night blindness,** always took a torch with him in the dark. (= My father, who suffered from .../Since my father suffered from ...)

Present and past participle constructions function here as insertions in the main clause. They are therefore marked off by commas in writing (and pauses in speaking). They are confined to written English and formal style.
Non-defining attributive participle constructions can also be regarded as adverbials inserted in the middle of a sentence (cf **292** Note 2). They may therefore be replaced by adverbial clauses (of reason, for example).

Chapter 9: Subordinate Clauses

302–303 Subordinate Clauses and their Functions in the Superordinate Clause (Summary)

302 Types and Functions of Subordinate Clauses

One or more subordinate clauses and a superordinate main clause together form a complex sentence. The subordinate clauses are usually linked to the main clause by function words (conjunctions, relative pronouns, interrogatives). There are various types of subordinate clauses:
a) *that*-clauses (indirect statements), which begin with the conjunction *that* (Ger. *daß*) (cf **304–305**)
b) indirect questions, which begin with interrogatives, such as *how, what, who,* etc. (cf **306–307**)
c) relative clauses, which begin with relative pronouns, such as *who, which, that,* etc. (cf **308–315**)
d) adverbial clauses, which begin with conjunctions, such as *after, where, because, if,* etc. (cf **316–318**).

In some cases certain function words can be omitted, e.g. the conjunction *that* and some relative pronouns.

Subordinate clauses are embedded in the main clause – i.e. they are either constituent parts of the main clause, or are attributes to a noun in it. This is demonstrated by the following sentences. The phrases in brackets have the same function as the subordinate clauses and are included for comparison:

subject	
That the new national park will be opened in June **When** the new national park will be opened (The date of the opening of the new national park)	has not been finally decided.

	direct object
The commission have decided	**that** the new national park will be opened in June. **when** the new national park will be opened. (the date of the opening of the new national park).

adverbial	
When the new national park has been opened (After the opening of the new national park)	tourists are expected in large numbers.

	attribute	
The film	**which** was made about the opening of the new national park (on the opening of the new national park)	will be shown next week.

Note:
Subordinate clauses can not only be part of a main clause (as they are in the above examples), but can also be part of another subordinate clause. They are then called second (third, etc.) degree subordinate clauses.

Everybody applauded	Main clause
when the speaker said	1st degree subordinate clause (adverbial)
that the amount of litter had greatly decreased	2nd degree subordinate clause (direct object)
since enough litter bins had been provided.	3rd degree subordinate clause (adverbial)

303 Function Words and Subordinate Clauses

There are a number of function words (*that, when,* etc.) which, without any alteration in their form, introduce more than one type of subordinate clause. For example:

		that
Nowadays everybody knows **that** evolution took place.	*(. . ., daß . . .)*	*that*-clause
The theory **that** Darwin expounded was at first widely ridiculed.	*(. . ., die . . .)*	relative clause
Fossil remains are so numerous **that** scientists are able to trace the development of certain species.	*(. . . so . . ., daß . . .)*	adverbial clause
		when
Nobody knows **when** life began.	*(. . ., wann . . .)*	indir. question
The late Paleozoic was the period **when** lungs evolved.	*(. . ., in der . . .)*	relative clause
There was great excitement **when** the first Neanderthal skull was found.	*(. . ., als . . .)*	adverbial clause
		if
If conditions had been different, the dinosaurs might have survived.	*(Wenn . . .)*	adverbial clause
The experts were not sure **if** the bones were those of a man or an ape.	*(. . ., ob . . .)*	indir. question
		who
The speaker was an anthropologist **who** had just returned from Africa.	*(. . ., der . . .)*	relative clause
We don't know **who** will finance the expedition.	*(. . ., wer . . .)*	indir. question

304–305 *That*-Clauses

304 Functions

Subordinate clauses which begin with the conjunction *that* can have various functions in the main clause. In all of these functions, they are not marked off by commas from the main clause, as German *daß*-clauses always are (exception: see below under 'Attribute').

Subject

That the Celtic languages are dying out is something that makes me very sad.
It is very sad **that the Celtic languages are dying out.**
It is a terrible pity **(that) I can't speak Welsh.**

In the function of subject of the sentence, *that*-clauses can precede the main clause. But, like German *daß*-clauses, they are mostly placed at the end of the sentence, as the notional subject. This is either because they are longer or because they contain new information (cf **6, 257** Note). In these cases the sentence begins with the structure word *it* as formal subject. The conjunction *that* can be omitted after some commonly used expressions.

Complementation of the predicate

I am told **(that) 1 % of the Welsh people speak no English.**
Many Welsh families are anxious **that their children should learn Welsh.**
Many people still have hopes **that a revival of Irish will take place.**
Gaelic-speaking Scots often complain **that their language is ignored in the media.**

When *that*-clauses are used to complement verbs and verbal complexes, they follow these verbs/verbal complexes directly. There is no preposition, such as would be needed to connect a noun phrase in the same function (cf. *to be anxious about s.th./to be anxious that . . .; to complain of s.th./to complain that . . .).* In this case as well, the conjunction *that* can be dropped after certain commonly used verbs and verbal complexes.

Attribute

The fact **that English is relatively easy to learn** makes it suitable as a world language.
The nationalists' original demand, **that English be banned,** was totally unrealistic.

That-clauses following abstract nouns like *answer, belief, demand, fact, feeling, knowledge, news, proposal, statement* etc. are attributes of these nouns.
When they are necessary for a correct understanding of the whole sentence, they must not be marked off by commas. *That*-clauses which are not necessary to complete the meaning of the sentence are, on the other hand, marked off by commas. (See also the comma rules for defining and non-defining relative clauses **308.1.**)

305 *That*-Clauses after Certain Verbs and Verbal Complexes

That-clauses occur as complementation of the predicate or as notional subjects after many verbs and verbal complexes:

1. Verbs and verbal complexes of reporting, opinion and supposition

We **were told** that "Gone with the Wind" was a best-seller in the thirties.
The author **was confident** that her novel would be a great success.
People **imagine that** romantic fiction **is** easy to write.
People **imagine** romantic fiction **to be** easy to write. (formal)

These verbs introduce statements and thoughts in reported speech. The rules for the use of tenses must be followed (cf **322–324**).

After verbs of opinion and supposition (*imagine, believe,* etc.), it is common to find an infinitive construction used in formal English instead of a *that*-clause with *be* (cf **266**).

Notes:

1. A construction with the structure word *it* and a following *that*-clause is possible after some verbs of opinion and supposition (verbs with object + object complement, cf **57.2**):
   I find it (to be) a fault that the play is so long.
   He considers it (to be) essential that the theatre should be subsidized.
Instead of the *that*-clause, an infinitive construction can sometimes be used:
   I thought it a splendid idea to join a drama group.

2. Verbs and verbal complexes which express an appearance or a degree of probability can take either a construction with the structure word *it* and a *that*-clause, or a construction with an ordinary subject and an infinitive (cf **267**):
   It is hardly likely that a book of poems will make a lot of money.
   A book of poems is hardly likely to make a lot of money.

2. Verbs and verbal complexes which express a demand, decision or wish

Our producer **proposed** that we **(should) perform** "Hamlet". It **was decided** that Bill **(should) play** the ghost. It **is necessary** that some of us **(should) take** two parts./It is necessary for some of us to take two parts. They **were** all **anxious** that the performance **(should) go off** well./They were all anxious for the performance to go off well.	After all these verbs (with the exception of *I wish, I'd rather*) one uses *should* (cf **234.**1) or the present subjunctive (cf **213.**2 a). Most of the verbal complexes can also be followed by an infinitive construction as an alternative to a *that*-clause (cf **268**).
I wish I **could** act like Meryl Streep. *(Ich wünschte, ich könnte . . .)* **I'd rather** people **didn't eat** chocolates in the theatre. **She'd rather** we **hadn't sat** so near the back.	*Wish* in a hypothetical sense and *I'd rather (he'd rather,* etc.) are followed by a subordinate clause (mostly without *that*) containing the past subjunctive or the modal past or modal past perfect (cf **214.**2 c)
When do you **want** us to turn the lights on? *(Wann sollen wir . . .)* The cast **wish** me to thank you for all your help. *(Die Mitwirkenden wünschen, daß ich . . .)*	After *want* only an infinitive construction is possible, never a *that*-clause. *Wish*, when used like *want* to denote a request or a realistic wish, is also followed by an infinitive construction. It occurs mainly in formal English.

Note:
Should or the present subjunctive are also used after **nouns** which express a demand, decision or wish:
His **suggestion** that everybody **(should) join** in the singing was taken up with enthusiasm.

3. Verbs and verbal complexes which express an emotional effect or an evaluation

It is not surprising that Australia **should have attracted/has attracted** many immigrants since the war. *(. . . angelockt hat.)* **It seems strange** to us that Christmas in Australia **should be/is** at the height of summer. I **regret** that we **(should have) missed** visiting a sheep station during our stay.	The *that*-clause in such sentences contains either *should* (formal) or the indicative (cf **234.**2). (For infinitive and gerund constructions after these verbs and verbal complexes see **268, 271.**3, **273, 278.**)

306–307 Indirect Questions

306 Structures and Functions

Somebody asked me **where the bus station was.**
They want to know **whether there'll be a coach to Dover soon.**

Indirect questions have the following features in common:

a) They begin with an interrogative (*where, how, when, why,* etc.) or with the conjunctions *whether* or *if* (German *ob*).
b) Unlike direct questions, they have the same word order as statements, i.e. no inversion, no *do*-auxiliary.
c) They obey the rules for the use of tenses in reported speech (cf **322–324**).
d) They are not marked off by commas from the main clause. (Exception: see below under 'Attribute')

Indirect questions can have the following functions in the superordinate main clause (see also **304**):

Subject

When the excursion will take place has not yet been decided.
It has not yet been decided **when the excursion will take place.**

Indirect questions can either come before the main clause as its subject, or, as its notional subject, after it. In the latter use, the main clause starts with *it* as formal subject (cf **304**).

Complementation of the predicate

The passengers wondered **why the driver had been gone so long.**
They inquired at the travel agency (about) **how much the fare would be.**
The children are quarrelling about **who is going to sit by the window.**
We were uncertain (about) **whether it was best to travel by coach or by train.**

When indirect questions are used to complement verbs and verbal complexes (e.g. *be uncertain*), they are sometimes (unlike *that*-clauses) preceded by a preposition. (For details see **307.2**.)

Attribute

There was no information about **when the relief bus would arrive.**
The usual question, **whether a new bus service can pay its own way,** was raised at the meeting.

Indirect questions can be attributes to certain abstract nouns. They are not marked off by commas, except when they are not necessary to complete the meaning of the sentence (see also **304**).

Note:
As an alternative to an indirect question with a modal auxiliary, one can often use an infinitive construction with an interrogative or *whether* (cf **290–291**):

We didn't know **where we could/should put** our luggage. – We didn't know **where to put** our luggage.

307 Indirect Questions after Certain Verbs, Verbal Complexes and Nouns

1. Meanings

I **asked** him why so many people were waiting at the station waving flags.
The question of who would win the election was hotly debated.
A grey-haired man **explained** to me what he thought of all political parties.
Nobody **had any idea** when the President's train would arrive.
It **was doubtful** whether many people would bother to come to the public meeting.

Indirect questions can be used to report direct questions (cf **327–328**) but can also refer to thoughts, ideas or facts. They therefore occur not only after certain phrases (verbs, verbal complexes and abstract nouns) which express the idea of asking, but also after some which express the ideas of saying, explaining, knowing.

2. The linking of indirect questions with or without a preposition

Everyone **was talking about** who would take over the leadership of the party.
The opinion polls caused much **confusion about/as to** who the winner would be.
There were **conjectures about/as to** why the minister had resigned.

Indirect questions can follow prepositional verbs or be linked to verbal complexes or nouns by means of a preposition. *As to* often occurs instead of the appropriate preposition after verbal complexes and nouns.

Many people had doubts **about/as to whether** a general election was necessary.
(Compare: They wondered **if/whether** it was necessary.)
It all **depends (on)** whether the new measures are popular or not.
The government **is not certain (about/as to)** how the voters will react.
No one **is sure** if and how soon the situation will improve.
She **had no idea** what his politics were.
I **don't care** if you do think differently.

Prepositions (including *as to*) can never be followed by *if;* one uses *whether* instead.

In some cases, the preposition can be omitted without a change of meaning.

Some verbs and verbal complexes hardly ever have a preposition before the indirect question. In case of doubt, most English dictionaries give examples of usage.

308–312 Attributive Relative Clauses

The term relative clause normally refers to attributive relative clauses – i.e. those which qualify a noun phrase in the main (or other superordinate) clause: I read *the book* **that you recommended.** This noun phrase (here: *the book*) is called the antecedent of the relative clause. (For nominal and adverbial relative clauses see **313–315**.)

308 Defining and Non-Defining Relative Clauses, Choice of the Relative Pronoun

1. Types of relative clause

A relative clause can be classified according to the importance of the information it contains:

Defining relative clauses

Trees **which lose their leaves in winter** are called deciduous, those **that don't** are called evergreen.

Defining relative clauses specify who or what is meant by the antecedent (in this case, which trees). They thus contain information which is necessary for the correct understanding of the whole sentence.

Defining relative clauses are therefore not marked off from the main clause by pauses in speaking, nor by commas in writing.

Defining relative clauses are used in both written and spoken English.

Non-defining relative clauses

Trees, **which play such an important part in our environment,** are suffering more and more from pollution.

Non-defining relative clauses contain extra explanatory information (in this case, about trees in general) which is not necessary for the understanding of the antecedent and therefore of the whole sentence.

Non-defining relative clauses are marked off from the main clause by pauses in speaking and by commas in writing.

Non-defining relative clauses are used mainly in written or in formal English.

Note:
Colloquially, non-defining relative clauses are usually avoided. Two separate simple sentences would, for example, be preferred to a complex sentence of main clause and non-defining relative clause:
Sherwood Forest was the home of Robin Hood. It is now much smaller than in medieval times.
Sherwood Forest, which is now much smaller than in medieval times, was the home of Robin Hood.

2. The choice of relative pronoun

There are three criteria for choosing the correct relative pronoun. In the following, we just give some examples of their effects. (For the choice of the relative determiner see **314.**)

- **The type of relative clause: defining or non-defining**

  We ate all the wild strawberries **(that) we could find.**

  Wild strawberries, **which you often find in our forests,** are much tastier than the garden variety.

  For example, *that* can only be used in defining relative clauses (cf **309.1, 310**). Only in defining relative clauses can the relative pronoun be dropped under certain conditions (cf **309.2**).

- **The antecedent: person or thing**

  The woodcutters, **who had been hard at work since early morning,** stopped for a short break.

  Half the wood **which is used in the world** is burnt as fuel.

  For example, *who* can only be used for persons, *which* only for things (cf **309.1, 310**).

- **The function of the relative pronoun in the relative clause: subject or other part of the sentence**

  The storm **which raged over the country last night** uprooted hundreds of trees.
  (*which:* here, the subject)

  The oak **(that) they chopped down** was over 300 years old.
  (*that:* here, the object)

  The relative pronoun can, for example, never be dropped when it is the subject (cf **309.2**).

Note:
For the correct relative pronoun for groups, animals, vehicles, countries, etc. see **74, 80** Note 1, **81.**

309 Relative Pronouns in Defining Relative Clauses

1. *who, whom, which, that*

The girl **who/that** claims to have seen the Loch Ness monster yesterday was interviewed by the press. The tourists **that/who/whom** the lake attracts every year all hope to catch a glimpse of the animal.	For **persons** one uses • as the subject of the relative clause, *who,* or sometimes *that;* • as the object of the relative clause, *that* (stylistically neutral), *who* (colloquial) or *whom* (formal).
The fog **that/which** rose during the boat trip reduced visibility to less than ten yards. The picture **that/which** a journalist had taken of "Nessie" revealed only a log floating on the water.	For **things** one uses • as subject or object of the relative clause, *that* or *which.*

Notes:

1. When referring to things, *that* is mostly preferred to *which,* especially after *all/any/only/every/few/some/first/last/* superlative + noun, and after the pronouns *all, anything, everything, something, nothing, few, little, much:*
   The bookseller showed him **all** the books on space research **that** she had in stock.
   The **only** novels **that** interest him are science fiction.
   Is there **anything** here **that** you haven't read?
2. When *such* precedes the antecedent, *as* is used instead of a relative pronoun in the relative clause:
   He studied only **such** reports **as** would be useful to him.

2. Omission of relative pronoun: contact clauses

The relative pronoun can be left out in defining relative clauses, provided it is not the subject but has one of the following functions:

Examples	Functions
These are postcards of all the towns *(which)* **my brother visited** when he was in Europe.	• direct object
Here are the holiday brochures **the customer was asking for** (. . . *that* the customer was asking for.)	• prepositional object (For the position of the preposition see **311**.1.)
The café **they had arranged to meet in** shut at six. (. . . *in which* they had arranged to meet . . .) The person **I'm waiting for** is ten minutes late already. Are you sure the clock **you looked at** was right?	• part of an adverbial prepositional phrase.

Contact clauses are very common in colloquial English, especially short ones that have a personal pronoun as subject.

310 Relative Pronouns in Non-Defining Relative Clauses

Non-defining relative clauses cannot begin with *that*, and the relative pronoun cannot be left out. These clauses are always marked off by commas.

Examples	Usage
My father, **who** was driving, just managed to stop the car in time.	For **persons** one uses • as subject, *who*
They overtook a cyclist, **whom** they recognized as Charlie Jones.	• as object, *whom.*
The white Jaguar, **which** had been speeding, overturned at the next bend. The road conditions, **which** the driver blamed for the accident, were in fact very nasty.	For **things** one uses • as subject or object, *which.*

311 Prepositions in Relative Clauses

1. Prepositions in defining relative clauses

Examples	Explanation
Was the project **which** he worked **on** for so long really such a success? The economist **whom** we talked **to** about the firm's plans for expansion was very pessimistic.	In defining relative clauses, the preposition mostly comes after the verb. In colloquial English this is always the case.
The goods did not have the quality **(that)** we were looking **for**. The man **(who)** you were talking **to** just now was the export manager.	In relative clauses with *that* or *who* (as prepositional object) and in contact clauses, the preposition can only come after the verb.
Those experts **on whom** the government is dependent for advice are often biased in favour of industry. The figures **on which** the report is based were provided by a government agency.	In formal style, the preposition usually comes before the relative pronoun *(whom, which).*

2. Prepositions in non-defining relative clauses

> The Arabs, **from whom** the Europeans learned the decimal number system, were also great astronomers.
> The Mediterranean region, **in which** much of our civilization developed, is today relatively impoverished.

As non-defining relative clauses are mainly used in formal English, the preposition normally comes before the relative pronoun.

Notes:

1. Some prepositions can only come before the relative pronoun, and never after the verb: e.g. *during, by means of, because of, due to, owing to, in spite of:*
   The hours **during which** the hijackers negotiated with the police were particularly nerve-racking for the victims.
   The trick **by means of which** he obtained the money was a very old one.

The prepositions *after, between* and *around* must come before the relative pronoun when they refer to time:
   the day **after which** ..., the dates **between which** ..., the time **around which** ...

2. When a relative clause with *that* or a contact clause follows an antecedent referring to time, the preposition is usually left out:
   Nobody knew **the day** (that) he intended to arrive (on).

3. After many antecedents referring to place and time, relative clauses can be introduced by *where* or *when* (relative adverbs):
   The area where our house used to be has now been turned into a huge car park.
   Instead of: The area in which .../The area (that/which) our house used to be in ...
   Nobody knew **the day when** he intended to arrive.
   Instead of: ... the day on which .../... the day (that) he intended to arrive (on).

312 Relative Clauses with *whose, of whom, of which*

Relative clauses can begin not only with relative pronouns, but also with the relative determiner *whose* + noun as well as with a noun phrase + *of whom/of which.*
They are used to indicate most of those relationships which can be expressed by the genitive (e.g. possession):

> We should like to thank all those **whose** generosity has helped us to preserve this historic building.
> The duke, **whose** country house is now owned by the National Trust, lives in the west wing only.
> The ruined castle, **whose** massive remaining walls give a good impression of its former strength, is still an imposing sight.
> Visitors always admire the lawns, the upkeep **of which** costs so much.
>
> The first Earl had three sons, **the youngest of whom** eventually inherited the title.
> Tiverton House, **part of which** is now open to the public, was once the home of Lady Margaret Ashley.

To express the idea of possessing or belonging one uses
- for people, *whose;*
- for things, *whose* or *of which;* the latter is somewhat clumsier.

To express a partitive relationship one uses
- for persons (*one/two/.../both/either/some/each/.../*comparative/superlative +) *of whom;*
- for things (*one/two/.../both/either/...* +) *of which.*

Note:
As the examples above show, *of whom* and *of which* usually follow the word (denoting number, quantity, etc.) to which they belong. Sometimes, however, they come before it:
   There is an adventure playground for children, **of whom very few** are interested in a tour of the house.
   Be sure not to miss seeing the family portraits, **of which a number** are very valuable.

313 Function

Whoever takes the trouble to climb the tower (subject)	will have a magnificent view.

You can take	**whichever footpath you like.** (object)

Nominal relative clauses are those which have no antecedent in the main (or other superordinate) clause. Within a complex sentence, they function like noun phrases, that is, for example, as subject or object. These relative clauses begin with what are called generalizing relative pronouns or determiners: *who-ever, what, whatever, whichever.*

Note:
Subordinate clauses with *whichever, whoever* and similar compounds with *-ever* can sometimes function as adverbial clauses (mainly of concession):

> **Whichever** footpath you take, it will get you to the village. (= No matter which footpath you take . . .)
> **Whoever** you ask, you'll get the same answer. (= No matter who you ask . . .)

314 Relative Pronouns and Determiners in Nominal Relative Clauses

Generalizing relative pronouns combine the meaning of a noun and a relative pronoun:

There will be an ice-cream for **whoever** finds the nicest sea-shells.
Whoever I showed the dead jelly-fish to just shuddered in disgust.

- *Whoever* is used to refer to **persons.** It can mean 'the person who . . .' or 'any / every person who . . .' (Ger. *derjenige, welcher; wer (auch immer); jeder, der*).

He was staring at **what** he thought was a sailing-boat on the horizon.
What I like about this beach is that it's never crowded.
The seagulls will eat **whatever** you throw to them.

- *What* and *whatever* are both used to refer to **things.** *What* can mean 'some unidentified thing which . . .' or 'the thing that . . .' (Ger. *etwas, das; (das,) was / wofür / wonach / worüber / etc.*).
  Whatever means 'anything that . . .' or 'everything that . . .'. (Ger. *was (auch immer); alles, was*).

Whichever *of you* has a spare moment can pump up the air-bed.
Both ways lead to the camping site. You can take **whichever** you like.

- *Whichever* can refer to **persons or things** and is always used when selecting from a limited number. It is used when an *of*-phrase follows, or to avoid repeating a noun mentioned before (Ger. *welcher auch immer*).

Generalizing relative determiners are used before nouns. For persons and things one uses:

Whatever people were out on the streets at that late hour hurried silently along. He decided to stay at **whatever hotel** happened to have a vacancy. **Whichever person** he asked the way of turned out to be a stranger in the area. You can see the cathedral towers above the roofs from **whichever way** you approach the city.

- *whatever*... when selecting from an unlimited or unknown amount or number (Ger. *jeder, ... der; alle, ... die; welcher... auch immer);*
- *whichever* ... when selecting from a limited amount or a number known to the speaker (Ger. *welcher... auch immer).*

Notes:

1. In set phrases and proverbs one also finds *who* and *whom* as generalizing relative pronouns:
   Whom the gods love die young. (= Those whom the gods love ...)
   Who pays the piper calls the tune. (= The person who finances something can determine what is to be done.)
2. *What* occurs occasionally as a generalizing relative determiner before nouns:
   I gave her **what information** I could. (= ... all the information that I could give her.)
   What directions they received were not very helpful. (= The few directions ... were not very helpful.)

315 Relative Clauses Commenting on a Statement

Relative clauses can comment on the whole of a sentence (or on a part of it). They function then as commenting adverbials.
As these relative clauses are not necessary to complete the meaning of the sentence, they are non-defining relative clauses and as such are marked off by commas in writing and pauses in speaking.

In the European institutions all documents must be translated into several languages, **which** costs a great deal of money. *(..., was viel Geld kostet.)* All economies of the world are interrelated; and **what** is more to the point, they are dependent on one another. *(... und, was noch entscheidender ist, ...)*

When they come after the main clause, they begin with the relative pronoun *which.*

When they come before it, they begin with the relative pronoun *what.* (In German, *was* is used in both cases.)

Notes:

1. In formal English, adverbial relative clauses are occasionally introduced by *which* + an abstract noun. A corresponding construction does not exist in German:
   The Prime Minister announced that there would be a general election in October, **which decision** was not unexpected. *(..., eine Entscheidung, die nicht unerwartet kam.)*
   According to the polls, the opposition has a good chance of gaining power, **in which case** the country must expect many changes. *(...; in diesem Fall muß ...)*
2. Relative clauses beginning with *which* can refer to people when they are actually comments on the main clause:
   He looked like a student, **which** in fact he was. *(..., was er auch war.)*
   The following is, however, a true attributive relative clause:
   A student who lives at home needs less money.
3. *As* (like German *wie*) can also be used like a relative pronoun when it refers to a whole sentence:
   The professor's lecture, **as** was intended, provoked a good deal of laughter. *(... rief, wie beabsichtigt, viel Gelächter hervor.)*

Adverbial Clauses

316 Structures

> **When** I was in America, I visited some of my relatives there.
> They went to Washington **because** they wanted to see the White House.
>
> Subordinate clauses which function as adverbials normally begin with a conjunction.
> The subordinate clause can either come before the main clause, in which case it is usually marked off by a comma, or it can come after it, in which case there is usually no comma between the main and subordinate clauses.

Note:
After certain conjunctions (e.g. *though, when, once, while, if*) the subject and the linking verb *be* in the relative clause can be omitted if the subject is the same as that of the main clause:
Though (it is) not the largest country in the world, the USA is definitely the richest.
When in Rome, do as the Romans do. (Proverb)

317 Types of Adverbial Clauses and Conjunctions

Adverbial clauses fall into various categories. The ten main categories, with their appropriate conjunctions, are listed below.

1. Clauses of time (temporal clauses)

after	*nachdem*	before	*bevor*	till/until	*bis*
as	*als, während*	now (that)	*(nun) da*	when	*als, wenn*
as long as	*solange*	once	*sobald*	whenever	*wann auch immer, immer wenn*
as soon as	*sobald*	since	*seit*	while/whilst	*während*

Once the North had won the Civil War, slavery in the United States was abolished.

For which tenses to use see 197.2, 208–209.

2. Clauses of place and direction

where	*wo, wohin*	wherever	*wo/wohin auch immer*

Wherever the pioneers settled, they came into conflict with the native Indians.

3. Clauses of reason or cause

because	*weil*	as, since	*da*	when	*wenn, da* (cf **318**)

As/Since there are now 50 states in the Union, there are 50 stars on the American flag.
We will have a motor caravan on our Canadian trip **because** it comes cheaper than hotels.

As a rule, adverbial clauses with *as* and *since* contain information already known and so tend to come before rather than after the main clause. Adverbial clauses with *because* mostly come after the main clause because they contain the new information.

4. Clauses of condition (conditional clauses)

if	*wenn, falls*	in case (that)	*im Falle, daß*
unless	*sofern nicht, außer wenn, es sei denn, daß*	provided/providing that	*vorausgesetzt, daß*
		on condition that	*unter der Bedingung, daß*
as long as	*sofern, solange*	supposing (that), etc.	*angenommen, daß*

If we don't deal with this fruit quickly, it will go bad.
The grape harvest is expected to be very good, **provided that** the weather keeps up.

If can be used to introduce all types of conditional clauses, whereas the other conjunctions are only used in realistic conditional clauses. (For the different types of conditional clauses and the tenses used see **215–218.**)

Note:
In conditional clauses with *should, were*-subjunctive or modal past perfect, the conjunction *if* can be omitted in formal English. When it is omitted, the subject comes after the auxiliary verb (partial inversion):

Should there be a surplus of apples, prices will drop. (**If** there **should** be . . .)
Were the weather to improve, the harvest might be saved. (**If** the weather **were** to improve . . .)
Had they not received immediate help, many fruit farmers would have been ruined. (**If** they **had** not received . . .)

5. Clauses of concession

although/though	*obwohl*	while	*obwohl* (cf **318**)	when	*wo . . . doch, obwohl* (cf **318**)
even if/even though	*selbst wenn*	if	wenn . . . auch (cf **318**)		

Although vast sums have been spent, malaria is still widespread in many countries.

Note:
In formal English *though* can come as the second word of the clause, after an initial adjective or adverb. *As* can be used in this way as well, also with concessive meaning:

Incredible **as/though** it may seem, smallpox has finally been eradicated from the earth.
Much **as/though** it is to be deplored, the fact is that one third of the world's population is starving.

6. Clauses of contrast

whereas/while *während* (cf **318**)

Whereas tuberculosis is now rare in the West, it is still quite common in some Third World countries.

7. Clauses of purpose

in order that/so that; so (colloquial); that (formal) (with modal auxiliary or present subjunctive, cf **213**.2 b)	*damit*	lest (formal) (with *should* or present subjunctive)	*damit nicht*

Money is needed for education in the developing countries, **so that** these can be helped to help themselves.
Measures must be taken immediately to protect the tropical forests, **lest** it be too late.

(For infinitive constructions with *in order to/so as to* see **296.**)

8. Clauses of result

so that *so daß* so/such . . . that *so/solche . . . daß*

The population of the Third World continues to increase **so** much **that** the problem of poverty becomes ever greater.

9. Clauses of comparison

as *(so) wie*	as though/as if *als ob* (cf **214.2** b)

The peasants go on cultivating the land **as** their forefathers have done before them.
The old woman shook her head **as if** she wanted to show that she disapproved of our presence.

Note:
Comparison and purpose can be expressed at the same time by *as if to* + infinitive:
She shook her head **as if to show** she disapproved of our presence.

10. Clauses of proportion

as *in dem Maße wie*

As living standards improve, (so) life expectancy increases.

318 Conjunctions with Several Meanings

As can be seen from **317**, some conjunctions have several meanings. They can therefore introduce different types of adverbial clauses. To understand a text correctly it is important to be aware of these different meanings.

Example	German	Meaning
		as
As Thunderbolt was lame, he could not be ridden in the polo match.	*(Da . . .)*	reason
There was cheering **as** the first horse reached the winning post.	*(. . ., als . . .)*	time
In spite of many protests, foxhunting is as popular today **as** it has ever been.	*(. . ., wie . . .)*	comparison
The jockeys got muddier and muddier **as** the rain became heavier.	*(. . . in dem Maße wie . . .)*	proportion
		if
If we run out of paint, we'll have to go and get a new tin.	*(Wenn/Falls . . .)*	condition
I'll finish painting this room **if** it takes me all night.	*(. . ., selbst wenn . . .)*	concession
		since
The living-room has not been wallpapered **since** we moved in.	*(. . . seit . . .)*	time
Many people prefer to do their own decorating **since** it comes so much cheaper.	*(. . ., da . . .)*	reason
		when
When the train arrived, there was a mad dash to get in.	*(Als . . .)*	time
There's no point in telling her to book a seat **when** she refuses to hear of it.	*(. . ., da/wenn . . .)*	reason
Why are you standing in the corridor **when** there is plenty of room further up?	*(. . ., wo . . . doch/ obwohl . . .)*	concession
		while
Would you get the cups and saucers out **while** I put the kettle on?	*(. . ., während . . .)*	time
Some people like sugar in coffee **while** others can't stand it.	*(. . ., während . . .)*	contrast
While tea is still the most popular beverage in Britain, coffee is gaining ground.	*(Obwohl . . .)*	concession
		so that
Give me a ring **so that** I'll know when you're coming.	*(. . ., damit . . .)*	purpose
His number was engaged all afternoon **so that** I gave up trying to telephone him.	*(. . ., so daß . . .)*	result

Note:
Conjunctions must not be confused with the prepositions which correspond to them. Conjunctions introduce subordinate clauses; prepositions come before noun phrases.

conjunctions:	prepositions:
. . . **while** he was staying abroad . . .	. . . **during** his stay abroad . . .
. . . **because** he had travelled extensively . . .	. . . **because of** his extensive travels . . .
. . . **although** she liked foreign places . . .	. . . **in spite of** her liking for foreign places . . .

Chapter 10: Direct and Reported Speech

319–321 Direct Speech, Reported Speech and Inner Monologue (Summary)

319 Forms of Reporting

There are various ways of relating what someone has said or written:

Speech by the Mayor:
I think that every one of us here is proud of the fact that our town has built one of the finest leisure centres in the country. How many of you here have always felt the need for a centre like this? A place where you can meet your friends, play squash, go swimming or simply relax.
And now a big hand for the architect, Mr Jones, who, I know you will all agree, has done a marvellous job, an absolutely marvellous job. It's not every day that this can be said, is it?
I now declare this Leisure Centre open.

1. As direct speech
The original sentences are quoted word for word. Nothing is changed. All the grammatical and stylistic features of colloquial spoken English, such as question tags, exclamations, repetitions, etc, are retained.

The Mayor said that he thought that every one of those present was proud of the fact that their town had built one of the finest leisure centres in the country.
He wondered how many of his audience had always felt the need for a centre of this kind, a place where they could meet their friends, play squash, go swimming or simply relax.
He called for a round of applause for the architect, Mr Jones, who, he knew they would all agree, had done an absolutely marvellous job. It was certainly not every day that that could be said!
He then declared the Leisure Centre open.

In his speech the Mayor said that he thought every one present was proud of their newly built Leisure Centre, one of the finest in the country. Local residents had always felt the need for a centre of this sort, where they could meet their friends, play squash, go swimming or simply relax. The architect, Mr Jones, deserved a special round of applause for his work, which had received unanimous admiration, a rare thing these days. On this humorous note he declared the Leisure Centre open.

2. As reported speech
In reported speech proper (i.e. indirect speech), one can choose to

- **stay close to the original:**
  The main changes are those which are grammatically necessary to present the text as a report, e.g. changes in pronouns and tenses. Incomplete sentences are omitted or completed. Other sentence patterns, however, and most of the original vocabulary remain the same.
- **give a freer version:**
  Here the person making the report takes greater liberties with the wording of the text. There are changes in sentence patterns and vocabulary, which often result in a change in style. These free versions are much commoner than versions close to the original words.

Yesterday the Mayor opened the town's new Leisure Centre, which he claimed to be one of the finest in the country. He praised particularly the work of the architect, Mr Jones.

3. As a summary
This very free form of reporting (a borderline case of reported speech) is used when one wants to give only the important points of what has been said.

320 Direct and Reported Speech: Grammatical Differences

When converting direct speech into reported speech, the following changes may have to be made:

"We'**re testing** a new brand of toothpaste, and we **want** you to try this sample." → The market research worker said that they **were testing** a new brand of toothpaste and that they **wanted** me to try a sample. *(… sie prüften gerade … und hätten gern …)*	1. Backshift of tenses if the reporting verb is in a tense of the past tense group (cf **322–324**). (In German, subjunctive forms are used instead.)
"I' ll write a letter of complaint to the Consumers' Association about **my** new lawn-mower." → Roy said that **he** would write a letter of complaint to the Consumers' Association about **his** new lawn-mower.	2. Adaptation of personal pronouns and possessives to the point of view of the person reporting.
"I'm looking for a blouse to go with the skirt I bought **here yesterday.**" → The customer said she was looking for a blouse to go with the skirt she had bought **in the same shop the day before.**	3. Adaptation of adverbials and other expressions of time and place to the point of view of the person reporting (cf **325–326**).
"Would you be willing to answer a few questions, please?" → The young woman asked me if I would be willing to answer a few questions. "Mind your own business!" → Several people told the interviewer to mind her own business.	4. Changes in sentence type, e.g. question → indirect question, imperative → infinitive construction (cf **327**).
"And what about our advertising? We'll have to brighten that up, won't we?" → At the meeting the sales manager raised the question of their advertising and suggested that they would have to brighten it up.	5. Omission of certain features of colloquial speech (e.g. question tags); shortened sentences are expanded where necessary. (Cf **327** Note 2.)
"Let us please not lose our tempers over the colour of the packaging!" → John **pleaded with** the other members of the staff not to lose their tempers over the colour of the packaging.	6. Characterization of speech intentions by an appropriate reporting verb (cf **328**).

321 Inner Monologue

> ... but the thought of having to cook was too much for her. Elderly people didn't need much food, anyway – surely the doctor must realize that? A cup of tea, of course; that was a stimulant, and now that she had discovered tea bags it was so much less trouble. At the supermarket she had bought a packet of 144 tea bags which she reckoned ought to last her about seven weeks all but one day. But long before that she would be at the hospital; the card indicating the date of her appointment at Mr Strong's outpatients' clinic was on her mantlepiece. Not that she needed reminding, especially not after what she had just seen.
>
> (From Barbara Pym, *Quartet in Autumn*)

Inner monologue is a common stylistic feature in literature. It is used to reflect people's thoughts, impressions and associations, their 'stream of consciousness'. Grammatically, it is half-way between direct and reported speech:

- The sentence types of direct speech and the features of colloquial speech (shortened sentences, etc.) are retained. Time and place adverbials are not changed.
- Personal pronouns and possessives, however, are changed, as in reported speech. The tenses are backshifted (as they are in inner monologue in German, as opposed to true reported speech).

322–324 Tenses in Direct and Reported Speech

322 The Principle of Backshift

In reported speech, there is normally a backshift of tenses whenever the reporting verb is in a tense of the past tense group, that is, past tense, past perfect, etc. The verb forms of direct speech are changed as follows:

"I'**m** on my way to the letter box." → Eric *said* he **was** on his way to the letter box.	present tense	→ past tense
"Postage on letters **has gone up** again in spite of the fact that the last rise **took place** only two years ago." → My mother *complained* that postage on letters **had gone up** again in spite of the fact that the last rise **had taken place** only two years before.	present perfect past tense	→ past perfect
"The post office **is going to** issue a new series of stamps, which **will depict** ships through the ages." → I *read* in the paper yesterday that the post office **was going to** issue a new series of stamps, which **would depict** ships through the ages.	*will*-future, *going to*-future, etc.	→ future-in-the-past, *was/were going to,* etc.
"**Will** the mail **have arrived** by eight thirty?" → She *asked* me if the mail **would have arrived** by eight thirty.	future perfect	→ future-perfect-in-the-past
"I'm not sure whether you **can** send the parcel to your pen-friend by the cheap rate – it **may** be too heavy". → My sister *said* she was not sure whether I **could** send the parcel to my pen-friend by the cheap rate as it **might** be too heavy.	*can, may,* *shall, will*	→ *could, might,* *should, would*

Notes:

1. *Shall* and *should* can only be used as future auxiliaries in the first person *(I, we)*. *Shall* is therefore backshifted to *would* when the grammatical person (i.e. the pronoun) is changed:

"**We shall** be sending you a card tomorrow."

→ They *told* us on the phone that **they would** be sending us a card the next day.

Shall is only backshifted to *should* when it is used in an enquiry as to another person's wishes:

"**Shall** I put the letter in the post box for you?"

→ She *asked* me if **she should** put the letter in the post box for me.

2. The following forms cannot be backshifted any further and therefore remain the same: past perfect, future-in-the-past (conditional), future-perfect-in-the-past (conditional perfect), *might, should, would, ought to, used to* and also *could* when it is equivalent to a German subjunctive (*könnte:* cf **225–226**).

"I noticed immediately that the parcel **had been opened.**"

→ She *said* that she had noticed immediately that the parcel **had been opened.**

"His telephone **could be** out of order again."

→ Brian *thought* that John's telephone **could be** out of order again.

When *could* is equivalent to a German indicative *(konnte)*, i.e. when it expresses an ability, etc. (cf **223–224**), a backshifted substitute *(had been able to, had managed to,* etc.) is normally used in reported speech:

"Until the introduction of the Penny Post in 1840 poor people **couldn't communicate** easily with one another."

→ The lecturer *said* that until the introduction of the Penny Post in 1840, poor people **had not been able to communicate** easily with one another.

323 Speech Situations in which Backshift is not Necessary

If the reporting verb is in the present tense, the present perfect or the *will*-future, i.e. a tense of the present tense group, there is no backshift; instead, the same tense is used as in direct speech:

I shan't mention the matter to Richard again. He *will* only *tell* me that he **knows** what he **is doing** and that no one **will find out** whether he **was involved** or not.

But even if the reporting verb is in the past tense or the past perfect, a backshift of tenses is not always necessary or meaningful.

1. Retaining the present tense, present perfect and future forms

The weatherman *said* that at present a depression **is/was moving** over the British Isles from the Atlantic. It *said* in the news that a new weather satellite **has/had been launched.**	The present tense and the present perfect can be retained in order to emphasize that something is still true at the time of reporting. (Here: the depression and the satellite are still there.)
It took a long time before everybody *was convinced* that the earth **revolves/revolved** round the sun. Peter *assured* us that on summer mornings he **likes/liked** to get up and watch the sun rising.	The simple present is, for example, often used to express that something is permanently the case (laws of nature, characteristics, habits). A backshift to the past tense, or past perfect, is, however, possible in all cases.
It *was announced* that the landing of the spacecraft **will/would be transmitted** live on TV. We *listened to* some madman *prophesying* that the world **is/was going to end** at midnight tonight.	The *will*-future and other future forms can also be retained in reported speech to stress that an event is still a future event at the time of reporting. Otherwise the future-in-the-past, etc. is used.

2. Retaining the past tense

He *told* me last month that he **(had) tried out** his new mountaineering boots during his last holidays and they **gave / had given** him blisters. He *said* that after he **(had) packed** his rucksack, one of the straps **broke / had broken.** The Browns *were telling* us a few weeks ago that they **had gone** for a walking tour in Cornwall the year before and **(had) enjoyed** themselves immensely. They **(had) followed** the track running along the cliff tops and **(had) spent** the night at bed and breakfast places along the way. They **were / had been** lucky with the weather – it **(had)** only **rained** once the whole week.	**a) Past tense to express 'time before'** The past tense forms of direct speech can be retained if 'time before' in relation to the reporting verb is made clear by other means, e.g. by time adverbials (*during his last holidays,* etc.) or conjunctions (*after,* etc.). It can, of course, be backshifted to past perfect, and this backshift is preferred in formal style. A long run of past perfect forms can be avoided by changing back to the past tense (as in the second text example).
"If I **lived** near the mountains I'd go climbing every weekend." → I *heard* one of the tourists *say* that if she **lived** near the mountains, she would go climbing every weekend. "I wish it **weren't** such a long way to the next youth hostel." → The hiker said he wished it **weren't** such a long way to the next youth hostel.	**b) Past tense: modal use** In sentences containing hypothetical conditions or expressing hypothetical wishes or comparisons, the past tense is not backshifted, because here it indicates not 'time before' but the idea of non-fact (cf **212, 214**). For the same reason the *were*-subjunctive is retained (as are the forms *might, would, should,* etc: cf **322** Note 2).

324 *Must* and *Need* in Direct and Reported Speech

Must and *need* only have a so-called present tense form, which refers to either present or future time. These two auxiliaries can, however, be used in reported speech introduced by a verb in the past tense.

"There's the door-bell. It **must** be the doctor." → Mum *said* that the door-bell was ringing and that it **must** be the doctor.	When *must* expresses a **supposition** (cf **230**), it is always retained in reported speech.
"You **must** stay at home the rest of this week." → The doctor *said* this morning that Tim **must** stay at home the rest of this week. → When the doctor had examined him, he *said* that Tim **would have to** stay at home the rest of that week.	When *must* expresses a **necessity** (cf **229**), it can be retained if the necessity still exists at the time of reporting. If the necessity no longer exists, the following forms are used (depending on the speech intentions): *had to, would have to, should, was to / were to.*
No, you can't watch TV. I *said* you **mustn't** get up for another two days. I *told* Jill she **shouldn't** get up for another two days, but she wouldn't listen.	*Mustn't* can also be retained, if a prohibition is still valid: otherwise it is replaced by *shouldn't, wasn't to / weren't to.*
The specialist said this morning that I **needn't** take any more of these tablets after tomorrow. (Three days later:) The specialist *told* me that I **didn't have to** take any more of those tablets from yesterday on.	The same applies to *needn't* and its substitutes *didn't have to/didn't need to, wouldn't have to / wouldn't need to.*

Note:
When *must* und *mustn't* express a command or a prohibition, infinitive constructions may be used instead of *that*-clauses:

"You must take things easy for a few days." → He *told her* **to take** things easy for a few days.
"You mustn't go back to work too soon." → He *told her* **not to go back** to work too soon.

325–326 Time and Place Adverbials in Direct and Reported Speech

325 Changes in Time and Place Relationships and How they are Expressed

A time adverbial can determine a period or point in time in two ways:

- in absolute terms, e.g. with dates (*on February 21st, in the 19th century,* etc.);
- in relative terms, either relative to present time, that is, the time of speaking (*yesterday,* etc.) or relative to a point in past time (*the day before, that month,* etc.).

Place adverbials are also either absolute (*in Munich,* etc.) or relative (*here, there,* etc.).
Only the adverbials of **relative** time and place undergo a shift in the change from direct to reported speech.

Direct Speech	Reported Speech	
	Time relationship unchanged	**Time relationship changed**
Sheila (on Thursday): I had my first driving lesson **yesterday.** – I'm feeling rather proud of myself.	Keith (on Thursday): Sheila told me that she (had) had her first driving lesson **yesterday** and that she is / was feeling rather proud of herself.	Keith (on Sunday): Sheila told me on Thursday that she (had) had her first driving lesson **the day before / on Wednesday** and that she was feeling rather proud of herself.

Adverbials of relative **time** are not changed in reported speech if the original time relationship (here: *yesterday*) is still valid for the person reporting. (In this case the tenses can be either retained or backshifted, depending on what one means to say; cf **323.**)
If the original time relationship is no longer valid, the time adverbials are replaced

- by other, backshifted, relative time adverbials *(yesterday → the day before)*
- or by absolute time adverbials *(yesterday → on Wednesday).*

Direct Speech	Reported Speech	
	Place relationship unchanged	**Place relationship changed**
Sheila (in Sandwich): The Golf Championships are being held **here** this year.	Keith (staying in Sandwich): Sheila told me that the Golf Championships are being held **here** this year.	Susan (in London): Sheila phoned from Sandwich and told me that the Golf Championships are being held **there** this year. Or: Sheila told me on the phone that the Golf Championships are being held **in Sandwich** this year.

Adverbials of relative **place** are also changed in reported speech if the original place relationship (in our example: *here*) is no longer valid, i.e. if the person reporting is not in the same place as the person whose words are being reported.

- The adverbials may sometimes be replaced by other relative place adverbials *(here → there).*
- Normally, the place concerned can only be indicated clearly by using absolute place adverbials *(here → in Sandwich).*

326 Changes in Expressions of Relative Time and Place

The following list shows the changes that may occur in reported speech. However, this is only a general guideline. The context will determine the choice of adverbial, etc. in each individual case. This is particularly important with adverbials of relative place (or noun phrases such as *this country, our town*). For instance *there* is only meaningful if the context shows what place is meant.

"Here is the twelve o'clock news. The fog blanket has become so thick that no planes are landing in London at all **now.** Other airports have so far been coping well with the extra traffic **this week,** although there was chaos at Manchester **yesterday. Tomorrow** the fog is expected to lift a little and there is hope that **next week** all will be back to normal."

→ Recalling the great fog catastrophe last winter, I remember hearing on the twelve o'clock news that Sunday that the fog blanket had become so thick that no planes were landing in London at all **then.** The newsreader went on to say that other airports had so far been coping well with the extra traffic **that week,** although there had been chaos at Manchester **the day before.** The fog was expected to lift a little **the next day** and there was hope that **the following week** all would be back to normal. But that was only the beginning . . .

Expressions of relative time

Direct speech	Reported speech
	commonly:
now/at this moment	→ *then/at that moment*
today	→ *(on) that day*
*this week/ these hours/*etc.	→ *(in) that week/ (in) those hours*, etc.
yesterday	→ *(on) the day before/ the previous day*
last week, etc.	→ *the week before/ the previous week*, etc.
two months ago, etc.	→ *two months before/ two months earlier*, etc.
tomorrow	→ *the next day/ the following day*
next year, etc.	→ *the next year/ the following year*, etc.

"You may have read in the paper about the floods **here.** Well, **our area** has been affected as well. **This village** was cut off from the outside world for nearly two weeks. Several families **here** are now homeless."

→ In her last letter, my Indian pen-friend mentioned the floods **in her country,** and told me that **their area** had been affected as well. **Her own village** was cut off from the outside world for nearly two weeks and several families **there** are now homeless.

Expressions of relative place

Direct speech	Reported speech
here/ (in) this village/ (in) this country/ etc.	→ usually: *(in) his/her/their village/ (in) India/*etc. occasionally: *there/ (in) that village/ (in) that country/*etc.

Note:
With time adverbials containing the word *next* it is important to note the effect of the definite article. *Next month* (no article) relates a time to the present, *the next month* relates a time to the past.

"I'll buy a new car **next month.**"	direct speech
→ John said that he will/would buy a new car **next month.**	reported speech with no change in the adverbial
→ John told me last August that he would buy a new car **the next** (= the following) **month.**	reported speech with a change in the adverbial

327–328 Different Sentence Types in Direct and Reported Speech

327 Converting Different Sentence Types into Reported Speech

The different sentence types of direct speech are normally reported in the form of either (finite) subordinate clauses or infinitive constructions:

	Direct speech	Reported speech
"I've been watching the news on TV." → Derek said (that) he'd been watching the news. "I'll videotape the Chaplin film for you tonight." → My brother promised to videotape the Chaplin film for me tonight.	statement (sometimes, e.g. after verbs expressing an intention)	→ *that*-clause (*that* can be omitted) → infinitive (cf **328.2**)
"How did the play end?" → Sylvia asked me how the play (had) ended. "Which programme shall I put on?" → I asked Toby which programme to put on.	question with an interrogative (in a request for instructions with *shall I, can we,* etc. normally)	→ indirect question with an interrogative (same word order as in a statement!) → interrog. + infinitive
"Do you always watch the Eurovision Song Contest?" → I asked Mary if she always watched the Eurovision Song Contest. "Would you please switch over to BBC 2?" → Bob asked me to switch over to BBC 2.	*yes/no* question (sometimes, e.g. in requests)	→ indirect question with *if/whether* (same word order as in a statement!) → infinitive (cf **328.2**)
"Turn the sound up a bit, will you?" → Mother asked me to turn the sound up a bit. "Go to bed now, Tony." → Father told Tony that he should go to bed.	imperative (less commonly)	→ infinitive → *that*-clause with *should*

Notes:

1. Constructions with gerunds or noun phrases may be used in certain instances for the sentence types of direct speech, especially in the freer kind of reporting (cf **319**):

"Take a walk every morning." → The doctor advised taking a walk every morning.
The doctor advised a walk every morning.
"I have a headache." → She complained of a headache.

2. Incomplete sentences (verbless exclamations and questions, greetings, etc.) are either made into complete sentences or paraphrased:

Ann:	Hello Bob. What about a game of table tennis?	Ann greeted Bob and suggested playing a game of table tennis.
Bob:	Oh, no. Too tired.	Bob refused and complained that he was tired.
Ann:	You lazy thing.	Ann called him a lazy thing.
Cathy:	Now, now, no quarrelling you two.	Cathy said soothingly that they shouldn't quarrel.
Ann:	Please, just for half an hour, Bob.	Ann pleaded with Bob to play for just half an hour.
Bob:	Oh, well, all right then.	Bob consented rather reluctantly.

3. In spoken English it is quite common for the word order of a direct question to be retained in reported speech:
"What's your name?" → He asked me what was my name (instead of the more correct: what my name was).

328 Choice and Position of the Reporting Verb

1. Direct speech

"I dreamt about you last night," Charles **said.** "It was a nice dream, too," he **added.**

"Whatever's the matter?" **asked** Beryl anxiously. "Thank goodness I'm awake again," **answered** Susan. "I was having a nightmare."

"You're daydreaming again," **exclaimed** his teacher, Mrs Walker.
"Daydreaming?" **echoed** Fred. "No, I wasn't," he **protested,** "I was just thinking."
Other verbs: remark, declare, inquire, continue, repeat; murmur, stammer, whisper, shout, cry, smile, laugh; agree, object, insist, etc.

When a person's words are quoted as direct speech, the reporting clause (*he said*, etc.) occasionally comes at the beginning. But it is more common to put it after or within the words quoted. In such cases the noun and verb of a reporting clause can change places (inversion); pronoun / verb inversion *(said he)* is archaic or literary.
Instead of the neutral *say* or *ask* other verbs are often used to give additional information, e.g. about
- the manner in which s.th. was said (*exclaim*, etc.)
- its function in the conversation (*answer, add, echo,* etc.)
- the speaker's intentions (*protest*, etc.).

Note:
Subject / verb inversion in a reporting clause preceding direct speech is sometimes found in journalism:
Declared the dog's owner: "His bones must be made of rubber to survive being run over like that."

2. Reported speech

Bob **said / stammered** that he was sorry he was late. He **added / promised** that he would be on time in future.
The boy **asked** a man in the street if he had the correct time on him.

If one wishes to stay **as close as possible** to the original words, subordinate clauses (*that*-clauses or indirect questions) are used. The reporting verbs are essentially the same as for direct speech.

"We shall resign if our demands are not met," two members of the committee said / threatened.
→ Two members of the committee **threatened to resign** if their demands were not met.

The chairman said / suggested, "I think we should try and work towards a compromise."
→ The chairman **suggested trying** to work towards a compromise.

In **freer versions** using, for example, infinitive or gerund constructions or noun phrases, one generally chooses reporting verbs which reflect the speaker's intentions.

The most frequent speech intentions can be expressed by the following verbs (for verbs taking an infinitive or a gerund see also **264–272**):

Our neighbours **invited me to come** and have a swim in their pool.
His uncle **encouraged Denis to take up** diving.
The experts **recommend using** a good snorkel.
If someone hadn't **reminded us of the incoming tide,** we would have been cut off.

- commands, requests, advice
  tell, order, command, urge, warn, encourage, invite, ask s.o. to do s.th.;
  advise, recommend s.o. to do s.th. / doing s.th.
  With other structures: *remind s.o. of s.th., encourage s.o. in (doing) s.th., ask (s.o.) for s.th.*

When the boatman **proposed crossing** over to the island, everyone was very enthusiastic.

- suggestions
  suggest, propose (doing) s.th.

The boss is mad. He was **expecting you to have** finished the job by four.
Mr Black has just phoned. He **wants to know** if his car is ready yet.

- expectations, wishes, intentions
  expect, want / wish (s.o./s.th.) to do s.th.

The garage man **offered to change** the oil.
The car dealer **promised me a trial run** in the latest model.

- offers, promises, threats
  offer, promise (to do) s.th., threaten to do s.th.

Chapter 11: Cohesion and Emphasis

329–331 Ways of Achieving Cohesion (Summary)

329 Features of a Cohesive Text

> Dear Sir Basil,
> I would like to apply for the position of personal assistant *that* you advertised in last Saturday's Daily Telegraph.
> There are numerous reasons why I think I could be of considerable help to you in researching your forthcoming book on Lloyd George.
> **First and foremost,** I have taken a life-long interest in both *his* political achievements and *his* colourful private life. What fascinates me most about *the man* are *his* powers of leadership. Equally impressive was the personal charm *he* possessed. **On the one hand,** *it* undoubtedly enabled *him* to cast a spell over the general public and political opponents alike; **on the other hand, however,** the power *it* gave *him* over women clearly played no small part in *his* subsequent downfall ...
> It is, **however,** the prospect of working with an author of your eminence, Sir, *that* I find most exciting, and I sincerely hope that you will give me the opportunity of doing *so.* **Meanwhile,** I look forward to having the opportunity of discussing *the matter* further with you in person.
> **Though** you did not specially ask for them in your advertisement, I enclose a curriculum vitae and the names of two referees.
> Yours faithfully,
> Jeremy D. Johnson

As you read through the example on the left it very soon becomes clear that this is not an arbitrary collection of sentences but a piece of connected text, namely a letter.
The most obvious sign is that it begins and ends in a way which is typical of letters. On closer examination you realize that the writer has presented his thoughts step by step, so that it is easy for the reader to follow what he wants to say. The cohesion of the text is achieved mainly by

- referring back to what has been mentioned previously, e.g. by means of noun phrases *(the man, the matter),* personal pronouns and possessive determiners (*his, he, it,* etc.), relative pronouns *(that)* or pro-forms such as *so* (all in italics in the text);
- expressing logical connections between sentences with the aid of linking adverbs and adverbial phrases (*first and foremost, on the one hand,* etc.) or conjunctions *(though)* (all printed in bold type);
- choosing the appropriate sentence construction. Both the normal word order (subject – predicate – complementation, as in the first sentence) and deviations from this (e.g. *Equally impressive was ...*), but also constructions with *there, it* or *what* (all underlined in orange) have been chosen deliberately to structure the information and give each part the right weight, thus making the relations between the sentences more explicit (cf **330, 332–342**).

Note:
"Text" is used here not only for written but also for spoken texts, e.g. conversations. The latter are characterized, for instance, by sequences of questions and answers (especially shortened answers). (Cf Chapter 1.)

Word order is important not only for showing how the various elements of a sentence are related to one another, but also as a means of achieving cohesion in a text. The first element of a sentence plays a major part in this. One can see how this works by looking at the two most common ways of beginning sentences:

- beginning with the subject
- beginning with an adverbial which is not a necessary part of the sentence pattern (cf **41**).

(For other word orders and constructions with *it, what, there* cf **337–342.**)

Subject in front-position

The destruction of Britain's countryside is proceeding at an appalling rate, according to the latest official report.	◀ link to what is already known
The facts and figures reveal the havoc wrought in particular by modern farming methods.	◀ link to *the latest official report*
Their effects can most clearly be seen in the damage done to wildlife by the spraying of the country's chalk downlands with fertilizer and weed-killers.	◀ link to *modern farming methods*
Another serious problem is acid rain. ...	◀ introduction of a new idea

By beginning with the subject one **leads directly to the main statement** of the sentence.
The subject usually picks up something that has been previously mentioned or is assumed to be known. This is indicated by the use of the definite article, possessive determiners, demonstrative pronouns, etc.
A subject in front-position can also introduce something new, if it contains an indefinite article or other indefinite determiner (e.g. *another*), for instance. (The *there*-construction has a similar function of introducing something new, but in a much more explicit way: *There is another serious problem: acid rain.* Cf **341–342.**)

Adverbial in front-position

According to an official report, 90 per cent of our landscape is at present under threat of destruction.	◀ 'setting the scene' for what follows
In the past Britain's countryside was very varied and teeming with plant and animal life.	◀ contrast to *at present*
In the national nature reserves something of this may perhaps survive intact;	◀ contrast to Britain as a whole
(but) unfortunately even this is doubtful.	◀ contrast *may perhaps – doubtful*

When one begins a sentence with an adverbial, one is **'setting the scene'** (place, time, point of view, etc.) for the main statement of the sentence. The listener is, as it were, being prepared for what follows. Within the text this scene-setting often introduces a contrast to what has been said or implied before. This contrast can sometimes be underlined by using *but* or *however.*

Note:
The above examples show only the most common uses of subjects and adverbials in front-position. Sentences beginning with the subject may also express a contrast to a preceding sentence. And time and place adverbials in front-position may function as links to previously mentioned time and place adverbials. (This is usually done to make a reference to a time or place quite clear.):

Country dwellers are still flocking to the cities, **many city-dwellers** (however) are dreaming of going back to the land.
Industrialization started in the early 19th century. **At that time** nobody foresaw the radical social changes the new machines would bring about.

331 Cohesion through Complex Sentences

A train of thought can often be expressed either by a sequence of simple sentences or by one complex sentence. (For the function of subordinate clauses or non-finite constructions as elements in the complex sentence see **257** and **302.**)
A complex sentence will often sound rather formal, and is more typical of written language. Compare the following examples:

Don't leave your purse around **or** it'll get stolen.	**If** you leave your purse around, it'll get stolen.
Mary gets a large allowance. **But/Nevertheless** she always seems to be short of money.	**Though** Mary gets a large allowance, she always seems to be short of money./**In spite of** getting a large allowance, Mary always seems . . .
I had no change. **So** I had to borrow some.	**As** I had no change, I had to borrow some./Having no change, I had to borrow some.

Here, simple sentences have been linked together by conjunctions or adverbials.
(For linking adverbials see **161–162.**)

Alternatively, one can use complex sentences with adverbial clauses (cf **317**) or non-finite constructions (cf **292–297**).

Possible changes in our climate are a worry to scientists. **Some of them** are expecting catastrophic effects from atmospheric overheating.	Possible changes in our climate are a worry to scientists, **some of whom** are expecting catastrophic effects from atmospheric overheating.
Global temperatures are expected to rise generally. **This** could cause the polar ice caps to melt noticeably by the end of the century, and **then** large-scale flooding would occur.	Global temperatures are expected to rise generally, **which** could cause the polar ice caps to melt noticeably by the end of the century, **when** large-scale flooding would occur.

In each case, the introductory element in bold type links the sentence or main clause with something that has been mentioned in the preceding sentence. This is made clear by the use of the personal pronoun *them,* the demonstrative pronoun *this* and the adverb *then.*

The alternative here is to use complex sentences with non-defining relative clauses.
(For relative clauses with an antecedent see **308,** for relative clauses commenting on a statement see **315.**)

Computer technology has become a major growth industry. **It** is closely watched by business and trade unions alike.	Closely watched by business and trade unions alike, computer technology has become a major growth industry.
Computer science is developing at an ever-increasing speed, and only a few insiders can actually grasp the possibilities it offers.	With computer science developing at an ever increasing speed, only a few insiders can actually grasp the possibilities it offers.

In the above examples, one of each pair of sentences contains the main statement and the other expresses either accompanying circumstances or a reason.
In the first example, *it* refers back to *computer technology*; in the second, *only a few insiders* introduces something new.

A complex sentence with a participle construction can be used instead. The first example contains a related participle construction, the second an absolute participle construction. (Cf **293–294.**)

Notes:

1. Sometimes the content of a simple sentence can be expressed by using a noun phrase or a prepositional phrase. Instead of a sequence of short simple sentences it is therefore possible to use one longer sentence (which is strictly speaking still a simple sentence); however, this usually sounds more formal:
   In spite of a large allowance, Mary always seems to be short of money.
   The general rise in global temperatures could cause the polar ice caps to melt noticeably.
2. In addition to linking adverbials and conjunctions, there are also certain linking infinitive and participle constructions such as *to begin with, supposing,* etc. which can be used to connect sentences and clauses (cf **298–299**).

Emphasis (Summary)

332 Normal Word Order, Normal Stress, Special Emphasis

In English, the order in which the necessary constituent parts of a sentence can be arranged is fairly rigidly fixed (in a statement: subject – predicate – complementation). Normally, the last part of the sentence carries special weight, and this is where the syllable with the greatest stress will be (underlined in the following examples; cf **6**). The same applies to adverbials in end-position, except adverbials of place and time which are not necessary to complete the sentence pattern. These are usually unstressed:

He is always complaining of **headaches.**

He complained **bitterly.** (**But:** He complained of **a headache** yesterday.)

If a sentence has two objects, then the longer of the two will normally occur in end-position (cf **50**):

He prescribed the patient **some nasty-tasting green medicine.**

However, in order to give special emphasis to some part of the sentence a speaker may deviate from the pattern described here, or use additional words.

333 Means of Expressing Emphasis

1. Emphatic stress and emphatic words

Today the three children are doing the cooking. (Mother is ill.)
It says you add a teaspoon of salt (not a tablespoon).

When speaking, one can give something special emphasis by shifting the main stress to a word which would not normally be given so much stress.

Now you must all lend a hand with the work.
Do clear the table and start the washing-up.
They didn't do any dusting, but they did go round with the vacuum cleaner.

The main stress can also be put on an auxiliary verb. In the case of predicates without an auxiliary an emphatic *do* can be used. (Cf **335–336.**)

Only a minority of households are still without a washing-machine.
Try this brand. We always use it **ourselves.**
Elsie has made a **complete** mess of the soufflé.
She spoiled it **completely.**
I wasn't **at all** satisfied with my sherry trifle.

Emphasis can also be achieved by using focusing adverbs (*only, even, chiefly,* etc., cf **150–151**), pronouns ending in *-self/-selves* (cf **87.2**), intensifying adjectives, adverbs and adverbial phrases (*complete(ly), (not) at all, by no means,* etc., cf **147**).

2. Achieving emphasis by changing the word order

Here, one usually moves an element that would normally not be stressed to the stressed end of the sentence.

They paid the £1,000 reward for the recovery of the stolen goods **to the wrong man.**

Sometimes this change in word order only affects the parts of the sentence after the predicate. For example, a short object can be emphasized by putting it after a longer object.

From a member of the underworld came **the crucial tip leading to the capture of the gangsters.**
Decisive for the solving of the case was **the co-operation of the public.**

Greater emphasis can be achieved by word order changes affecting the whole of the sentence. For instance, in some cases the subject can be emphasized by putting it in the end-position (cf **337.2**, **338.1**).

3. Achieving emphasis by using cleft sentences (constructions with *it* and *what*)

Who do you think was responsible for the bank robbery? – It must have been **the IRA** who was behind it.
What they tried to do was **smuggle the stuff out of the country.**

In this case, the sentence is divided into two parts. The part of the sentence which is to be given special emphasis is placed at the end of one of the two parts.
For further details of this see **339–340.**

Note:
Questions introduced by interrogatives can be given emphasis by reinforcing the interrogative with *ever* or expressions such as *on earth, the devil,* etc. These can express emotional reactions such as astonishment, anger, and so on. Imperative sentences can be made more emphatic by adding expressions such as *in heaven's name, for God's sake,* etc.:

Who **ever** is this? Where **the devil** have you been? **For God's sake,** shut up!

334 Emphasis in Texts

Text 1:	
Everybody now realizes that we are living in a finite world. But by the end of this century there will be six billion people on the face of this earth, most of whom will be very poor.	Arguments leading to main statement
What is needed to feed, clothe and house that population adequately is **a sane distribution of the earth's resources.**	Emphasis of main statement by means of cleft sentence
The more money that is spent on the nuclear arms race, however, the less there is available for getting development programs going.	New idea
Text 2:	
Anyone who has first-hand knowledge of Third World countries knows that a massive transfer of capital and advanced technology is **by no means the best form of development aid.**	Emphasis (with *by no means*) to prepare for a contrast
Rather, it tends to disrupt traditional societies and impose on them problems we have as yet failed to solve in the West.	Contrast

Emphatic word order and emphatic constructions generally fulfil two functions at once: emphasis and cohesion (cf **330**). They are used both in speaking and writing to highlight the main points of a text. But in order to be fully effective, emphasis has to be either well prepared for in the text (see Text 1, where the emphatic cleft sentence forms a link to the preceding sentence) or else justified afterwards (see Text 2). What effect the various ways of achieving emphasis have on cohesion is described in **335–340**.

35–336 *Do*-Emphasis and Other Ways of Emphasizing the Predicate

335 Structures

In spoken language, a speaker can emphasize the predicate, just like any other element in the sentence, by stressing it. There are two possible ways of doing this:

He **can swim,** but he **can't dive.** You'll make it if you **run**, but not if you **walk.**	**1. Stressing the main verb**
You are ['ɑː] **taking** your time, aren't you? They **will** ['wɪl] **be** surprised when they see you. He **must** ['mʌst] **have been held up** somewhere.	**2. Stressing the auxiliary verb** With predicates consisting of one or more auxiliary verbs and a main verb the (first) auxiliary can be stressed. The full, unshortened form of the auxiliary is then used.
I **did bring** my umbrella with me, didn't I? I **do believe** it's going to be fine today. **Do take** your mackintosh with you.	If the predicate consists only of a main verb, a stressed *do*-form (+ infinitive) can be used. This makes the emphasis clear in the written language, too.

Note:
For ways of emphasizing the predicate by using a cleft sentence construction with *what*, see **339**.

336 Use in Texts

A stressed main verb normally expresses a contrast between the meaning of this verb and that of another verb *(They're just arguing, not quarrelling)*. The effect of using emphatic *do*-forms and other stressed auxiliaries is different:

I *don't* care for Indian food, but I **do like** Chinese food.
They've got *no* Chop Suey left, but they **do** still **have** Sweet and Sour Prawns.

I **did enjoy** that curry. It was delicious. (= I really enjoyed . . .)
You **must try** some of my bird's nest soup. It's awfully good. (= You really must try . . . .)

- They can emphasize the affirmative character of a statement, in contrast to a negative statement. They therefore normally follow such a negative statement.
- A stressed auxiliary can also express a particularly strong emotional reaction or attitude. This may be quite spontaneous, and therefore needs no preparation beforehand in the text.

337–338 Emphasis through Deviations from the Usual Word Order

337 Structures

There is a certain amount of freedom with regard to the positioning of the different constituent parts in a sentence:
Adverbials which are not necessary to complete the sentence pattern can be used in various positions (cf **142.1**).
Some variation is also possible in the order of two objects following the predicate (cf **49–51**).
The word order of the basic sentence pattern (subject – predicate – complementation) is generally invariable, but even here, certain deviations are sometimes possible:

1. Word order: complementation – subject – predicate – complementation

Complementation	Subject	Predicate	Complementation	
For their third baby	they	chose	the name Victoria Alberta.	
Vicky	her friends	called	her	for short.
Onto her granny's lap	they	put	the squalling infant.	
His hundreds of photos	the proud father	showed	to anyone who was interested.	

If a sentence contains two pieces of necessary complementation, one of these may occur in front-position; the other then comes at the end of the sentence after the predicate. The word order subject – predicate remains unchanged, unlike in German. In such cases a direct object is usually put at the end of the sentence (sentences 1–3); only occasionally is it put at the beginning (last sentence).

2. Word order with inversion of subject and main verb (full inversion)

Complementation	Predicate	Subject
From the radio	came	the schmaltzy tones of David Dobson's latest hit.
Equally inexplicable	remains	this second-rate group's continued popularity.
At the top of the charts	is	'Sweet Dreams'.
Onto the stage	leapt	the band.

This word order only occurs when there is only **one** piece of complementation in the sentence. In this case the subject comes at the end of the sentence after the predicate. However, this type of inversion, which is called **full inversion**, is only used when one wants to emphasize the subject (normally a noun or a noun phrase). But the subject – predicate word order is not changed when the subject (usually a pronoun) is given less emphasis than the verb or the front-position complementation:

To this they **didn't reply.** Out of the room the two of them **stormed.**
Embarrassing it was. **A terrible mess** these people left.

3. Word order with inversion of subject and auxiliary (partial inversion)

Adverbial/ complementation	Auxiliary/*be* as a main verb	Subject	(Aux.)	Main verb	Rest of the sentence
Not for anything in the world	would	John	have	entered	that room again.
Scarcely	had	they		arrived	when mysterious things started to happen.
Not a single word	did	he		speak	for the rest of the evening.
So great	was	her relief			that she burst into tears.

This word order is only used if the front-position element contains a negation, restriction (*scarcely, hardly,* etc.) or intensification (*so* + adjective, etc.).
With this word order, the subject comes after the (first) auxiliary or after *be,* just as in questions (partial inversion, cf **21**). If there is no auxiliary verb, a *do*-form is used (except with *be* as a main verb, which does not take a *do*-auxiliary, cf **19** Note 1).

Notes:

1. A special type of inversion is possible with the progressive form and the passive form of verbs. Here, the main verb and its complementation are at the beginning of the sentence and the subject at the end:
   Dancing a Scottish reel **are** a group of folk-dancers from Braemar.
   Slung round his neck **was** a tartan scarf.
2. Sometimes, complementation from a following subordinate clause may be placed at the beginning of the whole sentence; this is more common in spoken than in written English:
   Chocolate I don't think I'll ever be able to give up. (Compare: I don't think (that) I'll ever be able to give up chocolate.)
3. The different variations in word order apply mainly to statements, but certain deviations are also possible in imperative sentences:
   Down you come. (Compare: Come down.) Out you go. (Compare: Go out.)

338 Use for Cohesion, Emphasis and the Structuring of Information

By deviating from the subject – predicate – complementation word order, the following aims can be achieved:

1. Emphasis of the element placed in end-position

This is usually the intended effect if one of two pieces of complementation occurs on its own at the end of the sentence (cf **337.1**), and it is always the effect achieved when placing the subject in the emphatic end-position (cf **337.2**). The 'end weight' of this part of the sentence is often reinforced by further additions (e.g. attributes, a list of details).
What function this emphatic word order has for text cohesion depends on the element which is placed at the beginning:

New York's subway is showing its age. **To this indisputable fact** must be attributed *its numerous failings:* it is smelly, dirty, smeared with graffiti and prone to breakdowns.
(Compare subject in front-position: **This indisputable fact** explains *its numerous failings . . .* .)

- The element in front-position may form a link to something that has been mentioned already and that will now be further discussed (cf **330**, functions of the subject in front-position).
  The use of the demonstrative determiner *this* in our example makes it clear that the speaker is referring back to something mentioned before.
  This kind of cohesion occurs mainly in formal style.

A lot has been talked about the failings of the New York subway. **Much more to the point,** however, is *the essential contribution it makes to the functioning of a city of over ten million people.*

- The element in front-position may also express a contrast to what has been said (or implied) before, with further details of the contrast to follow (also mainly in formal style).

It was shortly before eight when we arrived breathless on platform 2 of Times Square Subway Station. **In** came *the train.* The doors opened and **onto the platform** surged *a huge crowd of commuters from the Bronx all in a hurry to get to work.*

- When a necessary adverbial of place or direction is used at the beginning of a sentence, the effect is usually to highlight the climax of a narrative. The preceding sentence will have been building up to this climax.

2. Emphasis of the element placed in front-position

This effect is achieved particularly by changes of word order in short sentences which contain little or no really new information. Complementation in front-position (in this case often an adverbial of direction) generally expresses a speaker's emotional attitude, and it will carry the main stress. The subject which follows it (usually a personal pronoun, cf **337**.2) and the verb convey information that is known or, at least, expected and are therefore given no particular emphasis. This type of sentence is used mainly as follows:

... He had never been on a 10 m diving-board before. Cautiously he moved towards the edge of the board. He closed his eyes and, taking a deep breath, **down** he jumped.

Policeman to driver going wrong way down one-way street: "Didn't you see the arrows?"
Driver: **"Arrows** you said? I didn't even see the Indians."

- as the climax in a piece of narrative, a climax which actually only confirms what has already been anticipated. This is found typically in action narratives, sports commentaries, etc.
- as a spontaneous reaction to something that is said; here, the remainder of the sentence is simply added on to the element placed in front-position. This kind of construction is more typical of spoken language.

Notes:

1. In imperative sentences beginning with *in, out, up, down,* etc., it is again the front-position adverbial which carries the main force of what is being said:

   Out you come. **Down** you come. **On** you go. etc.

2. Stressed complementation in front-position can both form a link to what has already been mentioned and, at the same time, indicate that what follows later is in contrast to this:

   The crossword's easy. – **Easy** it may be, but it's taking me an awful long time.
   I showed him two ways of doing the puzzle – **one** he understood right away, but **the other** he couldn't make head or tail of.

3. Bringing forward the negative, restricting or intensifying element

Negative, restricting and intensifying elements do not normally occur at the beginning of the sentence. They can be placed in this position, however, if one wants to indicate right from the start that what follows is to be seen from a particular negative or positive point of view. In most cases the element in question will be an adverbial. (Compare the 'scene-setting' function of other adverbials in front-position, **330**.)
When an element of this kind is placed at the beginning of the sentence, it causes partial inversion (auxiliary – subject – main verb, cf **337**.3). This is found quite often in formal style, but is otherwise fairly rare.

Around 1920 the decline of the British Empire began. **No longer** was Britain's dominance of the seas unquestioned, **nor** could Britain maintain its industrial and financial supremacy. **In vain** did some politicians try to uphold the idea of Britain's special role in the world.

Ghandi was the most influential figure India had produced for centuries. **So highly** revered [-'-] *(verehrt)* was he by millions of his countrymen that they treated him as a saint.

When a **negative** adverbial is placed in front-position, it often announces that the content of the preceding sentence is about to be continued with greater force. Elements with negative meaning include *nor/neither, never, in vain, no longer* and other combinations with *no.*

Intensifying adverbials have a similar effect. These include *well, many a time, so highly, to such an extent* and other combinations with *many, so, such.*

India's struggle for independence lasted many years. **No sooner** was it granted, however, than terrible violence broke out. **Only after much suffering** was an uneasy peace established.

Restricting adverbials, e.g. *hardly/scarcely/barely/little/no sooner* and combinations with *only* are often used to introduce a sudden, dramatic development in a course of events (i.e. a contrast).

Notes:

1. In colloquial English, the above adverbials – if they are used at all – either take mid-position or end-position (cf Ch. 5). Short sentences beginning with *nor/neither* are however, very common in colloquial speech (cf **34**):

Independence had **scarcely** been granted when terrible violence broke out.
I've never been to India. – **Nor** have I.

2. Even when such adverbials are positioned at the beginning, the most important information, and therefore the main stress, will normally be at the end of the sentence or clause. The same applies when complementation intensified by *so* or *such* (or *such* used on its own) is placed in front-position. This usually indicates that what has been said in the preceding sentence is going to be continued with greater force:

The two figure skaters left the ice after their programme. **So breathless** were they that they could hardly speak.
They waited expectantly for the judges' verdict. **Such good marks** did they get that the medal was almost certainly theirs.
Such was the grace and musicality of the ice-dancers' performance that the spectators applauded frantically.

However, if there is a negated object at the beginning of the sentence, this will be given the main stress. The object here forms a link to what has just been said and reinforces it, while the subject and predicate convey only known or expected information (cf the type of cohesion described in **338**.2):

The trainer was very pleased. **Not one mistake** had his young pupil made.

339–340 Cleft Sentences

339 Structures

The idea behind the term 'cleft sentence' is that an underlying sentence is divided into two parts without any further 'content words' being added.
There are two types: '*it* cleft sentences' and '*what* cleft sentences':

(Underlying sentence: Jim broke his leg last week when he was skiing.)

'*It* cleft sentences':
It was **Jim**//who broke his leg last week.
It was **his leg**// (that) Jim broke last week.
It was only **last week**//that Jim broke his leg.
It was **when he was skiing**//that Jim ...

The *it* cleft sentence is introduced by the structure word *it* and the verb *be* in the singular (even when followed by a noun in the plural: *It was both legs that Peter broke).*
Except for the predicate, virtually any constituent part of the underlying sentence (including an adverbial clause) can be placed at the end of the first part of the cleft sentence.
The remaining elements are added on in the form of a relative clause or a *that* clause. (A *that* clause is used if the *it* in the first part is introducing an adverbial (or adverbial clause), e.g. *last week, when he was skiing.)*

'*What* cleft sentences':
What Jim broke (last week) //was **his leg**.
What Jim did (last week) //was **(to) break his leg!**
(Underlying sentence: He was skiing at the time. →)
What he was doing at the time//was **skiing**.

The first part of a *what* cleft sentence is introduced by *what*, the second part by a form of the verb *be*. There are two possibilities:

- the second part contains only the complementation to the predicate (usually a direct object, but never a noun or pronoun referring to a person). The predicate itself comes in the first part of the cleft sentence;
- the second part contains the main verb of the underlying sentence (an infinitive with or without *to*, or a participle) and its complementation. In the first part a form of *do* is substituted for the main verb.

Notes:

1. *It* cleft sentences can also be used as questions:
   Was it last week that Jim broke his leg? When was it that Jim broke his leg?

2. For *what* cleft sentences containing two pieces of complementation (here: two objects) there are two possible patterns:
   What she brought *me*//was *a magazine to read.* (predicate + one object in the first part, the other object in the second part)
   What she did//was bring *me a magazine to read.* (*do*-form in the first part, both objects in the second part)

340 Use for Cohesion, Emphasis and the Structuring of Information

1. The '*it* cleft sentence'

The metric system is used in most European countries. It was **Napoleon**//who introduced *it.* new known	The first part of the *it* cleft sentence contains the element with the most important new information, and this carries the main stress. Generally speaking, the second part simply picks up something that is already known.
The earliest measurements were based on the size of a man's thumb, foot, step, etc. and varied from country to country and even from place to place. It was **the metric system** which put an end to this diversity. You must have packed a lot of clothes in this suitcase. It weighs a ton. – No, it's **all those books** that are in it that make it so heavy.	The element which carries the emphasis usually expresses a contrast, and this must develop logically from what has been said before. It is therefore rare to find *it* cleft sentences at the beginning of a written text or a conversation. But **within the text** they are one of the most commonly used means of emphasis, both in spoken and written English.
The theory of universal gravitation was first developed by Newton. It was **a falling apple** that made him hit on the idea. *(Ein fallender Apfel brachte ihn auf den Gedanken.)*	(The German construction with *es* is far less common than the English equivalent. Instead, one normally uses simple sentences, indicating by means of stress which element carries the emphasis.)

Notes:

1. In formal style *it* cleft sentences can also be used when both parts of the sentence contain new information. The second part of the sentence is often very long and contains the more important new information, although, by using the cleft sentence construction, the speaker or writer presents it as known or obvious. The first part of the sentence generally contains an adverbial which 'sets the scene' for the rest of the sentence. When used in this way, *it* cleft sentences do occasionally occur at the beginning of a text or passage:
   It was at the turn of the century that the first films appeared: mainly newsreels and simple short comedies.

2. By using an '*it* cleft sentence' it is possible to avoid the even more formal construction with a restricting adverbial in front-position and partial inversion (cf **337**.3, **338**.3):
   Not until the late fifties **did** television really **catch on** in Britain.
   It was not until the late fifties **that** television really **caught on** in Britain.

2. The '*what* cleft sentence'

She hates living alone in that isolated house. What she *fears* most//is **burglary.** known new	The first part of a '*what* cleft sentence' picks up something that is known or has been implied in order to give it more emphasis or greater force. The new information is contained in the second part of the sentence. Each of the two halves of the sentence contains a stressed syllable.
When our neighbours returned from holiday, they found their house stripped of all its furniture. *What the thieves had done* was (to) come with a removal van in the night and simply load everything into it.	*What* cleft sentences, too, are usually found **within a text** rather than at the beginning. The *what* clause can, directly or indirectly, sum up what has been said previously in the text.

That petty crime is on the increase is a well-known fact. *What is really worrying,* however, is the fact that the number of young offenders is rising so much.

What we want to discuss today is the increase in shop-lifting and its possible causes.
What I wanted to tell you is that my purse wasn't stolen after all. It was found behind a bench.

What we need is a plan of the house. *(Was wir brauchen, ist ein Plan des Hauses.)*
What is most puzzling about the whole thing is that there were no footprints at all in the garden. *(Das Rätselhafte an der ganzen Sache ist, . . .)*

The *what*-part of the sentence may also have a 'scene-setting' function, expressing an evaluation of what follows; this often represents a contrast to what has been said or implied before.

At the beginning of a new section of a text or conversation one only finds stereotyped '*what* cleft sentences' which serve to catch the attention of the reader or listener.

In German there is a similar cleft sentence construction with *was, wofür, worüber,* etc., but it is more common to find simple sentences used here instead, especially ones with a nominalized adjective (cf **135**).

341–342 The *There*-Construction

341 Structures: *There* with *be* and Other Verbs

The structure word *there* (which is always unstressed) is normally followed by some form of *be*, but sometimes other verbs can be used as well.

1. *There* with *be*

Formal subject	Form of *be*		Notional subject		Participle	Adverbial or complementation
There	**is**		a bus stop			across the road.
		(Cf:	The bus stop	is		across the road.)
There	**are**		lots of people		**queuing**	already.
		(Cf:	Lots of people	are	queuing	already.)
There	**have been**		many complaints		**made**	about the new fares.
		(Cf:	Many complaints	have been	made	about the new fares.)

If *be* is a main verb, it comes before the notional subject (example 1).
Be can also be used as an auxiliary verb to form the progressive form and the passive form (examples 2 and 3). Here, the *be*-form comes before the notional subject, and the present or past participle comes after it.
The construction with a present participle does not, however, always correspond to a progressive form; it can also correspond to a sentence with the simple present or simple past:

There	**is**	a coach	**leaving**	at ten.
		(Cf: The coach	leaves	at ten.)

2. *There* with simple present and simple past forms of other verbs

At last	**there appeared**	a speck of light	in the distance.
(Cf: At last		a speck of light appeared	in the distance.)
Suddenly	**there rose**	through the air an ear-piercing scream.	
(Cf: Suddenly		an ear-piercing scream rose through the air.)	

This *there*-construction is used mainly with the verbs *appear, remain, come* and *follow.* It also occurs – although generally only in literary style – with a number of other verbs, all of them intransitive (or used intransitively), e.g. *lie, spread, rise.*

Notes:

1. In *there*-constructions, there is normally number concord between the *be*-form and the notional subject which follows. In colloquial speech, however, the singular form *there is* is sometimes used together with a notional subject in the plural:

   There**'s** two cracks in the ceiling here. (Instead of: There **are** two cracks in the ceiling here.)

2. The structure word *there* may be left out in literary style if the sentence begins with a place or direction adverbial. This is an instance of the word order with full inversion described in **337.2**:

   On the floor (there) lay a shattered statue.
   From the damp walls (there) came a musty smell.

3. The *there*-construction can also be combined with an infinitive or a gerund (cf **263.2**, **277** Note 2):

   There is so much to do. There remains much to be discussed.
   There is no denying the fact that we haven't got very far yet.

342 Use for the Structuring of Information

The structure word *there* signals that the whole of the rest of the sentence (especially the notional subject) contains new information:

There was *a* large crowd of spectators waiting outside the courtroom when the prisoner arrived. He was hurried inside among jeers and catcalls. The street market was in full swing. **There was** *every kind of* commodity you could think of being offered. At one end **there were** fruit and vegetables for sale, and at the other puppies and cage-birds. **There were** stalls selling genuine antiques and **there were** stalls selling just junk. And above all **there was** *an* incredible noise.	The *there*-construction occurs mainly when somebody or something is being introduced for the first time. It is therefore often used in combination with an indefinite article or indefinite pronoun or determiner. The construction is frequently used to start a new section of a text or conversation. Within the main body of a text it is used to present a series of facts or observations.
Hot and thirsty though he was, he dared not stop for a rest. At the back of his mind **there was** always *the* fear of arriving too late to save his friend. (Compare: He was afraid of arriving too late to save his friend. *This fear* haunted him as he rode through the dark.)	The *there*-construction is only combined with the definite article or a possessive determiner, etc. when a particularly important point is being recalled. (Normally, sentences with the subject in front-position will be used if one is picking up something that is already known: cf **330.**)

Notes:

1. The *there*-construction also occurs in subordinate clauses, questions and in shortened answers and question tags (following complete sentences with *there* as a formal subject):

   I don't think (that) **there's** anything wrong with that.
   Is there any point in following it up? – No, **there isn't.**
   There aren't any other problems needing attention, **are there?**

2. The unstressed structure word *there* should not be confused with the stressed adverb of place and direction, which may also occur at the beginning of a sentence:

   There he comes. **There**'s our bus. **There,** on the mat, lay the long-awaited letter.

Appendix

343 Alphabetical List of the Most Important Irregular Verbs

arise [aɪ]	arose [əʊ]	arisen [ɪ]	*sich erheben*
awake [eɪ]	awoke [əʊ]	awoke(n), awaked	*erwachen*
be [iː]	was [ɒ]	been [iː]	*sein*
bear [eə]	bore [ɔː]	borne, born [ɔː]	*(er)tragen, gebären*
beat [iː]	beat [iː]	beaten [iː]	*schlagen*
become [ʌ]	became [eɪ]	become [ʌ]	*werden*
begin [ɪ]	began [æ]	begun [ʌ]	*anfangen*
bend [e]	bent [e]	bent	*beugen, biegen*
bet [e]	bet, betted	bet, betted	*wetten*
bid [ɪ]	bade [bæd]	bidden	*heißen, gebieten*
bid	bid	bid	*(Preis) bieten*
bind [aɪ]	bound [aʊ]	bound	*binden*
bite [aɪ]	bit [ɪ]	bitten [ɪ], bit	*beißen*
bleed [iː]	bled [e]	bled	*bluten*
blow [əʊ]	blew [uː]	blown [əʊ]	*blasen*
break [eɪ]	broke [əʊ]	broken [əʊ]	*(zer) brechen*
breed [iː]	bred [e]	bred	*brüten, züchten*
bring [ɪ]	brought [ɔː]	brought	*bringen*
broadcast [ɑː]	broadcast, broadcasted	broadcast, broadcasted	*senden (Radio, TV)*
build [ɪ]	built [ɪ]	built	*bauen*
burn [ɜː]	burnt [ɜː], burned	burnt, burned	*(ver) brennen*
burst [ɜː]	burst	burst	*platzen*
buy [aɪ]	bought [ɔː]	bought	*kaufen*
cast [ɑː]	cast	cast	*werfen, (Metall) gießen*
catch [æ]	caught [ɔː]	caught	*fangen*
choose [uː]	chose [əʊ]	chosen [əʊ]	*(aus) wählen*
cling [ɪ]	clung [ʌ]	clung	*sich (an) klammern*
come [ʌ]	came [eɪ]	come [ʌ]	*kommen*
cost [ɒ]	cost	cost	*kosten*
creep [iː]	crept [e]	crept	*kriechen*
cut [ʌ]	cut	cut	*schneiden*
deal [iː]	dealt [e]	dealt	*handeln (von), sich befassen (mit)*
dig [ɪ]	dug [ʌ]	dug	*graben*
do [uː]	did [ɪ]	done [ʌ]	*tun*
draw [ɔː]	drew [uː]	drawn [ɔː]	*zeichnen, ziehen*
dream [iː]	dreamt [e], dreamed [iː]	dreamt, dreamed	*träumen*
drink [ɪ]	drank [æ]	drunk [ʌ]	*trinken*
drive [aɪ]	drove [əʊ]	driven [ɪ]	*fahren, treiben*
dwell [e]	dwelt [e]	dwelt	*(ver) weilen, wohnen*
eat [iː]	ate [e/eɪ]	eaten [iː]	*essen*
fall [ɔː]	fell [e]	fallen [ɔː]	*fallen*
feed [iː]	fed [e]	fed	*füttern*
feel [iː]	felt [e]	felt	*(sich) fühlen, sich anfühlen*
fight [aɪ]	fought [ɔː]	fought	*kämpfen*
find [aɪ]	found [aʊ]	found	*finden*
flee [iː]	fled [e]	fled	*fliehen*
fling [ɪ]	flung [ʌ]	flung	*schleudern, werfen*

fly [aɪ]	flew [uː]	flown [əʊ]	*fliegen*
forbid [ɪ]	forbad(e) [æ]	forbidden [ɪ]	*verbieten*
forecast [ɑː]	forecast, forecasted	forecast, forecasted	*vorhersagen*
forget [e]	forgot [ɒ]	forgotten [ɒ]	*vergessen*
forgive [ɪ]	forgave [eɪ]	forgiven [ɪ]	*vergeben, verzeihen*
freeze [iː]	froze [əʊ]	frozen [əʊ]	*erfrieren*
get [e]	got [ɒ]	got	*bekommen, werden*
give [ɪ]	gave [eɪ]	given [ɪ]	*geben*
go [əʊ]	went [e]	gone [ɒ]	*gehen, fahren*
grind [aɪ]	ground [aʊ]	ground	*mahlen*
grow [əʊ]	grew [uː]	grown [əʊ]	*wachsen, anbauen*
hang [æ]	hung [ʌ]	hung	*(auf)hängen*
	hanged	hanged	*an den Galgen hängen*
have [æ]	had [æ]	had	*haben*
hear [ɪə]	heard [ɜː]	heard	*hören*
hide [aɪ]	hid [ɪ]	hidden	*(sich) verstecken*
hit [ɪ]	hit	hit	*schlagen, treffen*
hold [əʊ]	held [e]	held	*halten*
hurt [ɜː]	hurt	hurt	*verletzen, wehtun*
keep [iː]	kept [e]	kept	*(be)halten, aufbewahren*
kneel [iː]	knelt [e]	knelt	*knien*
knit [ɪ]	knitted, knit	knitted, knit	*stricken*
know [əʊ]	knew [juː]	known [əʊ]	*wissen, kennen*
lay [eɪ]	laid [eɪ]	laid	*legen, (Tisch) decken*
lead [iː]	led [e]	led	*führen, leiten*
lean [iː]	leant [e], leaned [iː]	leant, leaned	*lehnen*
leap [iː]	leapt [e], leaped [iː/e]	leapt, leaped	*springen*
learn [ɜː]	learnt [ɜː], learned	learnt, learned	*lernen, erfahren*
leave [iː]	left [e]	left	*(zurück-/ver) lassen, weggehen*
lend [e]	lent [e]	lent	*leihen*
let [e]	let	let	*lassen, vermieten*
lie [aɪ]	lay [eɪ]	lain [eɪ]	*liegen*
light [aɪ]	lit [ɪ], lighted	lit, lighted	*anzünden, erleuchten*
lose [uː]	lost [ɒ]	lost	*verlieren*
make [eɪ]	made [eɪ]	made	*machen*
mean [iː]	meant [e]	meant	*meinen, bedeuten*
meet [iː]	met [e]	met	*begegnen, (sich) treffen*
mistake [eɪ]	mistook [ʊ]	mistaken [eɪ]	*verwechseln*
mow [əʊ]	mowed	mown	*mähen*
pay [eɪ]	paid [eɪ]	paid	*(be)zahlen*
put [ʊ]	put	put	*legen, setzen, stellen*
quit [ɪ]	quit, quitted	quit, quitted	*aufgeben, aufhören, verlassen*
read [iː]	read [e]	read [e]	*lesen*
rend [e]	rent	rent	*zerreißen*
rid [ɪ]	rid	rid	*loswerden, befreien (von)*
ride [aɪ]	rode [əʊ]	ridden	*reiten, fahren*
ring [ɪ]	rang [æ]	rung [ʌ]	*läuten, anrufen*
rise [aɪ]	rose [əʊ]	risen [ɪ]	*aufstehen, aufgehen*
run [ʌ]	ran [æ]	run [ʌ]	*rennen, laufen*
saw [ɔː]	sawed [ɔː]	sawn [ɔː], sawed	*sägen*
say [eɪ]	said [e]	said	*sagen*
see [iː]	saw [ɔː]	seen [iː]	*sehen*
seek [iː]	sought [ɔː]	sought	*suchen*
sell [e]	sold [əʊ]	sold	*verkaufen*
send [e]	sent	sent	*schicken*
set [e]	set	set	*setzen, stellen*
sew [əʊ]	sewed [əʊ]	sewn [əʊ]	*nähen*

shake [eɪ]	shook [ʊ]	shaken [ei]	*schütteln*
shed [e]	shed	shed	*vergießen, sich entledigen*
shine [aɪ]	shone [ɒ]	shone	*scheinen, glänzen*
shoot [uː]	shot [ɒ]	shot	*schießen, erschießen*
show [əʊ]	showed [əʊ]	shown [əʊ], showed	*zeigen*
shrink [ɪ]	shrank [æ], shrunk [ʌ]	shrunk	*schrumpfen, zurückschrecken*
shut [ʌ]	shut	shut	*zumachen, schließen*
sing [ɪ]	sang [æ]	sung [ʌ]	*singen*
sink [ɪ]	sank [æ]	sunk [ʌ]	*sinken, versenken*
sit [ɪ]	sat [æ]	sat	*sitzen, sich setzen*
slay [eɪ]	slew [uː]	slain [eɪ]	*erschlagen*
sleep [iː]	slept [e]	slept	*schlafen*
slide [aɪ]	slid [ɪ]	slid	*gleiten*
sling [ɪ]	slung [ʌ]	slung [ʌ]	*schleudern, werfen*
slink [ɪ]	slunk [ʌ]	slunk	*schleichen*
slit [ɪ]	slit	slit	*(auf)schlitzen*
smell [e]	smelt [e], smelled	smelt, smelled	*riechen*
sow [əʊ]	sowed [əʊ]	sown [əʊ]	*säen*
speak [iː]	spoke [əʊ]	spoken [əʊ]	*sprechen*
speed [iː]	sped [e], speeded	sped, speeded	*schnell fahren, sich beeilen*
spell [e]	spelt [e], spelled	spelt, spelled	*buchstabieren*
spend [e]	spent [e]	spent	*ausgeben, verbringen*
spill [ɪ]	spilt [ɪ], spilled	spilt, spilled	*verschütten*
spin [ɪ]	spun [ʌ], span [æ]	spun	*spinnen*
spit [ɪ]	spat [æ]	spat	*spucken*
split [ɪ]	split	split	*(sich) spalten*
spoil [ɔɪ]	spoilt [ɔɪ], spoiled	spoilt, spoiled	*verderben*
spread [e]	spread [e]	spread	*(sich) aus-/verbreiten*
spring [ɪ]	sprang [æ]	sprung [ʌ]	*springen*
stand [æ]	stood [ʊ]	stood	*stehen*
steal [iː]	stole [əʊ]	stolen [əʊ]	*stehlen*
stick [ɪ]	stuck [ʌ]	stuck	*(an)stecken, (an)kleben*
sting [ɪ]	stung [ʌ]	stung	*stechen*
stink [ɪ]	stank [æ], stunk [ʌ]	stunk	*stinken*
stride [aɪ]	strode [əʊ]	stridden [ɪ]	*schreiten*
strike [aɪ]	struck [ʌ]	struck	*stoßen, schlagen*
string [ɪ]	strung [ʌ]	strung	*(auf einer Schnur) aufziehen, besaiten*
strive [aɪ]	strove [əʊ]	striven [ɪ]	*(an)streben*
swear [eə]	swore [ɔː]	sworn [ɔː]	*schwören, fluchen*
sweep [iː]	swept [e]	swept	*fegen, kehren*
swell [e]	swelled [e]	swollen [əʊ], swelled	*(an)schwellen*
swim [ɪ]	swam [æ]	swum [ʌ]	*schwimmen*
swing [ɪ]	swung [ʌ]	swung	*schwingen, schwenken*
take [eɪ]	took [ʊ]	taken [eɪ]	*nehmen, bringen*
teach [iː]	taught [ɔː]	taught	*lehren*
tear [eə]	tore [ɔː]	torn [ɔː]	*zerreißen*
tell [e]	told [əʊ]	told	*erzählen, sagen*
think [ɪ]	thought [ɔː]	thought	*denken, glauben*
thrive [aɪ]	throve [əʊ]	thriven [ɪ]	*gedeihen*
throw [əʊ]	threw [uː]	thrown [əʊ]	*werfen*
thrust [ʌ]	thrust	thrust	*stoßen*
tread [e]	trod [ɒ]	trodden [ɒ], trod	*treten*
understand [æ]	understood [ʊ]	understood	*verstehen*
upset [e]	upset	upset	*aus der Fassung bringen, umstoßen*
wake [eɪ]	woke [əʊ], waked [eɪ]	woken [əʊ], waked	*(auf)wecken, aufwachen*
wear [eə]	wore [ɔː]	worn [ɔː]	*(Kleider) tragen, abnutzen*
weave [iː]	wove [əʊ]	woven [əʊ]	*weben*

wed [e]	wedded, wed	wedded, wed	*heiraten*
weep [iː]	wept [e]	wept	*weinen*
win [ɪ]	won [ʌ]	won	*gewinnen*
wind [aɪ]	wound [aʊ]	wound	*winden, (Uhr) aufziehen*
wring [ɪ]	wrung [ʌ]	wrung	*auswringen*
write [aɪ]	wrote [əʊ]	written [ɪ]	*schreiben*

Note:
Verbs which are derived from irregular verbs almost always have the same irregular past tense and past participle forms as the verb base: compare the examples in the table *come – become, take – mistake,* etc. Other examples are *overcome, oversee, overhear, overrun; rebuild, rewrite, retell; outdo, outgrow, outshine,* etc.

344–348 The Alphabet, Spelling and Punctuation

344 The English Alphabet

a	b	c	d	e	f	g	h	i	j	k	l	m	n
[eɪ]	[biː]	[siː]	[diː]	[iː]	[ef]	[dʒiː]	[eɪtʃ]	[aɪ]	[dʒeɪ]	[keɪ]	[el]	[em]	[en]
o	p	q	r	s	t	u	v	w	x	y	z		
[əʊ]	[piː]	[kjuː]	[ɑː(r)]	[es]	[tiː]	[juː]	[viː]	[ˈdʌbljuː]	[eks]	[waɪ]	*Br.* [zed], *Am.* [ziː]		

345 Capitalization

Except at the beginning of a sentence, English words normally start with small letters. Apart from the personal pronoun *I* (and *He/Him/His* referring to *God*), the only types of word which are regularly capitalized are names and words used like names. This group includes:

Angela, Dave Allen, the Smiths, John F. Kennedy, Joan of Arc, Emmy Lou Harris, Tiny Tim, Bugs Bunny, Rover, etc.	• names of persons (first names and surnames, initials, nicknames; also animals' names, etc.);
Queen Elizabeth, Saint Peter, Ms Kelly, Dr Oates, General Sherman, Uncle Jack, Nurse Carey, etc. Please, Mother, don't tell Father what I said about Auntie! Mr President, what themes were discussed in your meeting with the Prime Minister? When appointed Secretary of State, he resigned his post as Professor of Political Science at Harvard.	• titles, words denoting family relationships and (sometimes) professions when they are used as parts of or instead of a person's name; (Words designating the holders of high office are capitalized even when they are used – often with an article – as common nouns.)
the United Nations, the Environmental Protection Agency, the Foreign Office, General Electric, the Mafia, the Sioux, the Conservatives, the Catholic Church, Christendom, the Middle Ages, World War II, etc.	• words used as the names of important groups of people (organizations, institutions, companies, ethnic groups, religions, political parties, etc.), historical periods and events;
Melbourne, Alaska, the Rockies, Ben Nevis, the North Sea, Venus, the Great Bear, Broadway, Tower Bridge, the Statue of Liberty, The Welcome Inn, etc.	• geographical names, astronomical names and the names of streets, squares, buildings, monuments, public houses, etc.;
Chess for Beginners, Newsweek, The Times, Murder Most Foul, The Garden Party, My Fair Lady, When the Saints Go Marching In, the Magna Carta, the Immigration Act, etc.	• titles of books, magazines, newspapers, novels, plays, films, TV programmes, songs, poems, documents, laws etc., and the headings of chapters, articles, etc.;
Tuesday, Good Friday, Easter, Halloween, May, etc.	• days of the week, holidays, holy days, months.

Notes:

1. Adjectives and common nouns derived from names are also capitalized:
   (Germany) – German efficiency – she is a German – to speak German
   (Queen Victoria) – Victorian morals – an eminent Victorian
   (the Catholic Church) – Catholic dogma – the Catholics – Catholicism

Some adjectives and common nouns which are not derived from names but which have a meaning similar to the words listed above (group membership, ideology, etc.) are sometimes capitalized, sometimes not (words denoting languages and nationalities – both as adjectives and nouns – are always capitalized):
   a **B**lack girl/a **b**lack girl, the **B**lacks/the **b**lacks, **S**ocialist ideals/**s**ocialist ideals, **C**ommunism/**c**ommunism, etc.
   an **E**speranto dictionary, to speak **E**speranto/**P**idgin/**D**utch, etc.

2. In the case of names and titles which consist of several words, it is the first word and the most important of the other words that are generally capitalized. This means that articles, prepositions and conjunctions are normally written small. An initial article is capitalized if it is regarded as part of the name:
   In **S**tratford **o**n **A**von we were introduced to **t**he **T**hird **E**arl **o**f **M**arlborough.
   Did you see *Bonny and Clyde* on TV last night?
   I read it in *The Guardian*. (Also: I read it in **t**he *Guardian*.)

346 Some Spelling Rules

When one adds an inflectional ending (e.g. to form plurals, tenses, comparatives, etc.) or suffix to a word base, this sometimes changes the spelling of the base. In some cases a change in spelling is necessary to avoid a change in pronunciation (*rip/ripper* [ɪ], *ripe/riper* [aɪ]), in other cases it is purely arbitrary *(dry/drier)*. The most important spelling rules are listed below. (For further details see **69, 143** Note 1.)

rescue – rescuer – rescued, late – later – latest, free – freer – freest – freed, true – truer – truest	● **Final *-e*** is never doubled and is therefore always dropped before endings beginning with *e-* (*-er, -ed,* etc.).
rescue – rescuing, move – moving – movable, convince – convincible, stone – stony, nerve – nervous, base – basic	It is also normally dropped before endings beginning with other vowels.
canoe [u:] – canoeing, tiptoe [əʊ] – tiptoeing, free – freeing, foresee – foreseeable	It is retained, however, to avoid a change in the pronunciation of *-oe* [u:/əʊ] and *-ee* [i:] before *-ing* and *-able,*
change – changeable, courage – courageous [-'eidʒ-] notice – noticeable, trace – traceable grace – gracious [ʃ]	to avoid a change in the pronunciation of *-g-* [dʒ] before *-able* and *-ous* and, for the same reason, after *-c-* [s] before *-able* (*-ce* becomes *-ci-* [ʃ] before *-ous*).
die – dying, lie – lying, tie – tying, etc. (**Note.** dye – dyeing: *färben*)	● **Final *-ie*** becomes *-y-* before *-ing*. (In *dye* the *-e* is retained before *-ing* to avoid confusion with the word *die*.)
dry – dried – dries – drier – driest shy – shied (**But:** shy – shyer – shyest) pity – pitied – pities – pitiful – pitiless happy – happier – happiest – happily – happiness city – citify, forty – fortieth	● **Final *-y*** following a consonant becomes *-i- (-ie-)* before the endings *-ed, -s, -er, -est* (except in the comparatives and superlatives of some monosyllabic adjectives). As an unstressed final syllable it also becomes *-i-* before *-ly, -ful, -less, -ness, -fy* and *-eth*.
go – goes, do – does, potato – potatoes. (**But:** radio – radios)	● **Final *-o*** often becomes *-oe-* before *-s* (cf **69**).
sad [æ] – sadder – sadden, shop [ɒ] – shopping, regret [e] – regretted – regretting – regrettable, bag [æ] – baggy, star [ɑ:(r)] – starred – starry, control [əʊ] – controllable, occur [ɜ:(r)] – occurred – occurring – occurrence, prefer [ɜ:(r)] – preferred – preferring (**But:** preference ['---])	● **Single final consonants** are doubled before most endings beginning with a vowel *(-er, -est, -en, -ed, -ing, -ish, -y, -able, -ence, -ance)* when preceded by a stressed single-letter vowel. (In most cases this is to avoid a change in pronunciation.)

suffer – suffered, develop – developer, open – opening
travel – travelled – traveller, pedal – pedalling, jewel – jeweller (*Am.:* traveler, pedaling, jeweler)
worship – worship**p**er, handicap – handicap**p**ed, zigzag – zigzag**g**ing, panic – panic**k**ed – panic**k**y

There is usually no doubling after **unstressed** vowels.
Exceptions: *-l* before *-ed, -ing, -er, -est* in British English; some (mostly compound) words ending in *-p* or *-g* (especially in British English); *-ic* becomes *-ick*-before *e, i* and *y.*

bench – benches, watch – watches, ash – ashes, box – boxes, buzz – buzzes, press – presses, lens – lenses, opus – opuses, gas *(v.)* – gasses, gas *(n.)* – gases, bus *(v.* or *n.)* – buses

- **After *-ch, -sh, -x, -z, -s,*** an *-es* is added instead of *-s* (plural or verb endings).
  A single final *-s* is sometimes doubled before the ending *-es* (according to the rule for final consonants given above) but not always.

347 List of Punctuation Marks

.	full stop, period	-	hyphen ['haɪfən] *(Bindestrich)*
,	comma	“ ”	(double) quotation marks, inverted commas
;	semi-colon [semɪ'kəʊlən]	‘ ’	(single) quotation marks, inverted commas
:	colon	’	apostrophe [ə'pɒstrəfɪ]
?	question mark	( )	(round) brackets, parentheses [pə'renθɪsi:z]
!	exclamation mark	[ ]	(square) brackets
–	dash *(Gedankenstrich)*	/	diagonal (stroke), slant

348 Use of Commas and Exclamation Marks

English punctuation is similar to German, except in the way commas and exclamation marks are used. In English these do not belong essentially to particular grammatical structures as they do in German; instead, they mainly serve as guides to comprehension by indicating the way the sentences are spoken (pauses, intonation).

Two cokes, three glasses of lager(,) and an orange juice, please.
Mr Fuller, the biggest bore in town, was telling jokes again(,) but nobody was listening.

In some cases **commas** are used as in German: in lists, before and after insertions, sometimes between coordinated main or subordinate clauses, etc.

On the other hand, we are very short of money.
We could ask my uncle to help us, of course.
Most of the others, however, were rather keen on the idea.

A comma is also used:
- before or after most linking adverbs and adverbs of viewpoint (in front-position or end-position or as insertions, cf **155, 162**);

On the open plains of the Mid-West(,) you can travel for hours without seeing a single settlement.
Approaching the town, the first thing I noticed was the veil of smog.
In better weather conditions, I would have cycled.
If the weather had been better, I would have cycled.

- in most cases after front-position adverbials, non-finite constructions or subordinate clauses when these ‘set the scene’ for the statement made in the main clause (cf **330**).
  (The decisive factor here is what function the introductory element has in the context of the sentence and the text, and not its grammatical structure.)

There is, however, **no comma** (in complex or simple sentences) before and after constituent parts of the sentence which are necessary for the understanding of the sentence as a whole and are therefore not separated from the rest of the sentence by pauses when speaking. These include:

I didn't know (that) Patricia wanted the job. She wasn't sure whether she would have the time. All those who had voted for him cheered. We noticed Ann straining her neck to see the clock. They looked as if they were impatient to leave. I've been a member since I was a student. I've been a member since my student days.	– *that*-clauses (cf **304**) – indirect questions (cf **306**) – defining relative clauses (cf **308**) – necessary non-finite constructions – most subordinate clauses and adverbials in end-position, since the information they contain is important for the meaning of the sentence.
And who do you think I met there? Molly, of all people! Get out of my sight! You are a disgrace to us all! Hello, Jack! Haven't seen you in ages! "But it isn't my birthday!" she cried.	**Exclamation marks** are only used to indicate strong emotions (astonishment, enthusiasm, anger, etc.) and particularly emotional ways of speaking.
Answer all the questions on the paper. Pass the salt, please. Oh dear, I've spilt some coffee. – Never mind.	Otherwise (with normal instructions, requests, commands and exclamations with no strong emotional force behind them) a full stop or comma is used.

Note:
In letter-writing commas are used:
- at the end of each line of an address (except the last line, which can have a full stop)
- in datelines (cf **359**)
- after the opening salutation (never an exclamation mark!)
- after the closing salutation

65(,) Griffith Avenue,
Dublin 9.
April 2nd, 1984

Dear Mary,
Have you heard the news ....
....
Yours ever,
Joan.

349–353 Word Formation

349 Types of Word Formation

New words are always being formed from already existing words (bases).
The most important types of word formation are:

happy → **un**happy to write → to **re**write	● derivation by adding **prefixes**
to treat → treat**ment** dark → to dark**en**	● derivation by adding **suffixes**
to walk → a walk a nurse → to nurse comic → a comic tidy → to tidy	● **conversion** to a different word class with no change in form
gold, smith → goldsmith to treat, ill → to ill-treat	● **compounding** of two or more words (often creating a new meaning).
unfriendliness (prefix + two suffixes) grey-haired (compounding + suffix) to wallpaper (compounding + conversion)	The formation of new words often involves two (or more) different types of word formation.

Notes:
1. Further types of word formation include:
   - back-formation, i.e. omitting what is (sometimes mistakenly) considered to be an ending: baby sitter → to baby sit; burglar → to burgle
   - shortening words ('clipping'): influenza → flu, automobile → auto
   - blending two words together: motor + hotel → motel, smoke + fog → smog
   - forming words from a set of initials (acronyms): National Aeronautics and Space Administration → NASA ['nɑːzə]

2. English contains many Latin and French derivations. Frequently, only the derived forms exist in English, but not the bases, e.g.:

include *(einschließen)* – exclude *(ausschließen)* – conclude *(abschließen, beenden)*

350 Derivation through Prefixes

Prefixes add a meaning to the base, but almost never change its word class. A selection of the more common prefixes and their main meanings is given below:

Examples	Prefix		Meaning	Function
non-flammable *(nichtbrennbar)*, **non**-resident	*non-*		before adjectives and abstract nouns (*dis-* also before certain verbs)	negation or opposite
independent, **im**mobile, **im**polite, **im**balance	*in-*	(before *m/p/b, l, r:*		
illogical, **il**legality, **ir**rational, **ir**relevance	*im-, -il, -ir*	respectively)		
uneven, **un**decided, **un**damaged, **un**happiness	*un-*			
disloyal, to **dis**like, to **dis**obey, **dis**belief	*dis-*			
to **un**fasten *(auf-/losmachen)*, to **un**lock	*un-*		before activity verbs and nouns derived from these verbs	reversal of an action
to **dis**appear, to **dis**arm *(entwaffnen)*, **dis**armament	*dis-*			
to **de**frost, to **de**code, **de**coder, **de**centralization	*de-*			
misshapen *(mißgestaltet)*, to **mis**spell, a **mis**print	*mis-*		'wrong'	denigration
malodorous *(übelriechend)*, **mal**nutrition	*mal-*	[æ]	'bad'	
subconscious, **sub**human, to **sub**divide, **sub**heading	*sub-*		'under, beneath'	spatial or abstract relations (degree, attitude, etc.)
supernatural, to **super**impose, **super**man	*super-*		'over'	
transatlantic, to **trans**plant, **trans**action	*trans-*		'beyond, across'	
intercontinental, to **inter**marry, **inter**play	*inter-*		'between, among'	
cooperative, to **co**exist, **co**-education	*co-*		'together'	
counterclockwise, to **counter**sign, **counter**spy	*counter-*		'in opposite direction'	
anticlockwise, **anti**social, **anti**-hero, **anti**-Semite	*anti-*		'against'	
pro-American, **pro**-rector (= substitute r.)	*pro-*		'for'	
to **fore**tell [-'-], **fore**father ['---], **fore**sight ['--]	*fore-*	[fɔː]	'before'	relations in time (sequence, repetition)
prehistoric, to **pre**pay, **pre**fabrication	*pre-*	[priː]	'before'	
postglacial, to **post**date, **post**position	*post-*	[pəʊst]	'after'	
to **re**consider, to **re**elect, **re**organization	*re-*	[riː]	'again'	
unilateral (= on/from one side), **mono**syllable	*uni-*	['jʊnɪ] / ***mono-*** ['mɒnəʊ]	'one'	number
bimonthly (= twice a month *or* every two months)	*bi-*	[baɪ]	'two'	
triangular, **tri**cycle, **tri**colour	*tri-*	[traɪ]	'three'	
polysyllabic, **multi**millionaire, **multi**racial	*poly*	['pɒlɪ] / ***multi-*** ['mʌltɪ]	'many'	

Notes:

1. *Non-* and *pro-* are almost always used with a hyphen. New words formed with *anti-, re-, co-* and some other prefixes are frequently hyphenated.

2. When used with verbs – and with nouns and adjectives derived from the verbs – the Latin prefix *in- (im-/il-/ir-)* has a spatial meaning (place or direction) and should not be confused with the negative prefix *in-*:

to inhabit *(bewohnen)*, inhabitant *(Bewohner)*, inhabitable *(bewohnbar,* not *unbewohnbar!)*
to inflame *(entzünden)*, inflammation *(Entzündung)*, inflammable *(leicht entzündbar,* not *unbrennbar!)*

3. The prefixes *en-* (*em-* before *b/p*) and *be-* generally change the word class of the base; they sometimes occur together with suffixes:

to enslave *(versklaven)*, to empower, to embody *(verkörpern)*, to enlarge, to enlighten *(aufklären)*
to besiege *(belagern)*, to bewitch *(verhexen)*, belated *(verspätet)*, beloved *(geliebt)*, bespectacled *(bebrillt)*

351 Derivation through Suffixes

Suffixes either alter the word class of the base or give the base a different type of meaning. In some cases the spelling and/or the pronunciation of the base is changed (e.g. *sane* [eɪ] – *sanity* [æ]). A selection of the more common suffixes and their most important meanings and functions is given below.
Abbreviations: V = verb, N = noun, A = adjective.

1. Nouns derived through suffixes

Examples	Base	Suffix	Meaning
baker, teacher, employer, actor, liar, beggar, hatter (← hat), furrier (← fur), lawyer	V/N	+ ***-er/-or/-ar/ (-ier, -yer)***	person engaged in or concerned with an occupation, activity or field of interest
engineer, novelist, zoologist, grammarian	N	+ ***-eer, -ist, -ian***	person engaged in or concerned with an occupation, activity or field of interest
addressee, employee, payee (s.o. who is paid) (**but:** escapee – s.o. who has escaped)	V	+ ***-ee:***	person affected by an activity (or, in a few cases, a person acting)
stewardess, actress, waitress, duchess, hostess	N	+ ***-ess:***	female person (cf **79**)
New Yorker, Londoner, villager, cottager, foreigner (← foreign), Northerner, Westerner	N/(A)	+ ***-er***	also: person of a certain origin, etc. (for other suffixes of origin see **361**)
freezer, mixer, computer, trailer, (tin-)opener	V	+ ***-er***	also: tool, machine, etc. which does a certain job
movement, beginning, arrival, liberation, contribution, hindrance, occurrence	V	+ ***-ment, -ing, -al, -(t)ion, -ance/-ence***	a process, or its result
ripeness, friendliness, sanity, cruelty intelligence, elegance, decency, bankruptcy	A	+ ***-ness, -(i)ty, -ence/-ance, -cy***	characteristic, state
freedom, kingdom, falsehood, childhood, boyhood, hardship, friendship, professorship	A/N	+ ***-dom, -hood, -ship***	characteristic, state, status, condition, etc.
idealism, patriotism, heroism, racism, socialism, Anglicanism, fanaticism, romanticism, fatalism	N/(A)	+ ***-ism:***	political, religious, philosophical, etc. attitude or movement

2. Adjectives derived through suffixes

Many of the suffixes used to derive adjectives have a number of different meanings which are often difficult to define. Only a rough guideline to the most important meanings can be given here. Some of the prefixes are added mainly to abstract nouns referring to characteristics, states, etc., others are added mainly to concrete nouns referring to materials, substances, etc. (See the information given in brackets.)

Examples	Base	Suffix	Meaning
useful, hopeful, beautiful, forgetful	N/(V)	+ ***-ful:***	'having . . .', 'full of' (a characteristic or state)
bearded, feathered, striped, gifted	N	+ ***-ed:***	'having . . .' (a thing or characteristic)
hairy, cloudy, snowy; watery, silky	N	+ ***-y:***	'like . . .', 'covered with . . .' (a substance)
burdensome, troublesome, quarrelsome	N/(V)	+ ***-some:***	'having a tendency to be/to do . . .'
poisonous, spacious, furious, gaseous	N	+ ***-(i/-e)ous:***	'characterized by . . .', 'full of . . .'
atomic, historic(al), educational	N	+ ***-ic, (ic)al:***	'belonging to . . .', relating to . . .'
earthen, silken, woollen, wooden	N	+ ***-en:***	'consisting of . . .' (a substance)
useless, countless, beardless, cloudless	N/(V)	+ ***-less:***	'without . . .' (opposite of *-ful, -ed, -y*)
childlike, ladylike, cowardly, manly	N	+ ***-like, -ly***	'having the qualities of . . .' (mostly a person; *-ish* is often derogatory here)
childish, boyish; greenish *(grünlich)*	N/(A)	+ ***-ish***	'having the qualities of . . .' (mostly a person; *-ish* is often derogatory here)
eatable, readable, acceptable	V	+ ***-able:***	'able to be done', 'possible'
interested, surprised, shocked	V	+ ***-ed:***	'in a certain state or condition'
interesting, surprising, shocking	V	+ ***-ing***	'having a tendency to do something'
attractive, talkative, constructive	V	+ ***-ive***	'having a tendency to do something'

3. Verbs derived through suffixes

dark**en**, black**en**, wid**en**, length**en**	A/(N) + ***-en:*** 'to become . . .' (intransitive) 'to make . . .' (causative-transitive)
pur**ify**, simpl**ify**, cit**ify**, fals**ify** modern**ize**, fertil**ize**, computer**ize**	A/(N) + ***-ify*** } 'to make . . .' (causative- A/(N) + ***-ize/ise*** } transitive)

352 Conversion

Conversion is a very common way of forming words in English, which is why there are a lot of English words which belong to several different word classes. In many cases it has been forgotten which was the original word class, but sometimes one is still aware of this: *choice,* for example, is primarily seen as a noun although as an adjective it is sometimes even used in the superlative form. The following table gives an idea of the wide range of conversions that exist in English:

Noun	Verb	Adjective	Adverb(ial particle)	Preposition
an **elbow**	to **elbow** s.o.			
a **swim**	to **swim**			
a **choice**		**choicest** quality		
a **criminal**		a **criminal** act		
	to **dry**	**dry** clothes		
		the **then** minister	**Then** he left.	
the **ups** and	to **up** a price	the **up** train	to bring **up** an idea	to walk **up/**
downs of life	to **down** tools	the **down** train	Prices went **down.**	**down** the street

Note:
Words within a particular word class may change from one sub-class to another. For instance, intransitive verbs may become causative-transitive verbs (cf **45**), or proper nouns may become common nouns, etc.:
to stand somewhere *(stehen)* – to stand s.th. s.wh. *(stellen)*; Biro (registered trademark) – a biro (any ball-point pen)

353 Compounds

Compounds are combinations of words that are regarded as a unit; they are therefore usually written as one word or hyphenated. They may consist of two or more base words (cf *ice-cream, ice-cream parlour*). The meaning of the expressions is generally clear from the meaning of the bases; in most cases the basic meaning is conveyed by the last word and this word determines the word class: *songbird = a bird that can sing; power-hungry = hungry for power, to bottle-feed = to feed with a bottle.*
The most important types of compound are illustrated in the table below.

	Nouns compounded from:
fingernail, steamboat, press conference, paper-mill, birch tree, waterway, sunrise, postman, vacuum cleaner, dishwasher	– noun + noun (some derived from verbs)
washing-machine, boiling point, chewing gum, driving licence; house-cleaning, sun-bathing, sight-seeing, window shopping	– gerund + noun (or vice versa)
blackbird *(Amsel),* goodwill, small talk, redskin, sweetheart	– adjective + noun
afterlife, by-stander, by-product, input, offprint, onlooker, overcoat, outburst, underlip, upsurge; looker-on, passer-by	– adverbial particle + noun (or vice versa)
	Adjectives compounded from:
bitter-sweet, deaf-mute, blue-black, light brown, dark red	– adjective + adjective
grassgreen, year-long, sea-sick, waterproof, power-hungry	– noun + adjective
good-looking, ready-made, far-reaching, everlasting, newborn, deep-rooted, heartwarming, English-speaking, man-made	– adjective/adverb/noun + participle
upright, over-careful, over-proud, undersized, underprivileged, outstanding *(außergewöhnlich),* outgoing, inborn, offshore	– adverbial particle + adjective/participle/noun

Verbs: Compound verbs are generally formed by

– back-formation from words ending in *-ing* or *-er*

to housekeep, to sightsee, to baby-sit, to bottle-feed, to stage-manage, to dry-clean, etc. (from *housekeeper, sightseeing,* etc.)

– conversion

to snowball, to wallpaper, to highlight, to waterproof (from *a snowball,* etc.)

or they are compounded from

– adverbial particle (expecially *out, over, under*) + verb/noun. For the so-called phrasal verbs, e.g. *bring up, go by,* see **47**.)

outnumber s.o. *(jdm. zahlenmäßig überlegen sein),* outdistance *(weit hinter sich lassen),* outgrow *(über den Kopf wachsen),* overflow, overload, overdo s.th. *(etw. übertreiben),* underline, understate *(herunterspielen),* underestimate, upset, uphold, update

Note:
For some more complex compounds, such as *good-for-nothing,* see **71**.

54-360 Numerical Expressions

354 Cardinal Numbers

0	nought	[nɔːt]/zero ['zɪərəʊ]	11	eleven	[ɪ'levn]	30	thirty	['θɜːtɪ]
1	one	[wʌn]	12	twelve	[twelv]	40	forty	['fɔːtɪ]
2	two	[tuː]	13	thirteen	['θɜː'tiːn]	50	fifty	['fɪftɪ]
3	three	[θriː]	14	fourteen	['-'-]	60	sixty	['sɪkstɪ]
4	four	[fɔː]	15	fifteen	['fɪf'tiːn]	70	seventy	['sevntɪ]
5	five	[faɪv]	16	sixteen	['-'-]	80	eighty	['eɪtɪ]
6	six	[sɪks]	17	seventeen	['--'-]	90	ninety	['naɪntɪ]
7	seven	['sevn]	18	eighteen	['-'-]	100	a/one hundred	['hʌndrəd]
8	eight	[eɪt]	19	nineteen	['-'-]	101	a hundred and one	
9	nine	[naɪn]	20	twenty	['twentɪ]	142	a hundred and forty-two	
10	ten	[ten]	21	twenty-one	[--'-], etc.	500	five hundred	

1,080	a/one thousand ['θaʊznd] and eighty	
913,053	nine hundred and thirteen thousand, eight hundred and fifty-three	
1,000,000	a/one million ['mɪljən]	
1,000,000,000	*Br.* a/one thousand million	*Am.* a/one billion (Ger. *Milliarde*)
1,000,000,000,000	*Br.* a/one billion	*Am.* a/one trillion

The following rules have to be borne in mind when writing cardinal numbers (in words or figures), or using them in speech:

– The words *one, two, three,* etc. are joined to *twenty, thirty,* etc. with a hyphen (see the numbers 21, 142 above). *And* is used before the numbers *one* to *ninety-nine* to link them with a preceding *hundred* or *thousand* (see the numbers 101, 142).

– When *hundred* and *thousand* are used as numbers they are always preceded by another number or by *a/ an.*

– *Hundred, thousand* and *million* have no plural *-s* when used as numbers (see the numbers 500 etc. above; but: *hundreds of people,* etc.).

– From 1000 upwards there is a comma after every three places from right to left: 5,732,999. Sometimes these numbers are printed with spaces instead: 5 732 999. Full stops are never used here (cf **356**, Decimal Fractions).

Notes:

1. The ways of saying the number 0 vary according to function:

– *nought* (Am.: *zero*) for the numerical value	Three minus three is *nought* (Br.)/ *zero* (Am.).
– *zero* for the point on a scale	The temperature is ten below *zero*.
– *o/oh* [əʊ] in years, code numbers, etc.	She was born in 1903 *(nineteen-oh-three)*.
– *nil* (occasionally *nothing*) for sporting results (but in tennis: *love*)	The match ended *five – nil (five – nothing)*. And now Tracy Austin is leading *forty – love*.

2. The figures in telephone numbers and other long code numbers are spoken singly. They can be divided into rhythmical groups of two (sometimes three) digits; when there are two identical digits in a group (e.g. 88), they are usually spoken as *double eight*, etc.:

207704 *two oh/double seven/oh four* or: *two oh seven/seven oh four.*

355 Ordinal Numbers

1st	(the) first	10th	tenth	30th	thirtieth
2nd	second	11th	eleventh	40th	fortieth
3rd	third	12th	twelfth	50th	fiftieth
4th	fourth	13th	thirteenth ['-'-]	60th	sixtieth
5th	fifth [ɪ]	14th	fourteenth	70th	seventieth
6th	sixth	15th	fifteenth	100th	hundredth
7th	seventh	20th	twentieth ['---]	106th	hundred and sixth
8th	eighth	21st	twenty-first	1,000th	thousandth
9th	ninth [aɪ]	22nd	twenty-second	1,000,000th	millionth

When writing and speaking ordinal numbers, note the following rules:

- *First, second* and *third* are irregular forms. They are also used with the compound numbers ending in 1, 2 and 3: *the twenty-second, the hundred and third,* etc.
- All other ordinal numbers are formed with *-th*. The *-ty* of *twenty, thirty,* etc. becomes *-tieth* [tɪɪθ] (cf **346**). Note the irregularities in the spelling/pronunciation of 5th, 8th, 9th and 12th.
- When writing in (Arabic) figures, the last two letters of the ordinal numbers are added: *first – 1st, second – 2nd, third – 3rd, fourth – 4th,* etc.
- Roman numerals after the names of people (monarchs, etc.) are spoken as ordinal numbers: *Henry VIII (Henry the Eighth),* Elizabeth II *(Elizabeth the Second).*

356 Fractions

Vulgar fractions

$\frac{1}{2}$ a/one half	$\frac{1}{4}$ a/one quarter (one fourth)
$\frac{3}{5}$ three fifths	
$\frac{7}{8}$ mile	seven eighths of a mile
$1\frac{3}{4}$ miles	one and three quarter miles or: a mile and three quarters

- With the exception of $\frac{1}{2}$ *(a half)* and $\frac{1}{4}$ *(a quarter, more rarely one fourth),* the ordinal numbers (cf **355**) are used for the denominators. In the plural, an *-s* is added.
- Units of measurement (*miles, litres,* etc.) have an *of* before them after fractions (exception: *half a mile*).
- Combinations of whole numbers and fractions may be spoken in two different ways, as is shown above.

Decimal fractions

3.853	three point eight five three
1.53 cm	one point five three centimetres
0.76	point seven six (or: oh/nought point seven six)
.007	point oh oh seven

- There is a point (never a comma!) before the decimal fraction. The decimal point is normally placed on the line, but in British usage may be placed above the line: 3.53 or 3·53.
- Units of measurement (*centimetres,* etc.) come directly after the decimal number.
- A nought before the decimal point is mostly not spoken, sometimes not even written. The numbers after the point are always spoken as single digits.

357 Mathematical Operations and Expressions

Basic mathematical operations

$7+15 = 22$	7 plus 15 is/equals 22 7 and 15 are/make 22	$7 \times 5 = 35$	7 multiplied by 5 is/equals 35 7 times 5 is/equals 35 7 fives are/make 35
$22 - 8 = 14$	22 minus 8 is/equals 14 22 less 8 leaves 14 8 from 22 leaves 14	$42 \div 7 = 6$	42 divided by 7 is/equals 6 7 into 42 goes 6 (times)

The first version of the above variations is in each case the more formal, and is preferred in mathematics. The other versions are more common in everyday usage.

Further mathematical expressions

x_1, x_2, x_n	**x** [eks] sub one, **x** sub two, **x** sub **n**	10 % (p.c.)	ten per cent
x', x''	**x** prime, **x** double/(two/second) prime	$a = b, a \approx b$	**a** is equal to **b**/is approximately **b**
x^2, x^3	**x** squared, **x** cubed	$a > b, a < b$	**a** is greater/less than **b**
x^{10}, x^{-10}	**x** to the tenth, **x** to the minus ten	$x = \frac{a+b+c}{d}$	**x** equals **a** plus **b** plus **c** (all) over **d**
x^{a+b}	**x** to the power of **a** plus **b**	$y = f(x)$	**y** is a function of **x**
$\sqrt{9}, \sqrt[3]{27}, \sqrt[n]{x}$	(square) root of 9, cubic root of 27, nth [enθ] root of **x**	$y = \sin/\cos/\tan/\cot x$	**y** is sine [saın]/cosine ['kəʊsaın]/ tangent ['tændʒənt]/ cotangent of **x**
		$x : a :: b : c$	**x** is to **a** as **b** is to **c**

358 Expressions of Frequency and Multiplication

once	(one time)	single	
twice	(two times)	double	twofold
(thrice)	three times	treble, triple	threefold
	four times	quadruple	fourfold
	five times	(quintuple)	fivefold
	six times	(sextuple)	sixfold
	seven times	(septuple)	sevenfold
	eight times, etc.		eightfold, etc.
Knock **five times.** I usually go shopping **twice** or **three times a week.**		It was a **treble/threefold** victory for him. He got his money back **fourfold.** (Or: . . . **four times over.**)	

Expressions of frequency are mainly formed from the cardinal number + *times*. Only the numbers 1, 2 and 3 have separate forms. (The less usual forms are given in brackets.) Expressions of frequency are used as adverbs or as adverbial phrases, often followed by a limiting unit of time. (For the indefinite article see 103.2.)

Expressions of multiplication which are regularly formed with *fold* can be used as adjectives or adverbs. The forms *single, double* etc. (which only exist or are only commonly used for the lower numbers) are practically always adjectives. Sometimes the appropriate expressions of frequency can be used in expressions of multiplication *(fourfold = four times over; double the amount = twice the amount).*

359 Dates

Written:			Spoken:
April 2nd, 1987	April 2, 1987	Apr. 2, '87	*April the second, nineteen eighty-seven*
2nd April(,) 1987	2 April(,) 1987	2 Apr. '87	*the second of April, nineteen eighty-seven*
Informally also:	2/4/87 *(Br.)*		Spoken as above, but also:
	4/2/87 *(Am.)*		*the second of the fourth, eighty-seven*

Note:
Years are spoken as two separate numbers: one for the century, e.g. 19, 18 (usually without *hundred*, which sounds stilted or very formal), one for the year e.g. 87, 01 (see also **354**). Exceptions are the years ending in 00. B.C. (= before Christ) is used for the years before the Christian era, and A.D. (= Anno Domini) for the first few centuries of it.

1801	*eighteen oh one* (rarely: *eighteen hundred and one*)	9 A.D.	*nine A.D.*
1800	*eighteen hundred*	44 B.C.	*forty-four B.C.* [ˌbiːˈsiː]
1066	*ten sixty-six*	*2000 B.C.*	*two thousand B.C.*
432 (A.D.)	*four thirty-two* (A.D. [ˌeɪˈdiː])		

360 Time of Day

7.00 a.m.	seven (a.m. [ˌeɪˈem])	seven (o'clock) (in the morning)
7.05	seven oh five (a.m.)	five (minutes) past seven (in the morning)
7.15	seven fifteen	(a) quarter past seven
7.30	seven thirty	half past seven
7.40	seven forty	twenty to eight
7.42	seven forty-two	eighteen minutes to eight
12.00	twelve (a.m.)	twelve (o'clock) (midday/noon)
12.01 p.m.	twelve oh one (p.m. [ˌpiːˈem])	one minute past twelve (midday/noon)
4.34	four thirty-four (p.m.)	twenty-six minutes to five (in the afternoon)
8.50	eight fifty	ten to nine (in the evening)
9.25	nine twenty-five	twenty-five past nine (in the evening/at night)
12.00 p.m.	twelve (p.m.)	midnight/twelve (o'clock) (midnight/at night)

There are two ways of giving the time of day in words:

- The previous hour can be named first and then the minutes (1–59) after it, as in the middle column. This is the way preferred when it is necessary to be exact or when reading digital clocks, timetables, TV programmes, etc.
- Ordinarily the more colloquial way with *o'clock, past* and *to* is preferred, as in the right-hand column: One starts by stating either the time after (= *past*) or before (= *to*) a full hour (*past* up to and including the first half-hour, and *to* after that point). The half-hour is given as *half past;* quarter hours are mostly spoken as *(a) quarter past* or *(a) quarter to.* The word *minutes* is usually dropped with numbers divisible by 5. In American English *after* can be used instead of *past* (6.10 = *ten after six*) and *of* instead of *to* (8.45 = *a quarter of nine*).

Normally one counts the hours up to 12 and then one starts again. To avoid misunderstandings, *a.m. (= ante meridiem)* can be used to mark the hours from midnight to midday, and *p.m. (= post meridiem)* for the hours from midday to midnight. Alternatively, one can use expressions such as *in the morning, yesterday morning, at night, tonight.* The use of *a.m.* and *p.m.* is limited to the more formal way of giving the time in figures, as in the left-hand and middle columns (9.30 = *nine thirty,* etc.) The other expressions of time can be used in all cases: *I'll meet you at a quarter past eight/eight fifteen tomorrow evening.*

Note:
The 24-hour clock is used for air (and increasingly rail and other) timetables. Times in this system are read as normal digital times, the full hours being read . . . *hundred hours.*

Depart Shannon	13.20	17.05	*(thirteen twenty; seventeen oh five)*
Arrive New York	15.15	19.00	*(fifteen fifteen; nineteen hundred hours)*

361 Nationality Words

The names of most countries and geographical areas (continents, regions, etc.) have corresponding adjectives and words for the people. These are mainly formed by adding suffixes. Note the following rules or tendencies:

- Adjectives ending in *-an/-ian/-ean* and *-i* are also used as nouns to denote individuals or, with an added plural *-s,* a whole people. A number of other adjectives are used in the same way:
  a Russian samovar, a Russian, the Russians – a Greek temple, a Greek, the Greeks
- Adjectives ending in *-ese* (plus *Swiss*) are used to refer to individuals or to the whole people, without the addition of a plural *-s* (cf **70**):
  a Japanese camera, a Japanese, the Japanese
- Adjectives ending in *-ish* and *-ch* can only be used for the whole people (with no plural *-s*; cf **134**). For individuals compounds with *-man* or *-woman* are formed or there are special nouns (whose plural forms can normally be used for the whole people):
  a French car, a Frenchman, a Frenchwoman, the French
  a Danish trawler, a Dane, the Danish/the Danes
- If there is no adjective, the name of the country can be used as an attribute before other nouns. For the people, *-er* is usually added:
  New Zealand butter, a New Zealander, the New Zealanders.

The following alphabetical list contains a selection of names of countries and geographical areas with their corresponding adjectives. The words for the people are also given if they differ from the adjective or do not obey the above rules.
Adjectives which are at the same time the names of languages (e.g. *to speak English/French*) are marked with an asterisk*.

Afghanistan	Afghan(i)*
Africa	African
Albania	Albanian*
Algeria [-dʒ-]	Algerian
America	American
Angola [-'--]	Angolan
Arabia	Arab/Arabian/Arabic* (the Arab countries, Arabian Nights, Arabic numerals); an Arab(ian)
Argentina [-'tiːnə]/ the Argentine	Argentinian [-'tɪnɪən]/ Argentine ['ɑːdʒəntaɪn]
Asia	Asian
Australia	Australian
Austria	Austrian
Belgium	Belgian
Bolivia	Bolivian
Brazil [-'-]	Brazilian
Britain/ Great Britain	British; a Briton, the British
Brittany	Breton*
Bulgaria	Bulgarian*
Cambodia	Cambodian
Canada	Canadian
Chad	Chadian ['tʃædɪən]
Chile ['tʃɪlɪ]	Chilean ['tʃɪlɪən]
China	Chinese*
Colombia	Colombian
Cuba	Cuban

Cyprus [aɪ]	Cyprian [ɪ]/Cypriot [ɪ]; a Cypriot
Czechoslovakia	Czech*, Slovak*/ Czechoslovak(ian)
Denmark	Danish* [eɪ]; a Dane, the Danes/the Danish
Egypt	Egyptian [-ʃən]
England	English*; an Englishman/ -woman, the English
El Salvador	Salvadorean
Finland	Finnish*; a Finn, the Finns/the Finnish
France	French*; a Frenchman/ -woman, the French
Germany	German*
Greece	Greek*
Holland (the Netherlands)	Dutch*; a Dutchman/ -woman, the Dutch
Hungary ['---]	Hungarian* [-'---]
Iceland	Icelandic*; an Icelander
India	Indian
Indonesia	Indonesian
Iran [-'-]	Iranian [-'reɪn-]
Iraq [-'-]	Iraqi
Ireland	Irish*; an Irishman/ -woman, the Irish
Israel	Israeli [ɪz'reɪlɪ]
Italy	Italian*
Jamaica	Jamaican
Japan [-'-]	Japanese*

Jordan	Jordanian
Kenya	Kenyan
Korea	Korean*
Lebanon	Lebanese
Luxemb(o)urg	(a Luxemburg village); a Luxemburger
Libya	Libyan
Malta [ɔ:]	Maltese*
Mexico	Mexican
Mongolia	Mongolian*; a Mongol(ian)
Morocco	Moroccan
New Zealand	(a New Zealand sheep); a New Zealander
Nicaragua	Nicaraguan
Norway	Norwegian*
Pakistan	Pakistani
Palestine	Palestinian
Peru	Peruvian
Poland	Polish*; a Pole, the Poles/the Polish
Portugal	Portuguese*
Puerto Rico	Puerto Rican
Rumania/Romania	Rumanian*/Romanian*
Russia	Russian*
Saudi Arabia	Saudi (Arabian) (cf Arabia)
Scandinavia	Scandinavian
Scotland	Scottish/Scots/(Scotch); a Scot(sman/-woman), the Scots/the Scottish
Spain	Spanish*; a Spaniard the Spaniards/the Spanish
the Sudan	Sudanese
Sweden	Swedish*; a Swede, the Swedes/the Swedish
Switzerland	Swiss
Syria	Syrian
Thailand [t]	Thai*; the Thai(s)
Tibet [-'-]	Tibetan* [-'--]
Tunisia	Tunisian
Turkey	Turkish*; a Turk, the Turks/the Turkish
Uganda	Ugandan
the U.S.A.	(a U.S. dollar)/American
Venezuela	Venezuelan
Vietnam [-'-]	Vietnamese*
Wales	Welsh*; a Welshman/-woman, the Welsh
Yugoslavia [a:]	Yugoslav(ian)

362–365 British and American English

The following four sections outline the main differences between the two most important standard forms of English.
The differences have arisen in the course of several centuries, when the relative isolation of the two nations from one another and different experiences, influences, attitudes, etc. all played their part. Due to modern methods of communication, the differences are being lost again to some extent, especially those of vocabulary, so that the following tables can only reproduce the current state of affairs.

362 Differences in Spelling

Apart from some isolated cases, the most important differences are listed below:

Br.	*Am.*
favour, colour, odour, neighbour, etc.	favor, color, odor, neighbor, etc.
centre, theatre, litre, etc.	center, theater, liter, etc.
defence, offence, pretence, licence	defense, offense, pretense, license
quarrelling, pedalled, carollers, etc.	quarreling, pedaled, carolers, etc.

- Words which end in unstressed *-our* in British English are always spelt *-or* in American English.
- Most of the words which in British English end in *-re* [ə(r)] are spelt *-er* in American English.
- Some words which end in stressed *-ence* (but also *licence*) in British English are spelt *-ense* in American English.
- When *-ing, -ed, -er* and *-est* are added to the unstressed syllables *-el, -al, -ol, -il* the *l* is doubled in British English but not in American English (cf **346**).

organise/organize, realise/realize, etc. analyse, paralyse	organize, realize, etc. analyze, paralyze	In British English the final syllable [-aɪz] can be spelt either *-ise* or *-ize*, but in American English only *-ize*. (The British *-alyse* corresponds to the American *-alyze*.)
prologue, catalogue, travelogue, etc.	prolog (ue), catalog (ue), travelog (ue) etc.	The ending [-lɒg] is always spelt *-logue* in British English, whereas in American English it can also have the simplified spelling *-log*.

Note:
In informal American English one often finds the simplified spellings *thru, tho, donut* for *through, though, doughnut*. Other such simplified spellings are *sox* for *socks, tonite* for *tonight*.

363 Differences in Pronunciation

The following table lists the most important differences between the British R.P. ('Received Pronunciation', cf **10**) and the pronunciation of General American (as it is spoken in the greater part of the U.S.A.). For General American we have used here the phonetic symbols of the British standard system, slightly adapted in some cases. (American dictionaries use a different system.)

	Received Pronunciation	*General American*	
ask, after, laugh	[ɑː]	[æ]	An [ɑː] in R.P. is generally (but not always) pronounced [æ] in American English.
But: father, calm	[ɑː]	[ɑː]	
grand, hat	[æ]	[æ]	
hot, bother, stop	[ɒ]	[ɑ]	The vowels [ɒ] and [ɔː] of R.P. are more open in American English.
call, claw, yawn	[ɔː]	[ɒː]	
so, old, boat	[əʊ]	[oᵁ]	The British diphthongs [eɪ] and [əʊ] correspond to the American sounds [eᴵ] [oᵁ], which are only slightly diphthongized.
way, great, name	[eɪ]	[eᴵ]	
neutral, duty, tune enthusiasm, assume	[juː]	[(j)uː]	After *n, d, t, th, s,* there is usually no [j] pronounced before [uː] in American English, as there is in British English.
for, art, burn	[ɔː, ɑː, ɜː]	[ɒr, ɑr, ɜr]	In R.P. an *r* before a consonant and at the end of a word is not pronounced: in American English it is.
here, there	[ɪə, eə]	[ɪr, er]	
poor, door, fireman	[ʊə, ɔː/ɔə, aɪə]	[ʊr, ɒr, aɪr]	
better, winner	[-ə]	[-ər]	
shelter, call	[ɫ]	[ɫ]	Dark *l* [ɫ], which in R.P. is only heard before consonants and at the end of words, is used by American speakers between vowels as well.
alley, jelly, college	[l]	[ɫ]	
water, better	[t]	[d̦]	Between vowels *t* is often pronounced 'weak' by American speakers, so that it sounds a bit like *d*.
docile, futile, missile	[-aɪl]	[-ɪl]	The final syllable *-ile* is pronounced differently in the two varieties of English.
melancholy,	['--kəlɪ]	['--ˌkɑlɪ]	In contrast to British English, all words of more than three syllables have a secondary stress in American English.
territory,	[' t(ə)rɪ]	[' ˌtɑrɪ]	
dictionary	['--n(ə)rɪ]	['--ˌnerɪ]	

364 Differences in Grammar

British and American English differ least in their grammar and the differences are mainly limited to the following grammatical features:

Br.	*Am.*
(1) **Have you (got)** a match?	(1) **Do you have/Have you got** a match?
(2) I**'ve** already **bought** the tickets.	(2) I already **bought/I've** already **bought** the tickets.
(3) She suggested that he **should take** the bus. (Occasionally: . . . that he take the bus.)	(3) She suggested that he **take** the bus.
(4) We should have **got** the tickets earlier. She **dived** into the cold water.	(4) We should have **gotten** the tickets earlier. She **dived/dove** into the cold water.
(5) One should always do **one's** best.	(5) One should always do **his/their** best.
(6) We sat down and talked **a bit.** His advice didn't help me **at all.**	(6) We sat down and talked **some/a bit.** His advice didn't help me **any/at all.**

(1) As an alternative to the question form *Have you got . . .?* the form *Do you have?* is common in American English but rarer in British English (cf **250**).
(2) In colloquial American English the past tense is often used where British English has the present perfect (cf **295**).
(3) After verbs expressing a demand or decision, the present subjunctive is more widely used in American English than in British English (cf **213**.2a).
(4) The verb *get* has an additional past participle form *gotten* in American English, mostly used only in the meaning 'provide oneself with, acquire, buy'. A few other verbs also have additional past participle or past tense forms in American English.
(5) In American English, *he, his, himself* or *they, them, themselves* are commonly used to refer back to the general pronoun *one* (German: *man*), where in British English only *one, one's, oneself* are possible.
(6) *Some* can be used in American English informally as an adverb, as can *any,* which in British English can only be used as an adverb before an adjective or before a comparative form *(not any better).* (Cf **115** Note 3.)

365 Differences in Vocabulary

There are only a few words which belong exclusively to one or the other form of English (e.g. *Br. lorry, petrol; Am. gasoline*). Often the same words exist in both varieties but are less common in one or the other, or are used with different meanings. In the selection below, each British/American pair of words refers to the same thing. Words for specifically British or American institutions or geographical features (e.g. *pub, drugstore, prairie*) have not been included in this selection.

Transport		**Public Life**	
Br.	*Am.*	*Br.*	*Am.*
petrol	gasoline	(limited) company	(business) corporation
car	car, auto(mobile)	government	(the Carter) administration, (democratic) government
lorry, truck	truck		
railway	railroad	public (*or* State) ownership	government ownership
goods train	freight train		
underground (railway)	subway, rapid transit (system)	to conscript *(zum Militär einziehen)*	to draft
tram, (streetcar)	streetcar, (tram)	a conscript	a draftee, a conscript
motorway	(interstate) highway, expressway, turnpike	conscription	the draft
		to post/(mail) a letter	to mail/(post) a letter
dual carriageway	divided highway		
aeroplane	airplane, (aeroplane)	postman	mailman, postman

Nature and landscape		Clothes and personal effects	
Br.	*Am.*	*Br.*	*Am.*
autumn	fall, autumn	trousers	pants, trousers
stream, small river, brook	creek, brook	pants, underpants	underpants, (pants)
insect	insect, bug	braces *(Hosenträger)*	suspenders
embankment *(Uferbefestigung)*	levee ['levɪ]	handbag	purse, handbag, pocket-book

Urban environment		Food and nutrition	
Br.	*Am.*	*Br.*	*Am.*
lift *(Personenaufzug)*	elevator	chips, French fries	French fries
ground floor *(Erdgeschoß)*	first floor	(potato) crisps	(potato) chips
(public) toilet(s)	restroom	maize, (corn) *(Mais)*	corn
launderette *(Waschsalon)*	laundromat	corn *(Getreide)*	grain
bookshop	bookstore	aubergine, (egg-plant)	egg-plant
shop-assistant	sales clerk [klɜrk]	cookery book, cookbook	cookbook
dustbin	garbage can	tin, can	can

366 Phonetic Symbols and Signs

Vowels and diphthongs

[ɪ]	sit	[iː]	see	[eɪ]	name
[ʌ]	cut	[ɑː]	ask	[aɪ]	time
[ɒ]	box	[ɔː]	broad	[ɔɪ]	boy
[ʊ]	put	[uː]	moon	[əʊ]	cold
[e]	let	[ɜː]	bird	[aʊ]	house
[æ]	hat			[ɪə]	here
[ə]	another			[eə]	chair
				[ʊə]	sure

Consonants

[s]	sun	[z]	easy	[l]	land
[ʃ]	ship	[ʒ]	vision	[m]	man
[tʃ]	chin	[dʒ]	Jim	[n]	new
[θ]	thin	[ð]	then	[ŋ]	long
[f]	fan	[v]	van	[r]	red
[p]	pig	[b]	big	[h]	hand
[t]	town	[d]	down	[j]	yes
[k]	car	[g]	gas	[w]	water

The stress mark ' is placed before the stressed syllable of a word with more than one syllable. Secondary stress is marked by ˌ before the syllable.
When only the stress and not the pronunciation of a word is shown, the syllables are represented by small dashes:

elect [ɪ'lekt]/[-'-] reelect [ˌriɪ'lekt]/[ˌ--'-] anomalous [-'---]

Index

The numbers given refer to the **paragraphs**. Sub-sections of a paragraph are marked off by a decimal point, e. g. 73.1.
N = Note(s)

Other abbreviations used:

adj.	=	adjective	ger.	=	gerund	pr.	=	present
adv.	=	adverb	Ger.	=	German	prep.	=	preposition
Ch.	=	Chapter	incl.	=	including	progr.	=	progressive
compl.	=	complement	indir.	=	indirect	pron.	=	pronoun
conj.	=	conjunction	inf.	=	infinitive	rel.	=	relative
constr.	=	construction	interr.	=	interrogative	rep. speech	=	reported speech
determ.	=	determiner	obj.	=	object	subj.	=	subject
esp.	=	especially	pers.	=	personal	vs.	=	versus

A

Q

R

S

List of Grammatical Terms

The following is a selection of grammatical terms used in this book, with their German equivalents and examples where appropriate. It is limited to those terms which are likely to be less familiar to students.

absolute participle construction	unverbundene Partizipialkonstruktion	*Ann having left*, they . . .
abstract noun	abstraktes Nomen, Abstraktum	*life, decision, arrogance*
activity verb	Tätigkeitsverb	*work, run, sit, shine*
adjective phrase	Adjektivgruppe	*very careful, glad to be here*
adverb phrase	Adverbgruppe	*very carefully*
adverbial *(n.)*	adverbiale Bestimmung	*Occasionally* she travels *to London.*
adverbial particle	Adverbialpartikel	go *out,* look *up*
adverbial phrase	adverbiale Gruppe	*very carefully, with care, to London*
agent ['əɪdʒənt]	Verursacher	*Jim* fixed it. It was fixed by *Jim.*
antecedent [ˌæntɪ'siːdənt]	Bezugswort (eines Relativsatzes)	the *man* who fixed it
assertive words	positive Wörter	*somebody, a lot of, already*
attribute ['ætrɪbjuːt]/attributive use [ə'trɪbjʊtɪv]	Attribut/attributiver Gebrauch	a *cheap* ticket *to London*
auxiliary (verb)	Hilfsverb	*can* swim, *will* write, *doesn't* know
backshift	Rückverschiebung (der Tempora)	"It *is* . . ." → She said it *was* . . .
cardinal number	Grundzahl	*one, eight, thirty-seven*
case (also → common case)	Kasus, (Subjekt-/Objekt-)fall	subject ~, object ~, common ~, possessive ~
clause	(Haupt-/Neben-)satz	main clause, subordinate clause
cleft sentence	Spaltsatz	*It was Pat who reminded us.*
cohesion [kəʊ'hiːʒn]	Textverknüpfung	–
collective noun	Sammelbegriff (im Singular)	*group, flock, audience, family*
colloquial [kə'ləʊkwɪəl]	umgangssprachlich	–
common case	Einheitskasus	*The dog* bit *the man. The man* bit *the dog.*
common noun (opposite: proper noun)	allgemeines Nomen	*table, boy, decision, advice, group*
comparison	1. Steigerung 2. Vergleich	*big – bigger – biggest* *as big as . . ., bigger than . . .*
complement → subj./obj. compl.		
complementation	Ergänzung (zum Verb, zum Adjektiv)	He put *it down.* It is easy *to read.*
complex sentence	Satzgefüge, komplexer Satz	*I believe he did it.*
compound ['--]	Zusammensetzung, zusammengesetztes Wort	*steamboat, good-looking*
concord (in number/gender) ['--]	Kongruenz (Numerus-/Genuskongruenz)	The *girl was* . . . / *she* raised *her* hand . . .
constituent [-'---] part (of a sentence)	Satzteil	subject, object, predicate, adverbial
conversion	Konversion	*to walk → a walk; dry → to dry*
countables	zählbare Nomen	*a cat – cats; a family – families*
defining attribute	notwendiges Attribut	We live in the house *with the green door.*
derivation [ˌderɪ'veɪʃn]	Ableitung	*happy → happily, derive → derivation*
determiner	Begleiter	*this* book, *my* coat, *each* person
down toning	Abschwächung, abschwächend	Close the door, *will you?* I'm *nearly* finished.
dynamic meaning (of verbs)	dynamische Verbbedeutung	*work, sit, become, disappear*
gender	Genus	persons (masculine/feminine) ⟷ things
hypothetical condition	irreale Bedingung	*If I were you,* I would . . .
inner monologue	erlebte Rede	–
intensifying	Verstärkung, verstärkend	*Do* come in. It's *very* late.
linking adverb	verknüpfendes Adverb	*however, similarly, otherwise*
linking verb	Kopulaverb	The milk *is/smells/went* sour.
main verb	Vollverb	can *swim,* she *writes, do* the dishes
modal past ['məʊdəl]	modales *Past Tense*	It would be better if you *took* a raincoat.
mood	Modus	indicative, imperative, subjunctive
negation	Verneinung	This is *not* true. *Nobody* called.

negative words	negative (verneinende) Wörter	*nothing, neither (of them), never*
non-assertive words	nichtpositive Wörter	*anywhere, yet, ever*
non-finite verb forms/constructions	infinite Verbformen/Konstruktionen	gerund, participles, infinitive
non-defining attribute	nichtnotwendiges Attribut	Our house, *with its green door,* is easy to find.
notional concord	Sinnkongruenz	The *family were* gathered round the table.
notional object	Sinnobjekt	I think it a waste of time *to complain.*
notional subject (of a sentence, of a non-finite construction)	Sinnsubjekt (eines Satzes, einer infiniten Konstruktion)	It's no use *complaining.* In spite of *her* complaining, they ...
noun head	Kern einer Nominalgruppe, Bezugswort	a tasty *meal,* John's *car*
noun phrase	Nominalgruppe	*a tasty meal, John's car*
number	Numerus	singular, plural
object complement	Objektkomplement	We call him *Paddy.*
ordinal number	Ordnungszahl	*first, eighth, thirty-seventh,*
part of speech	Wortart	noun, adjective, verb, etc.
particle → adverbial particle		
phrase	Wortgruppe	→ verb/noun/adjective/adverb ~
phrasal verb	Partikelverb	*go off, wake up, point out*
predicate ['predikət]	Prädikat	I *could lend* it to you. He *was* a fool.
predicative use (of an adjective) [-'---]	prädikativer Gebrauch	The ticket was *cheap.*
prefix ['pri:fɪks]	Vorsilbe	*in*dependent, *re*elect, *dis*belief
process verb	Vorgangsverb	*become, go (sour), disappear, dry (up)*
proper noun (opposite: common noun)	Eigenname	*Betty, San Francisco, the Nile*
prop-word	Stützwort	Not this book – the other *one.*
question tag	Bestätigungsfrage	It's a lovely day, *isn't it?*
referent	Bezugswort (eines Pronomens, eines Begleiters)	The *boys* came in, each carrying a flag. Each *boy* had a different flag.
register	stilistische Ebene	formal, literary, colloquial, etc.
relation verb	Beziehungsverb	*contain, possess, imply, cost*
reported speech	indirekte Rede	She told me *it was raining.*
retrospection	Erzählrückgriff	–
speech intention	Sprechabsicht	wish, request, reproach, etc.
state verb	Zustandsverb	*seem, exist, look (nice)*
stative meaning (of verbs)	statische Verbbedeutung	*understand, want, hear, seem, contain*
stress	Betonung	... but I <u>do</u> like <u>straw</u>berry ice-cream.
subject complement	Subjektkomplement	She is *an architect.*
subjunctive (present/past ~)	Konjunktiv	I suggested he *take* a walk. Wish you *were* here.
substitutes, substitute forms	Ersatzformen	*is able to* = can; *has to* = must
suffix ['sʌfɪks]	Nachsilbe	happi*ly*, govern*ment*, teach*er*
superordinate clause	übergeordneter Satz	*I don't know* if it is true. ... *if it is true* that he did it.
tense	Tempus, Zeitform	present tense, future perfect, etc.
uncountables	nichtzählbare Nomen	*butter, furniture, advice, physics*
verb phrase	Verbgruppe	*has taken, may be working*
verbal complex	Verbverband	*be fond of* = like; *have a rest* = rest